VISUAL QUICKSTART GUIDE

C#

WEB DEVELOPMENT WITH ASP.NET

Jose Mojica

 Peachpit Press

Visual QuickStart Guide
C# Web Development with ASP.NET
Jose Mojica

Peachpit Press

1249 Eighth Street
Berkeley, CA 94710
510/524-2178
800/283-9444
510/524-2221 (fax)
Find us on the World Wide Web at: http://www.peachpit.com/
Peachpit Press is a division of Pearson Education
To report errors, please send a note to errata@peachpit.com
Copyright © 2003 by Jose Mojica

Editor: William Rodarmor
Production Coordinator: Lisa Brazieal
Proofreader: Corbin Collins
Compositor: Christi Payne
Indexer: Julie Bess
Cover design: The Visual Group

ISBN 0-201-88260-4

9 8 7 6 5 4 3 2 1

Printed and bound in the United States of America

Dedication

To my boys Alex and Andy who know nothing about C# except that it is not a video game I can play with them.

Acknowledgments

I would like to thank Fritz Onion, who offered his expertise in the area of Web programming, and was able to give us the fastest technical edit I have ever seen.

Special thanks to my wonderful wife who always does a lot of work on my books without getting paid.

Honorary mention to Mike Woodring and Craig Andera who have not blocked me yet from instant messenger and are always more than happy to answer my questions.

I would also like to thank the people at Peachpit (William, Lisa, Marjorie, Nancy, and Christi) who hung in there to see this book through to the end.

TABLE OF CONTENTS

TABLE OF CONTENTS

Chapter 10: **Delegates and Events** **303**

Chapter 11: **Error Handling** **331**

INTRODUCTION

What is C#? Pronounced "see-sharp," C# is a brand-new language from Microsoft. It looks a lot like a mixture of C++ and Java, but it's as easy to use as Microsoft Visual Basic, and can be used to build Web applications, desktop Windows applications, and Console Applications, which are applications that look like DOS applications.

C# is one of the languages for Microsoft's new development platform: the .NET Framework; some would argue that it's the premier language for the .NET Framework. Media reports have made .NET sound like the latest marketing buzz word from Microsoft to describe any Web-related product they might have, sort of like their obsession with the letter X (as in ActiveX or even Xbox), but the press is usually clueless when it comes to programming products. Web technology is only part of the purpose of the .NET Framework. The .NET Framework is a replacement for classic technologies such as COM, DCOM, and ASP.

Because C# is part of the .NET Framework, to learn about the C# language, it's good idea to learn a little about the .NET Framework. But before we talk about what the .NET Framework has, let's talk some gossip first.

.NET Framework Gossip

Why did Microsoft develop the .NET Framework? There are many theories. Here I present two of them.

The first theory is that Microsoft's .NET predecessor, the Component Object Model (COM), had a number of flaws, and that .NET was introduced to fix those flaws.

COM was introduced around 1992. One of the goals of COM was to simplify C++ development. In those days C++ developers would write programs for Windows using several kinds of C++ compilers. The compilers would take the C++ source code and turn it into an executable (an EXE file). If a programmer constantly had to write the same code for different executables, the compilers had an option to create a dynamic link library (a DLL file). The DLL would contain a group of the most commonly used functions that all the programs could share. The problem was that the formats for C++ DLLs were different depending on which compiler you used. One of the goals of COM was to provide a technology by which you could create C++ DLLs that worked with programs produced from any C++ compiler.

Around the same time a language called Visual Basic started gaining momentum. C++ programming for Windows was often difficult. The Windows operating system (OS) offers a set of functions that developers can use to develop applications. These functions are called the Windows 32-bit Application Programming Interface (Win32 API). Unless they used a predefined library of functions, C++ developers would often code to use the Win32 API directly, but this was too time-consuming. For example, creating a single form with the APIs alone requires you to declare many variables and structures and monitor messages from the OS such as Paint, MouseDown, MouseUp,

etc. There were a lot of functions to remember and a lot of work to be done just to display the smallest thing. People who programmed exclusively in the Win32 APIs tended to suffer from severe vitamin C deficiency and carpal tunnel syndrome.

Visual Basic programming was simpler. With Visual Basic you don't work with structures and messages to create a form. You simply draw it, and the VB compiler changes the "drawing" into calls to the Win32 API. Because of the popularity of VB, the language was changed to produce and use COM components easily. That served as a bridge between C++ code and Visual Basic code.

Life was good for the most part, except that COM had some "flaws." For one thing, if you wrote COM code in C++ it wasn't guaranteed to be compatible with Visual Basic, and if you wrote it in Visual Basic it wasn't guaranteed to be easy to use in C++. In addition COM DLLs suffered from lack of information. A developer could include with their DLL a file called a type library that described the contents of the DLL, but this was optional, and even if the type library was supplied the information in it was limited. But perhaps the worst part of COM was the phrase "DLL hell." COM relied heavily on the registry, and what was worse, there could only be one version of each COM class registered in the machine. So if someone replaced a new version of a COM component for an older version (or many times even a newer version) chances were that all the applications that needed that COM component would break. Another problem with COM was that it only worked under Windows. This is fine for a lot of desktop developers, but what about the Web developers who used UNIX or Linux, and what about those Mac developers (the few, the proud)?

In this theory, the .NET Framework was introduced to eliminate problems with COM, and in fact, the .NET Framework provides mechanisms to solve a number of these problems.

But here is another theory of why we have the .NET Framework, and this one falls more on the category of gossip than the first.

One of Microsoft's competitors, Sun, developed a language called Java. Java lets you write code once and then deploy it in any operating system because Java programs aren't compiled to machine code directly. Instead they are compiled to Java byte code, and a piece of software called the Java Virtual Machine (JVM) converts the Java byte code to machine code at the time the program is run. Vendors of the OS can provide virtual machines for their operating system, so in theory the same Java program can run in any operating system that has a virtual machine.

Java programs don't depend on the Win32 API. Programmers code to the Java Class Library (JCL). If the program is running under Windows, the JCL calls are then translated into Win32 APIs but if the program runs under another OS, the same calls would be translated to the functions native to that OS.

Companies like IBM, for whom I was working, began to ask themselves, "Why would we want to write new applications using C++ for Windows and be shackled to the Windows OS, and then have to rewrite the application for Linux or Mac later? Why not code once in Java and use the same code in every OS?"

At the beginning Microsoft was interested in the Java language, and they developed their own JVM and their own Java compiler. However, one of the biggest problems Microsoft had with Java was that Java programs did not have the look and feel of traditional Windows programs. Also they felt that the language could use some extensions. Some of those extensions facilitated COM interactions. When Microsoft attempted to extend the Java language, with the idea of making it work better under Windows (which some people argued was just a pretense to try to force people to use Microsoft's extensions for the language), Sun sued to keep Microsoft from adding the enhancements.

The legend goes that at that point, even if Microsoft had not been serious before about writing their own version of the .NET Framework, not being able to extend the JVM surely put them over the edge. It could have been that Microsoft said, "Fine, we'll just do our own virtual machine, and our own language for the virtual machine."

This has become a theory because the .NET Framework shares similar programming paradigms to the Java virtual machine, and the C# language shares many similarities to the Java language. In fact as an instructor whenever I teach C# programming, and I have Java developers in the room, I usually hear during the week, "ah, that is just like Java."

So the truth is out there and probably somewhere in between those two theories, but regardless of why we have the .NET Framework today, the .NET Framework is a great programming platform. It does a good job at solving the problems of its predecessors while at the same time providing a language that is as easy to use and as powerful as Java and provides a mechanism by which we can write code once and deploy it in multiple operating systems.

THE .NET FRAMEWORK GOSSIP

What Is the .NET Framework?

The .NET Framework has two main elements: a virtual machine called the Common Language Runtime (CLR) and the Base Class Libraries (BCL). When you program for .NET, your compiler doesn't generate machine code, the way it used to. It now generates Intermediate Language (IL), which looks a lot like assembly language, except that it's meant to be OS- and CPU-independent. You write code in a high-level language like C# or VB.NET, and the compiler turns your code into IL. The CLR then takes code in IL form and converts it to machine code, which it executes. The code that it generates is called *managed code*. It's managed code because the CLR controls all aspects of allocating memory, lifetime of objects, etc.

The idea is that later companies will write their own versions of the CLR for different operating systems. This is a strong possibility because Microsoft submitted the specification for the CLR to the standards committee ECMA. The Common Language Infrastructure (CLI) (ECMA-335) and C# Language Specification (ECMA-334) became ECMA standards in December 2001 and are available for download as PDF files from www.ecma.ch. Companies can use the ECMA specification to write their own versions of the CLR. At the time of this writing, Microsoft has shipped source code for a scaled-down Intel version and a scaled-down FreeBSD version of the CLR. So it's even mostly open source!

(There is another effort going on called the Mono Project [www.go-mono.com], an open-source effort to port the CLR to Linux and other platforms.)

The BCL is a set of classes and functions that enable you to talk to the operating system and to other technologies, such as XML, ASP.NET, and ADO.NET. The BCL eliminates the need to code to the Win32 API directly.

So Microsoft's goal with the .NET Framework is to get you to use the BCL instead of traditional Win32 APIs. This way, when vendors port the CLR to other platforms along with the BCL, your programs will work in other operating systems and other processors. The same will be true even within the Windows world when new flavors of Windows appear. For example, wouldn't it be nice to write one program that works equally well in Windows XP and Windows CE? To achieve that, at the end of 2002, Microsoft released a version of the CLR and BCL for Windows CE, called the Compact Framework.

So What Is C#?

Microsoft and Sun both offer similar platforms with similar goals. Sun offers the JVM (with the JCL), and Microsoft offers the CLR (with the BCL). Where they differ in focus is in the role of the languages.

Sun offers Java as the language for their platform. It's possible for other languages to compile to Java byte codes and work with the JVM, but Sun doesn't endorse those efforts. They strongly believe that if you're going to use the JVM, you should program in Java.

Microsoft calls its virtual machine the Common Language Runtime because it believes that you shouldn't be tied down to a single language to work with its framework. Microsoft wants all the major compilers (C++, Visual Basic, Java, COBOL, etc.) to compile their code to IL so that they work with the CLR. In other words, BYOL—"bring your own language." You use the language of your choosing, and if the vendor of that language compiles the source to IL, then you can work in the Microsoft Framework.

Some 30 language compilers are being changed to generate IL in order to work with the .NET Framework. This is good because you aren't tied down to one language. The main languages at the moment for .NET are C# and VB.NET. So if you're interested in job security you will probably want to learn one of those two languages or both.

As I noted above, C# is derived from C++ and has the look and feel of Java. It follows the C++ syntax in the way that you declare classes, declare functions, declare variables, write loops, derive classes from others, etc. It's also case sensitive. But it's a much simpler version of C++. It doesn't have pointers (unless you use unsafe code, which is hardly ever needed); it uses single inheritance (a class can only derive from at most one other class),

which eliminates some of the headaches of inheritance; it doesn't have macro support, which a lot of experienced C++ developers detested; and it doesn't have template support, which actually many C++ developers miss, but did complicate programming a bit.

C# is a very compelling language for a number of reasons.

◆ Microsoft submitted the language to ECMA for standardization, and it officially became a standard in December 2001, which means other companies can write compilers for it.

◆ Most of the BCL classes were actually written in C#.

◆ There is a lot of documentation for C# and some would argue that there's more documentation for C# than for the other .NET languages.

◆ It's a cool new language, with a lot of Microsoft marketing effort behind it.

The other main language for the .NET Framework is Visual Basic.NET, which uses the syntax of older versions of Visual Basic and has been greatly changed to account for all the object-oriented features of the BCL. Before .NET came along, there were many more VB developers than C++ developers— as many as 4 million registered users, compared to about 2 million for C++. Both C# and VB compile to IL, so in terms of performance, they are mostly the same.

Some VB developers argue that because VB.NET is so different from previous versions of VB, that if learning VB.NET takes the same amount of effort as learning C#— and Microsoft is pushing C# heavily—why not just learn C#?

It will be interesting to see in the future which language becomes the main development language for the framework.

ASP.NET

A lot of the .NET Framework has to do with Web programming. In the past, developers working with Microsoft's Web Server (IIS) had a choice of writing CGI programs or ISAPI extensions. ISAPI extensions were DLLs, as opposed to CGI programs that were done as EXEs.

DLLs perform better than EXEs in IIS. By writing an ISAPI extension, a programmer could intercept requests made to the Web server, analyze the request, and then tell the server how to respond to the client. So rather than just returning static content to a client, a programmer could return dynamic content with ISAPI extensions. For example, a developer could read a database and use the database information to build the response. However, it was nearly impossible to write a good ISAPI extension. It required knowledge of C++ and writing code that could handle many simultaneous requests.

For that reason, Microsoft wrote one general-purpose ISAPI extension called Active Server Pages (ASP). ASP.DLL executes when clients request documents that end with the .asp extension (other extensions also come into play, but .asp is the main one). A developer would interact with ASP.DLL by writing a script in VBScript or JavaScript. A client would make a request from the server in the form of www.server.com/hello.asp.

IIS would get the request and ask ASP.DLL to handle it. ASP.DLL would then process the script in the page requested (hello.asp). This script would then use ASP-provided objects such as the Request object and the Response object to interact with the Web server. A developer might write a script such as the following:

```
Welcome to Widget's USA Bank:

<%
'code here to open a database table and
'read client's balance
'then store balance in a variable like
'"bal"
%>

Your current balance is <%=bal%>
```

The code would have portions in HTML and then placeholders for code to be processed by ASP.DLL. Code segments would be enclosed between <% %> tags. The client would never see the code for the page, only the HTML generated from the code in his or her browser.

ASP had three main limitations, however. The first was speed. Every time a page was requested, the extension would have to process the script. The second was that ASP had no knowledge of HTML. It enabled the developer to read a request and build a response, but if you wanted to include a table to display figures as part of your response you needed to know how to write the HTML for a table. For example you would need to write a script like the following for a table, and as you'll see, it's a lot of work:

```
<%
'first open database and create a
recordset
'read all records from the authors table
in
'the pubs database
Dim rs
Set rs = CreateObject("ADODB.RecordSet")
rs.Open "select au_id,au_lname from
authors",
"provider=sqloledb;server=.;initial
catalog=pubs;user id=sa;password=;",0,1
```

```
Response.Write("<table
cellspacing=""0"" rules=""all""
border=""1"" id=""DataGrid1"">")

'print headings
Response.Write("<tr>")
Response.Write("<td>ID</td><td>Last
Name</td>")
Response.Write("</tr>")

'loop through all the records. Display
'records in an HTML table.
While rs.EOF <> True
   Response.Write("<tr>")
   Response.Write("<td>" & rs("au_id")
&

"</td>")
   Response.Write("<td>" &
rs("au_lname") &

"</td>")
   Response.Write("</tr>")
   rs.MoveNext
Wend

'finish the table
Response.Write("</table>")
%>
```

I've highlighted the lines that build the table. The rest of the script makes a connection to a SQL Server database and reads all the records from the authors table in the pubs database (one of the sample databases installed with SQL Server).

The third limitation with ASP was that the languages such as VBScript and JavaScript weren't full-featured languages; they lacked some of the essential features of other object-oriented languages.

To overcome the problems associated with ASP, Microsoft created ASP.NET, a brand-new ISAPI extension that works with the .NET Framework. It's mostly contained in aspnet_isapi.dll, one of the DLLs installed when you install the .NET Framework. The function of this DLL is to handle requests for documents that end with the .aspx extension (among others). It can be installed alongside ASP. ASP.NET pages are written in one of the languages for the .NET Framework. They can be written in C#, VB.NET, or even a new version of JavaScript.

The advantage of ASP.NET is that you can use all the features of the language; C# for ASP.NET is no different than C# for desktop applications. Another advantage is that the ASP.NET pages are compiled the very first time they are requested. From then on, any other requests are handled by the compiled version of the page. This makes them as much as three or four times faster than traditional ASP pages.

Finally, ASP.NET lets you use two styles of programming. You can rely on knowing HTML and build things like tables from scratch, or you can develop using Web Forms. Web Forms are pages in which you specify the location of full controls. Say "place table here," and the architecture then generates the HTML necessary to produce the element. Here is an example of a Web Form:

```
<%@Page Language="C#" %>
<%@Import
Namespace="System.Data.SqlClient"%>

<form id="Form1" method="post"
runat="server">
   <asp:DataGrid id="DataGrid1"
runat="server"/>                </form>
```

```
<script runat="server">

private void Page_Load(object sender,
                    System.EventArgs
e)
{
  //first open database and create a
recordset
  //read all records from the authors
table in
  //the pubs database

  SqlConnection conn = new
SqlConnection(

"server=.;database=pubs;uid=sa;pwd=;");

  SqlCommand cmd = new SqlCommand(
  "select au_id,au_lname from
authors",conn);

  conn.Open();
  SqlDataReader rs =
cmd.ExecuteReader();

  DataGrid1.DataSource=rs;
  DataGrid1.DataBind();
}
</script>
```

Look at the highlighted code lines in the preceding example. Notice first the line that starts with the tag "asp:" This tag tells the ASP.NET code generator to declare a WebControl field called DataGrid1 of type System.Web.UI.WebControls.DataGrid1. The DataGrid control knows how to draw its contents as an HTML table. To set the contents of the grid we use another feature of the DataGrid control called *databinding*.

(The lines that use the databinding feature are also highlighted.) With databinding, you set the control's datasource property to a collection of records like a datareader (the equivalent of a read-only forward-only recordset in old ADO) and then call the DataBind function. The grid takes care of setting its contents to the records in the datareader. (A complete discussion of databinding is beyond the scope of this book.)

In addition to Web Forms knowing HTML, they simulate classical desktop development. ASP development used to require that you learn one way of programming for desktop applications and a different one for Web applications. With ASP.NET, Web programming uses the same event-driven style as desktop application programming. In the example above, when the page loads, the Page_Load event fires, similar to the Load event in typical Visual Basic forms and even the new .NET Windows Forms. All these new features make ASP.NET a much better choice for Web development than its predecessor.

ASP.NET

What Is this Book About?

My goal in this book is to teach you the C# language. But as a writer, I had a choice to make in presenting the code examples to illustrate the language. One: I could show the examples in the context of console applications. C# enables you to write "DOS-looking" applications that run in the Command Prompt Window—boring! Two: I could show the examples in the context of Windows Forms applications. Or three: I could show the examples in the context of Web programming. I chose the third option, because I believe that the majority of people using C# will be building Web applications.

This book makes no attempt to teach Web programming. It assumes that you're inter-ested in learning the language, but it also assumes that you're learning the language with a project in mind, and that that project would most likely be a Web application. There is very little Web programming used in the examples and the concepts can be used just as well in other types of applica-tions. The information is presented in refer-ence style. The idea is that you can say, "Here is what I'm trying to do, show me the steps to do it." The book then shows you the steps to do a particular task. The book is also built so that you don't have to read the chapters sequentially.

I present core concepts of the C# language in Chapter 1, "Getting Started," Chapter 2, "C# Building Blocks," and Chapter 3, "Conditionals and Loops." If you're new to C++ or to object-oriented concepts, you may want to read these chapters first, before jumping to the later sections. From then on, you can read chapters in any order you wish. Although the book is about the C# language, Chapter 13 will give you more information about building Web applications, and Web Services.

Whom Is this Book For?

This book is for beginners. If you know a little programming, especially in either JavaScript or VBScript, you're more than qualified to read it. The book assumes that you're new to object-oriented programming.

If you have experience with object-oriented principles you can still learn from this book, because a number of things work differently in C# from other languages like C++ or Java. But I'll warn you when I am about to cover material that you already know.

About the Author

I guess you may also want to know who I am. I am a programmer and instructor, and I teach C# classes to various companies. I have even taught Microsoft consultants about C# and the .NET Framework. I work for a company called DevelopMentor, and have written a number of books, including *C# & VB.NET Conversion Pocket Reference*, *COM+ Programming With Visual Basic*, and *Activex Controls With Visual Basic 5.0*. I've also co-authored *Distributed Applications with Microsoft Visual C++ 6.0: MCSD Training Kit*, and *Programming Internet Controls* (way back when).

I have been teaching C# since it was legal to do so, which was after its announcement at the PDC conference in 2000. I've tried to model this book around the things that have worked best when teaching C#.

When I teach, students often tell me that what they like best about my teaching style are the demos I do. I like to code my demos on the fly, from scratch. Here is what I normally do when I teach: At the beginning of each lesson I start a project. Then, as I cover a few slides, I add code to the project. I have tried to copy the same style in the book. At the beginning of each chapter I start a project. Then, after covering several topics, I ask you to add code to the project that relates to the concepts you've just learned.

What You Need in Order to Learn C#

There are two main ways to get the C# language and ASP.NET installed in your machine. Chapter 1, "Getting Started," guides you through both ways. To learn C# all you really need is the C# compiler (and this book, of course). The C# compiler is included as part of the .NET Framework. You can download the .NET Framework directly from Microsoft—it's a free download. The .NET Framework will also give you all you need to run ASP.NET applications, as long as your machine can run IIS (Windows XP and Windows 2000 Professional are enough. See Chapter 1 for details).

What you don't get with the .NET Framework is a nice C# editor. You would have to use Notepad and work with the command-line compiler if you're going the free route. But people are developing open-source editors for C# that look pretty nice, so you may want to try some of these before spending any money.

If you prefer the Microsoft editor, you need to buy Visual Studio .NET. Visual Studio .NET comes in many flavors: Visual C# Standard Visual Studio .NET Professional, VS.NET Enterprise Developer and VS.NET Enterprise Architect. The Standard version costs close to $100 as of the release of this book, but it is not recommended for serious development. The Professional version costs around $1,000. With the Standard editions you only get support for one .NET language; with Professional you get support for all of them.

Final Thoughts

There is a lot to learn in .NET, especially if you're going to do Web programming. You will need to learn one of the .NET languages first. Here is how I learned .NET. First I learned the language, then the base class libraries, and finally all the Web-specific things. Learning C# is half the battle. It's easy to switch from C# to other languages like VB.NET and you will find that a lot of .NET features are tailored for C#. So you're making a very good choice in spending time to learn the C# language. Have fun!

1

GETTING STARTED

In the Introduction, you learned about the .NET Framework and the origins of the C# language. Now it's time to start writing applications. The goal of this chapter is to install the software necessary to build and debug C# Web-based applications as well as stand-alone ones.

Even though the sample code throughout the book is presented in the context of Web applications, the focus of each sample is the C# language. You can certainly use the same code in the context of stand-alone console applications or stand-alone Windows Forms applications.

I am defining a stand-alone application as an .EXE that runs without the need of a Web browser. Microsoft Word is an example of a stand-alone application, but Microsoft Word is a native application rather than a .NET application.

Getting C#

The first step in building C# applications is making sure that you have the C# compiler installed in your machine. There are two ways to ensure that. One way is to install Visual Studio .NET from the Visual Studio .NET CDs. The setup program will first install the .NET Framework. (The .NET Framework includes the C# compiler csc.exe.) If you don't have the Visual Studio .NET CDs, you can download and install the .NET Framework for free from Microsoft.com.

To download and install the .NET framework:

1. Install Internet Explorer (IE) 5.5 or higher. Using your browser, navigate to the download area for Internet Explorer. The IE download section is at www.microsoft.com/windows/ie /default.asp (**Figure 1.1**).

2. Install Internet Information Services (IIS). (See "Installing Internet Information Services" later in this chapter.)

3. Using your Web browser, navigate to the .NET download section. The .NET Framework download section is at msdn.microsoft.com/netframework/ downloads/howtoget.asp (**Figure 1.2**).

4. Click the "Get the .NET Framework SDK" link.

5. Click the "Full SDK Download" link (**Figure 1.3**).

Figure 1.1 The .NET Framework requires Internet Explorer 5.5 or higher. If you're running Windows 2000, you may need to download the latest version of IE from Microsoft.

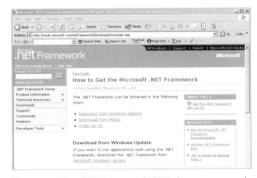

Figure 1.2 The .NET Framework SDK gives you enough tools to compile, run, and debug .NET applications, including ASP .NET pages. It doesn't provide a nice editor the way Visual Studio .NET does.

Figure 1.3 The .NET Framework is a free download. You could also download the redistributable runtime if you only need the files necessary to run .NET programs but not to write them.

GETTING C#

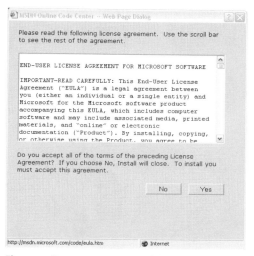

Figure 1.4 Does anyone ever read these things?

Running .NET Applications

You're now ready to write .NET applications with C#. The next question is, what do people need in their machines to run your .NET applications? Of course, any machine that has the .NET Framework SDK, or Visual Studio .NET, installed can run .NET programs. But what about machines that don't have or want any trace of the .NET development tools? Microsoft provides a program called dotnetredist.exe. It is known as the .NET Runtime Redistributable. When you run this program on a client machine, it installs the files necessary to run .NET applications. You can install the .NET runtime (not the SDK) in any flavor of Windows. To get dotnetredist.exe you can download it from the .NET download section. In fact, the download page for the redistributable is the page displayed after step 4 in the instructions above.

6. You will see a license agreement dialog. Click Yes to proceed if you agree with the licensing conditions (**Figure 1.4**).

7. After you click Yes, the browser will display the standard download dialog that asks if you wish to save or open the program. Choose Save or Open. If you choose Save, look for setup.exe in the download directory and run it.

8. Follow the directions of the setup program.

✔ Tips

■ The .NET Framework SDK includes the C# compiler, csc.exe (as well as other .NET compilers such as the Visual Basic .NET compiler, vbc.exe), and a visual debugger, dbgclr.exe. The only thing missing is a nice editor with intellisense, like Visual Studio .NET. (Intellisense is a Microsoft feature in the editor that displays choices for class names and function names as you type.)

■ The SDK is enough for you to build ASP .NET applications and stand-alone C# applications, but you will need to use a text editor to edit the code (notepad.exe is sufficient.), or one of the many third-party code editors. You can download a free editor called Web Matrix to build ASP .NET applications from www.asp.net/webmatrix/download.aspx

■ To install the .NET Framework SDK or Visual Studio .NET you must have Windows NT 4.0 (Service Pack 6a required), Windows 2000, or Windows XP Professional. These operating systems are sufficient to develop C# stand-alone or C# Windows Forms applications. To write ASP.NET applications you can't use Windows NT 4.0. You must have Windows 2000 or Windows XP Professional or higher.

GETTING C#

Installing Internet Information Services (IIS)

If you're going to build Web applications you must install the Microsoft Web Server, Internet Information Services (IIS) version 5.0 or higher. This tool is available in Windows 2000 Professional and higher and in Windows XP Professional and higher. In Windows 2000 Server edition and higher IIS is automatically installed with the operating system. In Windows XP Professional and in Windows 2000 Professional you must install IIS manually.

To install IIS:

1. Open the Windows Control Panel and click the Add or Remove Programs icon (**Figure 1.5**).

2. Click the Add/Remove Windows Components icon (**Figure 1.6**).

Figure 1.5 In Windows 2000 Professional and Windows XP Professional you must install IIS manually. You can do that from the Control Panel.

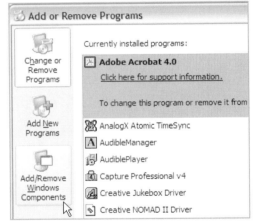

Figure 1.6 IIS is a Windows Component. Click the Add/Remove Windows Components icon to install it.

Figure 1.7 When you select IIS from the list, you will notice that the check box is grayed, indicating that not all related components are being installed. The only things missing from a full install are the Printers Virtual Directory component and the Remote Desktop Web Connection, neither of which is required for ASP .NET.

3. Select Internet Information Services from the list of components (**Figure 1.7**).

4. Click Next.

✔ Tips

■ Although you can also use Windows NT 4.0 and Windows XP Home Edition to build C# applications, you can't author ASP .NET applications with these products.

■ It doesn't matter if you install Visual Studio .NET or the .NET Framework SDK. As long as you have IIS installed, the setup program will install the files necessary to write and host ASP .NET applications.

■ If you don't install IIS before installing .NET Framework, the Web server won't be configured correctly. The file extensions for ASP.NET pages, such as .aspx, won't be associated with the correct ISAPI DLL. The .NET Framework program will warn you if you try to setup the SDK before IIS. However, if you choose to ignore the warning and install IIS after the SDK or if you uninstall and re-install IIS without re-installing the Framework SDK, you can run \Windows \Microsoft.NET\Framework\v1.0.3705\as pnet_regiis.exe to setup all the file associations in IIS for ASP.NET.

Creating a Web Project with Visual Studio .NET

This book focuses on C# in the context of creating ASP .NET applications, so it's fitting to show how to create a simple one. Perhaps the most common way to create ASP .NET applications is to use Visual Studio .NET.

To create an ASP.NET application with Visual Studio .NET:

1. Choose Start > All Programs > Microsoft Visual Studio .NET > Microsoft Visual Studio .NET to start Visual Studio .NET (**Figure 1.8**).

2. Click the New Project button. You will see the New Project Wizard (**Figure 1.9**).

3. On the Project Types side click Visual C# Projects. Then, on the Templates side choose ASP.NET Web application.

4. The Location field in the dialog will read "http://localhost/WebApplication1." Change WebApplication1 to the name you wish to give your application. For this example name it gettingstarted. Then click OK to continue. The project wizard will create a new project and display a Web Form in the editor (**Figure 1.10**).

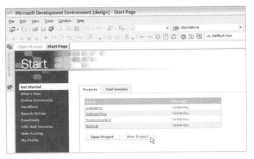

Figure 1.8 Start Visual Studio .NET to create a Web application. Click New Project.

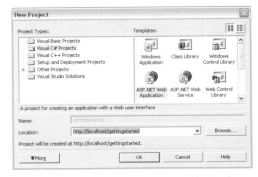

Figure 1.9 To create a Web application with visual elements select ASP.NET Web Application from the list of Visual C# Projects. Notice the ASP.NET Web Service icon. A Web service is a Web application that doesn't have visual elements. It enables a client program to execute a function in the Web application and get a result via XML rather than HTML.

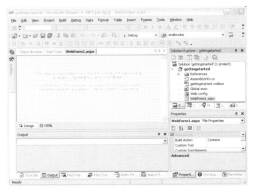

Figure 1.10 Creating an ASP.NET Web Application with the VS .NET Wizard creates a project with a Web Form. The editor displays the empty Web Form.

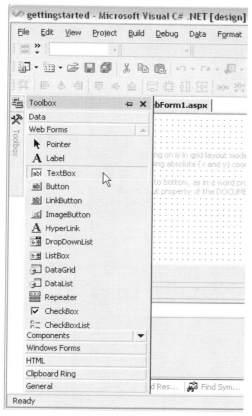

Figure 1.11 The Toolbox displays all the available Web controls.

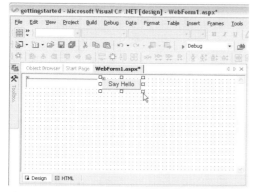

Figure 1.12 In essence, you can draw your Web Form. First you draw the controls onto the form, then you modify their properties.

5. Click View > Toolbox from the top menu. You will see the toolbox window on the left (**Figure 1.11**).

6. Double-click the TextBox icon in the toolbox to add a TextBox control to the form.

7. Double-click the Button icon in the toolbox to add a Button to the form.

8. Click on the newly created Button control to select it.

9. Click View > Properties Window from the top menu.

10. In the Properties window change the Text property to Say Hello, then move the button to the right of the TextBox (**Figure 1.12**).

11. Double-click the button control (which now reads Say Hello) to go into the code editor window. The editor will position the cursor inside a new function `Button1_Click`.

continues on next page

CREATING A WEB PROJECT WITH VS .NET

12. Type TextBox1.Text = "Hello there!"; (**Figure 1.13**).

13. Choose Debug > Start from the top menu bar. You will see Internet Explorer displaying your Web Form with a TextBox and a Button that reads Say Hello.

14. Click the Say Hello button, and the TextBox control should now read "Hello there!" (**Figure 1.14**).

✔ Tips

■ The Web Form you created has two elements to it. It contains an ASPX page with visual elements such as the TextBox and the Button. This page is named WebForm1.aspx by default. The code you typed is saved in a separate file, known as the code-behind file named WebForm1.aspx.cs.

■ When you choose Debug > Start from the menu, Visual Studio .NET enters debugging mode. However, VS .NET compiles your program before entering debugging mode. It takes all the code-behind files and combines them into a single DLL, which it then places into a subdirectory called bin. The DLL's name is the name of the project plus the DLL extension. VS.NET leaves the .aspx visual pages as text files. They will be compiled separately into DLLs by the ASP.NET architecture when requested by the client's browser.

Figure 1.13 Controls have events that trigger when the user interacts with them. For example, the Button control recognizes the Click action. You then write code for the Click event of the button. Double-clicking on the control in the visual designer causes VS .NET to open the code editor and add the control's default event.

Figure 1.14 Clicking the Say Hello button causes the Web browser to contact the Web server, IIS, and request a new page. IIS then runs your application and triggers the code you entered for the Click event. The code then sets the Text property of the TextBox to Hello there!, which causes the TextBox control to generate an HTML edit control with the phrase Hello there! in it.

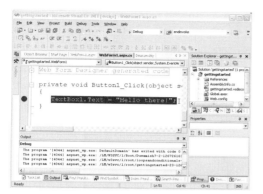

Figure 1.15 VS .NET highlights in red code that has a breakpoint, though it's hard to tell from this grayscale figure (they appear as reversed characters in the figure).

Debugging Web Projects with Visual Studio .NET

Visual Studio .NET offers an integrated environment for developing and debugging of ASP .NET applications. All you need to do to debug an application is add breakpoints to your code and run the application.

As you run the application, if the debugger encounters a line of code with a breakpoint, it pauses the execution of the program and puts you back in the edit window. From there you can step through the code one line at a time and analyze variables.

To debug a Web application using VS .NET:

1. Select a file that contains code you wish to debug. To do so, click View > Solution Explorer.

2. Right-click on the file and select View Code from the pop-up menu.

3. Place the cursor on the line of code you wish to stop.

4. Press F9 or right-click on the line of code and select Insert breakpoint from the pop-up menu. The line will be highlighted in red (**Figure 1.15**).

5. Choose Debug > Start from the top menu.

✔ Tips

- Once you run the program in the debugger, do something that will trigger the code where you put a breakpoint. If it is the code for the button, click the button. This will cause the debugger to halt at the breakpoint and put you back in the editor window with the line highlighted in yellow (**Figure 1.16**).

- Once you stop at a breakpoint, Press F11 to execute one line at a time.

- When you hit a breakpoint you can edit your code, but the changes won't take effect immediately. You have to restart the debugger for the changes to kick in.

- The Locals window within the development window (or in fancy terms, IDE for Interactive Development Environment) displays the variables available in the function that is currently executing.

- The Command Window lets you read or set the value of a variable. Type ? varname to print the value of a variable or varname = value to set the value of a variable, then press Enter.

- Even while the debugger is running, you can go back to the IDE, find a line of code, and place a breakpoint. The debugger will stop at that line without your having to restart the application.

- Choose Debug > Stop Debugging to stop the debugger.

- Press Ctrl-F5 to run the Web application without the debugger. This is useful when you want to run the program without stopping at each breakpoint and without first having to remove all the breakpoints.

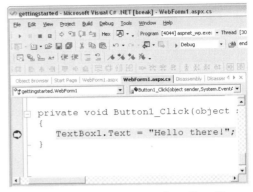

Figure 1.16 When the debugger reaches a line with a breakpoint, it pauses the program and puts you back to the code editor window. The line of code highlighted in yellow on your screen is the next line the debugger will execute.

Figure 1.17 This feature in Windows Explorer makes it easy to create Web virtual directories. Each Web virtual directory represents a separate ASP .NET application.

Figure 1.18 You don't have to name the virtual directory the same as your folder. The name you enter in this dialog is what goes after the .com part of the URL when a user is browsing. For example in www.microsoft.com/net, net is a virtual directory.

Writing a Simple ASP .NET Page

Earlier, you learned how to build a simple Web application with Visual Studio .NET. You don't need to use VS .NET to build ASP .NET applications. An alternative is to use everyone's favorite Web application editor, notepad.exe (though any other text editor is fine as well).

To author ASP .NET applications without VS .NET:

1. Create a directory in which to save your work.

2. With Windows Explorer, locate the directory you created and right-click on it.

3. Select Properties.

4. Click the Web Sharing tab (**Figure 1.17**).

5. Select the Share this folder option to view the Edit Alias dialog (**Figure 1.18**).

6. Press OK to accept the default settings.

7. Click OK to commit changes.

8. Left-click the directory you created in step 1.

9. Right-click in the right-hand pane.

continues on next page

WRITING A SIMPLE ASP .NET PAGE

10. Select New > Text Document.

11. Enter `default.aspx` for the filename and press Enter. Click Yes when asked if you're sure you wish to rename the extension for the file.

12. Right-click the newly created file and select Open With. Select notepad.exe from the list of programs.

13. Enter the code in **Figure 1.19** and save your changes.

14. From the Start menu, select Run and type `http://localhost/nameofdir/default.aspx`. Replace nameofdir with the name of the directory you created step 1 (**Figure 1.20**).

✔ Tips

■ If you don't see Web Sharing as a tab option (step 4), you may not have IIS installed in your operating system. See "Installing Internet Information Services" earlier in this chapter.

■ The first step in creating ASP .NET applications is to create a virtual directory in IIS. A virtual directory defines a Web application. You created a virtual directory for IIS in steps 2–7. The virtual directory you created is not accessible to anonymous users (users that don't have permission to access your machine). To allow anyone to access the site you would need to change the permissions for your virtual directory through IIS.

■ It's very important that you name your pages with an .aspx extension. This extension signals IIS to hand the request to the ASP .NET ISAPI extension. An ISAPI extension is a DLL (Dynamic Link Library) that communicates with IIS to analyze client requests and provide client responses. You don't have to name your page default, but IIS automatically looks for a page named default if the client forgets the name of the document.

Figure 1.19 Unlike older versions of ASP, you can now use strongly typed variables. That means that you can declare variables as strings or integers, like in this example.

```
<%@Page Language="c#" debug="true" %>
<%@Import Namespace="System.Text" %>

Thank you for purchasing C# VQS Guide:<br>

<%
StringBuilder str = new
StringBuilder("ASP .NET is so ");

for (int i = 0; i < 10 ;i++)
    str.Append("cool ");

str.Append("!");
Response.Write(str.ToString());
%>
```

Figure 1.20 The text passed to the program through the Response.Write command appears in the browser.

(side margin) WRITING A SIMPLE ASP .NET PAGE

Debugging ASP .NET Applications

You can also debug ASP .NET applications outside of Visual Studio .NET. That means that you can put breakpoints in your .aspx documents and have the program stop when the client requests that page. Then you can single-step through the code in the document.

There is one small limitation with debugging ASP .NET applications both in VS .NET and outside of VS .NET, but debugging outside VS .NET makes it apparent.

The application that runs your ASP .NET applications is ASPNET_WP.EXE. This program has to be run by the Web server (through the ISAPI extension) in order to work correctly. That means that you can't just ask the debugger to execute that application directly. Instead the debugger lets you attach it to a running instance of the application.

For the ASPNET_WP.EXE program to be running with your ASP .NET application executing, you must use the Web browser to navigate to the application first. This will make ASPNET_WP.EXE run, then you can attach the debugger to ASPNET_WP.EXE and debug your pages. That limitation is unfortunate because it means you can't debug in scenarios where a client launches your application for the first time.

To debug ASP .NET applications:

1. Build your application with debug information. When you do this, the compiler creates another file with the extension .PDB that helps it associate the compiled code with the source code. As you execute the compiled program, the debugger can use this file to identify the source code that produced the machine code that is currently executing. You tell the compiler to add debug information by adding debug="true" to the page directive at the top of the page (**Figure 1.21**).

2. Run Internet Explorer (or your Web browser of choice) and enter the URL for the first page in your application, for example: http://localhost/nameofdir /default.aspx. Don't close the browser after displaying the page.

3. Run the .NET SDK debugger. To do so, choose Start > Run, then type "C:\Program Files\Microsoft.NET \FrameworkSDK\GuiDebug\DbgCLR.exe" if you installed the Framework SDK only. If you installed Visual Studio .NET, type "C:\Program Files\Microsoft Visual Studio .NET\FrameworkSDK\GuiDebug \DbgCLR.exe" (**Figure 1.22**). Remember that when you enter paths with spaces and long names in the Run window you have to include quotation marks around the name.

4. Choose Tools > Debug Process from the menu bar (**Figure 1.23**).

Figure 1.21 Putting the debug="true" attribute in the Page directive tells the ASP .NET compiler to compile your code with the /debug+ switch. This enables you to debug your aspx documents.

Figure 1.22 The .NET SDK debugger works equally well for ASP .NET applications and for stand-alone applications.

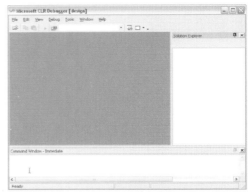

Figure 1.23 The processes dialog shows a list of running programs, including .NET programs and native (non-.NET) programs. However, the debugger only works with .NET code.

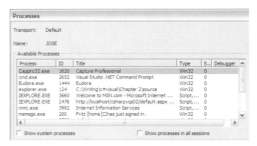

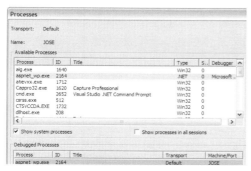

Figure 1.24 aspnet_wp.exe is the process that hosts your Web applications. It will appear on the list after you run an ASP .NET application.

Figure 1.25 You can open the source code file for any aspx page related to your application. Then you can put breakpoints in your code and have the debugger stop when a user requests the page.

Figure 1.26 Once the source code is displayed in the debugger, you can place breakpoints by clicking on the line you wish to stop and pressing the F9 key. The debugger will highlight the line of code in red.

5. Double-click aspnet_wp.exe from the list. You should see aspnet_wp.exe appear in the Debugged Processes list (**Figure 1.24**).

6. Click the Close button.

7. Choose File > Open > File from the menu bar.

8. Find and select the aspx page you're viewing in your browser. The debugger should now display the source code for the aspx page (**Figure 1.25**).

9. Select the first line of code and press F9 to place a breakpoint on that line. The debugger will highlight that line in red (**Figure 1.26**).

10. Go back to the Web browser and click the Refresh button.

11. Switch back to DbgCLR.exe. You should see the first line highlighted in yellow, indicating that the program has halted.

12. Press F11 to step into functions, F10 to step over functions, or F5 to run until the next breakpoint or until the end of the program.

✔ Tips

- If you stop the application from running (by selecting Debug > Stop Debugging) you will need to repeat the process of attaching to the running process (starting at step 3).

- If you continue to run the program until it ends (by pressing F5) you don't have to re-attach. You can simply click the refresh button in the browser to stop once again at your breakpoint.

Running the Compiler Manually

One of the programs included in the .NET SDK is the C# command-line compiler, csc.exe. ASP .NET uses csc.exe to compile your Web pages into DLLs when the client requests them for the first time from the browser. But you can also write stand-alone applications with Visual Studio .NET or with the text editor of your choice, then run the C# command-line compiler manually to produce an executable.

Using the command-line compiler:

1. If you installed Visual Studio .NET, choose Start >All Programs > Microsoft Visual Studio .NET > Visual Studio .NET Tools > Visual Studio .NET Command Prompt.

   or

   If you installed the .NET Framework SDK (and not Visual Studio .NET), choose Start > All Programs > Accessories > Command Prompt.

2. From the command prompt type: csc.exe /?.

✔ Tips

- The name of the C# compiler is csc.exe.

- If you run csc.exe /?, the program tells you all the command line options you can use with the compiler (**Figure 1.27**). For an example of some of the most important options see "Compiling and Executing a C# Program" later in this chapter.

Figure 1.27 Running csc.exe /? makes the compiler display the list of command line parameters for the compiler. For example /t specifies the target type: exe for console, winexe for a Windows Form application, library to create a DLL, and module to create a compiled file that can be combined with other modules to make an assembly.

Figure 1.28 All code in C# must be part of a class. For a console application, one of the classes must have a Main procedure. The runtime begins the program by executing the Main function.

```
Code                                    _ □ ×

using System.Text;

class HelloApp
{
    static void Main()
    {
        System.Console.WriteLine("Thank you for
purchasing C# VQS Guide:");

        StringBuilder str = new
        StringBuilder("ASP .NET is so ");

        for (int i = 0; I < 10; i++)
           str.Append("cool ");

        str.Append("!");

        System.Console.WriteLine(
        str.ToString());
    }
}
```

Figure 1.29 If you don't select All Files in the Save As Type field in notepad, notepad adds a .txt extension. Worse, if you have the option "Hide extensions for known file types" in the Windows Explorer folder options, you won't see the txt extension and will wonder why the ASP page isn't running properly.

Compiling and Executing C# Programs without VS .NET

There is no easier way to practice running the command-line compiler than to create a stand-alone console application outside VS .NET. A console application is an application that runs inside the command prompt window. The best way to describe it (if you're an old-timer like me) is that a console application looks like a DOS app rather than a Windows app.

To run the C# command line compiler:

1. Create a directory in which to save your work.

2. From the Start menu choose Run.

3. Type notepad.exe.

4. Type in the code shown in **Figure 1.28** and save the code as cstest.cs. Make sure that before you save you select All Files in the Save As Type field of the Save As dialog (**Figure 1.29**). Otherwise, Notepad will append .txt to the end of the filename.

5. If you installed Visual Studio .NET, choose Start > All Programs > Microsoft Visual Studio .NET > Visual Studio .NET Tools > Visual Studio .NET Command Prompt.

   or

   If you installed the .NET Framework SDK (and not Visual Studio .NET), choose Start > All Programs > Accessories > Command Prompt.

continues on next page

6. From the Command Prompt window change to the directory you created in step 1.

7. Type csc.exe /t:exe /out:cstest.exe cstest.cs.

8. Press Enter.

9. Type cstest.exe and then press Enter to execute the application (**Figure 1.30**).

✔ Tips

■ C# source files normally have the .cs extension, but you can give the source files any extension you like.

■ The parameter /t:exe tells the compiler to build a stand-alone application that runs inside the command prompt. Since /t:exe is the default option for csc.exe, omitting it also produces a console application.

■ To run a .NET EXE, the machine has to have the .NET runtime installed. This means that at the very least you must install the .NET Runtime redistributable file Microsoft provides. The concept is analogous to Java, where there must be a virtual machine installed on the machine for the Java code to run.

Figure 1.30 The compiler will display errors if you didn't type the code accurately. Otherwise the compiler will just display the copyright notice. When you run the program it displays its text in the console window.

COMPILING C# APPS WITHOUT VS .NET

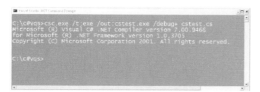

Figure 1.31 Compiling with the /debug+ has the effect of creating a debug file in addition to the executable. The debug file has the extension .pdb. The debugger uses this file to map the running program to the source code.

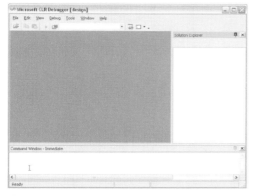

Figure 1.32 The .NET SDK ships with a visual debugger that has a similar look and feel to the debugger in Visual Studio .NET.

Figure 1.33 Enter the program you wish to debug. The debugger will run the program when you click the F11 key or the F5 key.

Debugging Applications Outside VS .NET

If you're using Visual Studio .NET to develop your application, you can easily run your application within the debugger by choosing Debug > Start from the menu options, or by pressing the F5 key.

If you're using another editor, the .NET Framework SDK includes a visual debugger you can use that has the same capabilities as the Visual Studio .NET debugger.

To use the SDK debugger:

1. Build your application with the debugging switch /debug+. If your source code name is cstest.cs, then the line to run the command-line compiler would resemble the following: `csc.exe /t:exe /out:cstest.exe /debug+ cstest.cs` (**Figure 1.31**).

2. Change directories to: C:\Program Files\Microsoft.NET\FrameworkSDK \GuiDebug.

3. Run DbgCLR.exe (**Figure 1.32**).

4. Choose Debug > Program to Debug.

5. Enter the path to the EXE you wish to debug in the program field. You can also search for the executable by clicking the [...] button next to the Program: field (**Figure 1.33**).

continues on next page

6. Press F11 to step into the program. The debugger will open the source code for the program and stop at the first line (**Figure 1.34**).

7. To set a breakpoint in the source code, select the line where you wish the program to halt, and press the F9 key. The debugger will highlight the source code line in red.

8. Press F11 to step into functions, F10 to step over functions, or F5 to run until the next breakpoint or until the end of the program.

✔ Tips

■ If the debugger won't let you place a breakpoint on the code, it is most likely because you didn't build your application with the /debug+ switch.

■ You can stop execution of the program by selecting Debug > Stop Debugging from the menu bar.

Figure 1.34 If you press F11, the debugger will run your program and stop in the first line of source code. The line of source code will be highlighted in yellow.

C# BUILDING BLOCKS

In the previous chapter you got a taste for how to run Visual Studio .NET, and how to enter some code and execute it. In this chapter you're going to start learning how to write C# code. In order to write code it's essential to learn a few of the basics. We'll start by learning how to declare variables and functions, and then we'll proceed to combining those variables and functions into classes. A class is a group of code that serves as a blueprint; the blueprint is used to create objects.

Working with C# Building Blocks

One way to learn the concepts in this chapter is to put them into practice. For that reason I will start a sample project at the beginning of each chapter. Some of the topics in the chapter show code from the sample project and tell you where to add the particular portion of code. Other sections show code that doesn't come from one of the examples. Whenever there is code that you need to add to the example to make it work, I will point that out in the tips for that particular section. At the end of the chapter you should have a small project that you can use later as a reference.

The purpose of the example program for this chapter is to maintain a list of tasks—a to-do list—and to display the list to the user as requested. The program has two Web pages. The first page enables you to add items to the to-do list. An item consists of a short name and a description. The second page displays a grid (a table) of all the items that have been added to the to-do list.

Building the project isn't necessary for learning the concepts in this chapter, but it is helpful.

To create a test project for this chapter:

1. Launch Visual Studio .NET. (Start > All Programs > Microsoft Visual Studio .NET > Microsoft Visual Studio .NET).

2. Select File > New > Project from the top menu bar to bring up the New Project dialog.

3. Under project types on the left side of the New Project window click the Visual C# projects folder.

4. Select the ASP.NET Web Application icon and change the name of the application to classesandmembers (**Figure 2.1**).

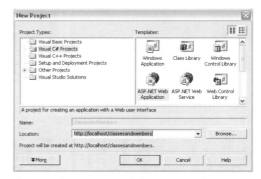

Figure 2.1 The New Project dialog lets you select among various project types. Most projects you will write in this book will be ASP.NET Web Applications. The dialog also remembers the last project type you selected.

Figure 2.2 Changing the filename through the property browser also renames the physical file.

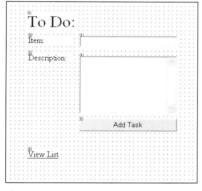

Figure 2.4 The purpose of this form is to add tasks to a ToDo list. A user assigns a name to the task and enters a description, then clicks the Add Task button. To view the list, the user clicks the View List link.

Figure 2.5 Notice how easy it is to toggle between HTML and Design view in the VS.NET editor. VS.NET keeps both the graphical representation and the HTML synchronized; changes to either one automatically get reflected on the other.

5. Visual Studio will create a new project and open WebForm1.aspx.

6. Change the form's name to entertask.aspx. Do so by choosing View > Solution Explorer from the top menu bar.

7. Right-click on WebForm1.aspx and choose properties. In the property grid below change the FileName property from WebForm1.aspx to entertask.aspx (**Figure 2.2**).

8. Create a form that looks like the form in **Figure 2.4**. Obviously this is a lot of work to do by hand if you aren't familiar with how to draw controls onto a Web Form (see sidebar on page 25). Instead you can enter the HTML directly into the editor. **Figure 2.3** (next page) shows the HTML necessary to create the form. To enter the HTML directly click the HTML button under the editor's window. The window will then look like the window in **Figure 2.5**. If books supported copy-and-paste, this option would work really well, but they don't. As an alternative you could download the skeleton file for this project (see Tips below).

✔ Tip

■ Skeletons for each project can be downloaded from Peachpit's Web site, http://www.peachpit.com/vqs/csharp.

Figure 2.3 The Visual Studio .NET lets you draw each control graphically, or manipulate the HTML script directly. If you add the HTML script shown here the editor will display the controls for the project.

Figure 2.3 *continued*

```
█ Code                                    _ □ ×
<%@ Page language="c#"
    Codebehind="entertask.aspx.cs"
    AutoEventWireup="false"
    Inherits="classesandmembers.WebForm1"
    %>
<HTML>
    <HEAD>
        <title>WebForm1</title>
    </HEAD>
    <body MS_POSITIONING="GridLayout">
        <form id="Form1" method="post"
        runat="server">
            <asp:hyperlink
                id="hypViewList"
                style="Z-INDEX: 107; LEFT:
                41px;
                POSITION: absolute;
                TOP: 287px"
                runat="server"
                NavigateUrl="viewlist.aspx">
                View List
                </asp:hyperlink>
            <asp:textbox
                id="txtItem"
                style="Z-INDEX: 101;
                LEFT: 138px;
                POSITION: absolute;
                TOP: 66px" runat="server"
                Width="184px">
                </asp:textbox>
            <asp:label
                id="lblToDo"
                style="Z-INDEX: 102;
                LEFT: 39px;
                POSITION: absolute;
                TOP: 22px" runat="server"
                Font-Size="X-Large">
                To Do:</asp:label>
            <asp:textbox
                id="txtDescription"
                style="Z-INDEX: 103;
                LEFT: 138px;
                POSITION: absolute;
                TOP: 105px" runat="server"
                Width="184"
                TextMode="MultiLine"
                Height="112px">
                </asp:textbox>

                        code continues
```

```
█ Code                                    _ □ ×
            <asp:label
                id="lblItem"
                style="Z-INDEX: 104;
                LEFT: 41px;
                POSITION: absolute;
                TOP: 66px" runat="server"
                Width="82px"
                Height="15px">
                Item:
                </asp:label>
            <asp:label
                id="lblDescription"
                style="Z-INDEX: 105;
                LEFT: 41px;
                POSITION: absolute;
                TOP: 100px" runat="server"
                Width="80px">
                Description:
                </asp:label>
            <asp:button
                id="btnTask"
                style="Z-INDEX: 106;
                LEFT: 138px;
                POSITION: absolute;
                TOP: 229px" runat="server"
                Width="184px"
                Text="Add Task">
                </asp:button>
        </form>
    </body>
</HTML>
```

Adding Controls to a Web Form

You can add controls to a Web Form by drawing the controls on the form. To do that, choose View > Toolbox from the top menu bar. Then select a control from the toolbox (**Figure 2.6**). Once the control is selected you can move the cross cursor to the form, left click and hold, move the mouse again and let go of the button when you're done drawing the control. Alternatively, you could drag-and-drop the control from the toolbox onto the form, or simply double-click on the toolbox control.

After you've added the control you can right-click on the control and choose properties. That will display a property grid like the one you saw in **Figure 2.2**.

Figure 2.6 The toolbox contains a list of the Web controls you can add to your Web form.

Writing C# Code

Before we start writing C# code, let's talk about some of the basic concepts of C# syntax.

To write C# code:

◆ C# is a case-sensitive language. That means that if the help says a command is written AddTwoNumbers, you can't write addtwonumbers; it won't work. You have to make sure you match the case of each letter to the original command (**Figure 2.7**).

◆ Statements are terminated with a semi-colon. In C# a single statement of code can be broken into many lines. The way the compiler knows you're done with a line is that you put a semicolon at the end. The semicolon isn't optional, it's mandatory (**Figure 2.8**).

◆ Multiple statements are grouped within curly brackets. One example is functions, which are blocks of code that act as one unit. To define a block of code you enclose the statements that form the function inside curly brackets. Another example is if statements. In Chapter 3, "Conditionals and Loops," you will learn about if statements. An if statement can execute a single statement, or a block of statements, enclosed in curly brackets (**Figure 2.9**).

Figure 2.7 C# is case sensitive. That means the compiler won't understand a command unless you match the casing for each character to the original declaration. Normally commands follow the standard that each word is capitalized. The editor also helps you case things correctly as you enter code.

```
void DoTask1()
{
    response.write("hello world"); //this is illegal

    Response.Write("hello world"); //this is legal
}
```

Figure 2.8 Each statement must end with a semicolon. Other languages like VB don't use semicolons. However, VB suffers from the opposite problem; you have to put the entire statement in one line or use a special character if you want to break up lines.

```
//these two statements are equivalent
int x = 10 + 20 + c;

int x
    = 10
    + 20
    +
    c;

//these two statements have
//errors, the are missing semicolons
int y = 30
int z = 40
```

Figure 2.9 Curly brackets are used to create code blocks.

```
//both "Response" statements are part of
// the WriteLetter function
void WriteLetter()
{
    Response.Write("Dear Mr. William");
    Response.Write("Thank you for your
    recent inquiry.");
}
```

Figure 2.10 You can't break up a string into multiple lines. The exception to that are special strings called literal strings. You will learn about these in Chapter 4, "Strings."

```
Code                                    _ □ ×

//illegal to say
string name = "Old Altered
              Karate Frogs";

//must all be in one line when strings
//are involved
string name = "Old Altered Karate Frogs";
```

Figure 2.11 You don't have to put a semicolon at the end of a code block, only at the end of single statements.

```
Code                                    _ □ ×

if (Age > 18)
   Adult = true; //semicolon used

if (Name == "James")
{
   Author = true;
   Age = 32;
} // no semicolon at the end
```

✔ Tips

■ Many languages are case sensitive. The best-known exception is Visual Basic, which has always been case insensitive. In case-insensitive languages you don't have to be careful to match the casing of your code to the actual command. It may seem easier to be case insensitive, but Visual Basic has its own share of problems with this scenario. Sometimes the language gets confused when one developer cases a statement one way and another developer cases it a different way. In these situations, the language may not know that both developers meant to type the same statement.

■ Most statements of code can be split into multiple lines. The biggest exceptions are statements that contain strings (**Figure 2.10**).

■ You don't have to use a semicolon when you use code blocks, only when you use single statements (**Figure 2.11**).

Declaring Variables

In programming lingo a *literal value* is a value that is entered by hand such as: 3.5, 50, or even a string like "Hello World." (String literal values are enclosed in quotation marks.) Sometimes you will use literal values when calling functions (**Figure 2.12**) or when setting the property of a control (**Figure 2.13**). But most of the time you'll use variables and constants. (We'll discuss constants below.)

A *variable* serves as a container. The container can store a value, such as a number, or a memory address where an object resides, depending on the type of variable. Some variables can be set to a literal value (**Figure 2.14**) or to the contents of another variable (**Figure 2.15**). Variables have a type. For example, they could be integers, strings, etc.

Figure 2.12 Many times you can pass literals as parameters when calling functions. However, most of the time it is preferable to use variables or constants (more on this later).

```
AddTwoNumbers(4.5, 10.7);
```

Figure 2.13 To represent a string in literal form put quotes around it.

```
TextBox1.Text = "Hello World";
```

Figure 2.14 A variable can be used to store a value or an object. Then you can use the variable instead of the actual value throughout your code.

```
string LastName = "Smith";
```

Figure 2.15 A variable can point to another variable. You might use this to store the value of another variable before changing it.

```
int count = 5;
int lastCount = count;
count = 6;
```

Figure 2.16 Variables are declared by first writing the type of the variable, then the name of the variable. There are a number of predefined numeric types. Notice that sometimes a letter is required at the end of a numeric value when assigning the value to the variable.

```
Code                                    _ □ ×

bool isOpened;
byte age;
int numRecords;

float rate = .33F; //use F at the end for floats
double sinAngle = 0.70710678;
decimal balance = 1072.45M; //use M at the end
for decimals

string firstName = "Jose";
string lastName = "Mojica";
string fullName = firstName + " " + lastName;
```

To declare a variable:

1. Type the name of the class of which you wish to declare a variable. You could choose a type from **Table 2.1** or—as you will see later—you could also use a class name for the variable type. The class name can come from a class you declare, or from a class that someone else declared and which you're referencing in your project.

2. Add a space followed by the name of the variable. The variable name must start with a letter, or an underscore.

3. Type a semicolon (**Figure 2.16**).

Table 2.1

Core Types (Most Commonly Used Types)

NAME	C# TYPE	RANGE
Boolean	bool	True/False
Unsigned Byte	byte	8-bit unsigned integer, 0 to 255
Signed Byte	sbyte	8-bit signed integer -128 to 127
Short	short	16-bit integer, –32768 to 32767
Unsigned Short	ushort	16-bit unsigned integer 0 to 65535
Integer	int	32-bit integer, –2147483648 to 2147483647
Unsigned Integer	uint	32-bit unsigned integer 0 to 4294967295
Long	long	64-bit integer, –9223372036854775808 to 9223372036854775807
Unsigned Long	ulong	64-bit unsigned integer 0 to 18446744073709551615
Character	char	A 16-bit Unicode Character (a single letter).
Single	float	A 32-bit floating point number with 7-8 points of precision $-3.402823E+38$ to $3.402823E+38$
Double	double	A 64-bit floating point number with 15-16 points of precision $-1.79769313486232E+308$ to $1.79769313486232E+308$
Decimal	decimal	A 96-bit fixed point number with 28 points of precision. A very big number. Use decimal to store currency.
Date/Time	System.DateTime	A 64-bit integer in IEEE date format, 1/1/0001 12:00:00 AM to 12/31/9999 11:59:59 PM
String	string	A fixed array of characters.
Object	object	An object variable can be set to anything, including numeric types and objects created from classes.

✔ Tips

■ If you're declaring more than one variable of the same kind, type a comma followed by the next variable name, before the semicolon (**Figure 2.17**).

■ When you compile code that includes a variable declaration, the definition for the variable type must be available to the compiler. The types in Table 2.1 are part of a system DLL called mscorlib.dll. This DLL is automatically referenced in all projects. If the type used isn't one you declared by hand and it isn't one in mscorlib.dll, you must add a reference to your project for the DLL that contains the class definition.

Files that contain .NET code are called assemblies. An assembly is the smallest package of code that the .NET runtime will execute. For details, see "Including Class Definitions from Outside Sources" later in this chapter.

■ Variables are only declared inside of a class, as part of a function definition, or as part of the body of a function. Classes and functions are defined later in this chapter. Variables that are declared inside of a class are called *fields*; Variables that are used to define a function are called *parameters*; Variables that are declared inside of a function are called *local variables* (**Figure 2.18**).

Figure 2.17 You can declare multiple variables of the same type in one statement. You can even initialize the variables at the same time you declare them.

```
byte x,y,z;

int numMen=10,
    numWomen=20,
    people=numMen+numWomen;
```

Figure 2.18 Fields are variables declared inside classes, parameters are variables used in function declarations and local variables are variables declared inside functions. You can't declare variables outside of classes.

```
class ToDoItem
{
    bool active;          //field
    string description;  //field

                         //parameter
    void Complete(string finalComments)
    { //local variable
        DateTime now = DateTime.Now;

        active = false;
        description = description +
        now.ToString() +
                    finalComments;
    }
}
```

Figure 2.19 Constants are variables that are read-only. They are handy in making the intent of your code more obvious. For example, x = 3.14 isn't as clear as x = pi.

```
Code                                    _ □ ×

const double PI = 3.14;
PI = 3.1; //this line is illegal
```

Figure 2.20 Constants can store strings as well.

```
Code                                    _ □ ×

const string CLOSED_STATUS = "closed";
const string OPEN_STATUS = "open";
```

Figure 2.21 Using constants can also make your code easier to maintain. For example, if you were to use the constant Open_Status throughout your program, if at some point the constant value changes, it only needs to be changed in one place. If you used the literal value, you would have to change every line in which the value was used.

```
Code                                    _ □ ×

const string ClosedStatus = "closed";
const string OpenStatus = "open";

string toDoStatus = OpenStatus;
```

Figure 2.22 You refer to the constant by using the class name plus the constant name, in this case Math.pi.

```
Code                                    _ □ ×

class Math
{  //inside of class definition
   public const double PI = 3.14;
}

class Checking
{
   void OrderChecks(byte amount)
   {  //inside of function
      const byte MinChecks = 20;
      const byte MaxChecks = 250;

      if (amount >= MinChecks &&
         amount <= MaxChecks)
      {
         //do something here
      }
   }
}
```

Defining Constants

A *constant* looks like a variable, but the value behind the constant can't be changed. You assign a value to a constant that the compiler can resolve at compile time before executing your program. You can't set a constant equal to a function, because the result of the function would only be known when you execute the program. Constants can only be declared inside a class or inside a function. If declared inside a function, the constant can only be used inside that function. If declared in a class the constant can be used from anywhere (if marked as public).

To define a constant:

1. Type the word const followed by a space.

2. Enter the type of constant, which must be primitive: int, double, string, etc.

3. Set the constant equal to a literal value, or to a simple calculation that involves literal values (10 + 20, for example).

4. End the expression with a semicolon (**Figure 2.19**).

✔ Tips

- Although constants normally hold numeric values, they can also hold string values (**Figure 2.20**).

- Once you declare a constant, you can use the constant throughout your code (**Figure 2.21**).

- Constant values can't be changed at run time.

- Constants are usually named using what is called PascalCasing. In PascalCasing the first letter of each word is capitalized. Here's an example: FakePhone="555-1212."

- Constants can only be declared inside of a class or inside a function (which I will define later in this chapter) (**Figure 2.22**).

Grouping Constants into Enumerated Types

Enumerated types are a set of numeric constants related to one another. Suppose you wanted to represent the days of the week numerically. With enumerated types, you could declare constants like Sunday = 1, Monday = 2, Tuesday = 3, Wednesday = 4, Thursday = 5, Friday = 6, Saturday = 7 into one type called DaysOfTheWeek. Then you could use DaysOfTheWeek as a type for declaring variables.

To declare an enumerated type:

1. Type the keyword enum.

2. Type the name of the enumerated type, DaysOfTheWeek, for example, or KindsOfFood.

3. Type an open curly bracket {.

4. Type the name of each constant in the group separated by commas. You can assign each constant a value. If you don't assign a value, the compiler will assign sequential values starting at zero.

5. Type a close curly bracket } (**Figure 2.23**).

✔ Tips

- Unlike variables and constants that can only be declared inside of a class or inside of a function, enumerated types are stand-alone types, and as such can be declared either outside or inside a class. They can't be declared inside of functions.

- You can use enumerated types in variable declarations (**Figure 2.24**). When you use the enumerated type in a variable declaration, the compiler forces the developer to use one of the constants in the enum rather than a random value. This makes the code more readable and less error prone (**Figure 2.25**).

Figure 2.23 Enumerated types enable you to group several related constants.

```
enum DaysOfTheWeek
{
    None=0,
    Sunday=1,
    Monday=2,
    Tuesday=3,
    Wednesday=4,
    Thursday=5,
    Friday=6,
    Saturday=7
}
```

Figure 2.24 Enums become types. As types they can be used in variable declarations.

```
DaysOfTheWeek apptDay;
```

Figure 2.25 If your variable is of an enum type the compiler will only let you assign constants in the enum to the variable. You can't just use numbers.

```
//use the name of the enum plus the constant name.
DaysOfTheWeek apptday = DaysOfTheWeek.Tuesday;

//*** illegal ***
DaysOfTheWeek today = 15;
```

Figure 2.26 If you want to use the numeric value, you have to use a mechanism called casting. Casting converts the number into the constant in the enum.

```
Code                                    _ □ ×

DaysOfTheWeek apptDay = (DaysOfTheWeek)7;

//be careful, the compiler will not stop
//an incorrect value
DaysOfTheWeek apptDay = (DaysOfTheWeek)15;
```

Figure 2.27 Enums are integers by default, but if you're only going to need a short range of values you can change the type to something smaller, or bigger if you need a greater range.

```
Code                                    _ □ ×

enum DaysOfTheWeek : byte
{
    None,
    Sunday,
    Monday,
    Tuesday,
    Wednesday,
    Thursday,
    Friday,
    Saturday
}
```

Figure 2.28 The | and & operators are used to do bit arithmetic. The | operator is used to take the union of two values, while & is used to take the intersection.

```
Code                                    _ □ ×

[Flags]
enum EmailFormats
{
    plainText=1,
    HTML=2,
    Attachments=4
}

//constants are combined with
// the | symbol
EmailFormats userPreferences =
EmailFormats.plainText |
EmailFormats.HTML |
EmailFormats.Attachments;

//you can test for a value in the
// variable using the & symbol
bool allowAttachments =
(userPreferences &
 EmailFormats.Attachments) != 0;
```

- If you wish to assign to an enumerated type variable a value (rather than a constant name) you must use a procedure called *casting*. Casting means that you put the name of the enumerated type in parenthesis in front of the numeric value (**Figure 2.26**). Be careful with this technique. The compiler won't stop you from assigning a value outside of the range of the enum.

- Enum constants can hold integer values by default. You can change the type of the constants to byte, short or long (actually the complete list includes: byte, sbyte, short, ushort, int, uint, long, or ulong). The type of the constant is changed by putting a colon followed by the type after the name of the enumerated type (**Figure 2.27**).

- Enum constants aren't meant to be combined by default. For example in a variable declaration like DaysOfTheWeek today, today is supposed to hold a single value from the DaysOfTheWeek constants. However, imagine an enumerated type called EmailFormats and a variable declaration like EmailFormats userPreferences. It is possible that the user may want to combine some of the values. If the values are meant to be combined, two things need to happen. First, you have to add the attribute [Flags] in front of the enum, and second, you have to number the constants using a power of 2 (1, 2, 4, 8, 16, 32, etc.) (**Figure 2.28**).

GROUPING CONSTANTS

Declaring Functions

A *function* is a series of statements that can be invoked more than once. As you're writing your program, you may discover that certain lines of code are being repeated throughout the program (for example, the code needed to open a database connection). It makes sense to put that code into a function.

Functions have input variables known as *parameters* and they also have an output value known as the *result*. Adding parameters and a return to a function will be discussed in the next few topics. The simplest type of function is one that doesn't have any input parameters and doesn't have a result value.

To declare a function that takes no input and doesn't return a value:

1. Type void followed by a space.

2. Type the name of the function.

3. Type an open parenthesis, followed by a close parenthesis ().

4. Type an open curly bracket {.

5. Enter the code for the function.

6. Type a close curly bracket } (**Figure 2.29**).

Figure 2.29 The ClearFields function doesn't depend on any input to carry out its task. It also doesn't return any values to the caller.

```
Code
void ClearFields()
{
    txtItem.Text = "";
    txtDescription.Text = "";
}
```

Figure 2.30 Languages like C and C++ support stand-alone functions, but C# doesn't. In C# functions need to be part of a type like a class. The only code outside of a class is code that defines a type, like enum declarations.

```
Code
//it is illegal to have stand-alone functions in C#.
//Functions need to be declared inside of a class.

void DoTask1() //this is illegal
{
}

class TruthTeller
{
    //this is legal
    bool WillIGraduate()
    {
        return false;
    }
}
```

Figure 2.31 You invoke static methods using the class name-dot-function. To invoke instance method you first create a new instance of a class, assign it to a variable, then use variable-dot-function.

```
Code
class Account
{
    public void PrintBalance()
    {
    }
}

class TruthTeller
{
    public static bool AmIOld(byte Age)
    {
        if (age > 40)
            return true;
        else
```
code continues on next page

Figure 2.31 *continued*

```
                              _|□|×
 📷 Code
          return false;
     }
 }

 class App
 {
     static void Main()
     {
         //to use an instance method you
         //have to declare a variable of the
         //type of class the method is in
         //and set it equal to a new
         //instance of the variable
         Account acct = new Account();
         acct.PrintBalance();

         //with static methods you simply
         //use the name of the class, a dot,
         //and the name of the method.
         bool Old = TruthTeller.AmIOld(45);

         //this would be illegal:
         //can't call static method
         //through instance variable
         TruthTeller Truth =
         new TruthTeller();
         bool Old = Truth.AmIOld(45);
     }
 }
```

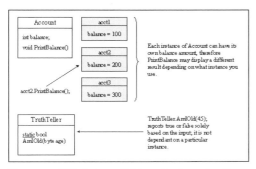

Figure 2.32 With instance fields and instance functions, it matters what variable you use to call the function. With static methods, it doesn't, you always use the class name to invoke it. Static functions aren't dependent on any one instance of the class.

✔ Tips

- In the old days of programming (before .NET, to be more accurate) developers would often declare their functions with a return parameter of int, rather than void, to return a success or failure code. Some developers would return zero if the function succeeded and a non-zero number if the function failed. Other developers would return a zero if the function failed and a non-zero number if the function succeeded. And that was the problem with error codes: No one ever knew whether a zero was a good thing to get or not. For that reason and others Microsoft decided to use exceptions (a type of class) to report error conditions in the .NET Framework and they recommend that you do so also.

- Functions must be declared inside classes. Other languages like C++ support stand-alone functions (functions that aren't part of a class), but C# doesn't (**Figure 2.30**).

- There are two main types of functions: *instance functions* and *static functions*. The above examples all include instance functions. These are functions that require you to create an instance of a class before using them. Static functions don't require you to have an instance of a class. You call static functions by using the name of the class plus the name of the function. **Figures 2.31** and **2.32** show you the difference between the two. Chapter 6, "Special Members," talks about how to declare and use static functions.

Declaring Functions with Parameters

Most of the time a function needs information from the programmer to do its task. For example, if you write a function to add two numbers, the function needs to know what two numbers to add. To be able to pass information to the function, and sometimes to receive information from the function, programmers declare variables as part of the function declaration. These variables are called *parameters*.

Parameters have a direction. The direction determines how the values are passed from the caller to the callee, and what information gets transmitted back from the callee to the caller. Parameters can have three different directions. These are: in (or by value), out, and in and out (by reference). By default parameters are "in" parameters.

It can be difficult to understand how parameters are sent between the caller and a function, even to a seasoned developer. Before understanding the differences between in, ref, and out parameters you have to understand that the .NET Framework makes a distinction between two types of data types: value types and reference types. *Value types* refer to primitive types, such as byte, int, book, double, float, etc., (almost every common type except for string, which is a special type of reference type), structures and enums. *Reference types* include object, string, and any custom types you define as a class (more on this later). The meaning of in, ref and out changes slightly depending on whether you're using value types or reference types.

First let's talk about using value types as parameters.

Figure 2.33 The receiving parameter only gets a copy of the original value. Changing the function's parameter has no effect on the value of the caller's variable.

```
Code                                    _ □ ×

void DoTask1(int x)
{
    x = 20; //this statement only changes
            //a copy of the original
            //variable, not the original
            //variable
}


void ProgramCode()
{
    DoTask1(5);    //can send literal to
                   //"in" parameter

    int num = 10; //the variable must be
                  //set to a value
                  //before calling DoTask1
    DoTask1(num);
    Response.Write(num); //prints 10,
                         //num is unchanged
}
```

Figure 2.34 With ref parameters the receiving function doesn't get a copy; instead it gets the location in memory of the original value. Changing the ref variable also changes the value of the caller's variable.

```
Code                                    _ □ ×

void DoTask2(ref int x)
{
    x = 20; //this statement changes the
    → original variable
}

void ProgramCode()
{
    DoTask2(ref 5); //*** illegal to send
    → literal to ref
                   //parameter

    int num = 10;   //the variable must be set
    → to a value
                   //before calling DoTask2
    DoTask2(ref num);
    Response.Write(num); //prints 20, num
    → changed
}
```

Consider the code in **Figure 2.33**. The x parameter in DoTask1 is an "in" parameter. (The absence of a direction modifier in front of the parameter. is what makes it an "in" parameter.) If you look at the code in DoTask1 you will notice that x can be set to a value. But the caller's variable, num, is unaffected by these changes. Also with "in" parameters you can send either a literal or a variable that has been set to a value.

Now look at the code in **Figure 2.34**. The x parameter is a ref parameter, or in-out parameter. It has the ref modifier in front of the parameter. Notice that if the value of the parameter is changed inside DoTask2, the original variable used, num, is also changed. With ref parameters you can't send literal values. You have to declare a variable and send the variable as the input for the parameter. Just like in the case of "in" parameters, you have to assign a value to the variable before using it. One main difference in the way you call the function is that you have to use ref in the call in front of the parameter.

DECLARING FUNCTIONS WITH PARAMETERS

Now look at **Figure 2.35**. Out parameters are similar to ref parameters in that when you change the value inside the function the original variable used is also changed. One difference is that when a function has an out parameter, it is assumed that the function will provide the value not the caller. Therefore, the compiler gives you an error if you forget to assign a value to the out parameter. You have to use the keyword **out** in front of the parameter you're sending. With out parameters you can't send literal values. Another difference from ref parameters is that you don't have to assign a value to the variable you're sending as a parameter.

Things are a little different when using reference types (classes) instead of value types as parameter types. However, there are a few concepts to learn before being able to talk about reference types being used as parameters. At the end of this chapter we will revisit the topic of parameter direction and talk about how things change with reference parameters.

To declare parameters:

1. Inside the parentheses for a function, type a parameter direction modifier. These are: (blank) for input-only parameters, ref for input-output parameters, or out for output-only parameters.

2. Then use the method for declaring variables in C# (see "Declaring Variables" earlier in this chapter).

3. Add a comma, and repeat steps one and two to add more parameters (**Figure 2.36**).

Figure 2.35 Out parameters are like ref parameters except that with out parameters the caller's variable doesn't have to be initialized beforehand; the value must be provided by the function.

```
void DoTask3(out int x)
{
    x = 20; //with out parameters you are
            //required to assign a value
            //to x.
}

void ProgramCode()
{
    DoTask3(out 5); //*** illegal to send
                    //literal to out
                    //parameter

    int num;        //num does not have to
                    //be initialized and
                    //if it is the value
                    //is ignored.
    DoTask3(out num);
    Response.Write(num); //prints 20, num
                         //is changed
}
```

Figure 2.36 A function can have more than one parameter, and each parameter can be of a different type and direction.

```
private void GetStudentInfo(int ID,
                            out int classRank,
                            out float GPA)
{
    if (ID == 10)
    {
        classRank = 2;
        GPA = 3.9F;
    }

    else
    {
        classRank = 1000;
        GPA = 0;
    }
}
```

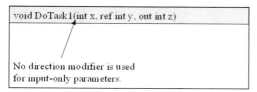

Figure 2.37 There is no direction modifier in C# to specify "in" parameters. To declare "in" parameters you simply don't add a modifier.

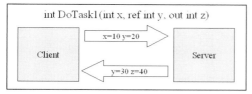

Figure 2.38 Out parameters are useful in remoting scenarios because they tell .NET that no value needs to be transferred from the client to the server, only from the server to the client.

✔ Tips

- If you don't use direction modifiers, the parameters will be input-only (**Figure 2.37**).

- Out parameters and ref parameters are close cousins; internally they work almost the same way. The reason we have out parameters is mostly because of remoting. In remoting, a client may be in one machine and the function being executed may be in a different machine. This isn't the same as ASP.NET applications.

  In ASP.NET applications the browser sends a request to the server. The server then creates objects and executes functions in the same machine. This is known as server-side execution. The same machine acts as both the client and the server. The Web browser only gets to see the output generated by each function. In true remoting a client program uses network communication to execute a command in another machine. In those scenarios, the less information you send across the network the better your application performs (usually, number of round trips across the network is another factor to consider). If we only had ref parameters, the client would always have to send a value to the server for the parameter, and the server would have to send the modified value back to the client. This is inefficient if the server doesn't care about the original value. Therefore in those cases out parameters are used to enable the client to forget the input value and minimize the amount of information sent (**Figure 2.38**).

Returning Function Values

In the previous section you saw that some parameters could be used to return data from a function. These parameters were `ref` and `out` parameters. In addition to using parameters, each function can also return a value as the outcome of the function. This special value is known as the *return value*. When you declare the function you can specify the type of value you wish to return. As you saw earlier, functions that don't return a value are declared with the `void` keyword.

To return a value from a function:

1. Instead of the word `void`, type the name of the type you wish to return before the function name.

2. Inside the body of the function, type `return` followed by a space and the value you wish to return.

3. Type semicolon to end the statement (**Figure 2.39**).

✔ Tips

- You can return a value using a literal or a variable (**Figure 2.40**).

Figure 2.39 Functions can also have a return value. Use return values when the function clearly has a single form of output. If you need to return more than one result, you should use out parameters.

```
class TruthTeller
{
    bool WillIEverBeRich(string profession)
    {
        if (profession == "Writer")
            return false;
        else
            return true;
    }
}
```

Figure 2.40 It is fine to return a literal or a value stored in a variable as the result of the function.

```
class Checking
{
    string GetAccountType()
    {
        return "Checking"; //returning a
                           //literal value
    }

    int MakeDeposit(int amt1, int amt2)
    {
        int total = amt1 + amt2;
        return total; //returning a
                      //variable
    }
}
```

Figure 2.41 If you put a return type in the function declaration, it becomes mandatory to return a value.

```
Code                                    _ □ ×

class Mother
{
    bool ApprovesOfGirlfriend(string name)
    {
        //error, Mother can't be silent, she
        //must return true or false
    }

    int AskForMoney(int Amount)
    {
        if (Amount > 20)
            return 20;

        //error, what if amount is less or
        //equal to 20, there is no return
        //for that case. All cases must return
        //something.
    }
}
```

Figure 2.42 return can be used even when the function doesn't have a return type to exit the function prematurely.

```
Code                                    _ □ ×

class Savings
{
    bool accountClosed;

    void CloseAccount(int accountNum)
    {
        if (accountClosed == true)
            return; //return here is used to
                    //exit function
                    //prematurely, in this
                    //case because the
                    //account is already
                    //closed.

        //...close the account

        //mark status as closed
        accountClosed=true;
    }
}
```

■ When you use **return**, not only do you set the output parameter of the function, but you also exit the function immediately. If there is code after the return, it won't be executed.

■ The C# compiler gives you an error if your function was declared to return a value but you forgot to use return (**Figure 2.41**).

■ Functions that use void for a return type can still use return without a value next to it (**Figure 2.42**).

RETURNING FUNCTION VALUES

Defining a Class

Classes are the primary blocks of object-oriented programming.

When writing applications, developers often attempt to solve a problem or *problem domain*, as it's often called. Problem domains can be broken up into pieces and each piece can be addressed with a class. Take the example program for this chapter. The purpose of the program is to maintain a list of tasks—a to-do list—and to display the list to the user as requested. We could write a class called ToDoItem to store each to-do item, and another class called ToDoList, to store an entire list of to-do items.

The class definition serves as a factory for objects. Each object can represent a different entity in the application. In our example, the ToDoItem class tells the language what ToDoItem objects contain. It is up to the developer to create objects from that class by using the new operator in C#:

```
ToDoItem item1 = new ToDoItem();
```

Classes have two main aspects: *state* and *behavior*. Those are two abstract terms that simply boil down to fields and functions.

Fields are variables declared inside a class. They are used to store information about each object. In the case of the application for this chapter, we create objects of type ToDoItem to hold the information for each to-do item. Fields are used to store the information about each to-do item. For example, we can add a field to store the name of the task and one to store the description. Fields enable each item object produced from the ToDoItem class to represent a different item in the list (**Figure 2.43**). On the other hand all we need is one object of type ToDoList to hold the collection of to-do items. This ToDoList class may have a single field that refers to a collection of ToDoItems.

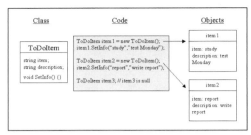

Figure 2.43 Each instance of the ToDoItem class can store its own item and description. If you don't set a reference variable equal to a new instance of the class or to another variable that already points to an object then the variable's value is null.

DEFINING A CLASS

Figure 2.44 The ToDoItem class serves as a factory for ToDoItem objects. It contains fields and functions specific to the class.

```
Code                                    _ □ ×
class ToDoItem
{
   //fields
   string item = "";
   string description = "";

   //function
   public void SetInfo(string item,
   string description)
   {
      this.item = item;
      this.description = description;
   }
}
```

In addition to the class defining the state information for each object the developer defines the behavior for the class. This is done by adding *functions* that make sense when using a ToDoItem object or a ToDoList object. For example, the ToDoList object may have a function called Add and another function called Remove. A programmer can use these functions to add to-do items to the list or to remove them from the list. A to-do item may also have functions such as SetInfo.

Classes are defined with the class keyword.

To declare a class:

1. Type the keyword `class` in lowercase letters followed by a space, and the name of the class (see sidebar).

2. Add an open curly bracket after the class name.

3. Add fields and functions as necessary.

4. Add a closing curly bracket at the end of the class definition (**Figure 2.44**).

Class Names

Class Names are referred to as identifiers under the C# ECMA Specification (section 9.4.2). There are a very large number of rules for which characters are allowed and which aren't, too many to cover here. The most important rule is that class names begin with a letter, an underscore _ or the @ symbol. Use the @ symbol in front of the name if you wish to use a language keyword as the class name. For example, suppose you want to name your class *class*, you would name your class as follows: `class @class`. This is a lot of fun to do, but may get you dirty looks from your coworkers (**Figure 2.45**).

Figure 2.45 Don't write code like this!

```
Code                                    _ □ ×
class @new
{
}

class Fun
{
   void JobSecurity()
   {
      @new @new = new @new();
   }
}
```

✔ Tips

- Classes are named using a technique called *intercaps*. With intercaps only the first letter in each word is capitalized. So in our example the class names are ToDoItem and ToDoList starting with a capital letter.

- Fields and functions inside of the class are referred to as *members* of the class. They are discussed later in this chapter.

- Classes have a scope. They are either internal or public. You control the scope by using an access modifier in front of the class keyword. Internal classes can only be used within the current project (more accurately, the current assembly). Public classes can be used from other assemblies as well (**Figure 2.46**).

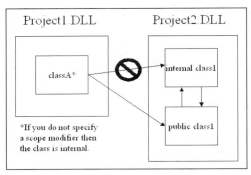

Figure 2.46 Classes can always be used by code in the same project (or assembly). By default they can't be used by another assembly. You can export them outside of the assembly by marking them public.

Figure 2.47 ToDoItem and ToDoList are two custom classes in the sample application.

```
namespace classesandmembers
{
    //add the highlighted class
    //definitions
    class ToDoItem
    {
    }

    class ToDoList
    {
    }

    public class WebForm1 : System.Web.UI.Page
    {
    //the code continues here
```

Adding Classes to the Sample Application

In this section you will continue the sample application by adding a few classes to the project.

To add classes to the sample application:

1. On the Solution Explorer window (View > Solution Explorer) right-click on the file entertask.aspx and choose View code.

2. Inside the namespace classesandmembers, before the class WebForm1, type the code in **Figure 2.47**.

✔ Tip

- In the later sections you will add members to the ToDoItem and ToDoList classes.

Creating and Using Objects

A class is only a type definiton. To do something useful with it, one must create objects from the definition. Each object can maintain its own state; every object from the class exhibits the same behavior.

To create an object and use it:

1. Declare a variable of the type of object you wish to use. If your class is called ToDoItem, your variable type will most likely be ToDoItem as well.

2. Use the new operator to create an instance of the class. Set the variable equal to new, a space, the name of the class you wish to instantiate and parentheses.

3. Type a semicolon.

4. Invoke a function in the object or use a field by using the variable name, followed by a dot, followed by the member's name (**Figure 2.48**).

Figure 2.48 You create objects based on a class by using the new operator and assigning the result to a variable. Then you can use the variable to set fields or call functions.

```
private void btnTask_Click(object sender,
                  System.EventArgs e)
{
    ToDoItem item = new ToDoItem();
    item.SetInfo(txtItem.Text,
            txtDescription.Text);
}
```

Figure 2.49 You don't have to declare the variable and create the object in the same statement. The declaration and instantiation can be separated.

```
protected void Application_Start(Object sender,
                                 EventArgs e)
{
    ToDoList todo;
    todo = new ToDoList();
}
```

Figure 2.50 You can't call a method or set a field through a null variable; the program gives you an error.

```
class Person
{
    void Talk()
    {
    }
}

class App
{
    void DoTask1()
    {
        //*** error ***
        //can't call method without
        //creating instance
        Person p1;
        p1.Talk();
    }
}
```

✔ Tips

- You don't have to put the **new** instruction in the same line as the variable declaration. It is possible to declare the variable first in one line, then later in the program set the variable equal to a new object (**Figure 2.49**).

- You can't invoke a function or set a field through a variable that has not been set to an object. The value of the variable before it has been set equal to a new instance of a class is null. Null is a reserved language keyword that means that a reference variable hasn't been set to an object (**Figure 2.50**).

- The variable type doesn't have to be the same type as the class you're creating. You can also choose a type that is a base class to the class you're creating. (See the "Inheriting a Class from Another" section in Chapter 5, "Class Inheritance.")

Creating Objects in the Sample Application

Now it's time to enhance the sample application a little. Let's add the code that creates instances of the ToDoItem class and the ToDoList class.

To create objects in the sample application:

1. From the Solution Explorer, double-click the file entertask.aspx. You should see the Enter Task Web page appear (**Figure 2.51**).

2. Click the Add Task button. The code editor should open up and add the btnTask_Click function.

3. Inside the function type the code in **Figure 2.48**. (We'll add more to this function later in the chapter.)

4. Back in Solution Explorer right-click on the file Global.asax and choose View Code from the context menu.

5. Locate the function Application_Start. Within the curly brackets, add the code for **Figure 2.49**.

✔ Tips

■   The application won't run yet. The code you have just added creates an instance of the ToDoItem class when you click the Add Task button. It then calls SetInfo passing the text from the item and description textboxes. However, you have not added all the functions needed to each class.

Figure 2.51 Double-clicking on an aspx file in Solution Explorer opens the graphical form for editing.

■   The code you added to Global.asax requires a little explanation, namely, what in the world is this Global.asax file? Well, when you execute your Web application, the ASP.NET framework creates an application object. The application object is an instance of the class defined in Global.asax. The first time the application is run, ASP.NET calls the Application_Start function. If you stop the Web server (not if you close the browser), or if you update any files in your project, the Application object will call the Application_End function. In Application_Start we are creating a ToDoList object to be shared by all users of the Web site. You haven't added the code yet to make it shared, but that is the intent, and the reason we are adding the code to Application_Start.

CREATING OBJECTS IN THE SAMPLE APPLICATION

Figure 2.52 A number of elements in Solution Explorer have context menus. If you right-click on the references element you can add a reference to another assembly in your project.

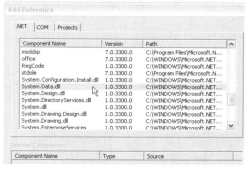

Figure 2.53 The Add Reference dialog lists all assemblies in \Windows\Microsoft.NET\Framework \ver and several other directories. Double-click on the entry you want to reference in your project.

Including Class Definitions from Outside Sources

Before you can declare a class, the compiler must know the definition of the class. Earlier in this chapter you learned how to define your own classes with the `class` keyword. But suppose you want to use someone else's class, like one that Microsoft has defined. For example, let's suppose that you want to talk to a database like SQL Server. Microsoft provides several classes to do so, one of which is called System.Data.SqlClient .SqlConnection. The definition for this class is in a DLL file called System.Data.DLL, which is an assembly. Remember that in .NET terms assemblies are files that contain .NET executable code. To use the definitions in an external assembly, you have to tell Visual Studio to reference this external file. Without the reference it won't understand when you ask it to create an instance of the SqlConnection class.

To reference another assembly:

1. In a Visual Studio Project, choose View > Solution Explorer.

2. Right-click on the References item and choose Add Reference (**Figure 2.52**).

3. You should see the Add Reference dialog. The dialog displays all the .NET assemblies stored in the installation directory \Windows\Microsoft.NET\Framework \ver and several other directories specified through registry keys under HKEY_ LOCAL_MACHINE\SOFTWARE \Microsoft.NET\Framework\Assembly Folders\ (**Figure 2.53**).

continues on next page

CLASS DEFINITIONS FROM OUTSIDE SOURCES

4. Click on the assembly you wish to reference and then click the Select button or double-click on the entry.

or

If the assembly you're looking for isn't in the list click the Browse button. This will display the typical Select Component dialog (**Figure 2.54**).

5. You can select multiple entries from the list by repeating step 4. When you're done, click OK.

✔ Tips

- Assembly is a term usually used to describe a DLL or an EXE that contains .NET-compatible code.

- Unlike other languages, in C# you don't reference source code to add a definition for another class not in your project. Instead, you reference something already compiled (an assembly) in the form of a DLL or an EXE.

- Web projects already have a number of assemblies referenced. If you look at your solution window (View > Solution Explorer) and expand the References branch (by clicking on the plus sign next to it) you will see several assemblies already referenced. Among them are assemblies for doing database work and for manipulating XML (**Figure 2.55**).

Figure 2.54 If the assembly you're looking for isn't in the GAC you can browse for it manually.

Figure 2.55 You can view a list of references in your project by opening the references branch in Solution Explorer.

Figure 2.56 VS.NET automatically creates a bin subdirectory in your application directory. It takes all the code you enter in the project and builds a DLL from it and copies it to the bin directory. Your Web forms are left in the application directory.

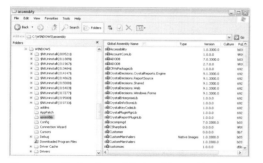

Figure 2.57 Navigating to Windows\Assembly shows a nice view of the GAC. If you were to navigate to the same directory through the command prompt, things would look a little different.

- Finding the assembly and referencing it when you're writing your application is one thing, but finding the assembly when you run the application is something altogether different. When you add a reference to another assembly to your project, all that does is help you compile your code. Without the reference, the compiler wouldn't know if the code you typed was in fact accurate. However, when you run your project, in order for your Web application to find the assembly at runtime the assembly must be in one of two places. Here is the first one: Under the directory your application is running from, you could create a subdirectory called bin and copy the referenced DLLs there (**Figure 2.56**). Visual Studio .NET automatically creates a bin subdirectory in your Web application directory when you first create the project. The second place is the Global Assembly Cache (GAC), a special directory for assemblies. It is one of the places the .NET Framework automatically looks for assemblies. The GAC is under your Windows\Assembly directory (**Figure 2.57**).

- If you add a reference to an assembly not in the GAC, Visual Studio .NET copies the latest version of the assembly to the bin subdirectory of your Web application every time you compile your Web project.

- You add an assembly to the GAC if you want to use the same assembly from multiple Web applications. If you didn't add the assembly to the GAC, each Web application would need its own copy.

- Adding an assembly to the GAC requires that you digitally sign your DLL. This will be explained in Chapter 13, C# Web Projects. Digital signatures make it possible for the .NET runtime to detect if a hacker has tampered with the code.

Grouping Classes into Namespaces

It is very likely for two different banking companies to have a class called Checking. If both companies then shared their code with other developers, it would be difficult for the developers to distinguish between the two classes. For that reason, Microsoft groups their classes in units called namespaces. They recommend that developers also do the same.

A *namespace* is a language feature that appends a prefix to every class name to make the class name unique. The resulting class name will be the name of the namespace, a dot, and the name of the class.

To add a namespace:

1. Add the word namespace in lower case followed by the name of the namespace, followed by an open curly bracket.

2. Place one or more class definitions in the namespace.

3. End the namespace declaration with a closing curly bracket (**Figure 2.58**).

✔ Tips

- When you create a project with Visual Studio, the wizard uses the project name as the default namespace. That means that every time you add a new file to your project, the wizard will add the declaration of the namespace to the file (**Figure 2.59**). You can change the name of the default namespace by choosing Project > Properties, then entering or deleting the default namespace in the general properties (**Figure 2.60**).

Figure 2.58 Namespaces can be used to group classes by company, and by functionality.

```
namespace Banking
{
  public class Checking
  {
    //code omitted for simplicity
  }

  public class Savings
  {
    //code omitted for simplicity
  }
}
```

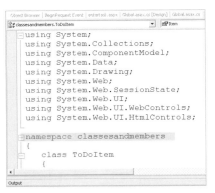

Figure 2.59 Whenever you generate a new class file, or Web Form in your project, the wizard adds a default namespace declaration with the name of the project and puts the new code inside it.

Figure 2.60 You can change the default namespace through the project properties dialog. However, this doesn't change the namespace names in files that have already been added to the project, only in new files. You can also set this property to blank.

Figure 2.61 Too much nesting results in carpal tunnel syndrome. Some classes in .NET are nested five or six namespaces deep. Make sure you have a comfortable wrist pad.

```
Code                          _ □ ×

namespace Nesting
{
    namespace CarpalTunnel
    {
      namespace Syndrome
      {
         class Wrist
         {
         }
      }
    }
}

//class name is now
//Nesting.CarpalTunnel.Syndrome.Wrist
```

Figure 2.62 The namespace names become part of the class names.

```
Code                          _ □ ×

namespace WidgetsUSA
{
  namespace Banking
  {
    public class Checking
    {
      //code omitted for simplicity
    }

    public class Savings
    {
      //code omitted for simplicity
    }
  }
}

class App
{
    void Program()
    {
       WidgetsUSA.Banking.Checking acct1 =
       new WidgetsUSA.Banking.Checking();

       WidgetsUSA.Banking.Savings acct2 =
       new WidgetsUSA.Banking.Savings();
    }
}
```

- Namespaces can be nested. That means you can declare a namespace inside another namespace declaration (**Figure 2.61**).

- Creating namespaces is optional, but it makes good programming sense to group related classes. The namespace serves as a prefix to every class name, so that if your namespace names are WidgetsUSA and Banking and your classes are Checking and Savings then your class names will end up being WidgetsUSA.Banking.Checking and WidgetsUSA.Banking.Savings (**Figure 2.62**).

continues on next page

GROUPING CLASSES INTO NAMESPACES

■ The using keyword in C# lets you omit the namespace name of the class when referring to the class in code (**Figure 2.63**). When you use using you can refer to the classes by their class names. All you're doing is saving keystrokes later on. You can always skip using and just use the full name of the classes when you write code.

Figure 2.63 When you use the using command, you can omit the namespace name and just type the class name.

```
using WidgetsUSA.Banking;

namespace WidgetsUSA
{
  namespace Banking
  {
    public class Checking {}

    public class Savings {}
  }
}

class App
{
  void Program()
  {
    Checking acct1 = new Checking();
    Savings acct2 = new Savings();
  }
}
```

Figure 2.64 An alias can be assigned to a namespace name in order to resolve ambiguity in cases where the same class name may appear in two different namespaces.

```
Code                                    _ □ ×

using ma=MyMath;
using ca=MyCollections;

namespace MyMath
{
    public class MyArray {}
}

namespace MyCollections
{
    public class MyArray {}
}

public class MyApp
{
    public void DoWork()
    {
        ma.MyArray arr1 = new ma.MyArray();
    }
}
```

■ When you use the keyword `using` you can assign an alias to the namespace name (**Figure 2.64**). This can help in two ways. First, it helps the compiler in cases where two classes with the same name may be in two separate namespaces. Imagine a class named MyArray. It is possible for the class to be defined in two namespaces: MyMath and MyCollections. If the developer writes:

```
using MyMath;
using MyCollections;
```

and then uses the class name MyArray directly, the compiler can't tell which class the developer is referring to. Second, it helps with intellisense. When you type the prefix, the Visual Studio .NET editor displays the list of classes in the namespace (**Figure 2.65**).

```
using ma=MyMath;

namespace MyMath
{
    public class MyArray {}
}

public class MyApp
{
    public void DoWork()
    {
        ma.
    }           MyArray
}
```

Figure 2.65 Aliases in namespaces also help you in entering code with the help of intellisense, which displays choices for class names as you type. With an alias, intellisense will display the names of classes in the namespace.

GROUPING CLASSES INTO NAMESPACES

Adding Fields to Classes

Fields serve as storage units. They are variable declarations within the class, outside of any functions.

To add a field to a class:

◆ Inside a class definition, outside of functions, declare a variable (see **Figure 2.66**).

✔ Tips

■ By default all fields are private. This means that only code within the class can access the fields. If code outside of the class tries to access a private field, the compiler issues an error (**Figure 2.67**).

■ You can change the access level for a field (from private to something else) using an access modifier (read "Exposing and Restricting Access to Members" in Chapter 5, "Class Inheritance," for details). For now, don't try to understand all the different scope rules, just realize that private means it can only be used inside the class, and public means it can be used everywhere.

■ **Figure 2.66** shows a field in the ToDoList of type HashTable. HashTable is a class in System.Collections. It is used to maintain a list of objects, and to assign a key to each item. The ToDoList class will use the HashTable class to keep a list of ToDoItem objects.

Figure 2.66 Fields in classes can be of any type. In this code item and description are strings while list is of a type declared by Microsoft called System.Collections.Hashtable.

```
class ToDoItem
{
    string item;
    string description;
}

class ToDoList
{
    Hashtable list;
}
```

Figure 2.67 Fields are private by default. They can only be read or changed by other code inside the same class. You can change the scope of the field by adding public in front of the declaration.

```
class Sibling
{
    //scope of _money is
    //private to class
    decimal _money;

    public void PurchaseItems(decimal
                             amount)
    {
        //PurchaseItems can change the
        //value of _money
        _money -= amount;
    }
}

class App
{
    void BorrowMoney()
    {
        Sibling brother = new Sibling();
        //this is illegal _money is private
        brother._money -= 100;
    }
}
```

Figure 2.68 Fields can be initialized in place. They can be set to a literal value, to a new object or to the result of a static function. In the case of the ToDoList class, every time we create an instance of ToDoList we also create an instance of the HashTable class, if we didn't, then list would be null every time we created a ToDoList.

```
class ToDoItem
{
    string item = "";
    string description = "";
}

class ToDoList
{
    Hashtable list = new Hashtable();
}
```

Initializing Fields in Place

C# enables you to initialize fields in place. This means that you can tell the compiler to automatically set a field to a certain value whenever someone creates an instance of the class. By default, the .NET Framework sets uninitialized fields to zero if they are numeric, `false` if they are Boolean, or `null` if they are reference types (like string or any variable of class you declare).

To add field initializers:

◆ After a field declaration, set the field equal to a literal value or to a function (**Figure 2.68**).

✔ Tip

■ You can set field initializers to literal values, to the result of static functions, to static fields, or to the result of an instance function if it is called through a static field. Static functions and fields will be covered in Chapter 6, "Special Members."

Adding Properties to Classes

Developers normally don't make fields in classes public. There are three main reasons why developers don't like to give everyone access to fields.

The first reason is that developers often want to validate the value the developer is assigning to the field. For example, if a class called Person has a field called Age, a developer may try to write the following:

```
Person p1 = new Person();
p1.Age = -99;
```

However, a person's age can't be negative. If the Age field is public, there is nothing to prevent the developer from setting the field to incorrect values.

A second reason developers don't like to expose fields is that sometimes the information needs to be calculated based on the result of another field. For example, taking the same class, Person, suppose that in addition to the field Age the class also had a field called IsAdult (true or false). The value of the field IsAdult could be calculated based on the Age. If Age is > 18 for example, then IsAdult should be true, otherwise IsAdult would be false. If IsAdult were public, a developer could set IsAdult to something without taking into consideration Age.

Figure 2.69 With information hiding you leave the field as private, then provide a function to set the value and one to read the value. This enables you to validate or calculate values before setting or reading the variable.

```
class Person
{
    byte age;

    public void SetAge(byte newage)
    {
        age = newage;
    }

    public byte GetAge()
    {
        return age;
    }
}

class App
{
    void Task1()
    {
        Person p1 = new Person();
        p1.age = 30; //***this is illegal
        //***this is also illegal
        Response.Write(p1.age);

        //to set or get the age field you
        //must go through the Set and Get
        //functions
        p1.SetAge(45);
        Response.Write(p1.GetAge());
    }
}
```

Figure 2.70 SetAge verifies that the age is greater than zero; if not, it sets the age to zero. IsAdult returns a calculated value based on the age.

```
Code                                    _ □ ✕

class Person
{
   byte age;

   public void SetAge(byte newage)
   {
      //with a SetAge function you can
      //now do validation of the value
      //before storing it in the age
      //field
      if (newage < 0)
         newage = 0;

      age = newage;
   }

   public byte GetAge()
   {
      return age;
   }

   public bool IsAdult()
   {
      //information obtained from
      //age field
      return (age >= 18); //returns true
                          //if age is
                          //greater than
                          //or equal to
                          //18
   }
}
```

The third main reason developers don't like to make a field public is that the field type may change in future releases. For example, it could be that a field called BouncedChecks begins as a type byte (0 through 255) and the bank later discovers that it needs to change the field's type to a long. If a field is made public, sometimes developers write their code assuming that the variable will contain a certain range of values. This makes it harder to change the type of the field later on.

For these reasons developers often use a technique called *information hiding*. It means setting the field to private and providing a pair of public functions, one to read the value, and one to set the value (**Figure 2.69**). These functions are normally called SetX and GetX where X is the name of the field that the functions manipulate.

A developer using the class would then be prevented from using the field directly. He or she would have to use the Set and Get function. This would enable the author of the class to validate, calculate, and even change the data type of the field later on (**Figure 2.70**).

The only problem with adding Set and Get functions is that they aren't as nice to work with as working with fields. When reading the value you have to call Get and put parenthesis after the function name. To set the value you have to use Set and send the value in parenthesis, rather than using the name of the field and the = sign. That's where properties come in.

Properties are functions that behave like fields. With a property you declare a get function and a set function. The get and set enable you to do things like validations and calculating fields. To the user of the class however, it looks and feels as if they were using a field.

To add a property to the class:

1. Start by following the syntax of adding a function. Type the return type, followed by a space and the name of the property, then stop. Don't add parentheses at the end of the property.

2. Add an open curly bracket.

3. Decide if the property will be read-only, write-only, or read-write.

4. If it is read-only add a get handler only (step 5), if it is write-only add a set handler only (step 6), and if it is read-write add both a get handler and a set handler.

5. Add a get handler as needed by writing the word **get** in a new line, followed by an open curly bracket, the code for the get handler and a close curly bracket. The code must at least return a value of the type of the property.

6. Add a set handler as needed by writing the word **set** in a new line, followed by an open curly bracket, the code for the set handler and a close curly bracket. The variable name value is a reserved word that will store the value to which the user of the class is attempting to set the property.

7. Add a close curly bracket (**Figure 2.71**).

Figure 2.71 Properties are functions that give the caller the feel of a field. You can add a set handler and a get handler to a property.

```
Code                                          _ □ ×

class Person
{
    byte age;

    public byte Age
    {
        get
        {
            return age;
        }

        set
        {
            //perform validation
            if (value < 0)
                value = 0;

            age = value;
        }
    }

    public bool Adult
    {
        //calculated read-only property
        get
        {
            return (age >= 18);
        }
    }
}

class App
{
    void ProgramCode()
    {
        Person p1 = new Person();
        p1.Age = 30;   //calls set portion
                       //of property;
                       //value keyword in
                       //set contains 30
        Response.Write(p1.Age); //calls get
                                //portion
                                //of
                                //property
    }
}
```

Figure 2.72 Properties, like fields, are private by default; they can only be used inside the class in which they were defined. You can change the scope by adding a scope modifier in front of the declaration, like the word public.

```
class NuclearPlant
{
    int _level;

    int Level
    {
        get
        {
            return _level;
        }

        set
        {
            _level = value;
        }
    }
}

class App
{
    void Task1()
    {
        NuclearPlant np = new NuclearPlant();
        np.Level = 50; //***this is illegal
                       //Level is private
    }
}
```

✔ Tips

■ By default properties are private. This means they can only be used by code inside of the class. Until you learn about scope modifiers you can declare the properties as public if you wish to use them outside of the class (**Figure 2.72**). A full explanation of scope modifiers requires an explanation of inheritance, found in Chapter 5, "Class Inheritance."

■ Properties must have a get handler, a set handler, or both.

continues on next page

ADDING PROPERTIES TO CLASSES

61

■ Read-only properties are properties that have a get handler but no set handler (**Figure 2.73**).

Figure 2.73 It's easy to add read-only properties. You just have to add a get handler to your property and not a set.

```
Code                                    _ □ ×
class ToDoItem
{
   string item = "";
   string description = "";

   public string Item
   {
      //read-only property
      //no set
      get
      {
         return item;
      }
   }

   public string Description
   {
      //read-only property
      //no set
      get
      {
         return description;
      }
   }
}
```

Figure 2.74 Write-only properties aren't very common. One possible use would be to set the parts of a larger property. In this case you set the first name and the last name of an individual, but then read the person's full name and not each part.

```
class Person
{
    string _firstName;
    string _lastName;

    //write-only property to set
    //person's first name
    public string FirstName
    {
        set
        {
            _firstName = value;
        }
    }

    //write-only property to set
    //person's last name
    public string LastName
    {
        set
        {
            _lastName = value;
        }
    }

    //read-only property to read
    //full name
    public string Name
    {
        get
        {
            return _firstName + _lastName;
        }
    }
}
```

■ Write-only properties are properties that have a **set** handler but no get handler (**Figure 2.74**). They aren't very common.

Adding Methods to Classes

Methods define the behavior of the class. There are two types of methods (also referred to as *functions*) in C#: instance methods and static methods.

Instance methods apply their behavior to a specific instance of the class. For example, imagine an instance method called Make-Deposit, a member of the Account class. If you create two account objects, you can invoke the MakeDeposit through either object; calling MakeDeposit through the first object only affects the balance of the first, while calling MakeDeposit through the second object only affects the balance of the second.

Static methods are global methods that don't apply their behavior to any particular instance of the class. (You will learn about static methods in Chapter 6, "Special Members.")

To add an instance method:

1. Inside a class definition, begin a new line.

2. Add a function to the class as you learned earlier in the chapter. Remember that functions can return a parameter of any type; or if you don't wish to return a value, type the word void (**Figure 2.75**).

Figure 2.75 Enhance the classes for the sample project by adding functions.

```
class ToDoItem
{
    string item = "";
    string description = "";

    public void SetInfo(string item,
    string description)
    {
        this.item = item;
        this.description = description;
    }

}

class ToDoList
{
    Hashtable list = new Hashtable();

    //adds the ToDoItem to the
    //hash table
    public void Add(ToDoItem tditem)
    {
        list.Add(tditem.Item,tditem.Description);
    }

    //removes the ToDoItem from
    //the hash table
    public void Remove(ToDoItem tditem)
    {
        list.Remove(tditem.Item);
    }
}
```

Figure 2.76 Functions, like fields and properties are private; they can only be invoked from other functions in the same class. To use it outside of the class you can mark the function public.

```
Code                                _ □ ×

class Cat
{
    public void Call()
    {
    }

    //function is private
    void Respond()
    {
    }
}

class Owner
{
    void LookForKitty()
    {
        Cat tiger = new Cat();
        tiger.Call(); //legal, Call is
                        //public
        tiger.Respond(); //***illegal,
                        //Respond
                        //is private

    }
}
```

✔ Tips

■ All methods inside a class are private by default. This means they can only be used by code inside of the class. Until you learn about scope modifiers you can declare the methods as public if you wish to use them outside of the class (**Figure 2.76**). A full explanation of scope modifiers requires an explanation of inheritance, found in Chapter 5, "Class Inheritance."

continues on next page

- You can't have a field with the same name as a function (**Figure 2.77**), but you can have two methods with the same name as long as you change either the number of parameters in the declaration, or the type of one of the parameters (**Figure 2.78**). This mechanism is called method overloading and it is discussed in Chapter 6, "Special Members."

Figure 2.77 You can't add a field and a method with the same name to the same class. But because C# is case sensitive you can essentially have the same name if you change the casing of one of the characters in one of the names.

```
class Toothbrush
{
    //this is illegal, you can't have
    //both a field and a method (or a
    //property for that matter) named
    //the same thing
    string Owner;

    void Owner(string name)
    {
    }
}
```

Figure 2.78 Method overloading is the idea that you can add multiple versions of the same method to the same class. To do method overloading at least one of the parameters in the declaration has to be different from the other declarations (either a different type or a different number of parameters.)

```
class Checking
{
    public void MakeDeposit(decimal amount)
    {
    }

    public void MakeDeposit(int amount)
    {
    }

    public void MakeDeposit(decimal amount,
                            decimal available)
    {
    }
}
```

Figure 2.79 Add the above code to the entertask.aspx file.

```
Code                                    _ □ ×
class ToDoItem
{
    //fields
    string item = "";
    string description = "";

    //properties
    public string Item
    {
        get
        {
            return item;
        }
    }

    public string Description
    {
        get
        {
            return description;
        }
    }

    //methods
    public void SetInfo(
    string item, string description)
    {
        this.item = item;
        this.description = description;
    }
}
class ToDoList
{
    //fields
    Hashtable list = new Hashtable();

    //methods
    public void Add(ToDoItem tditem)
    {
        list.Add(tditem.Item,
        tditem.Description);
    }

    public void Remove(ToDoItem tditem)
    {
        list.Remove(tditem.Item);
    }
}
```

Adding Members to the Classes in the Sample Code

Now that you know about the various members that classes can have, it's time to make the classes in the sample code more functional.

To add members to the classes in the sample code:

1. Right-click the file entertask.aspx in Solution Explorer, and choose View Code from the context menu.

2. Enter the code highlighted in **Figure 2.79** to your class definitions.

✔ Tips

- The code in **Figure 2.79** adds the fields, properties, and methods necessary to make the classes functional. Notice the use of the information-hiding technique. As you can see both classes use private fields. The classes expose properties or methods to enable the user to manipulate the fields, but the user can't manipulate the fields directly.

- The application isn't yet complete; see the next section, "Completing the Sample Application."

ADDING MEMBERS TO CLASSES

Completing the Sample Application

It's now time to add the remaining code to the sample application to make it fully functional. There are a few things missing. First of all, you might have noticed that the sample code thus far creates an instance of the ToDoList when the application starts, and creates instances of the ToDoItem class when the user clicks the Add Task button, but there is nothing there yet to connect the two instances. We need to add code that adds the ToDoItem to the list. To accomplish this you'll have to learn about the Application object.

The Application object is provided by ASP.NET. It enables you to maintain information for all the users that access your application. The Application object is like a large filing cabinet. It lets you add any object you want to the filing cabinet and assign a name to the item. The item is known as the *key*. In fact it works similarly to the HashTable class that you learned about previously. The key enables you to access the item later on, and even to remove it. The Application object makes it handy to pass information from one Web page to another.

All users using the Web application have the same Application object. Therefore, if one user adds tasks to the list, a different user will be able to see those items. When any user clicks View Tasks, that user sees all the tasks from all the users.

Another object that lets you save information is called the *Session object*. Session object works per user. Each user gets its own Session object; when you add information to the Session object, that information is only available to the current user.. We will use the Session object throughout this book.

Figure 2.80 Add this code to the Global.asax file. The code creates a ToDoList object and adds it to the Application object.

```
 Code                              _ □ ×
protected void Application_Start(
        Object sender, EventArgs e)
{
   ToDoList todo;
   todo = new ToDoList();
   Application.Add("list",todo);
}
```

Figure 2.81 This code retrieves the ToDoList object from the Application object and then adds a ToDoItem to it.

```
 Code                              _ □ ×
//ClearFields simply does
//what the name implies
//it resets the textboxes in
//the form. We call this function
//after adding a task to the list.
void ClearFields()
{
   txtItem.Text = "";
   txtDescription.Text = "";
}

private void btnTask_Click(object sender,
          System.EventArgs e)
{
   ToDoItem item = new ToDoItem();
   item.SetInfo(txtItem.Text,
   txtDescription.Text);

   //Retrieve the ToDoList from the
   //global Application object, and add
   //the newly created ToDoItem to the
   //list. Then clear the form fields.
   //Because many clients may be
   //accessing the same list
   //simultaneously make sure the code is
   //thread-safe with Lock and Unlock.
   Application.Lock();
   ToDoList list =
   (ToDoList)Application["list"];
   list.Add(item);
   Application.UnLock();
   ClearFields();
}
```

It would also be nice to be able to display the list of tasks when the user clicks the View Tasks link. For that we are going to add another page with a ListBox control in it.

So, let's get to it.

To connect the ToDoList to ToDoItems:

1. Right-click on Global.asax and choose View Code from the context menu.

2. In the function Application_Start add the highlighted code from **Figure 2.80** to complete it.

3. Right-click on entertask.aspx and choose View Code from the context menu.

4. Enter the highlighted code from **Figure 2.81**. Notice that some of the code is meant to be added as part of the btnTask_Click function. Then add the ClearFields function right before it.

The only thing left is to find a way to display the items in the task list. For this we are going to use a technique called *databinding*. Databinding makes it easy to display the items in the list. All we have to do is connect a "data-aware" control to the object that holds the list and the control reads and displays all the items in the list. Let's see how that's done.

COMPLETING THE SAMPLE APPLICATION

To display the items in the task list:

1. Select Project > Add Web Form from the main menu. You should see the dialog in **Figure 2.82**.

2. Change the default file name to viewlist.aspx and press Enter. The wizard adds viewlist.aspx to the Solution Explorer.

3. Double-click viewlist.aspx to reveal the form.

4. Add a ListBox control and a label control to the form. Customize the form so that it looks like the form in **Figure 2.84** (next page). Of course this is really hard to do without detailed instructions. You may want to enter the HTML in **Figure 2.83** directly, the way you learned at the beginning of the chapter, or even better, copy and paste the HTML from the downloadable sample code at www.peachpit.com/vqs/csharp.

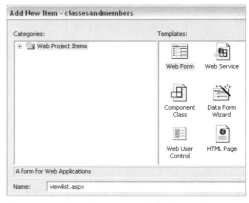

Figure 2.82 The Add New Item dialog is used to create a new Web Form file and add it to your project.

Figure 2.83 You can use this HTML to create a simple form that displays the list of to-do items.

```
<%@ Page language="c#"
        Codebehind="viewlist.aspx.cs"
        AutoEventWireup="false"
        Inherits="classesandmembers.viewlist" %>
<HTML>
    <HEAD>
        <title>viewlist</title>
    </HEAD>
    <body MS_POSITIONING="GridLayout">
        <form id="viewlist" method="post"
          runat="server">
            <asp:ListBox
                id="lstTaskList"
                style="Z-INDEX: 101;
                LEFT: 35px;
                POSITION: absolute;
                TOP: 46px"
                runat="server" Width="183px"
                Height="200px">
            </asp:ListBox>
            <asp:Label
                id="Label1"
                style="Z-INDEX: 102;
                LEFT: 39px;
                POSITION: absolute;
                TOP: 17px"
                runat="server"
                Width="175px">
                Items:
            </asp:Label>
        </form>
    </body>
</HTML>
```

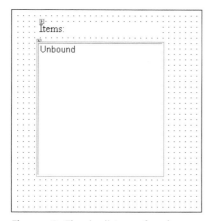

Figure 2.84 The viewlist.aspx form has a listbox that will display the to-do items. This listbox will be data bound. Data-binding is a quick way to populate a control from a collection, like a HashTable.

Figure 2.85 The listbox control has a DataSource property that you can set to a collection. Collections will be discussed in Chapter 9, "Arrays and Collections." By calling the DataBind method the control reads all the items in the collection and adds them to the list.

```
private void Page_Load(object sender,
System.EventArgs e)
{
    //grab the ToDoList object from the
    //Application and bind it to the
    //TaskList ListBox (lstTaskList)
    ToDoList list =
    (ToDoList)Application["list"];
    lstTaskList.DataSource =
    list.TaskList;
    lstTaskList.DataBind();
}
```

5. After adding the controls and naming them correctly according to **Figure 2.84**, double-click in an empty space on the form. Doing so should bring up the code editor positioned in the Page_Load function.

6. Add the code in **Figure 2.85** to the Page_Load function.

   The last thing to do is to make the internal list in the HashTable (the object the ToDoList object uses to maintain the list of ToDoItem's) available to the viewlist function. This is easily done by adding a read-only property to the ToDoList class.

7. Right-click on entertask.aspx and choose View Code from the context menu.

continues on next page

COMPLETING THE SAMPLE APPLICATION

71

8. Add the highlighted code from **Figure 2.86** to the ToDoList class.

9. Press F5 to build the code and execute.

✔ Tip

■ There are a couple of things in the sample code that have not been explained fully. Don't worry about knowing all the details at this point. Things like HashTables will be explored in more detail throughout the book. Other concepts like databinding are beyond the scope of this book. This book concentrates on the C# language itself and not on Web-specific concepts. Nevertheless, you should get a good understanding of those concepts just by trying the code in the examples. Consult the MSDN documentation that ships with Visual Studio for more information on databinding.

Figure 2.86 The HashTable stores objects. Each object has a key assigned to it. You can get the list of items using the Values property of the HashTable.

```
class ToDoList
{
    Hashtable list = new Hashtable();

    public void Add(ToDoItem tditem)
    {
        list.Add(tditem.Item,tditem.Description);
    }

    public void Remove(ToDoItem tditem)
    {
        list.Remove(tditem.Item);
    }

    public ICollection TaskList
    {
        get
        {
            return list.Values;
        }
    }
}
```

Figure 2.87 Inline comments are handy for describing the purpose of fields, functions, and local variables. They are also often used above parts of the code to tell the reader what the code does.

```
Code                                    _ □ ✕

class Account
{
    int _Balance;      //keeps track of
                       //overall balance
    int _LastDeposit;  //Amount of money
                       //last deposited
    int AccountNum;    //Account number
                       //(unique identifier
                       //for account)

    public int MakeDeposit(int Amount)
    {
        _Balance += Amount;
        return _Balance;
    }
}
```

Figure 2.88 Block comments are normally used before a function or class to provide a history of changes made and more robust information about the portion of code.

```
Code                                    _ □ ✕

class Account
{
    /*
    Function:  MakeDeposit
    Purpose :  Increase or decrease
               account's balance
    Input   :  int Amount - The amount to
                            deposit (can
                            be negative)
    Output  :  Total balance after
               deposit.
    */
    public int MakeDeposit(int Amount)
    {
        _Balance += Amount;
        return _Balance;
    }
}
```

Adding Comments

Last but not least is the issue of producing readable code. One way to make your code more readable is to add comments. You probably noticed the comments throughout the code in the examples. Comments don't affect the processing of your code; they just make it more readable. C# has two types of comments: *inline comments* and *block comments*.

To add inline comments:

◆ At the end of a code line type two forward slashes (//) followed by the text for the comment (**Figure 2.87**).

To add block comments:

1. Type a forward slash followed by an asterisk (/*).

2. Type the comment text. It can be as short as a single character or as long as several paragraphs.

3. Type an asterisk followed by a backslash (*/) (**Figure 2.88**).

✔ Tips

- You can insert block comments within a line of code (**Figure 2.89**).

- You can add inline comments to the end of every line even if the lines aren't complete program statements (**Figure 2.90**).

Figure 2.89 Block comments are also useful for describing the purpose of parameters.

```
class Account
{
    public int MakeDeposit
    (int Amount /*can be negative*/,
    int Available /*how much is
    immediately available */)
    {
        _Balance += Amount;
        return _Balance;
    }
}
```

Figure 2.90 C# lets you break up statements into multiple lines. Each line can have an inline comment at the end of the line.

```
class Account
{
    int _Balance;

    public int MakeDeposit
    (int Amount, int Available)
    {
        _Balance       //original balance
        +=             //equals to original
                       //balance plus
        (Amount        //amount deposited
        -              //minus
        Available);    //amount available
        return _Balance;
    }

}
```

Figure 2.91 Even though ch is an "in" parameter in the NameChild function, you can still change the fields of the object ch points to and the changes are reflected to caller.

```
Code                                    _ □ ×
class Child
{
    public string Name;
}


class Parent
{
    public void NameChild(Child ch)
    {
        ch.Name = "John";
    }
}


class App
{
    void ProgramCode()
    {
        Child ch = new Child();
        ch.Name = "Bill";

        Parent pr = new Parent();
        pr.NameChild(ch);

        Response.Write(ch.Name);
    }
}
```

Understanding Parameter Direction for Reference Types

In the section "Declaring Functions with Parameters" I introduced you to the different directions that parameters support. There we discussed what it meant to pass primitive types, like int, double, byte, etc. through in parameters, ref parameters, or out parameters. I also told you that things were different for reference types and that we would discuss the differences at the end of the chapter. Promise kept!

Consider the code in **Figure 2.91**. Take a close look at the highlighted lines. If you look at the function NameChild in the Parent class you will see that the function has an "in" parameter of type Child. The Child class has a public field called Name. The code in NameChild changes the Name field to "John." If you look down at the ProgramCode you will see that the child's name is first set to "Bill" before calling the function; the question is: what will the Name of the child be after calling NameChild? The answer is "John." Even though the Child parameter in NameChild is an "in" parameter you can still change the contents of the fields in the object. So what does it mean to have input parameters with reference types?

PARAMETER DIRECTION FOR REFERENCE TYPES

Look at the code in **Figure 2.92**. If you look at the highlighted line you will see that now the code in NameChild attempts to change the object the ch variable is pointing to. The question now is, after the call, will the original ch be pointing to the original child object or the one that NameChild is creating? The answer is that the original ch points to the original object, not the new one. What if the parameter were a ref parameter? Then in that case the original ch would point to the new object.

With reference types, "in" means that the object the variable is pointing to can't be changed. With ref parameters, pointing the variable to a new object changes what the original variable is pointing to; the same is true for out parameters. **Figure 2.93** shows the difference between in and ref parameters with reference types.

Figure 2.92 With an "in" parameter, when the code sets the ch variable to a different object from the caller's object, the caller's variable is unaffected.

```
class Child
{
    public string Name;
}

class Parent
{
    public void NameChild(Child ch)
    {
        ch = new Child();
    }
}

class App
{
    void ProgramCode()
    {
        Child ch = new Child();

        Parent pr = new Parent();
        pr.NameChild(ch);
    }
}
```

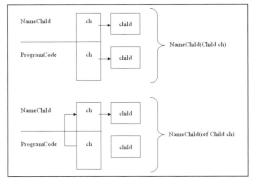

Figure 2.93 With "in" parameters, setting the variable in the function to a new object has no effect on the caller's variable. However, with ref parameters the caller's variable is also changed to point to the newly created object.

CONDITIONALS AND LOOPS

3

In the last chapter you learned how to write classes. Let's briefly review what we know about classes. A lot of the concepts in this section will feel somewhat simple if you have done programming in other languages, like JavaScript, VBScript, or C++.

You learned that classes are the building blocks of applications in C#. No code can exist outside of a class. Classes have two main characteristics—they have state and behavior. The *state* of the class is defined by the instance fields that the class has. The state is the information that is exclusive to each instance of the class. For example, each Checking account may have its own balance. The *behavior* is defined by the methods that a class has. The behavior is what you can do with the class: OpenAccount, CloseAccount, etc. For a method to do something useful you must have some code and that usually means writing loops and conditional statements.

Conditional statements enable you to execute code when a condition is true or false. Normally they are split into two code sections: the code to execute if the condition is true, and the code to execute if the condition is false. Loops enable you to execute a specific block of code a certain number of times. Loops fall into two categories: loops that execute for a specific number of times, and loops that execute while a condition is true or false.

Working with Loops and Conditionals

Like in all the other chapters in this book, the best way to learn about the topic at hand is to create a small project in which you can try new things.

In this chapter, we will create a very simple shopping-cart application. In the application you'll be able to select an item from among a list of items and then enter the quantity for the item you wish to purchase. The program will add the item to the shopping cart. After you're done adding items you can click on Place Order to view the total amount spent. The first half of the program will teach you how to use conditional statements to find a description and unit price for each item. The second half will teach you how to write a loop to calculate the total amount for the order.

To create a test project for this chapter:

1. Launch Visual Studio .NET. (Start > All Programs > Microsoft Visual Studio .NET > Microsoft Visual Studio .NET).

2. Select File > New > Project to bring up the New Project dialog.

3. Under project types on the left side of the New Project window click the Visual C# projects folder.

4. Select the ASP.NET Web Application icon and change the name of the application to loopsandconditionals (**Figure 3.1**).

5. Visual Studio will create a new project and open WebForm1.aspx.

6. Change the form's name to enterorder .aspx. Do so by choosing View > Solution Explorer from the top menu bar.

Figure 3.1 The New Project dialog lets you select among various project types. For this chapter you are writing an ASP.NET Web Application.

Figure 3.2 Changing the filename through the property browser also renames the physical file.

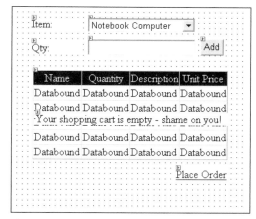

Figure 3.3 You're going to write a shopping cart application for this chapter. The user selects the item to purchase and the quantity and the items are seen in a grid (a table). Then you click place order to see the total amount purchased.

7. Right-click on WebForm1.aspx and choose Properties. In the property grid below change the FileName property from WebForm1.aspx to enterorder.aspx (**Figure 3.2**).

8. Create a form that looks like the form in **Figure 3.3**. Obviously this is a lot of work to do by hand. Instead you can enter the HTML directly into the editor. **Figure 3.4** (next page) shows the HTML necessary to create the form. To enter the HTML directly click the HTML button under the editor's window. As an alternative you could download the skeleton file for this project (see Tips below).

✔ Tips

■ Remember that like in any other projects in this book, building the project isn't necessary for learning the concepts in this chapter.

■ Skeletons for each project can be downloaded from Peachpit's Web site, http://www.peachpit.com/vqs/csharp.

Figure 3.4 The Visual Studio .NET lets you draw each control graphically, or manipulate the HTML script directly. If you add the HTML script below the editor will display the controls for the project.

```
🗗 Code                                                              _ □ ×
<%@ Page language="c#" Codebehind="enterorder.aspx.cs"
        AutoEventWireup="false"
        Inherits="loopsandconditionals.WebForm1"
        enableViewState="False"
        enableViewStateMac="False"%>
<HTML>
    <HEAD>
        <title>WebForm1</title>
    </HEAD>
    <body MS_POSITIONING="GridLayout">
        <form id="Form1" method="post" runat="server">
            <asp:TextBox id="txtQty"
                        style="Z-INDEX: 101; LEFT: 127px;
                        POSITION: absolute; TOP: 56px"
                        runat="server" Width="157"
                        Height="24"
                        EnableViewState="False">
                        </asp:TextBox>
            <asp:label   id="lblItem"
                        style="Z-INDEX: 102; LEFT: 45px;
                        POSITION: absolute; TOP: 25px"
                        runat="server"
                        EnableViewState="False"
                        Height="19"
                        Width="70">
                        Item:
                        </asp:label>
            <asp:label   id="lblQty"
                        style="Z-INDEX: 103; LEFT: 45px;
                        POSITION: absolute; TOP: 60px"
                        runat="server"
                        EnableViewState="False"
                        Height="19px"
                        Width="70px">
                        Qty:
                        </asp:label>
            <asp:button  id="btnAdd"
                        style="Z-INDEX: 104; LEFT: 291px;
                        POSITION: absolute; TOP: 56px"
                        runat="server"
                        EnableViewState="False"
                        Text="Add">
                        </asp:button>
            <asp:dropdownlist id="lstItems"
                        style="Z-INDEX: 105; LEFT: 127px;
                        POSITION: absolute; TOP: 25px"
                        runat="server"
                        EnableViewState="False"
                        Width="157">
                <asp:ListItem Value="Notebook">
                        Notebook Computer</asp:ListItem>
                <asp:ListItem Value="Desktop">
                        Desktop Computer</asp:ListItem>
                <asp:ListItem Value="FlatMon">
                        Flat Screen Monitor</asp:ListItem>
                                    code continues
```

WORKING WITH LOOPS AND CONDITIONALS

Figure 3.4 *continued*

```
                  <asp:ListItem Value="FatMon">
                        Big Fat Monitor</asp:ListItem>
                              </asp:dropdownlist>
              <asp:datagrid id="grdItems"
                          style="Z-INDEX: 106; LEFT: 47px;
                          POSITION: absolute; TOP: 103px"
                          runat="server"
                          EnableViewState="False"
                          Width="284px"
                          AutoGenerateColumns="False">
              <Columns>
                  <asp:BoundColumn DataField="Name"
                  HeaderText="Name">
                  <HeaderStyle HorizontalAlign="Center"
                  ForeColor="White" BackColor="Black">
                  </HeaderStyle>
                  </asp:BoundColumn>
                  <asp:BoundColumn DataField="Quantity"
                  HeaderText="Quantity">
                  <HeaderStyle HorizontalAlign="Center"
                  ForeColor="White" BackColor="Black">
                  </HeaderStyle>
                  </asp:BoundColumn>
                  <asp:BoundColumn DataField="Description"
                  HeaderText="Description">
                  <HeaderStyle HorizontalAlign="Center"
                  ForeColor="White" BackColor="Black">
                  </HeaderStyle>
                  </asp:BoundColumn>
                  <asp:BoundColumn DataField="Price"
                  HeaderText="Unit Price">
                  <HeaderStyle HorizontalAlign="Center"
                  ForeColor="White" BackColor="Black">
                  </HeaderStyle>
                  </asp:BoundColumn>
              </Columns>
            </asp:datagrid>
            <asp:label    id="lblEmpty"
                          style="Z-INDEX: 107; LEFT: 51px;
                          POSITION: absolute; TOP: 166px"
                          runat="server"
                          Width="284px"
                          Visible="False">
                          Your shopping cart is empty - shame
                          on you!
                          </asp:label>
            <asp:hyperlink id="lnkOrder"
                          style="Z-INDEX: 108; LEFT: 256px;
                          POSITION: absolute; TOP: 248px"
                          runat="server"
                          EnableViewState="False"
                          NavigateUrl="finishorder.aspx">
                          Place Order
                          </asp:hyperlink>
        </form>
      </body>
</HTML>
```

Comparing Numeric Types

Comparing numeric types is one of the primary ways of building conditional statements. In a comparison of numeric types, one checks to see if a variable's number is less than, equal to, greater than, or not equal to the value stored in another variable or to a literal value.

To compare two numeric types:

1. Type the name of a variable to store the result of the comparison of type bool. For example: bool bResult =.

2. Type the name of the variable to use for the first element in the comparison. The variable could be of any of the following types: byte, short, long, int, float, double, decimal, sbyte, ushort, ulong, etc.

3. Type a comparison operator. The comparison operator could be < (less than), <= (less than or equal to), > (greater than), >= (greater than or equal to), == (equals to), or != (not equal to).

4. Type a variable name or the literal value for the second element in the comparison.

5. Type a semicolon ; (**Figure 3.5**).

✔ Tip

■ The type for the second element doesn't have to match the type of the first element. You could, for example, compare an integer to a float, a byte to a double, a float to a double, etc. The only exception is that you can't compare the decimal type to a float or a decimal to a double without casting one of the variables to the type you are comparing against (**Figure 3.6**).

Figure 3.5 You can compare variables to literal numbers, to constants or to other variables. You can also compare a variable to the result of a function, for example. The result of the comparison is true or false.

```
Code                                    _ □ ×

int qty = 10;
bool validQty = (qty > 0); //validQty will be true

double balance = 0.0;
const double ZeroBalance = 0.0;
bool validBalance = (balance != ZeroBalance);
                    //validBalance will be false

int age1=15;
int age2=30;

bool Person1Older = (age1 > age2);
                    //Person1Older will be false
```

Figure 3.6 You can perform some comparisons of numeric types even if the types aren't the same for both variables. One exception is comparing decimals to doubles. In that case a conversion (or casting) is required.

```
Code                                    _ □ ×

int x=10;
double y = 30.54;
decimal z = 11.11M;

if (x<y)
{
    //does not require explicit casting
}

if ((double)z < y)
{
    //requires explicit casting
}
```

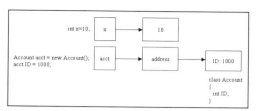

Figure 3.7 A variable that is a value type (numeric types, bool, char, etc.) points to the actual data in memory. Reference type variables on the other hand point to an address which then points to the object.

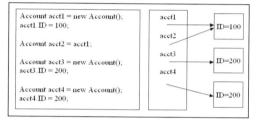

Figure 3.8 With reference types, two questions are important. Are the variables pointing to the same object in memory? If not, do the object's fields contain the same information? In the figure you see that acct1 and acct2 point to the same object, while acct3 and acct4 point to different objects but refer to the same information.

Comparing Reference Types

Comparing reference types is different than comparing numeric types. Reference types are variables that point to objects created as the result of using new on class type (for example: Account acct = new Account( ) where Account is a class definition). The reason it is different is that numeric types are allocated differently in memory than reference types. Whenever you use a variable that is a numeric type, the variable represents an address in memory where the value is stored. A variable that points to a reference type doesn't point to the object directly. Instead, it points to the place in memory that stores the address of the object (**Figure 3.7**).

Since a reference type points to an address that points to an object and not to the object directly there are two questions we can ask when comparing two reference variables: are the two variables pointing to the same object, and if they aren't, are the two objects referring to the same thing? For example if we are comparing two Account variables we can first ask: Are the two variables referring to the same object in memory? Then we can ask: If they aren't the same object, are they the same account, i.e. both have the same account number and the same balance? The first question (same object) is a question of identity, the second question (same data in the object) is a question of equivalence (**Figure 3.8**).

To compare two reference variables for identity:

◆ Type bool bResult = object.ReferenceEquals(var1,var2); where var1 and var2 are the two reference variables to compare (**Figure 3.9**).

   or

◆ Type bool bResult = (var1 == var2) where var1 and var2 are the two reference variables to compare.

Figure 3.9 Even though the data for the fields is the same in p1 and p2, ReferenceEquals only tests whether the variables are pointing to the same memory address. They aren't because we are creating two distinct objects.

```
class Person
{
   public string LastName;
   public string FirstName;
}

class App
{
   void DoTask1()
   {
      Person p1 = new Person();
      p1.LastName = "Mojica";
      p1.FirstName = "Jose";

      Person p2 = new Person();
      p2.LastName = "Mojica";
      p2.FirstName = "Jose";

      Person p3 = p2;

      bool bResult1 = object.ReferenceEquals(
                          p1,p2); //false
      bool bResult2 = object.ReferenceEquals(
                          p2,p3); //true
   }
}
```

Figure 3.10 The result statements are only true if the developer of the Person class overrides the default implementation of Equals and the default implementation of the == operator. Both Equals and == are intended to be for equivalence, but without the programmer implementing the methods the results are based on identity. You will learn how to override Equals and == in Chapter 7, "Types."

```
class Person
{
   public string LastName;
   public string FirstName;

   public override bool Equals(
   object obj)
   {
      //implementation discussed in a
      //later chapter
   }

   public static bool operator ==(
   Person p1, Person p2)
   {
      return p1.Equals(p2);
   }

   public static bool operator !=(
   Person p1, Person p2)
   {
      return !(p1==p2);
   }
}

class App
{
   void DoTask1()
   {
      Person p1 = new Person();
      p1.LastName = "Mojica";
      p1.FirstName = "Jose";

      Person p2 = new Person();
      p2.LastName = "Mojica";
      p2.FirstName = "Jose";

      Person p3 = p2;

      //true
      bool bResult1 = p1.Equals(p2);
      //true
      bool bResult2 = p2.Equals(p3);
      //true
      bool bResult3 = (p2 == p3);
   }
}
```

To compare two reference variables for equivalence:

◆ Type bool bResult = var1.Equals(var2); or bool bResult = var2.Equals(var1); where var1 and var2 are the two reference variables to compare.

or

◆ Type bool bResult = (var1 == var2) where var1 and var2 are the two reference variables to compare (**Figure 3.10**).

COMPARING REFERENCE TYPES

✔ Tips

■ Testing for identity is faster than testing for equivalence. Although no developer does this consistently, it makes sense to do a test for identity before doing a test for equivalence. That way, you eliminate the need for an equivalence test if the two variables are pointing to the same object. For that reason a developer who redefines the == sign should perform an identity check first and return true immediately if the two things compared are exactly the same object.

■ OK what gives? If you look at both the test for identity and the test for equivalence, in both cases I've said that you can use the == operator. So is == for identity or for equivalence? The answer: it's for both. By default, whenever you use the == operator the compiler writes code to do an identity check. However, a developer may override the way that == works as you will see in Chapter 7, "Types." Most of the time when developers use the == operator with reference types they're looking for the program to perform a test of equivalence.

■ Strings are a special kind of reference types that support comparisons with the == and != operators. For details, see Chapter 4, "Strings" (**Figure 3.11**).

■ In addition to using == you can use != to test for two things not being equal. If a developer redefines the == then the compiler forces the developer to also override the != operator. Thus if the == performs an equivalence test, the != will also. A common practice is to perform a test for != null (**Figure 3.12**).

Figure 3.11 Strings override the == operator as well as the != operator. When you compare two strings with == you are comparing the contents of the string, not whether the two variables point to the same string object. Unfortunately you can't use the < or > operators with strings.

```
class Person
{
    public string LastName;
    public string FirstName;
}

class App
{
    void DoTask1()
    {
        Person p1 = new Person();
        p1.LastName = "Mojica";

        Person p2 = new Person();
        p2.LastName = "Mojica";

        bool Same = (p1.LastName ==
        p2.LastName); //true

        p1.LastName = "Smith";
        bool Before = (p1.LastName <
                        p2.LastName);
        //*** Error < operator not
        //supported
    }
}
```

Figure 3.12 Be careful to test for null. A classic example is when you attempt to retrieve an item from the Session object. If the item is not found, the result is null.

```
class App
{
    void ContactFamily()
    {
        Person brother =
        (Person)Session["jarvx"];

        if (brother != null)
            WriteLetter(brother);
    }
}
```

Figure 3.13 C# enables you to combine clauses with either && (for and) or || (for or).

```
Code                                      _ □ ×
int qty = 10;
string item = "Computer";

bool ValidEntry = (qty > 0 &&
                   item != ""); //true
```

Figure 3.14 In an && clause if one of the parts is false, then the whole expression is false. In an || clause if one of the parts is true then the whole thing is true.

```
Code                                      _ □ ×
class App
{
    bool Task1()
    {
        return true;
    }

    bool Task2()
    {
        return false;
    }

    void ProgramCode()
    {
        bool result1 = (Task2()
                    && Task1());
        //only Task2 is executed

        bool result2 = (Task1()
                    || Task2());
        //only Task1 is executed
    }
}
```

Combining Test Clauses

In the previous section you learned how to compare two value types and how to compare two reference types. A lot of times you will want to make more than one comparison.

To combine multiple clauses in the same statement:

1. Type the first clause (for example, qty >= 0).

2. Type one of the following operators: && for and, or || for or.

3. Type the second clause (for example, sItem != "") (**Figure 3.13**).

✔ Tips

- When you use an and clause (&&) both sides have to be true in order for the expression to be true; in the case of an or expression (||) only one of the expressions needs to be true.

- C# uses a system called *short-circuiting*. With short-circuiting if the program figures out that the expression will be true or false after evaluating part of the statement, it stops evaluating the rest of the expression. This happens if, for example, the first clause is false in an and expression. Since both of the clauses need to be true, having a single false makes the entire expression false, so there's no need to evaluate the second half. The same is true if one of the clauses is true in an or expression, since only one of the clauses needs to be true for the expression to be true (**Figure 3.14**).

Writing if-else Statements

Now that you know how to write conditional clauses and even how to combine multiple clauses, it's time to write if statements. if statements enable you to execute some code, either a single line of code or a block of code if the conditional evaluates to true. You can optionally execute a line of code or even a block of code if the expression is false.

To write an if-else statement:

1. Type if.

2. Type an open parenthesis (.

3. Type a clause that evaluates to a Boolean value (bool in C#).

4. Type a close parenthesis).

5. If you wish to execute a single statement type the statement after the parenthesis (most of the time people write the statement in the next line) and type a semicolon (**Figure 3.15**), and skip to step 9.

6. If you wish to execute more than one statement, type an open curly bracket {.

7. Write the statements you wish to execute if the condition evaluates to true.

8. Type a close curly bracket } (**Figure 3.16**).

9. If you would like to execute alternate statements if the condition evaluates to false, then type the word else.

Figure 3.15 If statements have an expression inside parenthesis. If the expression results in true then you can execute a single statement as shown here.

```
if (items.Count == 0)
    HideGrid();
```

Figure 3.16 With if statements you can also execute an entire code block if the expression is true.

```
if (qty >= 0 && name != "")
{
    //create new purchased item
    PurchasedItem pi = new PurchasedItem();
    pi.SetInfo(name,qty);
    items.Add(pi);

    ShowGrid();
    UpdateGrid();
}
```

Figure 3.17 else is the evil counterpart of if. It gets executed when the expression results in false. You can see that you can execute a single statement if you like in the else.

```
🖪 Code                          _ □ ✕
if (balance > 0)
    PurchaseNewPhone();
else
    KeepOldPhone();
```

Figure 3.18 As with if, else also supports the execution of an entire code block.

```
🖪 Code                          _ □ ✕
if (balance > 0)
    PurchaseNewPhone();
else
{
    BegSpouseForMoney();
    PurchaseNewPhone();
}
```

Figure 3.19 In the code below there is a second if condition as part of the first else. The second else is part of the second if condition. It gets executed if the else if condition results in false.

```
🖪 Code                          _ □ ✕
if (balance > 0)
    PurchaseNewPhone();
else if (IsTodayBirthday())
    AskParentsForNewPhone();
else
{
    BegSpouseForMoney();
    PurchaseNewPhone();
}
```

10. If you have only a single alternate statement, then type the statement and end with a semicolon ; (**Figure 3.17**), then skip the remaining steps.

11. If you wish to execute more than one statement, type an open curly bracket {.

12. Type the statements for the else condition.

13. Type a close curly bracket } (**Figure 3.18**).

✔ Tip

■ If you want to add another if statement as part of the else clause, simply type if after the else clause and repeat steps 1–8 (**Figure 3.19**).

WRITING IF-ELSE STATEMENTS

Testing Multiple Conditions with switch

If you have multiple clauses to test, it makes sense to add a *switch* statement instead of many if statements. Internally the compiler treats switch statements as if they were multiple if statements. Code-wise, however, switch statements are normally easier to follow and to maintain than several if statements all in a row.

To write a switch statement:

1. Type the word `switch`.

2. Type an open parenthesis (.

3. Type the name of a variable that is either of an integral type (`byte`, `int`, `long`, `char`, etc.), or a `string` type.

4. Type a close parenthesis).

5. Type an open curly bracket {.

6. Type the word `case` followed by a space and a literal value, either a number, a string in quotes, or the name of a constant variable, then type a colon :.

7. In the next line type the statements that are to be executed if the variable contains the value in the case.

8. Type the word `break` and a semicolon ;.

9. Add other case statements. Repeat steps 6, 7, and 8 for as many cases as you like.

10. If you want to execute code for any value outside of the cases you specified type the word `default` followed by a colon :.

11. Type the commands to execute in the default case.

12. Type a close curly bracket } (**Figure 3.20**).

Figure 3.20 A switch statement is an easy way to condense a number of if statements. In this case a string variable is being evaluated. Depending on the value of name, the program will jump to a particular case statement and execute the code within.

```
Code                                    _ □ ×
public string Description
{
    get
    {
        string desc="";

        switch(name)
        {
            case "Notebook":
                desc = "A small computer";
                break;
            case "Desktop":
                desc = "A big computer";
                break;
            case "FlatMon":
                desc =
                "A sweet looking monitor";
                break;
            case "FatMon":
                desc =
                "An old-looking fat monitor";
                break;
            default:
                desc = "unknown item";
                break;
        }

        return desc;
    }
}
```

Figure 3.21 Don't forget to put the word break; at the end of each case. Failure to do so will result in great embarrassment.

```
Code                                    _ □ ×

public string Description
{
   get
   {
      string desc="";

      switch(name)
      {
         case "Notebook":
            desc = "A small computer";
            //<--error can't omit the break;
         case "Desktop":
            desc = "A big computer";
            break;
      }

      return desc;
   }
}
```

✔ Tips

■ In the old days of C++ if you omitted the break; statement in one of the case sections, the program would execute the statements in the following case; it would fall through to the next case. With C#, the compiler gives you an error if you forget to put the break statement (**Figure 3.21**).

■ In C# you can have multiple cases execute the same code by putting one case statement after another without code in between (**Figure 3.22**).

■ You can forward one case block to another by using the goto statement (**Figure 3.23**).

Figure 3.22 Several cases can do the same code. The trick is to not put any code between them. In the code below, if name is either Notebook or FlatMon the code below FlatMon will be executed. The same is true for Desktop and FatMon.

```
Code                                    _ □ ×

public string Description
{
   get
   {
      string desc="";

      switch(name)
      {
         case "Notebook":
         case "FlatMon":
            desc =
            "something cool I want";
            break;
         case "Desktop":
         case "FatMon":
            desc =
            "something old I don't want";
            break;
         default:
            desc = "unknown item";
            break;
      }

      return desc;
   }
}
```

Figure 3.23 After executing the code in one case, you can jump to another case using the goto statement followed by the name of the case.

```
Code                                    _ □ ×

public string Status
{
   get
   {
      string status="";

      switch(name)
      {
         case "Notebook":
            status = "A small computer";
            if (qty == 0)
               goto default;
            break;
         case "Desktop":
            status = "A big computer.";
            if (qty == 0)
               goto default;
            break;
         default:
            //append to status
            status += "(item unavailable.)";
            break;
      }

      return status;
   }
}
```

Conditional Operator

Many times in programming you want to set the contents of a variable to one value if the condition is true, or to another value if the condition if false. For example, consider the following code.

```
string status;
if (qty > 0)
  status = "Available";
else
  status = "Unavailable";
```

Notice that status could be available or unavailable depending on the value of qty. In C# these five lines of code can be condensed into a single line of code using the conditional operator (? :).

To use the conditional operator:

1. Enter the name of the variable you would like to set followed by an equal sign. For example: string status =.

2. Enter a Boolean expression in parentheses. For example: (qty > 0).

3. After the close parenthesis type a question mark ?.

4. Type the resulting value if the expression evaluates to true. For example: "Available".

5. Type a colon :.

6. Type the resulting value if the expression evaluates to false. For example: "Unavailable".

7. Type a semicolon ; (**Figure 3.24**).

✔ Tip

■ Instead of having literal values for the results you could use variables or invoke a function (**Figure 3.25**).

Figure 3.24 The conditional operator makes it handy to combine an "if" and an "else" clause in a single statement. If qty is greater than zero, then the status will be available, otherwise it will be unavailable. Be careful not to abuse this technique. To beginning developers, it's often easier to read an if-else statement than the conditional operator.

```
int qty = 10;
string status = (qty > 0) ?
      "Available" : "Unavailable";
```

Figure 3.25 You aren't limited to using literals with the conditional operator; it also works with functions and variables.

```
int balance = 20;
int withdrawal = 30;

int amount = (balance > withdrawal)
? MakeWithdrawal()
: BorrowFromSavings();

string managers = "Joe;Jane;Jill;John";
string everyone = managers + ";Rick;Sue";

bool managersOnly = true;
string meeting = (managersOnly)
? managers : everyone;
```

Figure 3.26 Beautiful isn't it? It is the sample application with a few items added to the shopping cart.

Figure 3.27 When the cart is empty, the application hides the grid and displays a label instead.

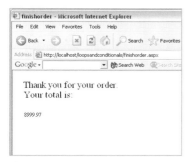

Figure 3.28 When the user clicks Place Order, the application jumps to another page that displays the total for the order and a thank-you message.

Adding Conditional Statements to the Sample Program

It's time to add code to our sample application. In this section you will add the conditional statements. Before adding the code however, a little explanation of what the application does is in order. You are writing a scaled-down version of a shopping cart. Here's how it works. You select an item to purchase from a list of items, then specify the quantity, and click the add button. As you add items, a table in the middle of the page displays the items purchased, their description, and their unit price (**Figure 3.26**). Before you purchase any items, the page displays that the shopping cart is empty (**Figure 3.27**). When you are done purchasing items, click the Place Order button. Clicking the button sends you to another page where you get a thank-you message and the total for the order (**Figure 3.28**).

To complete this program you're going to have to use one of the ASP.NET intrinsic objects—the Session object. I explained the `Session` object briefly in Chapter 2, "C# Building Blocks." The Session object works like a filing cabinet. It is similar to the `Application` object you used in Chapter 2 except that rather than storing information for all users, the `Session` object can store different information per user. You use it by adding objects to the `Session` object and associating each object with a key. It's easy to add objects to the `Session` object; all you have to do is enter a line like the following:

```
Person p1 = new Person();
Session["Jose"] = p1;
```

The above lines add the `Person` object in `p1` to the `Session` object and assign the key

continues on next page

"Jose" to the object. The information added to the Session object is only for the user accessing the page at the moment. If other users access the page, they may have something totally different in their Session object. To retrieve the information from the Session object you just reverse the process, like this:

```
Person p1 = (Person) Session["Jose"];
```

In this case Session returns something of type object. In order to assign the result to the Person variable we need to convert the result to a Person. The conversion only works if the thing we put into "Jose" was a Person to begin with. But the C# language requires you to be very explicit about conversions. What if there is no item in Session with the key "Jose"? Then, Session["Jose"] will return null.

In addition to the Session object, you are going to use another class called the ArrayList. The ArrayList is a class that can maintain a dynamic array of items. Its complete name (as written by Microsoft) is System.Collections.ArrayList. It's kind of like the HashTable that you used in Chapter 2, except that you don't assign a key to each item. It is just a place to store objects, and then navigate through them one by one. We are going to use the ArrayList to store the purchased items. Then we are going to put the ArrayList object into the Session object so that every user will have his own ArrayList (i.e. set of purchased items). When the user clicks on the Place Order link we are going to retrieve the ArrayList from Session and add the price times the quantity for the items in the ArrayList.

I hope this doesn't sound too complicated. Let's get to it.

Figure 3.29 The PurchasedItem class keeps information about a purchased item. When the user clicks the Add button to add the item to the shopping cart, the application creates an instance of this class to keep track of the item.

```
Code                                    _ □ ×
class PurchasedItem
{
    string name;
    int qty;

    public void SetInfo(string name, int qty)
    {
        this.name = name;
        this.qty = qty;
    }

    public string Name
    {
        get
        {
            return name;
        }
    }

    public int Quantity
    {
        get
        {
            return qty;
        }
    }
}
```

To add conditional statements to the sample application:

1. First let's add the definition for the PurchasedItem class. The PurchasedItem class will be used to store each item that the customer purchases. Right-click on the file enterorder.aspx in Solution Explorer and choose View Code from the menu.

2. Locate the lines that read:

   namespace loopsandconditionals

   {

   After that line, add the code in **Figure 3.29**.

   continues on next page

3. Now add a variable to your WebForm1 class of type ArrayList. Type ArrayList items; after the declaration for the fields that store the Web Controls (**Figure 3.30**).

4. After the declaration line in step 3, it would be handy to define a few support functions. In particular, one function to show the grid and one to hide the grid, depending on whether there are items on the list or not. These functions are called ShowGrid and HideGrid (**Figure 3.31**).

Figure 3.30 The ArrayList is a class that Microsoft provides to store a collection of objects. The objects can be of any type. The list grows automatically as you add objects to it.

```
Code                                    _ □ ×

using System.Web.UI;

public class WebForm1 : System.Web.UI.Page
{
    protected WebControls.Button
    btnAdd;
    protected WebControls.Label
    lblItem;
    protected WebControls.TextBox
    txtQty;
    protected WebControls.Label
    lblQty;
    protected WebControls.DataGrid
    grdItems;
    protected WebControls.DropDownList
    lstItems;
    protected WebControls.Label
    lblEmpty;
    protected WebControls.HyperLink
    lnkOrder;

    ArrayList items;
```

Figure 3.31 The ShowGrid function does what its name implies, shows the grid and hides the label that says that the cart is empty. The HideGrid function does the opposite.

```
Code                                    _ □ ×

private void ShowGrid()
{
    lblEmpty.Visible = false;
    grdItems.Visible = true;
}

private void HideGrid()
{
    lblEmpty.Visible = true;
    grdItems.Visible = false;
}
```

Figure 3.32 UpdateGrid binds the data grid to the array list. The grid control automatically updates itself to show the items in the array list. There will be one row for each purchased item. The columns of the grid will be bound to properties in each object.

```
Code                                    _ □ ×

private void UpdateGrid()
{
    grdItems.DataSource = items;
    grdItems.DataBind();
}
```

Figure 3.33 Every time the client requests a Web form, ASP.NET calls the Page_Load function in your code. In this form we see if there is a list of items already present in Session. If not we create a new array list and save it in Session. If the list (previously there or newly created) contains no items, then we hide the grid and show the label that says the cart is empty. If there are items, we show the grid and hide the label.

```
Code                                    _ □ ×

private void Page_Load(object sender,
System.EventArgs e)
{
    if (Session["items"] == null)
    {
        items = new ArrayList();
        Session["items"] = items;
    }
    else
        items = (ArrayList)Session["items"];

    if (items.Count == 0)
        HideGrid();
    else
    {
        ShowGrid();
        UpdateGrid();
    }
}
```

5. One more support function is needed, one to bind the grid to the array list. This code uses the grid's databinding feature. Databinding is a handy feature. You set the DataSource property of the grid to a list object, like the ArrayList. The grid takes care of navigating through the items in the list and updating its data to match the elements. Each column in the grid has a DataField property. The grid reads each object from the list and looks for a property in the object named the same as the DataField. So, all we have to do is make sure our class PurchasedItem has properties, and that we set the columns' DataFields to the names of the properties. The grid control will take care of displaying the data properly. Add the code in **Figure 3.32** after the HideGrid function.

6. In Solution Explorer, right-click on enterorder.aspx and choose View Designer from the context menu.

7. Double-click on an empty space on the form. This will make the code editor add a Page_Load function if it has not already been added.

8. In Page_Load, add the code in **Figure 3.33**. This code does two things. First it checks if Session already contains the ArrayList object. If it doesn't, we create the ArrayList object and add it to Session. The second part of the code checks if we have items in the ArrayList. If we don't have items, then we hide the grid (i.e. call HideGrid). If we do have items then we show the grid (i.e. call ShowGrid).

9. In Solution Explorer right-click on enterorder.aspx and choose View Designer from the context menu.

10. Double-click on the Add button. This will make the code editor add a `btnAdd_Click` function if it has not already been added.

11. Add the code in **Figure 3.34** inside the `btnAdd_Click` function. This code reads the contents of the fields (item selected and quantity) and if they are valid creates a `PurchasedItem` object with the information and adds it to the `ArrayList`.

12. Finally, let's enhance the `PurchasedItem` class. The `PurchasedItem` class needs to have two properties: `Description` and `Price`. Of these, `Description` gives the description for the item. It is a property that returns a different string using a switch statement depending on the item that `PurchasedItem` is storing. `Price` works in the same fashion. It reports a price for the current item based on a switch statement. Add the highlighted code in **Figure 3.35** (next page) to your project inside the `PurchasedItem` class.

✔ Tip

■ At this point your application should compile and run. The only code missing is the code that displays the total when the Place Order link is clicked.

Figure 3.34 When the user clicks the Add button, the code reads the contents of the item and qty fields. Notice that it needs to convert the qty text field into a numeric value. Then if the fields aren't empty, the code creates a new PurchasedItem, sets the information in the object, and adds it to the ArrayList.

```
private void btnAdd_Click(object sender,
                    System.EventArgs e)
{
    int qty = 0;

    if (txtQty.Text != null)
        qty = System.Convert.ToInt32
            (txtQty.Text);

    string name = lstItems.SelectedItem.
                Value;

    if (qty >= 0 && name != "")
    {
        PurchasedItem pi =
        new PurchasedItem();
        pi.SetInfo(name,qty);
        items.Add(pi);
        ShowGrid();
        UpdateGrid();
    }
}
```

Figure 3.35 The Description and Price fields are calculated based on the name of the item.

```
Code                                    _ □ ×

class PurchasedItem
{
   string name;
   int qty;

   public void SetInfo(string name,
                         int qty)
   { ... }

   public string Name { ... }

   public int Quantity { ... }

   public string Description
   {
      get
      {
         string desc="";

         switch(name)
         {
         case "Notebook":
            desc = "A small computer";
            break;
         case "Desktop":
            desc = "A big computer";
            break;
         case "FlatMon":
            desc =
            "A sweet looking monitor";
            break;
         case "FatMon":
            desc = "An old fat monitor";
            break;
         default:
            desc = "unknown item";
            break;
         }

         return desc;
      }
   }

   public double Price
   {
      get
      {
         double price = 0.0;

         switch(name)
         {
         case "Notebook":
            price = 1999.99;
            break;
                        code continues
```

Figure 3.35 *continued*

```
Code                                    _ □ ×

         case "Desktop":
            price = 899.00;
            break;
         case "FlatMon":
            price = 1500.00;
            break;
         case "FatMon":
            price = 300.00;
            break;
         default:
            price = 0.0;
            break;
         }

         return price;
      }
   }
}
```

Using while Loops

There are various ways of executing code a certain number of times. *While loops* enable you to loop until a certain condition is met.

To write a while loop:

1. The variables that are going to be used in the while statement must be declared first. For example: int count = 1;

2. Type while followed by an open parenthesis (.

3. Type an expression that results in true or false. For example: count < 10.

4. Type a close parenthesis).

5. Type an open curly bracket {.

6. Type the statements that you wish to execute while the expression is true.

7. Remember to change the variable used for the expression in step 3 so that at some point the expression will result in false and end the loop. For example: count++;

8. Type a close curly bracket } (**Figure 3.36**).

✔ Tips

- Writing the expression for the while loop is similar to writing an expression for an if statement. You can combine clauses with && and || (**Figure 3.37**).

- While loops continue to execute until the expression becomes false. Forgetting to change the variable in the expression is a common mistake that results in an endless loop.

Figure 3.36 The loop will continue as long as the start number isn't greater than the end number. Notice that the loop won't execute at all if the caller sends a start number greater that the end number to begin with.

```
void GenerateEvenNumbers(int startnum, int endnum)
{
    while (startnum <= endnum)
    {
        Response.Write(startnum + "<br>");
        startnum+=2;
    }
}
```

Figure 3.37 The conditional expression supports and statements and or statements just like if statements. You can put any expression in the parenthesis that evaluates to true or false.

```
void ForwardToVoiceMail(int maxRings)
{
    int rings = 0;
    bool answered  = HasPersonAnswered();

    while (rings < maxRings && answered == false)
    {
        Ring();
        rings++;
        answered = HasPersonAnswered();
    }
}
```

Figure 3.38 No matter how hard you try to put kids to bed on time, they always have an unlimited amount of excuses. Some would argue the above will result in an endless loop. Nonetheless, the code attempts to put the kids to bed first before finding out if there are excuses, then continues to try while the excuses continue, if they ever stop then the loop ends. This code came courtesy of my wife.

```
void NightRoutine()
{
   string childExcuse="";

   do
   {
      childExcuse = PutKidsInBed();
   } while( childExcuse != ""  );
}
```

Using do Loops

Do loops and while loops are closely related. *Do loops*, like while loops, also execute statements a number of times. However, a do loop always executes once regardless of whether the expression to test is true or false.

To write a do loop:

1. Type do.

2. In the next line type an open curly bracket {.

3. Type the statements to execute in the loop.

4. Remember to change the variable used for the expression in step 8 so that at some point the expression will result in false and end the loop. For example: count++;

5. Type a close curly bracket }.

6. Type while.

7. Type an open parenthesis (.

8. Type an expression that results in true or false. For example: count < 20. The variables that are going to be used in the while at the end of the do statement must be declared before the do in step 1. For example: int count=1;

9. Type a close parenthesis).

10. Type a semicolon ; (**Figure 3.38**).

Using for Loops

for loops are written to execute a loop for a fixed number of times.

for loops are very powerful constructs. They are divided into three parts. The first part is the initialization part. In the initialization part you can declare multiple variables that can be used as part of the loop. The second part of the for loop is the test part. The loop continues to execute while the test part is equal to true. The third part of the for loop is the execution part. At the end of each loop the code will execute the third portion of the for statement. When wanting to execute a series of statements in a loop a certain number of times a variable that serves as the counter is initialized in the first part of the statement; the second part of the statement tests to see if the counter variable is below a certain value; and the third part of the statement increases the counter by one in each iteration.

Figure 3.39 Assuming that items is an ArrayList, this code enumerates through all the items and calculates the total amount of the order.

```
Code                              _ □ ×
double total=0;

for (int i=0; i < items.Count; i++)
{
    PurchasedItem item = (PurchasedItem)items[i];
    total += item.Price * item.Quantity;
}
```

Figure 3.40 Don't write code like that. It's here to show you how flexible for statements are.

```
Code                              _ □ ×
//extremely confusing for loop
int m;
for (int count = 1, total = 500;
     count < 10 && total > 200;
     count++,total--,m = count * 100)
{
  //do something interesting here
  //I have no idea what
}
```

To write a for loop that executes for a specified number of times:

1. Type for.

2. Type an open parenthesis (.

3. Type int count=0, where count is the name of the variable that will be used for the counter.

4. Type a semicolon ;.

5. Type count < 10, where 10 is the number of times that you would like to loop. You can optionally use another variable for the comparison.

6. Type another semicolon ;.

7. Type count++.

8. Type a close parenthesis).

9. Type an open curly bracket {.

10. Type the statements that you wish to execute inside the loop.

11. Type a close curly bracket } (**Figure 3.39**).

✔ Tip

- The for statement is very flexible. You can declare several variables in the first portion of the for statement, you can test that multiple criteria are met before continuing the loop, and you can even execute multiple statements in the execution part of the for (**Figure 3.40**).

USING FOR LOOPS

Exiting and Continuing Loops

There are three commands that let you control the execution of loops: break, continue, and goto.

The break command enables you to exit the loop early. Rather than having to wait until a loop finishes, if you can determine that it isn't necessary to continue you can exit the loop.

The continue command lets you advance the loop at any point. Other languages like VB.NET don't offer this ability and so the entire loop has to be executed before advancing. With for loops, being able to advance the loop means that you can add one to the counter and go back to the beginning of the loop without having to execute the remaining statements.

C# enables you to assign labels to a segment of code in a function. You can then use the goto command to exit the loop and jump to a particular label in the code.

To use the break command:

1. Inside the loop, type break.

2. Type a semicolon ; (**Figure 3.41**).

To advance the loop:

1. Inside the loop type continue.

2. Type a semicolon ; (**Figure 3.42**).

Figure 3.41 In this example a number of items need to be copied from one directory to another. Ideally we want to move all the items, however, the user can cancel the copy midstream. If the cancel option is selected the break is invoked which causes the code to exit the loop.

```
void CopyItems(int totalItems,
               string src, string dest)
{
    for (int i = 0; i < totalItems; i++)
    {
        MoveFile(i, src, dest);

        bool cancel = CheckUserCancel();
        if (cancel)
            break;
    }
}
```

Figure 3.42 In the code below there is no sense doing anything if the item requested isn't in stock. Therefore, if the item isn't in stock, the code calls continue to go to the next item.

```
void ProcessOrder()
{
    for (int i=0; i < items.Count; i++)
    {
        bool inStock = (GetItemQty(i) > 0);

        if (inStock == false)
            continue;

        SubtractFromInventory(i);
        SendToShipping(i);
    }
}
```

Figure 3.43 You can put a label on a portion of the code. A label is a name followed by a colon. Then you can jump to that portion of the code with the goto command. You can only jump to labels in the same function.

```
Code                                    _ □ ×
void DailyWorkRoutine()
{
   bool havingFun = true;

   while (havingFun)
   {
      if (BossIsComing() == true)
         goto fundone;

      havingFun = CheckFunStatus();
   }

   fundone:
      CloseBrowser();
      ShutdownEmail();
      DoActualWork();
}
```

To jump to another part of the code:

1. First assign a label to the portion of code to which you would like to jump, for example: `cleanup:`.

2. Inside the loop type `goto` followed by the name of the label, for example: `goto cleanup` (**Figure 3.43**).

✔ Tips

■ If you have a loop inside of another loop, the break command only exits the inner loop (**Figure 3.44**).

■ Sometimes there are too many conditions that may warrant exiting from a loop. When this happens developers normally write an infinite while loop. The infinite while loop has the clause `while(true)` which always evaluates to true, and therefore always executes the loop. When one of the many condition that warrant exiting is met, then you issue a break statement or a `goto` statement (**Figure 3.45**).

■ Programmers typically stay away from `goto` statements, for one main reason: If `goto` statements are overused, the code becomes really hard to follow.

Figure 3.44 When you have nested loops, the break statement only applies to the innermost loop in which it was executed. Incidentally, as you type the break; statement in VS.NET, VS.NET highlights the loop to which it belongs in bold.

```
void PlanFoodForTrip(int totalFamilies)
{
    for (int i =0; i < totalFamilies; i ++)
    {
        for (int j = 0; j < famMembers(i); j++)
        {
            if (BringingFood(j))
                break; //<--only exits inner loop
        }
    }
}
```

Figure 3.45 These types of loops are usually written when keyboard or mouse input needs to be monitored. The code continues to loop indefinitely until something calls break or goto.

```
void TypeLetter()
{
    string msg = "";
    while(true)
    {
        char c = GetKeyboardInput();
        if (c=='q' || c=='x')
            break;
        else
            msg += c;
    }

    Response.Write(msg);
}
```

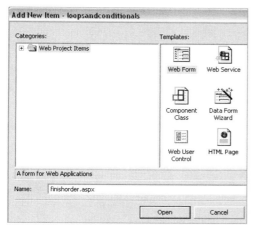

Figure 3.46 Use this dialog to add a new Web Form to your application.

Adding Loops to the Sample Program

It's time to put our new knowledge of loops into practice. In this section you will add the code to make the Place Order link work. First you need to add a new Web Form to your project. Then you can add the code to calculate the order's grand total. Calculating the total cost isn't difficult. All you need to do is get hold of the `ArrayList` that contains all the items.

Earlier you learned that the sample code stores this `ArrayList` in the `Session` object. So we need only retrieve it from the `Session` object, go through all the items in the list, calculate the price times the quantity, add them all up, and print the value. And that's where loops come in.

To add loops to the sample application:

1. Choose Project > Add Web Form. You will see the dialog in **Figure 3.46**. Enter `finishorder.aspx` for the file name and press Enter.

continues on next page

2. Create a form that looks like the form in **Figure 3.47.** Do so by entering the HTML directly into the editor (**Figure 3.48**) or by downloading the skeleton file for this project from Peachpit's Web site.

3. Double-click on a blank space in the form. This will cause VS.NET to open the code editor and add a `Page_Load` function.

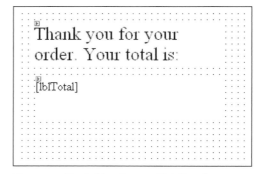

Figure 3.47 The finishorder.aspx Web Form has two labels. One is static and says thank you; the other reports the total amount for the order and is calculated at runtime.

Figure 3.48 You can recreate the form from the HTML, but it might be easier to download it from Peachpit's Web site.

```
Code                                    _ □ ×
<%@ Page language="c#"
    Codebehind="finishorder.aspx.cs"
    AutoEventWireup="false"
    Inherits="loopsandconditionals.
    finishorder" %>
<HTML>
    <HEAD>
        <title>finishorder</title>
    </HEAD>
    <body MS_POSITIONING="GridLayout">
    <form id="finishorder" method="post"
        runat="server">
    <asp:Label id="lblThankYou"
            style="Z-INDEX: 101;
            LEFT: 24px;
            POSITION: absolute;
            TOP: 22px" runat="server"
            Width="246px" Height="53px"
            Font-Size="Large">
            Thank you for your order.
            Your total is:
            </asp:Label>
    <asp:Label id="lblTotal"
            style="Z-INDEX: 102;
            LEFT: 26px;
            POSITION: absolute;
            TOP: 95px" runat="server"
            Width="243px"
            Height="53px">
            </asp:Label>
    </form>
    </body>
</HTML>
```

Figure 3.49 When the user clicks the Place Order link in the enterorder.aspx form, control is transferred to finishorder.aspx and ASP.NET calls the Page_Load function in your code. In this case we take the list of items from Session and add up all the prices times the quantities. Then we display the amount in the form's label.

```
Code                                    _ □ ×

private void Page_Load(object sender,
                   System.EventArgs e)
{
   ArrayList items =
   (ArrayList)Session["items"];

   if (items != null)
   {
      double total=0;

      for (int i=0; i < items.Count; i++)
      {
         PurchasedItem item =
         (PurchasedItem)items[i];
         total += item.Price *
                  item.Quantity;
      }

      lblTotal.Text = total.ToString();
   }
}
```

4. In the Page_Load function, add the code in **Figure 3.49**. This code retrieves the list of purchased items from the Session object, adds the cost for each entry, and then displays the total in a label.

5. Build and execute your program.

✔ Tips

- After clicking the Place Order link in your Web Form the results should look similar to **Figure 3.50**.

- This completes the sample code for this chapter, and the chapter as well.

Figure 3.50 If everything works correctly your results should resemble this, give or take a few thousand dollars.

4

STRINGS

Most applications require the use of strings in one way or another. Strings are required for building SQL statements when accessing a database, for example. Knowing how to manipulate strings is useful in analyzing requests from Web clients and in constructing a response for the client.

Strings are reference types. You've been learning about reference types little by little in each chapter. The category of reference types includes types you define with the class keyword. As you may recall, you have to create an object before you can use a variable of the type. For example:

```
Account acct = new Account();
```

Before you create an object, the variable holds the value of null. The same rule holds true for strings. String variables when declared are equal to null. However, what makes strings interesting is that they also have characteristics of value types (integers, longs, Booleans, etc., for example). C# lets you allocate a string object without using the new operator, like this:

```
string sqlAuthors = "SELECT * FROM
→ AUTHORS";
```

The above code creates a new string object. Other characteristics include the way that you can use the == and the != operators for comparing two string objects.

So what is a string? Internally you can think of a string as an array of characters. When you create a string object, in essence two objects are being created in one. The first object is an instance of the string class. The string class has members that describe the physical attributes of the string, such as the length of the string. The second object that gets created is a buffer to hold the characters of the string. The buffer is just a chunk of memory where the characters of the string are stored. The string variable you declare will point to the outer string object, which in turn points to the buffer of characters.

What makes string types really interesting is that in .NET strings are immutable—the contents of the buffer can't be changed. Languages like C# enable you to treat your string variable as a changeable type. For example, they let you append another string to the string in your variable. However, this is an illusion provided by the compiler. In reality, when you change the contents of your string, the compiler asks the .NET runtime to create a brand-new string object.

String objects consume memory, and if you're not careful, you can end up consuming too much memory. At some point that memory needs to be reclaimed. The .NET framework uses a mechanism known as *garbage collection* to reclaim the memory.

At the end of this chapter you will learn about `StringBuilder`, which lets you create a changeable string—a single buffer of characters that can be modified. When you're done modifying the `StringBuilder` buffer, you can ask `StringBuilder` to produce a single string object from the result. Using StringBuilder will help you minimize the number of string objects that need to be created, and this will in turn decrease the number of garbage collections that need to occur to delete those objects from memory.

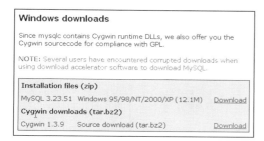

Windows downloads

Since mysqlc contains Cygwin runtime DLLs, we also offer you the Cygwin sourcecode for compliance with GPL.

NOTE: Several users have encountered corrupted downloads when using download accelerator software to download MySQL.

Installation files (zip)	
MySQL 3.23.51 Windows 95/98/NT/2000/XP (12.1M)	Download
Cygwin downloads (tar.bz2)	
Cygwin 1.3.9 Source download (tar.bz2)	Download

Figure 4.1 You can download the latest version of MySQL from the MySQL Web site.

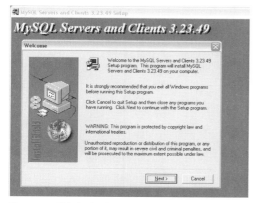

Figure 4.2 This looks familiar! Just change the title and you have the setup program of your choice.

Preparing Your Machine to Work with Strings

Like in all other chapters, the best way to learn about the topic at hand is to create a small project in which you can try new things. For this chapter, however, you may be getting more than you've bargained for. We are going to write a little database application. You don't need a commercially available database like SQL Server or even Access. All the database examples in this book will use MySQL. MySQL is a free, open-source, relational database. It doesn't have all the flashy administration tools that SQL Server has, but it is a very powerful database and it's free!

To talk to MySQL from C# you need to use a .NET database provider. One such tool is a tool called dbProvider by eInfoDesigns, Inc. dbProvider isn't free, but eInfoDesigns offers a scaled-down version of the tool for free. Because a lot of you probably don't have MySQL and dbProvider installed I've divided the instructions for writing the sample application into two topics "Preparing your machine to work with strings" (this one) and "Working with strings" (the next one).

To prepare your machine to run the database samples:

1. First download MySQL. The company that produces MySQL is called MySQL AB and their URL is www.mysql.com. The download section for the latest version as of the time of this writing is at: http://www.mysql.com/downloads /mysql-3.23.html (**Figure 4.1**).

2. Once you download the file mysql-3.23.51-win.zip, unzip its contents to a temporary directory.

3. Run setup.exe to install MySQL and follow the instructions (**Figure 4.2**).

continues on next page

4. After installing MySQL, install dbProvider. You can get dbProvider from the download section for this book at www.peachpit.com. The file is called dbProvider-Personal-1-5.msi. Double-click this file to install the dbProvider (**Figure 4.3**).

5. After installing dbProvider, run the file createdb.cmd, which is a script I wrote to create the database for the sample applications. It is also available in the download section in Peachpit's Web site. To run it, double-click on the file from Windows Explorer.

✔ Tips

- Although the sample code will use MySQL for a database backend, the techniques used for database programming are identical to those used for accessing SQL Server or Oracle, for example.

- The samples in this chapter will use ADO.NET to talk to the database. ADO.NET is a library of functions that Microsoft ships with the .NET framework for accessing databases. For you to access a database through ADO.NET, the vendor of the database has to write what is called a *data provider*. You may have heard of other technologies for accessing databases such as ODBC or OLE DB. ADO.NET data providers have the same goals as ODBC and OLE DB providers— to use the same functions to access any type of database. MySQL doesn't have any native ADO.NET providers as of the writing of this book, which is why we need a third-party tool like dbProvider.

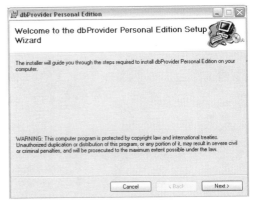

Figure 4.3 The setup program for dbProvider looks a little different from the standard setup programs. However, I have faith that readers will be able to successfully click the Next button.

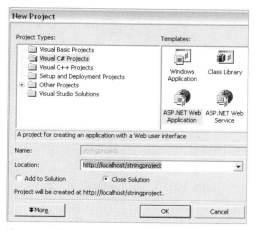

Figure 4.4 The sample application for this chapter will be an ASP.NET Web application.

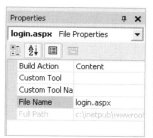

Figure 4.5 The property grid gives you an easy way to change the filename for your Web page without having to go through Windows Explorer.

Working with Strings

Now that you have set up the database software and installed the database, it's time to start writing the sample application.

To create a test project for this chapter:

1. Launch Visual Studio .NET. (Start > All Programs > Microsoft Visual Studio .NET > Microsoft Visual Studio .NET).

2. Select File > New > Project to bring up the New Project dialog.

3. Under project types on the left side of the New Project window, click the Visual C# projects folder.

4. Select the ASP.NET Web Application icon and change the name of the application to stringproject (**Figure 4.4**).

5. Visual Studio will create a new project and open WebForm1.aspx.

6. Change the form's name to login.aspx. You do that by choosing View > Solution Explorer from the top menu bar.

7. Right-click on WebForm1.aspx and choose properties. In the property grid change the FileName property from WebForm1.aspx to login.aspx (**Figure 4.5**).

continues on next page

8. Create a form that looks like the form in **Figure 4.6**. Obviously this is a lot of work to do by hand, so I suggest you enter the HTML directly into the editor instead. **Figure 4.7** (next page) shows the HTML necessary to create the form. To enter the HTML directly click the HTML button under the editor's window. As an alternative you could download the skeleton file for this project (see Tips below).

✔ Tips

■ As with the other projects in this book, building the project isn't necessary for learning the concepts in this chapter.

■ Skeletons for each project can be downloaded from Peachpit's Web site, http://www.peachpit.com/vqs/csharp.

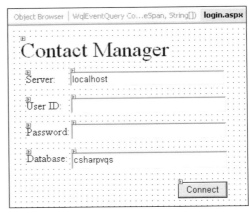

Figure 4.6 The login form lets you enter information that will be used in connecting to the MySQL database. The form has five labels, four textboxes, and one button.

Figure 4.7 The Visual Studio form editor enables you to edit the HTML for the page directly. This HTML is the source for the form in Figure 4.6.

```
<%@ Page language="c#"
Codebehind=
   "login.aspx.cs"
   AutoEventWireup="false"
   Inherits="stringproject.WebForm1"
   enableViewState="False"
   enableViewStateMac="False"%>
<HTML>
   <HEAD>
      <title>WebForm1</title>
   </HEAD>
   <body MS_POSITIONING="GridLayout">
      <form id="Form1" method="post"
      runat="server">
      <asp:Button id="btnConnect"
         style="Z-INDEX: 101;
         LEFT: 246px;
         POSITION: absolute; TOP: 237px"
         runat="server"
         Text="Connect">
      </asp:Button>
      <asp:Label  id="lblTitle"
         style="Z-INDEX: 102; LEFT: 18px;
         POSITION: absolute; TOP: 20px"
         runat="server"
         Font-Size="X-Large">
         Contact Manager
      </asp:Label>
      <asp:Label  id="lblServer"
         style="Z-INDEX: 103; LEFT: 25px;
         POSITION: absolute; TOP: 71px"
         runat="server" Width="56px"
         Height="19px">
         Server:
      </asp:Label>
      <asp:TextBox id="txtServer"
         style="Z-INDEX: 104; LEFT: 90px;
         POSITION: absolute; TOP: 69px"
         runat="server" Width="226px"
         Height="22px">
         localhost
      </asp:TextBox>
```

code continues

Figure 4.7 *continued*

```
      <asp:Label  id="lblUserID"
         style="Z-INDEX: 106; LEFT: 25px;
         POSITION: absolute; TOP: 111px"
         runat="server" Width="56px"
         Height="19px">
         User ID:
       <asp:TextBox id="txtUserID"
          style="Z-INDEX: 105; LEFT: 91px;
          POSITION: absolute; TOP: 108px"
          runat="server" Width="227"
          Height="24">
       </asp:TextBox>
      </asp:Label>
       <asp:Label id="lblPassword"
          style="Z-INDEX: 107; LEFT: 25px;
          POSITION: absolute; TOP: 150px"
          runat="server" Width="56px"
          Height="19px">
          Password:
      </asp:Label>
      <asp:TextBox id="txtPassword"
         style="Z-INDEX: 108; LEFT: 91px;
         POSITION: absolute; TOP: 147px"
         runat="server" Width="228"
         Height="26"
         TextMode="Password">
      </asp:TextBox>
      <asp:Label  id="lblDatabase"
         style="Z-INDEX: 109; LEFT: 25px;
         POSITION: absolute; TOP: 190px"
         runat="server">
         Database:
      </asp:Label>
      <asp:TextBox id="txtDatabase"
         style="Z-INDEX: 110; LEFT: 91px;
         POSITION: absolute; TOP: 190px"
         runat="server" Width="228px"
         Height="26px">
         csharpvqs
      </asp:TextBox>
      </form>
   </body>
</HTML>
```

Initializing Strings

When you declare a variable of type string, the runtime doesn't automatically create a buffer to hold that string. Like other reference types in which the actual object isn't created until you use the new operator, string buffers aren't created until you initialize the string.

To declare and initialize a string variable:

1. Type `string str` where str is the name of the variable to hold the string.

2. Type `="My String"` where "My String" is the string you wish to store in the string variable declared in step 1.

3. Type `;` (a semicolon) to end the statement (**Figure 4.8**).

✔ Tips

■ There are two ways of declaring string variables: You can use the C# keyword string or use the .NET Framework's class name System.String. Either way, you end up with the same thing—a string object. Having two ways of declaring a string object could be confusing in C#, especially because C# usually adds a using System; statement to each file. That means that you can omit the word System when specifying System.String. If you do so, then the two ways of declaring strings would be string (lowercase s) and String (capital s). So which one should you use? The C# ECMA specification says to use the language-provided keyword. However, other experts in the field say that you should use the class name from the Framework. I'm sticking with the language's reserved word, for consistency (**Figure 4.9**).

Figure 4.8 Whenever you set a string variable to a literal value, you create a new string object in memory.

```
string msg = "Your balance is $1000";
```

Figure 4.9 The class name for strings is System.String. However, the language provides an alias called string (lowercase letters). On top of that if you have a using statement for the System namespace you can also use String (capital S).

```
//you say tomato
string firstMsg = "Come here my son.";

//you say to-mah-toe
System.String secondMsg
            = "Come here now!";

//if there is a
//using System; statement
String thirdMsg = "Nevermind";
```

Figure 4.10 The .NET Framework makes a distinction between uninitialized strings and empty strings. A string variable that hasn't been set to any literal value or to another string variable is null.

```
Code                                    _ □ ×

string rat = "Splinter";  //rat declared
                          //and created in
                          //place.

string mouse;             //mouse is null

if (mouse == null)
   mouse = "Mickey";      //string object
                          //created and
                          //address stored
                          //in mouse

string dog = "";          //this is
                          //different from
                          //null. in this
                          //case a string
                          //object is
                          //created but
                          //its contents
                          //are empty.
```

Figure 4.11 Two girlfriends by definition can't share the same space. When you set the girlfriend variable to a different name, a new string object is created in memory and the variable points to the new object. The old string object is in memory until the system performs a garbage collection.

```
Code                                    _ □ ×

string girlfriend = "Rebecca";

//a new string object is created
//by the system silently
girlfriend = "Laurel";
```

Figure 4.12 String literals can't be broken into two lines.

```
Code                                    _ □ ×

string title1 = "The Grinch Who Stole Christmas";

string title2 = "Raiders of the Lost
                Ark"; //this is illegal
                      //you can't break a string
                      //into multiple lines
```

■ Before you initialize a string variable (setting it equal to the contents of a string), the variable is equal to null. **Figure 4.10** shows code that tests whether the value of the variable is null.

■ If you assign a different value to the string, the system silently creates a new string object (**Figure 4.11**).

■ You can't break a string initialization statement into multiple lines unless you use literal strings (see "Using Literal Strings" later in this chapter) (**Figure 4.12**).

119

Comparing Strings

There are a number of ways to compare two strings. Normally developers want to know whether two strings are equal. When comparing two strings for equality, sometimes casing is important and sometimes it isn't (is Jose the same as jose? for example). When sorting a series of strings, developers also want to know if a string comes before another string. In that case there are a couple of ways of comparing the strings. You can use a dictionary comparison in which lowercase "a" comes before uppercase "C," or you can use an ASCII-like comparison (using a code page) in which all uppercase letters come before all lowercase letters ("C" comes before "a").

To perform a case-sensitive test for equality:

◆ Use the == operator. Type if (s1 == s2) { } in which s1 and s2 are string variables you wish to compare for equality (**Figure 4.13**).

To perform a case-insensitive, dictionary-based string comparison:

1. Type int result = string.Compare(str1,str2,true); in which str1 and str2 are the strings you wish to compare and true means ignore casing (false means make a case-sensitive comparison).

2. Test the result of the Compare function. If result = 0 then the strings are equal. If the result is a negative number, then str1 comes before str2 alphabetically. If the result is a positive number, then str1 comes after str2 alphabetically (**Figure 4.14**).

Figure 4.13 The == operator lets you compare two strings for equality. When you use == case sensitivity matters.

```
string name1 = "James";
string name2 = "james";

if (name1 == name2)
    Response.Write("same name");
else
    Response.Write("not the same");

//prints out: not the same
```

Figure 4.14 The Compare method can be used to compare equality. With Compare you can control whether the comparison is case sensitive or not. Compare performs a dictionary comparison.

```
string name1 = "James";
string name2 = "james";

int result = string.Compare(name1,name2,true);
Response.Write( (result == 0) ?
                "same name<br>"
              : "not the same<br>");
//prints out: same name

name1 = "andrew";
name2 = "Bob";

result = string.Compare(name1,name2,true);
Response.Write( (result < 0) ?
                "andrew before Bob<br>"
              : "Bob before andrew<br>");
//prints out: andrew before Bob
```

Figure 4.15 CompareOrdinal performs a comparison based on the language's codepage. The codepage is a table that assigns a code to each character. In the English codepage, capital letters come before lowercase letters.

```
Code                              _ □ ×
string name1 = "James";
string name2 = "james";

int result =
string.CompareOrdinal(name1,name2);
Response.Write( (result == 0) ?
                "same name<br>"
              : "not the same<br>");
//prints out: same name

name1 = "andrew";
name2 = "Bob";

result = string.CompareOrdinal(name1,name2);
Response.Write( (result < 0) ?
                "andrew before Bob<br>"
              : "Bob before andrew<br>");
//prints out: Bob before andrew
```

Figure 4.16 Because string variables could be null, it's a good idea to make sure that the variable isn't null and not empty before using it.

```
Code                              _ □ ×
private void Search(string whereClause)
{
    if (whereClause != null && whereClause != "")
    { //do something
    }
    else
    {
       //do something else
    }
}
```

To perform a case-sensitive, ASCII-based string comparison:

1. Type `int result = string.CompareOrdinal(str1,str2);`

2. Test the result of the Compare function. If result = 0, then the strings are equal. If the result is a negative number, then str1 comes before str2 in the ASCII table. If the result is a positive number, then str1 comes after str2 in the ASCII table (**Figure 4.15**).

✔ Tips

■ A string variable that is null isn't equal to a string variable that contains an empty string. When you have functions with string parameters a programmer may send you a null or an empty string, so it's a good idea to test for both (**Figure 4.16**). When you read the Text property from a TextBox and the TextBox is empty, Text will return an empty string, not a null.

continues on next page

COMPARING STRINGS

- You can't use the < or > operators with two strings. The only way to test for the order of two strings is to use the Compare or CompareOrdinal functions (**Figure 4.17**).

- CompareOrdinal is always case sensitive. Compare can be either case sensitive (last parameter equal to false) or case insensitive (last parameter equals to true) (**Figure 4.18**).

- The string class also has a function called Equals. Throughout this book you'll learn that every class has this function. In the string class Equals does the same thing as == namely, it performs a case-sensitive test (**Figure 4.19**).

Figure 4.17 In my opinion, it's a shame that you can't compare strings with the < or > operators in C#, the way you can in other languages.

```
string s1="James";
string s2="Andrew";

//*** this is illegal   ***
//*** can't use < or >  ***
if (s1 < s2)
   Response.Write("James before Andrew");
```

Figure 4.18 The last parameter in Compare can be a little confusing. Instead of asking whether you want the comparison to be case sensitive or not, it asks whether you want the comparison to be case insensitive or not. So to do a case-sensitive search you have to resort to double negatives (not case insensitive).

```
string name1 = "James";
string name2 = "james";

//case-insensitive dictionary comparison
int result = string.Compare(name1,name2,true);
Response.Write( (result == 0) ?
                  "same name<br>"
                : "not the same<br>");
//prints out: same name

//case-sensitive dictionary comparison
int result = string.Compare(name1,name2,false);
Response.Write( (result == 0) ?
                  "same name<br>"
                : "not the same<br>");
//prints out: not the same
```

Figure 4.19 Using the Equals method is similar to using the == operator.

```
string name1 = "James";
string name2 = "james";

if (name1.Equals(name2))
   Response.Write("same name");
else
   Response.Write("not the same");

//prints out: not the same
```

Concatenating Strings

Figure 4.20 The Concat method creates a new string object from two or more pieces.

```
Code                                    _□×
string firstName = "John Jacob ";
string lastName = "Jingle Hymer Smith";
string name =
string.Concat(firstName,lastName);

Response.Write(name);
//prints: John Jacob Jingle Hymer Smith
```

Figure 4.21 Concat is a method in System.String available to all languages, but the C# language also provides a quick way to call the Concat function: using the plus sign.

```
Code                                    _□×
string firstName = "John Jacob ";
string lastName = "Jingle Hymer Smith";
string name = firstName + lastName;

Response.Write(name);
//prints: John Jacob Jingle Hymer Smith
```

Figure 4.22 If you're used to programming in VBScript whenever you want to take an existing variable and append to it, you end up writing an expression like var1 = var1 + newvar. In C# the same expression can be compacted into var1 += newvar.

```
Code                                    _□×
string firstName = "John Jacob ";
string lastName = "Jingle Hymer Smith";
firstName += lastName;

Response.Write(firstName);
//prints: John Jacob Jingle Hymer Smith
```

You can concatenate strings and produce a new string from the combination. There are two ways to combine strings. One way is using a method called Concat in the string class. The other is to use the + or the += operator. The compiler then does the work of changing + and += to calls to the Concat function. In essence, there is one function to concatenate, and two ways of calling it.

To build one string from the combination of two or more strings:

1. Declare a string variable to hold the result of the concatenation.

2. Type
   =System.String.Concat(piece1,piece2);
   where piece1 and piece2 are either string literals or string variables (**Figure 4.20**).

   or

   Type =piece1 + piece2; where piece1 and piece2 are either string literals or string variables (**Figure 4.21**).

   or

   Instead of declaring a new variable to hold the result you can use an existing variable and just append to it by typing piece1 += piece2, where piece1 is the variable that contains the original string and piece2 is the variable you wish to append to the end of piece1 (**Figure 4.22**).

CONCATENATING STRINGS

✔ Tips

- The Concat function is a static function. Static functions will be explained in more detail in Chapter 6, "Special Members." For now it's enough to know that to invoke a static function you don't need to create an instance of the class. You simply use the name of the class plus a dot plus the name of the function, as in the examples above.

- There are nine versions of the Concat function. You can pass to the Concat function as many segments as you like. It's also possible to pass objects to the function that aren't strings. The Concat function will turn the objects into strings by calling the ToString function on each object. See "Representing Objects as Strings" later in this chapter (**Figure 4.23**).

- When you use the plus operator or the plus equal operator, the compiler turns the code into calls to the Concat function. The compiler is smart enough to know that if you glue three pieces together with a plus sign, it should use the version of the Concat function that accepts three parameters, instead of concatenating the first to the second and then concatenating the result to the third, which would be inefficient.

- Remember that string buffers can't be changed, so when you concatenate to a string using any of the above mechanisms, the result is that the .NET Framework allocates a new string object in memory to store the characters from all the pieces in the string.

Figure 4.23 The parameters for the Concat function are of type Object which means that you can pass in strings, numbers, instances of classes, etc.

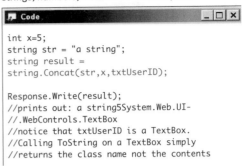

```
int x=5;
string str = "a string";
string result =
string.Concat(str,x,txtUserID);

Response.Write(result);
//prints out: a string5System.Web.UI-
//.WebControls.TextBox
//notice that txtUserID is a TextBox.
//Calling ToString on a TextBox simply
//returns the class name not the contents
```

Figure 4.24 The nice thing about having a framework that every language uses is that you use the same command, Length, to get the size of the string in every language.

```
Code                           _ □ ×
string str="this is a very long string. Don't
→ you think?";

Response.Write(str.Length);
//prints out: 44
```

Figure 4.25 This is exactly the reason you should check for null before calling a method in string. In this case if you call Length before the string has been initialized you will get a runtime exception.

```
Code                           _ □ ×
string str;

//error str has not been initialized
//str is currently null
if (str.Length > 0)
  Response.Write(str);

str = "";
//no error but length is zero
//so the if is not executed
if (str.Length > 0)
  Response.Write(str);
```

Finding the String Length

There are times when it's important to find out the length of a string. Usually developers want to know if the string variable has been initialized, and, if it has been initialized, if the length of the string is greater than zero.

To find the length of a string:

◆ Use the Length property of the string class. Since Length is a property, you don't put parenthesis after the property name (**Figure 4.24**).

✔ Tip

■ A string variable that has not been initialized doesn't have a length—its length isn't zero. If you try to ask for the Length of a null variable you will get an error. However, if you initialize the variable to " " then its length will be zero (**Figure 4.25**).

Comparing and Concatenating Strings in the Sample Application

It's time to hit the keyboard and put some of these principles into practice. In this section you will implement the login screen for the application.

First, let's talk about database stuff. We are going to connect to a small table called contacts in the csharpvqs database. At the beginning of the chapter you ran a script called createdb.cmd. This script talks to MySQL and tells it to create the csharpvqs database and add the contacts table and some records to the table. The contacts table has the following fields: ID, LastName, FirstName, and Phone. ID is a string field that basically stores social security numbers without the dashes. LastName, FirstName and Phone should be self-explanatory.

The first step in talking to a database is to connect to it. Each database provider has a connect class. In dbProvider, the connect class is called `eInfoDesigns.dbProvider.MySqlClient.MySqlConnection`. To connect to the database you need to create an instance of this class and tell it four things: what machine you're connecting to, what database, who you are, and your password. We build one string with this information, as you will see later, and feed it to the Connection object. This string is called the *connection string*. Then we open a connection. For the most part everyone will have the same string. For machine you can specify localhost, which means the current machine. The database doesn't require a password so you can leave the user id and the password blank. The database is going to be csharpvqs, which is the database that contains all the tables for the sample code in this book. So let's get to it.

Figure 4.26 Using the conditional operator, you can set the variables equal to the contents of the textbox, or if the textbox is empty, to a default value.

```
Code                              _ □ ×
private void btnConnect_Click(object sender,
                              System.EventArgs e)
{
    string server = (txtServer.Text == "") ?
                    "localhost" : txtServer.Text;

    string database = (txtDatabase.Text == "") ?
                    "csharpvqs" :
txtDatabase.Text;
}
```

Figure 4.27 This code constructs a connection string. Building a connection string is the first step in connecting to a database. It tells the connection object what database to connect to, the user id, the password, etc.

```
Code                              _ □ ×
private void btnConnect_Click
(object sender, System.EventArgs e)
{
    string server = (txtServer.Text == "")
    ? "localhost" : txtServer.Text;

    string database =
    (txtDatabase.Text == "") ?
    "csharpvqs" : txtDatabase.Text;

    string ConnectionString =
    "server=" + server +
    ";uid=" + txtUserID.Text +
    ";pwd=" + txtPassword.Text +
    ";database=" + database + ";";

    Session["ConnectionString"] =
    ConnectionString;
}
```

To implement the login screen:

1. In Solution Explorer, right-click on the file login.aspx and choose View Designer from the popup menu. You will see the form you created at the beginning of the chapter.

2. Double-click on the connect button to open the code editor. The wizard adds the btnConnect_Click event.

3. Add the code in **Figure 4.26**. This code checks to see if the server and database fields have been set. If they haven't been set to anything, this code will use the default values of localhost and csharpvqs correspondingly.

4. Now enter the code in **Figure 4.27**. This code concatenates several strings to create one connection string. Notice the format for the connection string. All .NET database providers follow a similar format. In fact, this connection string is identical to a connection string you would use for SQL Server. This code also stores the connection string in the Session object so that other forms can use it. You learned about the Session object from Chapter 3.

continues on next page

COMPARING AND CONCATENATING STRINGS

5. Enter the code in **Figure 4.28**. This figure contains the code to jump to another HTML page: contacts.aspx. You'll write this page later in the chapter.

✔ Tip

■ The application at this point checks the contents of a couple of fields, and then creates a connection string from the values of the fields. It saves the connection string in the Session object. One new command is Response.Redirect. This command tells the client's browser to go to a different page. The result is that the client will click the connect button and their browser will refresh with a page to view the contacts in the contacts table.

Figure 4.28 Response.Redirect tells the client browser not to display output for the current page, but to rather transfer to another page.

```
private void btnConnect_Click
(object sender,
System.EventArgs e)
{
    string server = (txtServer.Text == "")
    ? "localhost" : txtServer.Text;

    string database =
    (txtDatabase.Text == "") ?
    "csharpvqs" : txtDatabase.Text;

    string ConnectionString =
    "server=" + server +
    ";uid=" + txtUserID.Text +
    ";pwd=" + txtPassword.Text +
    ";database=" + database + ";";

    Session["ConnectionString"] =
    ConnectionString;

    Response.Redirect("contacts.aspx");
}
```

Figure 4.29 To save you from having to type all 25 asterisks, the string class provides an easy way to construct a string by repeating a character a number of times.

```
string s = new string('*',25);
Response.Write(s);
//outputs: *************************
```

Creating Strings from Characters

You can think of strings as collections of characters. The string class provides several mechanisms for creating strings from characters using the new operator. One way to create a string is by repeating the same character a certain number of times.

To create a string by repeating a character a number of times:

1. Type string str where str is the name of the variable to hold the string.

2. Type = new string('A',5), where 'A' is any character (characters are represented in single quotes), and 5 is the number of times you wish to repeat that character. This form will create a string by repeating one character a specified number of times. (**Figure 4.29**)

Another way to create a string from characters is to first create an array of characters.

We haven't talked about what an array is. An array is a fixed list of elements. Arrays will be discussed in detail in Chapter 9, "Arrays and Collections." The following instructions first show you how to create an array of characters, and then how to create a string from those characters.

To create a string from an array of characters:

1. Type `char[] title`. `title` is a variable that can point to an array of characters. The way you tell C# that you want many characters (an array) instead of a single character is by putting square brackets after the data type (`char[]` instead of `char`).

2. Type `= new char[] {'C','S','H','A', 'R','P','V','Q','S'};` new in this case tells the compiler to create an array of characters and we can initialize each character in the array in place by putting the characters separated by commas inside curly brackets.

3. Type `string str` where str is the name of the variable to hold the string.

4. Type `= new string(title);` where `title` is the name of the array you declared in step 1.

   or

   Type `= new string(title,1,5);` where title is the name of the array you declared in step 1, 1 is the zero-based position of the first character you want from the array, and 5 is the number of characters to take from the array. In this example str will end up with the word "Sharp" (**Figure 4.30**).

Figure 4.30 Strings are essentially arrays of characters. Thus, the string class provides a way to create a string from a buffer.

```
Code                                    _ □ ×

char[] title = new char[]
{'C','S','H','A','R','P','V','Q','S'};

string str1 = new string(title);
//contains CSHARPVQS
string str2 = new string(title,1,5);
//contains SHARP
```

Figure 4.31 Constructing a string by repeating the same character a number of times is useful when you need to make all the strings the same size. In this case we are repeating the space character a number of times.

```
Code                                    _ □ ×

string name1="John Smith";
string name2="Q";
string name3="Jackie Chan";

//make all names 40 characters long
name1 += new string(' ',40-name1.Length);
name2 += new string(' ',40-name2.Length);
name3 += new string(' ',40-name3.Length);
```

Figure 4.32 ToCharArray is a function in the string class that creates an array of characters from the characters in the string. The first parameter is the starting character index (zero based) and the second parameter is the number of characters to copy.

```
Code                                    _ □ ×

string record=
"SS#: 111-11-1111  Name: James T. Kirk";
string ssNum =
new string(record.ToCharArray(5,11));
```

✔ Tip

■ You may be wondering whether these techniques for creating strings from characters are ever useful. Trust me, they are. The first technique is normally used for *padding*. Padding is when you need all your strings to be the same length because you want to display them in a table and you want each column to have a certain width. In this case you can add spaces at the end of the string by repeating the space character a number of times (**Figure 4.31**). The second technique is useful when you want to create a string from part of another string. You can treat any string as a collection of characters; therefore, you can take some of the characters from the original string and use them to create a second string (**Figure 4.32**).

CREATING STRINGS FROM CHARACTERS

Using Escape Characters

A number of characters have been labeled as special characters. Take for example, the quote character. How would you represent a quote within a string, since the compiler interprets a quote as the beginning or end of the string? Whenever you want to use one of these special characters you need to use a technique known as *escaping the character*. Escaping the character means typing a backslash (\) in front of the character (**Figure 4.33**).

To use special characters in your string:

1. Type a backslash \ before the special character.

2. Enter one of the characters from **Table 4.1**.

Figure 4.33 Escape characters have been a part of languages like C and C++ since the beginning of time. In C# they are used also to represent line breaks, quotation marks, and other special characters.

```
Code                                    _ □ ×
string letter = "Dear Mr. Jones,\n\t "
letter += "The purpose of this letter ";
letter += "is to discuss your ";
letter += "so-called \"work\" in this "
letter += "company.";

/*
shows the following text:
Dear Mr. Jones,
      The purpose of this letter is to discuss
your so-called "work" in this company.
*/
```

Table 4.1

Escape Sequences (Special Characters in C# Strings)	
SEQUENCE	PURPOSE
\n	New line
\r	Carriage return
\r\n	Carriage return—new line
\"	Quotation marks
\\	Backslash character
\t	Tab

Figure 4.34 It may look strange, but even though you have to type a couple of characters to represent an escaped character, each escape sequence is treated as a single character.

```
char newline = '\n';
char backslash = '\\';
```

Figure 4.35 Carriage returns, tabs, and spaces are treated as white space in HTML. In HTML all white space is condensed into a single character. To break lines you have to use HTML tags such as <br>.

```
//the \n character is ignored
Response.Write("first line\nsecond line");

//the \n character is preserved. To see it
//you need to set TextMode to Multiline
txtMessage.Text = "***first line\nsecond line***";

//<br> character translated to line break
Response.Write("first line<br>second line");

//<br> character printed verbatim
txtMessage.Text = "first line<br>second line";
```

✔ Tips

■ Even though escaped characters involve two characters (backslash \ plus the escaped character) the compiler treats the sequence as one character. That means that \n is a single character and the same is true for \", \\, etc (**Figure 4.34**).

■ There are two main ways of outputting text to a Web client. You can set the text property of a control like a label or a textbox, or you can use a command like `Response.Write`. When you use `Response.Write` to output text, the browser treats the text as HTML. In HTML spaces, tabs, and carriage returns are known as *white space*. In HTML, if you have multiple spaces or a tab, the characters are converted to a single space, and carriage returns are ignored. That means that characters like \n are just ignored. This also happens when you set the text of a label, because label Text is outputted to the browser as HTML. However, when you set the text of a textbox the characters are displayed as raw text and the white space is preserved (**Figure 4.35**).

Using Literal Strings

Table 4.1 showed a list of special characters. These characters are characters that must be represented using the escape character (****). In C# it is also possible to create literal strings. Literal strings enable you to use special characters like the backslash or double quotes without having to use special codes or the escape character.

To create a literal string:

1. Type `string str` where `str` is the name of the variable to hold the string.

2. Type `= @"the string";` (the @ character followed by double quotes, followed by any string context, followed by another double quote) (**Figure 4.36**).

✔ Tips

■ You can use backslashes in literal strings without having to use two backslashes (**Figure 4.37**).

■ To specify the double-quote character you can put two double-quote characters together (**Figure 4.38**).

Figure 4.36 Literal strings enable you to represent special characters without using escape sequences.

```
string lit = @"this is a boring literal string";
```

Figure 4.37 Because the backslash is used to represent escape sequences, to add a backslash you need to type two backslashes. However, with literal strings you don't use escape sequences, so you can use the backslash as a backslash.

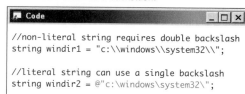

```
//non-literal string requires double backslash
string windir1 = "c:\\windows\\system32\\";

//literal string can use a single backslash
string windir2 = @"c:\windows\system32\";
```

Figure 4.38 The double-quote character is a problem no matter what type of string you use, because it tells the compiler where the string begins and ends. With literal strings to use a double quote as part of the string all you have to do is put two double quotes together.

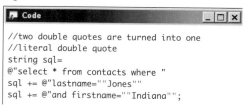

```
//two double quotes are turned into one
//literal double quote
string sql=
@"select * from contacts where "
sql += @"lastname=""Jones"""
sql += @"and firstname=""Indiana"";
```

Figure 4.39 When you break a literal strings into multiple lines the carriage returns you put in the editor are preserved. However, they aren't visible in HTML because white space is condensed into a single space.

```
Code                                    _ □ ×

string msg = @"Welcome to WidgetsUSA
               First Bank of Cyberspace.
               Your Balance is $1000.";

txtMessage.Text = msg;
//output:
// Welcome to WidgetsUSA
//             First Bank of Cyberspace.
//             Your Balance is $1000.


Response.Write(msg);
//output:
//Welcome to WidgetsUSA First Bank of
Cyberspace. Your Balance is $1000.
```

- If you use literal strings you can split a string into multiple lines of code; however, keep in mind that doing so inserts a carriage return character into the string (**Figure 4.39**).

- The rules for when white space is preserved, which we discussed in the previous section, also apply to literal strings.

Accessing the String's Characters

We learned earlier that you can think of a string as an array of characters. In Chapter 9, "Arrays and Collections," you will learn how to allocate arrays and navigate through arrays. In this chapter you will get a little preview of navigating through character arrays.

To access the characters of a string:

◆ Type char c = str[x]; where c is a variable to hold the character from the string, str is the string variable and x is the zero-based position of the character you wish to save (**Figure 4.40**).

✔ Tips

■ There are two ways of enumerating through all the characters in a string. One way is to write a loop where you maintain an index with an integer variable. The index begins at zero and increases until the index is equal to Length −1 (see "Finding the String's Length" earlier in this chapter) (**Figure 4.41**). The other way is to use a function called foreach, which will be explained in detail in Chapter 9, "Arrays and Collections" (**Figure 4.42**).

■ If you ask for an index greater than Length −1, the string class generates an exception (see Chapter 10, "Exceptions," for details). The exception (or error) is IndexOutOfBoundsException.

■ You can access the characters of the string, but you can't modify them since strings are immutable (**Figure 4.43**).

Figure 4.40 Because strings are essentially arrays of characters, you can address any character in the array by specifying its zero-based index in square brackets.

```
string sInfo = "Gender: M";
char Gender = sInfo[8];
```

Figure 4.41 This code shows a common way to parse the characters of the string in a loop. It searches for commas to count names.

```
string sName=
"Jose Mojica, Javier Mojica, ";
sName += "Ricardo Mojica,";
int TotalNames = 0;
for (int index=0;
    index < sName.Length;
    index++)
{
   if (sName[index] == ',')
      TotalNames++;
}
```

Figure 4.42 An easier way to navigate through the characters of the string is to use the foreach method.

```
string sName=
"Jose Mojica, Javier Mojica, ";
sName += "Ricardo Mojica,";
int TotalNames = 0;

foreach (char ch in sName)
{
   if (ch == ',')
      TotalNames++;
}
```

Figure 4.43 You can reassign a string variable to another string but you can't really change an existing string.

```
for (int index=0;
    index < sName.Length;
    index++)
{
   if (sName[index] == ',')
      sName[index] = '\n'; //compiler
                           //error,
                           //string is
                           //readonly
}
```

Figure 4.44 The IndexOf and LastIndexOf functions let you search for a character in the string.

```
Code                                 _ □ ×
string filename =
@"c:\documents and settings\";
filename += "picard\my documents\";
filename += "captainslog1.txt";

int driveMark = filename.IndexOf(@"\");
int fileMark =
filename.LastIndexOf(@"\");
```

Figure 4.45 Without specifying an index, IndexOf always searches from the same character. However, you can specify a starting position, as you can see from the examples above.

```
Code                                 _ □ ×
string filename =
@"c:\documents and settings\";
filename += "picard\my documents\";
filename += "captainslog1.txt";

int driveMark = filename.IndexOf(@"\");
int baseDirMark =
filename.IndexOf(@"\",driveMark+1);
int captNameMark =
filename.IndexOf(@"\",baseDirMark+1);
```

■ If the `IndexOf` or `LastIndexOf` functions don't find any occurrences of the substring, the functions return –1.

■ There are a few variations of the `IndexOf` and `LastIndexOf` functions. One variation lets you specify a location within the string where you want to start the search. This is useful for cases in which you wish to scan the string for one character, then when you find it, you want to get the next occurrence of the same character. In that case you specify that you want to begin the search in the position after the first occurrence (**Figure 4.45**).

Finding a Substring within a String

The topic of finding a character within a string and the following topic "Extracting Part of the String" normally go hand in hand. Often in string manipulations a developer will search for the first occurrence or the last occurrence of a character and extract the piece either before the character or after the character. For example, let's say you have a string that contains the path to a file, such as C:\Windows\System\regsvr32.exe. What if you wanted to place the path to the file and the filename itself into two different string variables? One way to do that is to find the last instance of the backslash character, then extract the characters before the backslash and put those characters in a variable, and then put the characters after the backslash into another variable.

To find the first or last occurrence of a character within the string:

◆ Using a string variable type `int index = str.IndexOf(@"\");` where index is a variable that will store the zero-based position of the character within the string, `str` is the variable you want to search, and `@"\"` is the string you are searching for.

or

◆ Type `int index=str.LastIndexOf(@"\");` to search for the last occurrence of a substring within the string (**Figure 4.44**).

✔ Tips

■ You can search for a single character or for a substring. Here's how to search for a substring. Let's say you were searching for .exe in a string containing "MyProgram.exe." The `IndexOf` function returns the index of the first character in the substring, in this case nine.

Extracting Part of the String

If you read the section titled "Finding a Substring within a String" you know that developers often want to find the index of a certain character within the string, then place a portion of the string up to that character into a separate variable. Suppose you have a path to a string like "C:\Dir1\SubDir2\SubDir3\MyFile.txt." What if you wanted to extract the filename minus its extension and put that into a separate variable? First you would find the index of the last occurrence of the backslash character, then you could find the index of the ".txt" segment. Once you had those two indices, you could tell the system to give you the characters that are within them.

To extract part of a string based on indices:

◆ Using a string variable type `string segment = str.Substring(index1,len);` where segment is a variable to store the substring, str is the original string, index1 is the zero-based starting position of the substring that you want to extract, and len is the number of characters you wish to extract (**Figure 4.46**).

✔ Tips

■ In the example code you see that sometimes to get the number of characters you wish to extract you obtain the index for the character before the first character of the substring, then the index for the character after the end of the substring, and then you use the formula: `lastindex - firstindex - 1` to get the number of characters.

Figure 4.46 The Substring function can be used to extract a segment of the string. You simply specify the starting index and the number of characters and the function builds another string from that portion of the original string.

```
string filename =
@"c:\documents and settings\picard\my
documents\captainslog1.txt";

int driveMark = filename.IndexOf(@"\");
string drive =
filename.Substring(0,driveMark);

int baseDirMark =
filename.IndexOf(@"\",driveMark+1);
string baseDir =
filename.Substring(driveMark+1,
            baseDirMark - driveMark)

int captNameMark =
filename.IndexOf(@"\",baseDirMark+1);
```

Figure 4.47 If you specify only a starting index, Substring gives you a string from the index until the end of the original string.

```
string filename =
@"c:\documents and settings\picard\my
→ documents\captainslog1.txt";

int extMark = filename.IndexOf(".");
string ext = filename.Substring(extMark+1);
```

■ One other variation of the Substring function lets you type `string segment = str.Substring(index1);` without specifying the length for the substring. This variation assumes the substring will be all the characters starting at index1 (**Figure 4.47**).

Figure 4.48 The Split function makes it easy to divide one string into multiple segments.

```
Code                              _ □ ×
string
namelist="Frodo,Gandalf,Aragorn,Samwise";
string[] names = namelist.Split(',');
```

Figure 4.49 The Split function is flexible enough to split based on any number of delimiters. In this example the function splits the original string each time it finds a comma or a semicolon.

```
Code                              _ □ ×
string food="Apples,Bananas,Grapes;
→ Rice,Potatoes,Noodles;";
string[] items = food.Split(',',';');
//array contains six string elements.
```

Figure 4.50 If you don't specify a delimiter character, Split uses spaces and carriage returns as delimiters.

```
Code                              _ □ ×
string food="Apples Bananas Grapes   Rice
→ Potatoes Pizza";
string[] items = food.Split();
foreach(string item in items)
{
    Response.Write(item + "<br>");
}

/*
prints out:
Apples
Bananas
Grapes


Rice
Potatoes
Pizza
*/
```

Splitting a String

Suppose you have a list of names in a single string, with each name separated by a comma. Then suppose you wanted to extract each name from the string. The hard way to do this is to scan all the characters for commas, then copy the characters before the comma to another string. The easy way is to use the Split function in the string class. You can tell the Split function what character or characters to use as delimiters—the split function then creates substrings for each segment before and after each delimiter. The Split function returns an array of strings.

To split strings into an array of substrings:

1. Type string[] pieces, where pieces is the name of the string array variable that will hold all the segments resulting from the split.

2. Type = str.Split(','); where str is the name of the string variable containing the buffer you wish to split, and ',' is the delimiter character (**Figure 4.48**).

✔ Tips

■ You can specify more than one delimiter to use in the split. For example if your string contains "Apples,Bananas,Grapes; Rice,Potatoes,Noodles;" you can specify both a single quote and a semicolon as delimiter characters (**Figure 4.49**).

■ You can omit the delimiter character altogether, in which case the Split function treats spaces and carriage returns as delimiter characters (**Figure 4.50**).

continues on next page

SPLITTING A STRING

- If the Split function finds two delimiter characters next to each other then the function returns an empty string to represent the segment between the two delimiters (**Figure 4.51**).

- If you specify one or more delimiter characters in the Split function, and the Split function doesn't find any of the characters in the string, the Split function returns an array of one element in which the element is the entire original string (**Figure 4.52**).

Figure 4.51 When you have two delimiters next to each other, in this case a space and a carriage return, you end up with an empty string.

```
string food="Apples Bananas Grapes \nRice
→ Potatoes Pizza";
string[] items = food.Split();
foreach(string item in items)
{
    Response.Write(item + "<br>");
}

/*
outputs:
Apples
Bananas
Grapes

Rice
Potatoes
Pizza
*/
```

Figure 4.52 If Split doesn't find the delimiter you specified, it simply returns an array with a single element containing the original string.

```
string food="Apples,Bananas,Grapes,Rice,
→ Potatoes,Pizza";
string[] items = food.Split(';');
foreach(string item in items)
{
    Response.Write(item + "<br>");
}

/*
outputs:
Apples,Bananas,Grapes,Rice,Potatoes,Pizza */
```

Figure 4.53 Join does the opposite of Split—it creates one string from an array of strings and uses a delimiter to join each piece.

```
Code                                    _ □ ×
string[] characters = new string[5];
characters[0] = "Mickey";
characters[1] = "Minnie";
characters[2] = "Pluto";
characters[3] = "Goofy";
characters[4] = "Donald";

string Disney = string.Join(",",characters);
Response.Write(Disney);
/*
outputs:
Mickey,Minnie,Pluto,Goofy,Donald
*/
```

Figure 4.54 When you put strings together with Join you aren't limited to a single character to put in between each segment.

```
Code                                    _ □ ×
string[] phrases = new string[5];
phrases[0] = "Hi";
phrases[1] = "How are you";
phrases[2] = "";
phrases[3] =
"Like we got to get together";
phrases[4] = "ok";

string collegeTalk =
string.Join(" dude ",phrases);
Console.WriteLine(collegeTalk);

/*
outputs:
Hi dude How are you dude  dude Like we got to
⟶ get together dude ok
*/
```

Joining a String

Joining a string is the opposite of splitting a string. It's done by invoking the Join function in System.String and passing an array of strings containing all the pieces you wish to join, and a string with the characters to use as a delimiter. The Join function then returns a single string by gluing all the segments from the array together and placing the delimiter between them.

To create a string by joining other strings:

1. Type `string[] pieces = new string[10];` where pieces is a variable to store a set (array) of strings, and 10 is the number of segments that you wish to glue together.

2. Type `pieces[0] = "any string";` where pieces is the variable declared in step 1 and `[0]` is the element in the array that you wish to set. You can set each element in the string array by specifying the index from zero to the number of elements minus one.

3. Declare a string variable to hold the new string resulting from the join.

4. Type `=System.String.Join(",",pieces);` where "," is the character to use as a delimiter and pieces is the array of strings (**Figure 4.53**).

✔ Tip

■ The delimiter string doesn't have to be a single character. It can be a series of characters, as in **Figure 4.54**.

Uppercasing and Lowercasing

You can easily produce a version of a string where all the characters are uppercase or all the characters are lowercase.

To produce a string in either uppercase or lowercase form:

1. Declare a new string variable.

2. Type =str.ToUpper(); or =str.ToLower() accordingly, where str is a variable holding the original string (**Figure 4.55**).

✔ Tip

■ The ToUpper and ToLower functions don't change the original string. They produce new strings (and therefore new string buffers) with the characters' case modified.

Figure 4.55 The ToUpper function creates a new string object from the original where all characters are in uppercase.

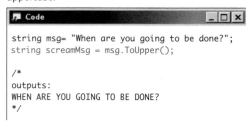

```
string msg= "When are you going to be done?";
string screamMsg = msg.ToUpper();

/*
outputs:
WHEN ARE YOU GOING TO BE DONE?
*/
```

Figure 4.56 You can build a format string to serve as a template. In the format string you specify placeholders for each segment. The placeholders are specified with curly brackets.

```
string firstName = "Bill";
string lastName = "Smith";

string templ =
"Select * from contacts where ";
templ +=
"LastName={0} and FirstName={1}";

string SQL =
string.Format(templ,firstName,lastName);
Response.Write(SQL);

/*
outputs:
Select * from contacts where
LastName=Bill and FirstName=Smith
*/
```

Figure 4.57 Each placeholder has an index number. You can insert the same word in many places in the string if you repeat the index number that corresponds to the word.

```
string company = "Federation";
string customer = "Chewbacca";

string templ = "Dear Mr. {1},<br>";
templ += "Welcome to the {0}. ";
templ += "The {0} is glad that you have become ";
templ += "a warp capable species.";

string letter =
string.Format(templ,company,customer);
Response.Write(letter);

/*
outputs:
Dear Mr. Chewbacca,

Welcome to the Federation. The Federation is
 → glad that you have become a warp capable
 → species. */
```

Formatting Strings

Formatting enables you to define templates for strings. The template tells the string class the text that doesn't change. In the template you also specify placeholders for the text that does change. The string class then fills in the placeholders with text that you provide. This makes it easier for you, because the string class does the hard work of concatenating the parts of fixed text with the parts of variable text.

To format strings:

1. Type `string str` where str is the name of the string that will hold the formatted text.

2. Type `=string.Format(`.

3. Type a formatting string enclosed in quotes. The formatting string tells the string class the fixed text.

4. Within the formatting string, type `{0}`, `{1}`, `{2}`, etc. to set placeholders for the variable text. For example: `"LastName={0} and FirstName={1}"`.

5. Type a comma.

6. Type the name of the variable that contains the dynamic text for the string.

7. Repeat steps 5 and 6 for each placeholder in step 4.

8. Type `);` to end the statement (**Figure 4.56**).

✔ Tip

■ You can use the same placeholder more than once. For example, if you were writing a form letter, you could repeat the recipient's name more than once. To accomplish that you simply use the placeholder string, for example {0} more than once (**Figure 4.57**).

Finishing the Sample Application

A lot of database programming involves running queries. Queries are statements written in SQL, the language of databases. They are phrases that almost read like plain English, and that tell the database how to select, edit, insert or delete records to a table. A common SQL statement is a statement that selects a number of records based on a criterion, normally called a Where clause.

Here is a typical SQL statement: `"select * from contacts where LastName='Mojica' and FirstName='Jose'"`. The word select does what it implies, brings back some information. The asterisk after the select tells the database that you want all fields from the table. If we only cared about the phone field we could have said: `"select Phone from…"`. After the fields we tell the database what table to run the query on, that is, the from contacts part. Then comes the Where clause. Without a Where clause the query would return every record in the table. With the Where clause the query returns only the records that match the criteria.

So why are we talking about queries and SQL? Because in this part of the sample application, you're going to use your knowledge of the Split and Format commands to build some good old SQL statements. We're going to display a form in which users can search for a person in the contact list. They will enter the person's first and last name in the search field. Your job will be to separate the first name from the last name, then build a query to search for that first name and last name. If they enter a blank in the search field, the program should display all the records in the table.

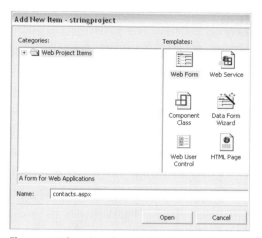

Figure 4.58 If you have been doing the sample applications in each chapter you are now quite familiar with this dialog. It enables you to add a new file to your project.

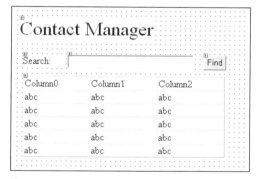

Figure 4.59 The Contacts Web page has a table with contact information. The search field lets you enter a name (first name and last name), then when you click the Find button the grid shows the matching records.

To finish the sample application:

1. Choose Project > Add Web Form. You will see the dialog in **Figure 4.58**. Enter `contacts.aspx` for the file name and press Enter.

2. Create a form that looks like the form in **Figure 4.59**. Do so by entering the HTML directly into the editor (**Figure 4.60** (on next page). You can also download the skeleton file for this project from the Peachpit Web site.

continues on next page

3. Double-click on a blank space in the form. This will cause VS.NET to open the code editor and add a `Page_Load` function.

4. Scroll up to the top of the file, and under the last using statement add the following: using eInfoDesigns.dbProvider .MySqlClient;

5. Right before the `Page_Load` function after all the variable declarations add the following declaration:

   `private string ConnectionString;`

   This line declares a string variable to hold the connection string.

Figure 4.60 You can recreate the Contacts Web page using the HTML here.

```
Code                                    _ □ ×
<%@ Page language="c#"
        Codebehind="contacts.aspx.cs"
        AutoEventWireup="false"
        Inherits="stringproject.contacts"
%>
<HTML>
    <HEAD>
        <title>contacts</title>
    </HEAD>
    <body MS_POSITIONING="GridLayout">
    <form id="contacts"
     method="post" runat="server">
        <asp:Label id="lblTitle"
            style="Z-INDEX: 101; LEFT: 20px;
            POSITION: absolute; TOP: 21px"
            runat="server"
            Font-Size="X-Large">
            Contact Manager</asp:Label>
        <asp:DataGrid id="grdContacts"
            style="Z-INDEX: 104; LEFT: 26px;
            POSITION: absolute; TOP: 117px"
            runat="server" Width="327px"
            Height="119px"></asp:DataGrid>
        <asp:Label id="lblSearch"
            style="Z-INDEX: 102;
            LEFT: 25px; POSITION: absolute;
            TOP: 82px"
            runat="server" Width="67px">
            Search:</asp:Label>
        <asp:TextBox id="txtSearch"
            style="Z-INDEX: 103;
            LEFT: 98px; POSITION: absolute;
            TOP: 81px"
            runat="server" Width="204px">
            </asp:TextBox>
        <asp:Button id="btnFind"
            style="Z-INDEX: 105;
            LEFT: 318px;
            POSITION: absolute; TOP: 82px"
            runat="server" Text="Find">
            </asp:Button>
        </form>
    </body>
</HTML>
```

Figure 4.61 Upon loading the page we check to see if the connection string already exists. If it doesn't that means some sneaky user tried to bypass the login screen and go directly to the Contacts page. Therefore, we redirect back to the login screen. If everything is fine we display all records from the Contacts table.

```
private void Page_Load(object sender,
                       System.EventArgs e)
{
    ConnectionString =
    (string)Session
    ["ConnectionString"];

    if (ConnectionString == null ||
    ConnectionString == "")
        Response.Redirect("login.aspx");

    Search(null);

}
```

Figure 4.62 This is the master Search function. It ultimately opens a connection to the database, runs the query to search for a contact, then binds the grid to the result set, which makes the grid display all the records returned by the query.

```
private void Search(string whereClause)
{
    string SQLCmd;

    if (whereClause != null &&
        whereClause != "")
    {
        string[] segments=
        whereClause.Split(' ','-');
        SQLCmd = string.Format(
        "select * from contacts where" +
        " LastName='{0}' and" +
        " FirstName='{1}'",
        segments[1],segments[0]);
    }
    else
        SQLCmd = "select * from contacts";

    MySqlConnection conn = new
    MySqlConnection(ConnectionString);
    conn.Open();
    MySqlCommand cmd = new
    MySqlCommand(SQLCmd,conn);
    grdContacts.DataSource =
    cmd.ExecuteReader();
    grdContacts.DataBind();
}
```

6. Inside the `Page_Load` function, add the code in **Figure 4.61**. This code checks to see if there is a connection string stored in the Session object. If there isn't, it redirects back to the login window. This is a common practice in programs where there is a login window, because it protects against the situation in which a user enters the URL for the second page with the idea of bypassing the login page. The second thing that this code does is run a function called Search passing the value of null. You'll add this function next.

7. Above the `Page_Load` function, add a new function described in **Figure 4.62**. This code is for the Search function. The Search function takes in a Where clause as a parameter. If the Where clause is null or empty, then the function creates an SQL statement that selects all records. If the Where clause contains text, then the function uses `Split` to divide the text into first name and last name. The `Split` function looks for a space or a dash for the delimiter. It then builds an SQL statement using the `Format` command.

continues on next page

FINISHING THE SAMPLE APPLICATION

8. In Solution Explorer, right-click on `contacts.aspx`, then select Show Designer from the pop-up menu.

9. Double-click the Find button to bring up the code editor. The wizard will add the `btnFind_Click` function. Add the code in **Figure 4.63**. This code will just invoke the Search function you've added, passing the text from the search field as the input parameter.

✔ Tips

■ The sample code should now be fully functional and ready to be tested.

■ SQL Server uses the same scheme for fetching data. The only difference between the code above and code for SQL Server would be that you would drop the "My" from all the class names. Instead of `MySqlConnection` you would use `SqlConnection`; in place of `MySqlCommand` you would use `SqlCommand`, etc. All the SQL Server classes are under the `System.Data.SqlClient` namespace.

Figure 4.63 With the Search function in place, all we need to do now is call the function when the user clicks the Find button passing the contents of the search textbox as input to the function.

```
private void btnFind_Click(object sender,
                           System.EventArgs e)
{
    Search(txtSearch.Text);
}
```

Fetching Data from a Database

The last five lines of code in the `Search` function have to do with data access, and haven't been discussed yet. The first line of the bunch creates a new `MySqlConnection` object and passes the connection string as a parameter to the new. The line after that one calls the Open function. The Open function does the actual connection to the database. Following that line is a statement that creates a `MySqlCommand` object. This object runs the query in the database. The two parameters used in creating the command are the command's SQL statement and an instance of the connection object. To actually run the query you call `ExecuteReader`. `ExecuteReader` returns a result set and that result set can be handed to the grid control, which reads through the records and displays a table with the information. That's all there is to it! Of course, there are a lot more things you can do with a database but they are all beyond the scope of this book.

Figure 4.64 Every class has a default ToString function. However, by default this function only outputs the class's name. To make it more useful you can override the default behavior as illustrated here.

```
Code                                    _ □ ✕

class CheckingAccount
{
    private string LastName = "Gates";
    private string FirstName = "William";
    private string AccountType =
    "World Domination Free Checking";

    public override string ToString()
    {
        string format =
        "Name: {0} {1}<br> Account:{2}";
        return string.Format(format,
        LastName,FirstName,AccountType);
    }
}
```

Figure 4.65 The Date class and the Decimal class have different versions of ToString that enable you to pass format characters in order to get different representations of the variable's contents.

```
Code                                    _ □ ✕

DateTime dt = new DateTime(1999,12,25);
string christmas = dt.ToString("D");
Response.Write(christmas);
//outputs: Saturday, December 25, 1999

Decimal balance = 1050.55M;
string balinfo = balance.ToString("C");
Response.Write(balinfo);
//outputs: $1,050.55
```

Representing Objects as Strings

Representing an object as a string means different things depending on the object. The .NET framework provides a function called ToString by which you can turn any object into a string. Every object has a ToString function because ToString is a function in System.Object. Every class in .NET has System.Object as its root parent. If you write a class like Account and a programmer creates an object of type Account and calls ToString, by default the system prints the name of the class, which isn't very useful. However, you can override the default implementation of the ToString function to return something more meaningful, like the Account's balance for example. (For a full explanation of overriding methods see Chapter 5, "Class Inheritance.")

To implement your own ToString function:

1. In a new line within your class type
   public override string ToString().

2. Type {.

3. Type return "some string";, where "some string" is the string representation of your object—you can return either a literal value or a string variable.

4. Type } (**Figure 4.64**).

✔ Tip

■ Some programmers provide more than one version of ToString in the class. The other versions have input parameters that enable the user of the class to specify a formatting string. Some examples of such classes are the Date class and the Decimal class (**Figure 4.65**).

Allocating Strings with StringBuilder

Every time you manipulate a string using one of the string commands, the system silently allocates new string buffers. Say you initialize a string variable to a certain string, then you use the Concat command to add some characters to the string. The .NET runtime doesn't adjust the original string buffer; it creates a new string buffer that contains the original string plus the appended piece. Eventually, if you aren't careful, you can use up the memory for allocating objects and force the runtime to do a garbage collection. Doing a garbage collection isn't too time-consuming, but too many collections can affect the performance of your program. For that reason Microsoft created a class called StringBuilder, which lets you manipulate a single buffer of characters. You can insert, append, and remove characters from the buffer. Then, when you're done using the buffer, you use the ToString function in the class to obtain a string object from the buffer.

To create strings with StringBuilder:

1. Type System.Text.StringBuilder sb where sb is the variable name.

2. Type = new System.Text.StringBuilder();.

3. Use StringBuilder's Append, Insert, Remove, and Replace functions to manipulate the string buffer.

4. Use the ToString() function to retrieve the final contents of the buffer (**Figure 4.66**).

Figure 4.66 StringBuilder lets you manipulate the characters of a string without creating multiple string objects in memory. When you're done manipulating the string, you call the ToString method to obtain the end result.

```
System.Text.StringBuilder sb = new
System.Text.StringBuilder();
sb.Append("I love Macs");
sb.Insert(10,"Donald'");
sb.Remove(8,1);
string msg = sb.ToString();
Response.Write(msg);
//outputs: I love McDonald's
```

Figure 4.67 StringBuilder's internal character buffer expands as you append characters. Too much expanding can affect performance. For that reason you can specify the initial size of the buffer. In this case the buffer is 1024 characters at the beginning. StringBuilder will only expand the buffer if you add more than 1024 characters.

```
System.Text.StringBuilder sb = new
System.Text.StringBuilder(1024);
```

✔ Tip

■ The StringBuilder's buffer begins with enough space for 16 characters. If you go beyond 16 characters the class creates a new buffer with double its current space and fills it in with the old characters. Going beyond the capacity of StringBuilder too many times defeats the purpose of using StringBuilder because you then create multiple buffers in memory. You can minimize the number of times this happens by starting with a larger buffer (**Figure 4.67**).

CLASS
INHERITANCE

Inheritance is one of the core concepts in object-oriented programming and in the .NET framework. Inheritance is the idea that a developer can create a class to serve as a building block for other classes. When a class inherits from another class it gains all the methods from the class it inherited from. The class the author inherits from is referred to as the *base class*. The class that inherits from the base is referred to as the *derived class* or the *child class*.

In this chapter you will learn how to inherit from another class and what happens when both the base and the derived class have a method with the same name.

Another feature related to inheritance that is crucial in object-oriented programming is *polymorphism*. With polymorphism, a variable of a base type can point to two different derived types. Each derived type may have a slightly different implementation for a method. In this chapter you will learn one way to achieve polymorphism by using *virtual functions*.

Working with Class Inheritance

Imagine an application in which you have to fill out an entry form. For example, suppose you are creating a work order application that records maintenance requests for a building. When something in the building needs to be fixed, a user would create a work order and enter the building code the problem is in along with the department that will be responsible for handling the problem. The application can also have other fields, such as priority for the work order, estimated cost, a description of the problem, etc.

Let's also say that we want to make the application flexible enough so that if the user keys in a building code and discovers that the building doesn't exist, the user may enter a new building code on the fly. This can be done by displaying what I call a "quick entry" form (a smaller second browser window) that asks for the new building code.

Now, instead of writing the code for each button it would be better to write the code in one class, then use the class as a base class for each "quick entry" button. In addition, it would be nice to write a generic form that encapsulated the basic functionality of all entry forms and use it as a base to every entry form in the project.

The sample application shows how to implement both cases of inheritance. You will first write a simple class that will encapsulate the functionality of the Page_Load event for all the forms in your project. Then, you will write a generic class that serves as a button. When the button is clicked the program will display a lookup form that lets you enter a new building or department code.

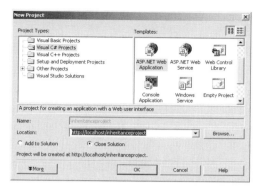

Figure 5.1 The sample application for this chapter will show you how to use inheritance to encapsulate the code of Page_Load for every form in the project, and how to use inheritance to create a custom button control.

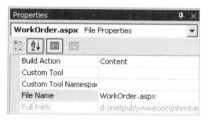

Figure 5.2 Change the name of the main form to WorkOrder.aspx.

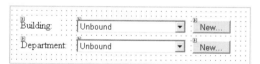

Figure 5.3 The WorkOrder form has two drop-down lists: one for building and one for department. Initially the drop-down lists don't have any values; to enter the values you click the New button to display a quick entry form that enables you to add items to the drop-down list.

To create a test project for this chapter:

1. Launch Visual Studio .NET. (Start > All Programs > Microsoft Visual Studio .NET > Microsoft Visual Studio .NET).

2. Select File > New > Project to bring up the New Project dialog.

3. Under project types on the left side of the New Project window click the Visual C# projects folder.

4. Select the ASP.NET Web Application icon and change the name of the application to inheritanceproject (**Figure 5.1**).

5. Visual Studio will create a new project and open WebForm1.aspx.

6. Change the form's name to WorkOrder .aspx. Do so by choosing View > Solution Explorer from the top menu bar.

7. Right-click on WebForm1.aspx and choose properties. In the property grid below change the FileName property from WebForm1.aspx to WorkOrder.aspx (**Figure 5.2**).

8. Create a form that looks like the form in **Figure 5.3**. This may be a lot of work to do by hand, so you may want to enter the HTML directly into the editor. **Figure 5.4** (on next page) shows the HTML necessary to create the form. To enter the HTML directly click the HTML button under the editor's window. As an alternative you could download the skeleton file for this project (see Tip on next page).

continues on next page

✔ Tip

■ A skeleton for this project can be downloaded from Peachpit's Web site, http://www.peachpit.com/vqs/csharp.

Figure 5.4 The form is composed of two label controls, two drop-down lists, and two buttons.

```
Code                              _ □ ×

<%@ Page language="c#"
  Codebehind="WorkOrder.aspx.cs"
  AutoEventWireup="false"
  Inherits="inheritanceproject.WorkOrder"
%>
<HTML>
  <HEAD>
    <title>WorkOrder</title>
  </HEAD>
  <body MS_POSITIONING="GridLayout">
  <form id="WorkOrder" method="post"
           runat="server">
  <asp:label id="lblBldg"
           style="Z-INDEX: 101; LEFT:
           22px; POSITION: absolute;
           TOP: 23px" runat="server"
           Height="22px" Width="61px">
           Building:
           </asp:label>
  <asp:label id="lblDepartment"
           style="Z-INDEX: 106; LEFT:
           23px; POSITION: absolute;
           TOP: 55px" runat="server"
           Height="22px" Width="61px">
           Department:
           </asp:label>
  <asp:dropdownlist id="lstBuilding"
           style="Z-INDEX: 102; LEFT:
           113px; POSITION: absolute;
           TOP: 23px" runat="server"
           Height="26px"
           Width="176px">
           </asp:dropdownlist>
  <asp:dropdownlist id="lstDepartment"
           style="Z-INDEX: 103; LEFT:
           113px; POSITION: absolute;
           TOP: 55px" runat="server"
           Height="26px"
           Width="176px">
           </asp:dropdownlist>
  <asp:button id="btnNewBldg"
           style="Z-INDEX: 104; LEFT:
           299px; POSITION: absolute;
           TOP: 23px" runat="server"
           Height="21px" Width="61px"
           Control="lstBuilding"
           Text="New...">
           </asp:button>
  <asp:button id="btnNewDept" style="Z-
           INDEX: 105; LEFT: 299px;
           POSITION: absolute; TOP:
           56px" runat="server"
           Height="21px" Width="61px"
           Text="New...">
           </asp:button>
  </form>
  </body>
</HTML>
```

Figure 5.5 Both Checking and Savings receive the MakeDeposit method from Checking.

```
Code                                    _ □ ×

class Account
{
   decimal balance;

   void MakeDeposit(decimal amount )
   {
      balance += amount;
   }
}

class Checking : Account
{
   // Inherits Account functionality
}

class Savings : Account
{
   // Inherits Account functionality
}
```

Figure 5.6 Notice that even though we are creating a Savings object, we can still call the methods in the Account class because Savings inherits its functionality from Account.

```
Code                                    _ □ ×

class Account
{
   decimal balance;

   void MakeDeposit(decimal amount )
   {
      balance += amount;
   }
}
class Savings : Account
{
   // Inherits Account functionality
}

class Bank
{
   static void CreateAccounts()
   {
      Savings s = new Savings();

      // MakeDeposit is defined in
      // Account
      s.MakeDeposit(500.00m);
   }
}
```

Inheriting a Class from Another

In order not to have to duplicate code, C# and other object-oriented languages support *code inheritance*, by which you can use one class as the base of another class. For example, let's say that your banking Web application requires a Checking class and a Savings class. When authoring these classes you realize that aside from a few fields and functions, they have a number of members in common. It would not be practical to create the Checking class and then copy most of the code to the Savings class. Simply copying the code can result in maintenance headaches; consider what would happen if after copying the code to five different classes, you discover a bug in one of the functions. Instead of copying and pasting code it is possible to create a class called Account. The Account class would contain all the code that every type of Account would have in common. Then you simply write a Checking class or a Savings class that derives from the Account class. *Deriving* from a class means that you gain all the functionality of the base class plus you can add functions that are specific to each derived class.

To inherit a class from another:

1. Add a colon at the end of the class name, before the open curly bracket.

2. After the colon, add the name of the base class you want to inherit from (**Figure 5.5**).

✔ Tips

■ If you don't specify a class you want to inherit from, the class automatically inherits from a system class called System.Object.

■ Inheriting from a class means that you gain all the functionality from that class (**Figure 5.6**).

continues on next page

- It's legal to assign a variable of the base type to an instance of the derived class. The opposite isn't true—you can't assign a variable of the derived type to an instance of the base class (**Figure 5.7**).

Figure 5.7 Whenever you have a base-child class relationship, you can always declare a variable using the base type and assign it to an instance of the child class. The opposite isn't true. You can't have a variable of the child class be equal to an instance of the base class.

```
class Account
{
    decimal balance;

    void MakeDeposit(decimal amount )
    {
        balance += amount;
    }
}
class Savings : Account
{
    // Inherits Account functionality
}

class Bank
{
    static void CreateAccounts()
    {
        Savings s = new Savings();

        // it's OK to do this
        Account a = s;

        a = new Account();

        // it's NOT OK to do this
        s = a; // won't compile
    }
}
```

Figure 5.8 With refactoring, you find all the code that Checking and Savings have in common and move it to a class like Account, then derive Checking and Savings from the Account class.

```
📰 Code                                    _ □ ×

//****************************
//********* BEFORE ***********
//****************************
class Checking
{
   public void MakeWithdrawal(
               decimal amount)
   {
      if(balance >= amount)
            balance -= amount;
      else
         throw new
         InvalidOperationException(
         "Not enough Money");
   }
}

class Savings
{
   public void MakeWithdrawal(
               decimal amount)
   {
      if(balance >= amount)
            balance -= amount;
      else
         throw new
         InvalidOperationException(
         "Not enough Money");
   }
}

//****************************
//********* AFTER ************
//****************************
class Account
{
   public void MakeWithdrawal(
               decimal amount)
   {
      if(balance >= amount)
            balance -= amount;
      else
         throw new
         InvalidOperationException(
         "Not enough Money");
   }
}

class Checking : Account
{
}

class Savings : Account
{
}
```

- Inheritance is used for a mechanism known as *refactoring*, in which you find all the code you have in common in related types and create a base class and move all the common code to it. For example, you start with Savings and Checking. You discover the code that you have in common between the two, then create an Account class and move the common code to Account (**Figure 5.8**).

Exposing and Restricting Access to Members

The members of a class are private by default. When designing your class it's a good idea to leave as many things as possible private. This is called *information hiding*. When you mark something public, a developer using your class will have dependencies on those public members, and sometimes that prevents you from modifying your class the way it needs to be in future releases.

For example, in **Figure 5.9**, suppose that we decided to make Balance public. A developer could set the Balance field directly outside the class. This may be okay in the first release but imagine if later we want to have some code trigger if the Balance is ever set to a negative number. By having exposed the Balance field we can no longer inject code that triggers automatically based on how that field changes. A better approach is to keep the Balance field private, and add public functions like MakeDeposit and MakeWithdrawal (**Figure 5.10**). These two functions in turn set the value of the Balance field. The fact that the developer doesn't get direct access to the Balance field means that we can change the code that affects the field in later releases.

Figure 5.9 You should assume that if you mark a field as public, the programmer using the class will most likely use it and then have a dependency on that field in future versions of the class.

```
class Account
{
    public decimal balance;
}

class Bank
{
    static void CreateAccount()
    {
        Savings s = new Savings();

        // direct access to balance
        s.balance += 1000m;
    }
}
```

Figure 5.10 Rather than exposing a field like Balance, it is better to hide it by marking it private and then create public functions that enable the programmer using the class to access the field indirectly.

```
class Account
{
    private decimal balance;

    //A better way to access balance
    public void MakeDeposit(
            decimal amount)
    {
        balance += amount;
    }

    public void MakeWithdrawal(
            decimal amount)
    {
        if(balance >= amount)
            balance -= amount;
        else
            throw new
            InvalidOperationException
            ("Not enough Money");
    }
}

class Bank
{
    static void CreateAccount()
    {
        Savings s = new Savings();

        // no direct access to balance
        s.MakeDeposit(1000m);
    }
}
```

Figure 5.11 By default, classes are internal. That means that only other classes within the same project (or assembly, to be more accurate) can access the class.

```
Code                                    _ □ ✕

// class is only visible within the
// assembly
internal class Checking : Account
{
    // Checking implementation
}

// if not specified, default
// accessibility is internal
class Savings : Account
{
    // Savings implementation
}
```

To change the scope of a member:

◆ **Table 5.1** shows the different scope modifiers. Add one of these modifiers in front of the member declaration. Apply to fields, properties, functions, events, nested classes, etc.

✔ Tips

■ Classes also have a *scope*. The scope for classes is either `internal` (default) or `public`. A public class can be used by any other code. An internal class can be used by any code that lives in the same assembly. Assembly is an abstract boundary for types. It normally refers to a DLL or an EXE. In C# Web Applications all the code in the same project ends up in a single DLL. A class marked as internal can only be used by other code in the same DLL. If you wanted to use the DLL from one project in another project (you'll learn how to do this in various chapters of the book), you need to mark the class as public. For the most part it's best to keep classes as the default, internal, until there's a need to make them public (**Figure 5.11**).

continues on next page

Table 5.1

Member Scope Modifiers (Modifiers that Enable You to Expose or Hide Class Members)	
MODIFIER	EXPLANATION
private (default)	Member can only be used inside of the class.
protected	Member can be used inside of the class, and by code in a class that derives from the class. The derived class can live in a different project. For example, you can write a DLL (Class Library Project) and place the class there, then inherit from it in a class of a Web Application project. The inherited class would be able to access protected members.
internal	Member can be used by any code that lives in the same project (assembly). If the class lives in an ASP.NET Web Application then the members are accessible only to other classes in the same ASP.NET Web Application.
protected internal	It is the combination of protected and internal. Member can be seen used outside of the project (assembly) if the class inherits from this class, and the member can be seen used by any class in the same project.
public	Members can be used by any code.

■ You should always keep as much as possible private. If you feel you should expose a field to developers, keep the field private, but add a property to access the field. Then make the property protected or public depending on how much access developers require (**Figure 5.12**).

Figure 5.12 Adding a public property is another way of hiding a data member. Notice that in this case m_balance is private.

```
class Account
{
    // m_balance is accessed via balance
    // property
    private decimal m_balance = 0.0m;

    // this is the balance property
    public decimal balance
    {
        get
        {
            // could put business logic here
            return m_balance;
        }
        set
        {
            // could put validation logic
            // here
            m_balance = value;
        }
    }
}
```

Figure 5.13 The quick entry form is displayed in a separate window. It is a modal window, which means that you have to close it before you are able to interact with the main window.

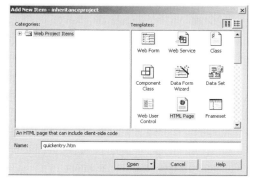

Figure 5.14 The quick entry form doesn't need to do any server-side processing, so rather than creating an aspx page, we're just going to add a simple HTML page.

Enhancing the Sample Application

It's now time to enhance the sample application. One thing we want to do in the sample application is display a "quick entry" form (**Figure 5.13**). As you can see, the "quick entry" form is a page displayed in another browser window. For us to open a new browser window we need to use client-side scripting. So far our applications have been using ASP.NET controls which generate server-side code. The difference is that with server-side code the client never sees our code. The server-side code generates HTML and the client sees the end result. Some things in HTML can only be done with client-side code. Client-side code is composed of functions that are part of the HTML end result, and are visible to the end user. To display a pop-up form, we will use a DHTML function called window.showModalDialog.

But how do we generate client-side scripts using our server-side code? With ASP.NET, it's easy. You only need to call the function Page.RegisterClientScriptBlock and pass the HTML for the client-side script.

We're going to start by adding the client-side script to the Page_Load function of the WorkOrder.aspx form. Then, because we may have other entry forms that need the same functionality, we're going to create another class, move the Page_Load to there, and inherit the form class from this new class.

To add a client-side script to the WorkOrder form:

1. First add the "quick entry" form to your project. Choose Project > Add HTML Page and enter quickentry.htm for the filename (**Figure 5.14**).

continues on next page

2. Add controls to the page to make it look like the page in **Figure 5.15**.

   Alternatively you can enter the HTML in **Figure 5.16** directly or download the finished product from Peachpit's Web site.

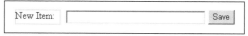

Figure 5.15 All we need for the quick entry form is a label, a textbox (to enter the new values), and a Save button. If the user closes the window without clicking the Save button then the new item is discarded.

Figure 5.16 Notice the use of client-side scripting in the quick entry form. The script sets the window's returnValue to the text the user entered in the TextBox, then closes the window. The main form will then obtain the return value and add the item to the drop-down list that corresponds to the button clicked.

```
Code                                    _ □ ×

<meta name="vs_showGrid" content="True">

<SCRIPT>
function btnSave_onclick()
{
    window.returnValue = txtNewItem.value;
    window.close();
}
</SCRIPT>

<DIV id="lblNewItem"
    ms_positioning="FlowLayout"
    style="Z-INDEX: 100; LEFT: 10px;
    WIDTH: 74px; POSITION: absolute;
    TOP: 15px; HEIGHT: 24px">
    New Item:
</DIV>

<INPUT id="btnSave" type="button"
    value="Save" name="Button1"
    onclick="return btnSave_onclick()"
    style="Z-INDEX: 101; LEFT: 324px;
    POSITION: absolute; TOP: 14px">

<INPUT id="txtNewItem" type="text"
    size="32" name="Text1" style="Z-
    INDEX: 102; LEFT: 93px; POSITION:
    absolute; TOP: 16px">
```

Figure 5.17 The code in Page_Load declares a client-side function called fnOpen. It calls window.showModalDialog to display the quick entry form; showModalDialog blocks until the user closes the quick entry form; it then returns the value the user entered in the quick entry form and adds it to the corresponding drop-down list. The name of the drop-down list is being passed in as a parameter to the function.

```
private void Page_Load(object sender,
            System.EventArgs e)
{
    // Put user code to initialize
    // the page here
    string script = @"<SCRIPT>
    function fnOpen(control){
    var result = window.showModalDialog(
'quickentry.htm','','dialogHeight=10');

    if (result != null)
    {
    var oOption = document.createElement(
                'OPTION');

    window.document.forms[0].elements[
    control].options.add(oOption);

    oOption.innerText = result;
    oOption.Value = result;
    oOption.selected = true;
    }
    }
    </SCRIPT>";

    this.Page.RegisterClientScriptBlock(
    "quickentry",script);
}
```

3. Open the WorkOrder.aspx form in the editor and then double-click on the form itself. This will cause the editor to show the Page_Load function. In the Page_Load function add the code in **Figure 5.17**. This code registers a client-side script that uses the window.showModalDialog function to display the quickentry.htm function in a pop-up window. (The code isn't fully functional yet.)

ENHANCING THE SAMPLE APPLICATION

Because this code may be repeated to multiple Page_Load's, let's create a generic class that encapsulates this code.

To create a generic class to encapsulate Page_Load:

1. Choose Project > Add Class from the top-level menu. Enter InputForm.cs for the class name. The editor will open up a code window displaying the new class.

2. Add code to have the InputForm class derive from System.Web.UI.Page (**Figure 5.18**). This is necessary because all Web Forms derive from System.Web.UI.Page. Since we are going to make the WorkOrder form derive from InputForm we want to make sure InputForm contains all the functionality of System.Web.UI.Page.

3. In the code for WorkOrder.aspx, change the declaration of the WorkOrder class so that it inherits from InputForm instead of System.Web.UI.Page (**Figure 5.19**).

4. Cut the entire Page_Load function from the WorkOrder class (**Figure 5.20**) and paste it inside the InputForm class (**Figure 5.21** on next page).

Figure 5.18 Because the InputForm is going to serve as a base to all Web forms in the application we need to derive InputForm from System.Web.UI.Page which is the class that turns a regular class into a Web form.

```
public class InputForm :
            System.Web.UI.Page
{
```

Figure 5.19 With InputForm deriving from System.Web.UI.Page we can change the base class of WorkOrder to be InputForm.

```
public class WorkOrder : InputForm
{
```

```
public class WorkOrder : InputForm
{
    protected System.Web.UI.WebControls.Label lblBldg;
    protected System.Web.UI.WebControls.DropDownList lstDepartment;
    protected System.Web.UI.WebControls.Button btnNewDept;
    protected System.Web.UI.WebControls.Button btnNewBldg;
    protected System.Web.UI.WebControls.Label lblDepartment;
    protected System.Web.UI.WebControls.DropDownList lstBuilding;

    Web Form Designer generated code

}
```

Figure 5.20 The Page_Load function will be moved to the InputForm class.

Figure 5.21 At this point the Page_Load function is in the InputForm class without any code modifications. The only problem is that it is private by default, which means that derived classes don't have access to it.

```
Code                           _ □ ×

public class InputForm :
      System.Web.UI.Page
{

   private void Page_Load(object sender,
                  System.EventArgs e)
   {
      // Put user code to initialize the
      // page here
      string script = @"<SCRIPT>
      function fnOpen(control){
         var result = window.
                  showModalDialog(
                  'quickentry.htm',
                  '',
                  'dialogHeight=10');
         if (result != null)
         {
            var oOption = document.
                     createElement(
                     'OPTION');
            window.document.
            forms[0].elements[control].
            options.add(oOption);

            oOption.innerText = result;
            oOption.Value = result;
            oOption.selected = true;
         }
      }
      </SCRIPT>";

      if (!this.Page.
         IsClientScriptBlockRegistered(
         "quickentry"))
         this.Page.
         RegisterClientScriptBlock(
         "quickentry",script);
   }
}
```

Figure 5.22 Changing the scope modifier of the function to protected makes Page_Load visible to classes that inherit from InputForm.

```
Code                           _ □ ×

protected void Page_Load(object sender,
            System.EventArgs e)
{
   //code omitted for simplicity
}
```

5. Change the access modifier for the Page_Load function to be protected instead of private (**Figure 5.22**).

✔ Tip

■ The code isn't fully functional at this point. We need to add code to the New buttons in order to display the "quick entry" form. However, it should compile correctly at this point with Build > Build Solution.

Hiding Methods from the Base Class

When you derive one class from another the derived class inherits all the non-private members of the base class. The derived class can then declare methods specific to the derived class to extend the base class. But what happens if the author of the base class adds a method with the same name as a method in the derived class? And what happens if the base class and the derived class have members that have the same name? The answer is that C# by default uses a mechanism called *hide-by-signature*.

Hide-by-signature means that the compiler will try to combine all the methods from the base class and the derived class as long as the methods don't conflict in some way. Two methods would conflict if they had the exact same name and parameters. Another source of conflict would be if one of the members of the class were a field and the derived class had a method with the same name. This would be a conflict because you can't have a method and field with the same name. When there is a conflict, the compiler will choose what version of the method to use depending on how you declare the variable to use the class. If the variable is of the type of the base class, then only the base class method can be invoked. If the variable is of type of the derived class, then only the derived version of the function can be invoked. Even though this is the default behavior, the compiler issues a warning that hiding is occurring—which leads us to the steps of this topic.

Figure 5.23 When a method in the derived class is identical to a method in the base class the compiler warns you that method hiding is taking place. You can tell the compiler that you meant to do that by adding the new keyword in front of the function's return type.

```
Code                              _ □ ✕

class Account
{
    protected decimal m_balance = 0.0m;

    // default implementation of
    // MakeDeposit
    public void MakeDeposit(decimal
                            amount)
    {
        m_balance +=amount;
    }
}

class Checking : Account
{
    // specialized Checking implementation
    // of MakeDeposit
    public new void MakeDeposit(decimal
                                amount)
    {
        if (amount > 500.0m)
            m_balance +=amount;
        else
            // do some validation first
            if (ValidateDeposit())
                m_balance +=amount;
            else
             throw new
             InvalidOperationException();
    }

    public bool ValidateDeposit()
    {
        // include some validation on the
        // deposit
        return true;
    }
}
```

To suppress the warning resulting from hiding:

◆ In the derived class's method type **new** after the access modifier and before the function's type (**Figure 5.23**).

✔ Tips

■ Hiding isn't usually done on purpose; normally what you want to do is override a function from the base class instead. Overriding means that you replace a function in the base from one in the derived class. With hiding there is basically a duplicate function. Hiding normally happens backwards: a person writing the derived class adds a method called Connect, for example, and later the developer of the base class decides to add a method with the same name. If the developers are from different companies, there is no way for the base class developer to know that the derived class already has a method with the same name.

■ Using the **new** keyword in a function declaration isn't just for suppressing a warning; it is also for suppressing method overriding, as you will see in the next section.

HIDING METHODS FROM THE BASE CLASS

Overriding Functions in a Derived Class

In the last section, we described hiding methods. But developers often want to be able to override methods from the base class. For example, in a banking application, let's say a developer defines a class called Account with a method called MakeDeposit. The author of the class writes a default implementation of the MakeDeposit method. Later a developer creates a class called Checking that inherits the methods from the Account class, but the MakeDeposit method needs to work differently. What's more, the same developer creates a Savings class and the Savings class would also like to have a different version of MakeDeposit. For this reason the author of Account may decide to make the MakeDeposit function virtual.

To override functions from a base class:

1. The developer of the base class must first grant permission to override a function. To do this type `virtual` after the access modifier of the function and before the function's return type (**Figure 5.24**).

2. In the derived class, enter a function declaration that is identical to the function you want to override.

3. Type `override` after the function access modifier and before the function's return type (**Figure 5.25**).

Figure 5.24 To enable programmers to override the code in a function, you have to mark the function as virtual.

```
class Account
{
    protected decimal m_balance = 0.0m;

    // default implementation of
    // MakeDeposit
    public virtual void MakeDeposit(decimal
                                    amount)
    {
        m_balance +=amount;
    }
}
```

Figure 5.25 To override a virtual function you have to use the override keyword; otherwise the compiler will use the hiding mechanism as described earlier.

```
class Checking : Account
{
    // specialized Checking implementation
    // of MakeDeposit
    public override void MakeDeposit(
                decimal amount)
    {
        if (amount > 500.0m)
            m_balance +=amount;
        else
            // do some validation first
            if (ValidateDeposit())
                m_balance +=amount;
            else
                throw new
                InvalidOperationException();
    }

    public bool ValidateDeposit()
    {
        //include some checking account
        // validation
        return true;
    }
}
```

Figure 5.26 Notice that the DepositMoney function has a parameter of type Account. With polymorphism we can pass to this function either a Checking object or a Savings object and the function will call MakeDeposit in the corresponding class.

```
class Account
{
  protected decimal m_balance = 0.0m;

  public virtual void MakeDeposit(
                    decimal amount)
  {
    m_balance +=amount;
  }
}

class Checking : Account
{
  public override void MakeDeposit(
                    decimal amount)
  {
    // specialized Checking
    // implementation of MakeDeposit
  }
}

class Savings : Account
{
  public override void MakeDeposit(
                    decimal amount)
  {
    // specialized Savings
    // implementation of MakeDeposit
  }
}

class Bank
{
  static void CreateAccount()
  {
    Savings s = new Savings();
    DepositMoney(s);
    Checking c = new Checking();
    DepositMoney(c);

  }

  // Can pass in anything that "IS A"
  // Account
  static void DepositMoney(Account acct)
  {
    acct.MakeDeposit(1000.0m);
  }
}
```

✔ Tips

■ The virtual function mechanism is used for polymorphism (**Figure 5.26**). Notice from the example that the PrintBalance function accepts any class that derives from Account, however, the implementation of PrintBalance in both Checking and Savings differs. Polymorphism means that the execution of a function may be different depending what object you send to the function.

continues on next page

OVERRIDING FUNCTIONS IN A DERIVED CLASS

■ When you use virtual functions and make a method call, the method to be executed depends on the type of object that you create, not on the type of variable pointing to the object (**Figure 5.27**).

Figure 5.27 Even though the variable in DepositMoney is of type Account because we are passing an object of type Savings and because Savings is overriding MakeDeposit, the code will execute the version of MakeDeposit in Savings.

```
Code                                    _ □ ×

class Account
{
  protected decimal m_balance = 0.0m;

  public virtual void MakeDeposit(
                    decimal amount)
  {
    m_balance +=amount;
  }
}

class Savings : Account
{
  public override void MakeDeposit(
                    decimal amount)
  {
    // specialized Savings
    // implementation of MakeDeposit
  }
}

class Bank
{
  static void CreateAccount()
  {
    Savings s = new Savings();
    DepositMoney(s);
  }

  static void DepositMoney(Account acct)
  {
    //Even though the variable is of
    // type Account the call to
    // MakeDeposit calls the overridden
    // method in Savings
    acct.MakeDeposit(1000.0m);
  }
}
```

Figure 5.28 The code in Bank creates a Savings object, then calls the DoBanking method. DoBanking is part of Account not Savings. This is legal, because Savings derives from Account. However, when DoBanking calls MakeDeposit the code executes the version in Savings because the object type is really Savings.

```
class Account
{
    protected decimal m_balance = 0.0m;

    // default implementation of
    // MakeDeposit
    public virtual void MakeDeposit(
                    decimal amount)
    {
        m_balance +=amount;
    }

    public void DoBanking()
    {
        // This will call the Savings version
        // of MakeDeposit
        this.MakeDeposit(200.0m);
    }
}

class Savings : Account
{
    public override void MakeDeposit(
                    decimal amount)
    {
        // specialized Savings implementation
        // of MakeDeposit
    }
}

class Bank
{
    static void CreateAccount()
    {
        Account s = new Savings();
        s.DoBanking();
    }
}
```

■ Even code within the base class that calls the function will execute the version in the derived class if the code created an instance of the derived type (**Figure 5.28**).

■ A class author may choose to override a function in the base class but may want to invoke some of the default functionality in the original method (**Figure 5.29**).

Figure 5.29 You can call a method in your base class by using the base keyword.

```
class Checking : Account
{
    public override void MakeDeposit(
                    decimal amount)
    {
        // specialized Checking
        // implementation of MakeDeposit

        // after specialized code, call
        // base class's version
        base.MakeDeposit(amount);
    }
}
```

Adding a Generic Button to the Sample Application

Now that we have discussed overriding methods we are ready to create a generic "New..." button for "quick entry" forms. The way to accomplish this is to create your own button control. This sounds more difficult than it actually is.

A *custom control* is a class that derives from System.Web.UI.WebControls.WebControl. When you derive the class from WebControl you first have to call the base class's constructor and tell it what type of control you are creating. (Remember, a constructor is a function that executes when we create an instance of a class.) In this case you are going to tell the base class that we are creating a button control (System.Web.UI .HtmlTextWriterTag.Button).

Next we have to override two functions in WebControl. The first function is called AddAttributesToRender. In this function we're going to tell ASP.NET that whenever we generate the HTML for our control we want the tag for our button to have the onClick attribute to invoke the client-side script we wrote in Page_Load. In other words, when the user clicks the button, the code should invoke the client-side script. The second function we have to override is the RenderContents function. In this function we tell ASP.NET how to generate the HTML for our control. We don't have to worry about generating the HTML to make our control a button because we do that in the constructor. But by default our button will be blank, so in the RenderContents function we'll add code to set the text for the button to "New...".

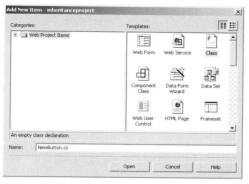

Figure 5.30 The NewButton class will wrap a custom button control that we're going to use in the WorkOrder form to display the quick entry form.

Figure 5.31 The Control property will store the name of the drop-down list control that will be associated with the button.

```
Code                                    _ □ ×
public class NewButton
{
    string _control;

    public string Control
    {
        get
        {
            return _control;
        }
        set
        {
            _control = value;
        }
    }
}
```

Figure 5.32 Web controls are classes that derive from System.Web.UI.WebControls.WebControl.

```
Code                                    _ □ ×
public class NewButton :
System.Web.UI.WebControls.WebControl
{
```

To create a generic button class:

1. Choose Project > Add Class. When asked for the class name, enter NewButton.cs (**Figure 5.30**).

2. Add the code in **Figure 5.31**. This code adds a string property called *control*. The purpose of this property is to store the id of a listbox to which we're going to add the new "quick entry." In summary, the user will click the New button to bring up the "quick entry" form, then enter a new value in the textbox; click the Save button in the form and the new value will appear inside the listbox next to the button.

3. After the NewButton class declaration, add the code in **Figure 5.32** to make the class inherit from System.Web.UI .WebControls.WebControl.

continues on next page

ADDING A GENERIC BUTTON

4. After the code for the constructor add code to invoke the base class constructor as seen in **Figure 5.33**. This tells the base class that we mean to draw a button control.

5. Now add code to override the AddAttributesToRender function as seen in **Figure 5.34**. This code tells ASP.NET to add an onClick attribute to our button that invokes the client-side script function we added earlier to Page_Load.

6. Override the RenderContents function (**Figure 5.35**). This code tells ASP.NET to make the contents of the button display the word "New...".

✔ Tips

- In the next section, we will add the code to actually use the button.

- Notice that the code in **Figure 5.34** and in **Figure 5.35** both make calls to a function in the base class. AddAttributesToRender calls base.AddAttributesToRender before writing the onClick attribute and RenderContents calls base.RenderContents after drawing the text for the button. The only way to know whether you have to call the base class function before or after you do something is by consulting the documentation.

Figure 5.33 First we need to tell the base class what type of control we are using. This is necessary because the base class will do the initial rendering of our control into HTML. So this line tells it what type of HTML tag to use for our control, in this case an input tag of type button.

```
public NewButton() : base(
  System.Web.UI.HtmlTextWriterTag.Button)
{
}
```

Figure 5.34 We are overriding the AddAttributes ToRender function to add a call to the fnOpen function when the button is clicked.

```
protected override void
        AddAttributesToRender(
        System.Web.UI.HtmlTextWriter
        writer)
{
  base.AddAttributesToRender(writer);
  writer.AddAttribute("onclick",
  "fnOpen('" + _control + "');");
}
```

Figure 5.35 We are overriding the RenderContents function to tell ASP.NET to set the text for our button to New....

```
protected override void
        RenderContents(
        System.Web.UI.HtmlTextWriter
        writer)
{
  writer.Write("New...");
  base.RenderContents(writer);
}
```

```
<%@ Page language="c#" Codebehind="WorkOrder.aspx.cs" AutoEventWireup="fa
<!DOCTYPE HTML PUBLIC "-//W3C//DTD HTML 4.0 Transitional//EN" >
<HTML>
    <HEAD>
        <title>WorkOrder</title>
        <meta content="Microsoft Visual Studio 7.0" name="GENERATOR">
        <meta content="C#" name="CODE_LANGUAGE">
        <meta content="JavaScript" name="vs_defaultClientScript">
        <meta content="http://schemas.microsoft.com/intellisense/ie5" nam
    </HEAD>
    <body MS_POSITIONING="GridLayout">
        <form id="WorkOrder" method="post" runat="server">
            <asp:label id="lblBldg" style="Z-INDEX: 101; LEFT: 22px; POSI
        </body>
</HTML>
```

Figure 5.36 We need to switch to HTML view in the editor in order to add information for our custom control to the form.

Figure 5.37 The Register directive registers a new tag that will represent our custom control. Whenever you use one of the standard controls, you use the <asp:control> tag. In this line we are registering <SuperControl:control> for our custom control.

```
<%@ Register TagPrefix="SuperControls"
    Namespace="inheritanceproject"
    Assembly = "inheritanceproject" %>
```

Using the Generic Button in the WorkOrder Form

We have created a generic button to display a "quick entry" form, but so far we have not used it anywhere. In this section you'll learn how to use the generic button in the WorkOrder form.

To do so, you're going to change the New buttons currently on the form that are of type Button to NewButton, the class you created in the previous section.

To replace all buttons on the WorkOrder form with NewButton:

1. Open the WorkOrder form in the designer and click the designer's HTML button to display the HTML for the form (**Figure 5.36**).

2. After the line that <%Page...%> add the <%Register...%> tag from **Figure 5.37**. This line tells ASP.NET that there are custom controls in our project. To use the custom control all we have to do is use the tag we registered with the <%Register...%> directive. In this case the tag is SuperControls.

continues on next page

continues on next page

3. Replace the HTML for the two buttons on the form with the HTML in **Figure 5.38**. Notice that this HTML uses SUPERCONTROL:NEWBUTTON for the tag name rather than asp:Button. The SuperControl portion of the tag comes from the Register command in step 2 and tells ASP.NET that the control comes from our own DLL; and the NewButton part of the tag tells ASP.NET the class name of the control which is NewButton. The two new entries also set the Control property of the New button to the listbox control next to the buttons.

Figure 5.38 All we have to do to turn the standard button control into our control is to change the asp:button tag to SuperControl:NewButton. Also we can add an attribute for the Control property of NewButton.

```
Code                                    _ □ ×
<%@ Page language="c#"
  Codebehind="WorkOrder.aspx.cs"
  AutoEventWireup="false"
  Inherits="inheritanceproject.WorkOrder"
%>
<HTML>
    <HEAD>
        <title>WorkOrder</title>
    </HEAD>
    <body MS_POSITIONING="GridLayout">
    <form id="WorkOrder" method="post"
            runat="server">
    <asp:label id="lblBldg"
            style="Z-INDEX: 101; LEFT:
            22px; POSITION: absolute;
            TOP: 23px" runat="server"
            Height="22px" Width="61px">
            Building:
            </asp:label>
    <asp:label id="lblDepartment"
            style="Z-INDEX: 106; LEFT:
            23px; POSITION: absolute;
            TOP: 55px" runat="server"
            Height="22px" Width="61px">
            Department:
            </asp:label>
    <asp:dropdownlist id="lstBuilding"
            style="Z-INDEX: 102; LEFT:
            113px; POSITION: absolute;
            TOP: 23px" runat="server"
            Height="26px"
            Width="176px">
            </asp:dropdownlist>
    <asp:dropdownlist id="lstDepartment"
            style="Z-INDEX: 103; LEFT:
            113px; POSITION: absolute;
            TOP: 55px" runat="server"
            Height="26px"
            Width="176px">
            </asp:dropdownlist>
    <SUPERCONTROLS:NEWBUTTON
            id="btnNewBldg"
            style="Z-INDEX: 104; LEFT:
            299px; POSITION: absolute;
            TOP: 23px" runat="server"
            Height="21px" Width="61px"
            Control="lstBuilding">
            </SUPERCONTROLS:NEWBUTTON>
    <SUPERCONTROLS:NEWBUTTON
            id="btnNewDept"
            style="Z-INDEX: 105; LEFT:
            299px; POSITION: absolute;
            TOP: 56px" runat="server"
            Height="21px" Width="61px"
            Control="lstDepartment" >
            </SUPERCONTROLS:NEWBUTTON>
    </form>
    </body>
</HTML>
```

Figure 5.39 All that is left to do is replace the fields in our WorkOrder class that the wizard generated to be of type NewButton instead of Button.

```
//using System.Web.UI.WebControls
protected Label lblBldg;
protected DropDownList lstDepartment;
protected NewButton btnNewDept;
protected NewButton btnNewBldg;
protected Label lblDepartment;
protected DropDownList lstBuilding;
```

4. In the code for the WorkOrder form, replace the field declarations for the two buttons with the code in **Figure 5.39**. This code changes the variable types from System.Web.UI.WebControls .Button to NewButton.

✔ Tips

■ In this section, we told ASP.NET about our control by adding a Register tag to the HTML of the WorkOrder form. We can then use the new button by using this new tag in the HTML. The last step was to make sure that the variables that represent our buttons in the code were changed to NewButton types instead of Button.

■ The application is now finished and should be fully functional. Experiment by clicking the "New" button next to the Building listbox, then adding a new Building name in the quick entry form and pressing Save. The new entry should appear in the Building listbox.

Adding Functions that Must Be Overridden

A class may declare a method that doesn't have a default implementation, but which must be overridden. For example a class called Account may have a method called `PrintInfo`, and the method may use a property called `AccountType`. The `AccountType` property would have a different implementation in each class. Therefore the author of the Account class may define the `AccountType` function as a function that must be overridden.

To add a function that must be overridden:

1. Type `abstract` in the function definition after the access modifier for the function and before the function's return type.

2. Type a semicolon after the method declaration. Don't add curly brackets (**Figure 5.40**).

3. Mark the class as a class that must be inherited. See the next section "Requiring Inheritance" for details.

✔ Tip

■ If you have too many functions that require overriding it is best to define interfaces for the set of overridable functions (**Figure 5.41**).

Figure 5.40 PrintInfo uses the GetAccountType function. However, GetAccountType is specific to each derived class. Therefore, we can mark GetAccountType as abstract which means that derived classes must override it. Virtual means that it is optional to override and that there is a default implementation; abstract means that it is required to override and there is no default implementation.

```
abstract class Account
{
    public void PrintInfo()
    {
        Response.Write("Account Type:" +
                    GetAccountType);
    }

    // declared without curly braces or
    // code
    public abstract string
                GetAccountType();
}
```

Figure 5.41 If you end up with too many abstract function and properties, it is better to declare an interface instead. Interfaces are discussed in Chapter 8.

```
interface IAccount
{
    void PrintInfo();
    void LogInfo();
    void CheckBalance();
    void FileReport();
}
```

Figure 5.42 When you mark a class as abstract, you are telling the compiler not to allow a developer to create the class directly. It is only meant to be used as a template for other classes.

```
Code                                    _ □ ×
abstract class AbstractAccount
{
    // you can declare variables in
    // abstract classes
    protected decimal m_balance;

    // default implementation of
    // MakeDeposit
    public virtual void MakeDeposit(
                        decimal amount)
    {
        m_balance +=amount;
    }

    public decimal GetBalance()
    {
        return m_balance;
    }
}
```

Figure 5.43 It is illegal to create an instance of an abstract class. However, it is perfectly legal to use the abstract class as a data type and then assign it to an instance of a class that derives from the abstract class.

```
Code                                    _ □ ×
abstract class AbstractAccount
{
}

class Checking() : AbstractAccount
{
}

class Bank()
{
    static void CreateAccount()
    {
        //you can declare a variable of
        //type AbstractAccount
        AbstractAccount acct =
                new Checking();

        //but you can't create an instance
        //of the AbstractAccount directly
        //this is illegal
        AbstractAccount acct =
                new AbstractAccount();
    }
}
```

Requiring Inheritance

Certain classes are meant to be used as base classes. For example, in the case of a banking application, a developer may define a class called Account that has default implementations for methods like MakeDeposit and GetBalance. However, the intention of the class may be for other developers to build derived classes like Checking and Savings. You can require developers to derive from your class and prevent developers from creating instances of the class directly.

To require inheritance in your class:

◆ Type abstract after the access modifier of the class and before the word class in the class declaration (**Figure 5.42**).

✔ Tip

■ Abstract classes can be used for declaring variables; you just can't create an instance of the abstract class (**Figure 5.43**).

Blocking Inheritance

Blocking inheritance is the opposite of requiring it. Certain classes block inheritance to prevent derived classes from overriding virtual methods that come from interfaces or from other base classes. For example the string class in .NET blocks inheritance. One reason may be that the string class overrides functions that determine things like equality. The class may make certain assumptions as to how these methods work. If the string class didn't block inheritance, any developer would be able to create a subclass and override how equality is determined and potentially invalidate some of the assumptions made in the original string class.

To block inheritance:

◆ Type `sealed` after the access modifier of the class and before the word class in the class declaration (**Figure 5.44**).

Figure 5.44 There are at least three reasons why you may want to seal a class: 1) It doesn't make sense to inherit from the class; 2) All members are static (you should then also add a single private constructor to prevent creation); 3) You want to prevent overriding of all virtual methods.

```
sealed class Business : AbstractAccount
{
  public override void PrintInfo()
  {
    string s = "Savings - balance is: "
         + this.m_balance.ToString();
    System.Console.WriteLine(s);
  }
}
```

SPECIAL MEMBERS

At this point, if you have been reading the book sequentially, you probably know the basics of writing classes—how to define a class, and how to add members such as fields and functions to a class. In the last chapter you also learned how to build one class by inheriting code from another class.

Aside from the basic members that you can add to a class, there are a few members that fall into the "special members" category. These are members that add functionality beyond what a basic member provides. For example, there are functions known as *constructors* that can trigger automatically when you create an instance of the class. There are also function definitions that enable the user of the class to pass a variable number of parameters. These special members are discussed in this chapter.

One more thing before we get started. Every chapter in this book has a sample application you build for the chapter. However, this chapter doesn't create a whole application. Rather, for this chapter you're going to write a single class at the end that will be useful in writing Web applications and will illustrate a lot of the principles in the chapter.

Adding Functions with the Same Name (Method Overloading)

It is possible to add two or more functions with the same name to the same class. This is called *method overloading*. Programmers normally use method overloading in order to have multiple versions of the same function that accept different numbers of parameters.

To do method overloading:

1. Add another function with the same name.

2. Change the type of one of the parameters in the new function (**Figure 6.1**).

   or

   Change the number of parameters in the new function (**Figure 6.2**).

   or

   Change the direction of one of the parameters (**Figure 6.3** on the next page).

Figure 6.1 One way to overload functions is to change the type of at least one of the parameters.

```
class Account
{
    public void MakeDeposit(int Amount)
    {
    }

    public void MakeDeposit(double Amount)
    {
    }
}
```

Figure 6.2 Another way to overload functions is to change the number of parameters in the function.

```
class Account
{
    public void MakeDeposit(int Amount)
    {
    }

    public void MakeDeposit(int Amount,
                            bool Available)
    {
    }
}
```

Figure 6.3 Remember that in C# the caller of the function has to use the word ref in front of any by-ref parameters being sent to the function. In this way the compiler can distinguish between a call to the first version of MakeDeposit (no ref in the call) and the second version (ref in the call).

```
Code                              _ □ ×

class Account
{
    int Balance=0;

    public void MakeDeposit(int Amount)
    {
        Balance += Amount;
    }

    public void MakeDeposit(
                       ref int Amount)
    {
        Balance += Amount;
        //Amount is a reference parameter
        //which means you can change it.
        //change it to the actual balance.
        Amount = Balance;
    }
}
```

Figure 6.4 You can change the output parameter type only if you also change something in the parameter list.

```
Code                              _ □ ×

class Account
{
    int Balance=0;

    public void MakeDeposit(int Amount)
    {
        Balance+=Amount;
    }

    public int MakeDeposit(int Amount,
                      bool Available)
    {
        if (Available) Balance+=Amount;
        return Balance;
    }
}
```

3. If you make one of the changes in step 2 you can also change the return type of the function (**Figure 6.4**).

✔ Tips

- You can overload functions, constructors, events and indexers (events and indexers are explained in later chapters).

- You can't overload functions by making one function static and the other an instance function. You must change something in the parameters of the function as well in order to overload the functions.

Which Function Gets Called When?

The difficult part when overloading functions is trying to figure out which function the compiler is going to call. Consider the code in **Figure 6.5**. The code in that figure has three functions: one that accepts a double, one that accepts a float, and one that accepts any object. (All types are compatible with the object type.) The code calls MakeDeposit but passes an integer as the parameter. Which of the functions gets called? The rules are described in the C# ECMA Specification under section 14.4.2 *Overload Resolution*. However, the short version of the rules is that functions are selected based on which function results in a better conversion. Essentially, a better conversion is one where the type you are converting to is closest in memory consumption to the type you are starting from. So in the case of numeric values one can follow the following list: byte, short, int, long, float or decimal, double, object. In this list, byte consumes the least amount of memory and object consumes the most. You pick the smallest type that fits the value you are converting without data loss. In C# all literal integral numbers are of type int by default. However if there is no integer function to invoke, C# checks to see if the number is within the range of a smaller data type (short for example). All decimal numbers are of type double by default. In Figure 6.5, the closest data type is float.

Figure 6.5 Decisions, decisions. The 500 value is type integer, so which of the MakeDeposit version actually gets called? The answer is double. Double is the closest data type to Integer, memory-wise.

```
Code                                    _ □ ×

class Account
{
    public void MakeDeposit(double Amount)
    {
    }

    public void MakeDeposit(float Amount)
    {
    }

    public void MakeDeposit(object Amount)
    {
    }
}

class Bank
{
    public void CreateAccount()
    {
        Account acct = new Account();
        acct.MakeDeposit(500);
    }
}
```

Figure 6.6 It's a well-known fact that Santa uses C# to make up his list, and because there is a variable number of names each year that are part of the Nice list he needs to use a "params" parameter.

```
class Santa
{
    public void AddToNiceList(
              params string[] names)
    {
    }
}
```

Figure 6.7 When Santa is done adding names to the list he can treat the names as an array. One way to navigate through all the names of the array is to use the foreach function.

```
class Santa
{
    public void AddToNiceList(
              params string[] names)
    {
        foreach( string onename in names)
        {
            WriteToNamesDB(onename);
        }
    }
}
```

Defining Functions with a Variable Number of Parameters

The C# language also has a way to pass a variable number of parameters to a function. (A variable number of parameters could be zero parameters as well).

To add a function that accepts a variable number of parameters:

1. Add a function with any return type.

2. In the parameter list type `param int[] args` where int[] is an array of any type, and args is any variable to hold the arguments (**Figure 6.6**).

3. Retrieve the parameters using the same mechanisms that you would use when retrieving values from an array (**Figure 6.7**).

✔ Tips

- You can call a function that has a params argument in one of two ways. You could call the function passing a number of arguments of the same type separated by commas (**Figure 6.8**), or you could call the function passing a single array of the type of the function parameter (**Figure 6.9**).

- If you pass a variable number of parameters to the function, the C# compiler invisibly builds an array with all the parameters and passes the array to the function.

Figure 6.8 When working with params parameters you can call the function passing any number of values, or no values. The compiler creates an array from the values and calls the function.

```
class Santa
{
   public void AddToNiceList(
                   params string[] names)
   {
   }
}

class Christmas
{
   void PrepareLists()
   {
      Santa Nick1 = new Santa();
      Nick1.AddToNiceList(
         "Tom", "Sue", "Jane", "Bill");
   }
}
```

Figure 6.9 Another way to call a function that has a params parameter is to take matters in your own hands and create an array yourself, then pass the array as a single parameter.

```
class Santa
{
   public void AddToNiceList(
                   params string[] names)
   {
   }
}

class Christmas
{
   void PrepareLists()
   {
      Santa Nick1 = new Santa();
      string[] names =
      { "Tom", "Sue", "Jane" ,"Bill"};
      Nick1.AddToNiceList(names);
   }
}
```

Figure 6.10 Constructors are usually used to initialize values. In this case Balance is being initialized to 100.

```
class Account
{
    int Balance;

    public Account()
    {
        Balance=100;
    }
}
```

Figure 6.11 Balance has only one constructor and it has a parameter called InitialBalance. This means that when you create an Account you have to pass in a value for initial balance—it isn't optional.

```
class Account
{
    int Balance;

    public Account(int InitialBalance)
    {
        Balance = InitialBalance;
    }
}
class Bank
{
    void OpenAccount()
    {
        Account acct = new Account(100);
    }
}
```

- You can add multiple constructors to the class, but only one is triggered when the developer creates an instance of the class. The way the compiler knows which constructor to invoke is based on how the developer uses the new operator. For example, if the class has a default constructor and a constructor that accepts one integer parameter, then when the developer writes Account acct = new Account(), the compiler will invoke the default constructor; and when the developer writes Account acct = new Account(100), the compiler will invoke the constructor that accepts one parameter.

Adding Constructors

Constructors are functions that are triggered automatically when an object is created. You can also use constructors to require the developer using the class to set initial values for the class. For example, with a Checking class it makes sense to require a developer to set the initial balance for the account. You can have more than one constructor by using method overloading, a technique discussed earlier in this chapter.

To add a constructor:

1. Add a function to your class that doesn't have a return type and is named the same as the class name (**Figure 6.10**).

2. Change the scope of the constructor by adding one of the scope modifiers: public, private, protected, internal or protected internal. (Constructors are private by default.)

3. When using the new operator to create an object, pass the parameters for the constructor in parentheses after the class name (**Figure 6.11**).

✔ Tips

- If you don't add a constructor to your class, the compiler will add a default constructor automatically.

- If you add a constructor, the compiler doesn't add a default constructor. That means that if you add a single constructor that accepts a parameter (like in **Figure 6.10**), the only way to create an instance of the class is to pass the parameter in the new operator. This is a good technique to use if you want to require developers to pass a value whenever they create an object of the type.

Invoking Base Constructors

Suppose you write a class called Account to be a base class, and then write a class called Checking and have Checking derive from Account. When a developer creates a new Checking class the compiler invokes the constructor for Checking, the derived class. What about the constructor for Account, the base class?

When you derive a class from another class, the derived class inherits all the non-private functions of the base class, as well as all non-private fields. However, the functions in the base class may have been written assuming that certain fields were initialized prior to their execution.

For that reason it's important for the compiler to also execute the code in the base constructor when the developer creates an instance of the derived class. So the compiler does a little trick: It inserts a line to every constructor that invokes the constructor of the base class automatically. The problem is that this trick is limited—the compiler can only invoke the default constructor of the base. If the base class doesn't have a default constructor, or if you want to invoke a different constructor than the default, you must do it yourself with code.

Figure 6.12 Checking is derived from Account, but Account has a single constructor that requires a parameter. You need to call the constructor explicitly in Checking by adding a constructor to it and using base to pass a parameter to Account's constructor.

```
class Account
{
    public Account(int InitialBalance)
    {
    //code omitted for simplicity
    }
}

class Checking : Account
{
    public Checking() : base(100)
    {
    }

    public Checking(int InitialBalance) :
        base(InitialBalance)
    {
    }
}
```

To invoke a base constructor:

1. Add a constructor to the derived class. It can be a default constructor or a parameterized constructor.

2. Before the curly brackets after the closing parenthesis of the constructor's parameters, add a colon followed by a space.

3. Type base, in lowercase, followed by the parameters for the base constructor you want to invoke in parentheses (**Figure 6.12**).

✔ Tips

- Use this technique when the base class doesn't have a default constructor (a constructor that takes no parameters), or when you want to invoke a different constructor.

- When using the base keyword you can specify in parentheses a literal value or simply use one of the parameters sent in to the constructor. In **Figure 6.12**, the second constructor in Checking has a parameter called InitialBalance and forwards this parameter in the base function.

- You can't use a field or specify a function of the class as the parameter for the base function unless the field or function is marked as static (see "Building Code Libraries with Static Members," later in this chapter). If the member isn't marked as static, the compiler will issue an error.

Adding Finalizers

Finalizers are functions that trigger when the .NET Framework recognizes that the program no longer needs the object. Whenever you create an instance of a class, the resulting object consumes a little bit of memory. The more objects you create, the more memory is consumed. The .NET Framework uses garbage collection to reclaim this memory. It identifies when objects are no longer needed and removes them from memory. A finalizer is a function that executes before the memory is reclaimed. You should add finalizers sparingly, and only when absolutely necessary, as they can significantly decrease the performance of your application.

To add a finalizer:

1. Add a function without a return type. Name the function the same as the class name with a tilde symbol in front of the name.

2. Don't add parameters to the function (**Figure 6.13**).

✔ Tips

- Classes can only have one finalizer.

- In C#, the finalizer function also calls the finalizer function of the base class if there is one.

Figure 6.13 If you have used C++, you may be tempted to call ~Account a destructor; however, in C# this is called a Finalizer. Destructors in C++ are always guaranteed to execute. In C# finalizers are not guaranteed to get called, and sometimes they may get called more than once. They are mostly used to clean up operating system resources.

```
class Account
{
    int Balance;

    ~Account()
    {
        //clean OS resource
    }
}
```

Building Code Libraries with Static Members

All the functions and fields discussed so far in the code examples have been *instance* members. These are members that can only be invoked if you create an instance of the class. In other words, before you call MakeDeposit, for example, you must create an Account object.

Sometimes a function or a field doesn't need to be attached to a certain object. In the case of the Account class one can envision each object storing a Balance and each time you call MakeDeposit, the MakeDeposit function must execute in the context of the object through which the function was executed. In other words, if you write `acct1.MakeDeposit(500)` then you are increasing the balance for the object stored in acct1.

But suppose that you want to create a Math library—a class that contains a number of math functions. The functions must be part of a class because in C# all code must be part of a class. The Math class may have an Add function and a Subtract function. The Add function takes two numbers, adds them and returns the result; the Subtract function takes two numbers, subtracts the second from the first and returns the result. In this scenario it would be awkward to have to create objects of type Math just to invoke these functions.

So you might use a static function instead. *Static functions* are functions that can be invoked without creating an instance of the class. Along the same lines, static fields are global fields that store a single value for all the objects of the same type. Static functions are limited in that they can only invoke other static functions and only use static fields.

To add and call static members:

1. Type static in front of a field to make it a type field.

   or

   Type static in front of a function to make it a type function.

2. Make sure the code for the static function doesn't reference non-static fields or non-static functions (**Figure 6.14**).

3. To call a static function in code, use the class name plus a period plus the name of the function. If the code is inside the class where the static functions are declared, you don't have to use the class name (**Figure 6.15**).

✔ Tips

- Use static fields when you need to store information that relates to all of the instances of the class and not just to a single instance. In **Figure 6.14** this is done to store the total number of account objects that have been created.

- The value stored in a static field lives for the duration of the program.

Figure 6.14 You can't have global variables in C#, but you can simulate them with static variables. Static variables are more manageable than old global variables because they are attached to a particular type.

```
class Account
{
    static public int TotalAccounts;

    static public int
    GetNextAccountNumber()
    {
        TotalAccounts++;
      return TotalAccounts;
    }
}
```

Figure 6.15 To call a static function you don't create an instance of the class that contains the static function, you simply use the name of the class plus the name of the function.

```
class Bank
{
    void CreateAccount()
    {
      //add this code to the code
      //in Figure 6-14
      int iTotal =
      Account.GetNextAccountNumber;
      Response.Write(
      "Total number of Accounts=" +
      iTotal.ToString());
    }
}
```

Figure 6.16 One reason people use static functions is to create a library of global functions. Notice that the Math class serves as a library of Math-related functions.

```
class Math
{
    static public int Add(int x1, int x2)
    {
      return x1+x2;
    }

    static public int Subtract
                        (int x1, int x2)
    {
      return x1-x2;
    }
}

class Homework
{
    void DoMath()
    {
        int iTotal = Math.Add(5,7);
        Response.Write("5 + 7 = " +
        iTotal.ToString());
    }
}
```

■ Use static functions when building code libraries (**Figure 6.16**). Code libraries are groups of functions that can be invoked without creating instances of the class.

■ You can add a static constructor to your class. The constructor must be marked public and must not have any parameters. A static constructor is also referred to as a type initializer. The static constructor will trigger only once during program execution, and normally triggers the first time any of the code refers to the class.

Redefining the Meaning of Operators (Operator Overloading)

In certain classes it makes sense for the developer to redefine operators like +, -, *, /, ++, —, etc. Take the built-in string class (System.String), for example. It is possible to take two string variables and add them together and put the result in a third string variable (**Figure 6.17**). In the case of strings, Microsoft has redefined the + operator so that when used, the class simply takes the string to the right of the plus and concatenates it to the string to the left of the plus. You can do the same thing in your classes—you can redefine what it means to add, subtract, multiply, divide, etc. instances of your class. This technique is called method overloading.

Operators fall into two categories: unary operators and binary operators. *Unary* operators are operators that can be applied directly without taking into consideration another type. An example of a unary operator is ++; a developer writes var++. (See **Table 6.1** for a complete list of unary operators.)

Figure 6.17 Although it looks like you can add string variables, the truth is that this is only a compiler trick. The string class has a definition for the + operator that calls the string Concat function.

```
Code                                    _ □ ×
string first = "Indiana";
string last = "Jones";
string full = first + " " + last;
```

Table 6.1

Unary Operators (Operators that Can Be Applied Directly to the Type)	
OPERATOR	COMMON PURPOSE
+	Make type positive (return value of the type)
–	Make type negative
!	Negate value. If value is true applying this operator should return false and vice versa.
~	Return bitwise complement. In a numeric value, this means turn the number to binary (zeros and ones) then take each zero and turn it into a one and take each one and turn it into zero.
++	Increase by one unit.
– –	Decrease by one unit.
true, false	These operators are not applied to the variable directly, but are used whenever the type is compared to the Boolean values true and false.

A *binary* operator is one that involves two variables. An example of a binary operator is +, a developer writes var1+var2. (See **Table 6.2** for a list of binary operators.)

Table 6.2

Binary Operators (Operators that Require Two Variables)	
OPERATOR	COMMON PURPOSE
+, -, *, /	Add, Subtract, Multiply and Divide two types.
%	Calculate remainder after dividing the first variable by the second.
&	Computes bitwise intersection. With numbers it means turn both numbers into binary (ones and zeros) then take the intersection of both numbers (two ones equals one, anything else equals zero). For example 3 & 5 = 1. That is because 3 = 11 and 5 = 101 in binary. The intersection of the two numbers is 001 in binary which is also 1 in decimal.
|	Computes bitwise union. Same principle as & operator except if at least one of the bits is one then the result is one. If both numbers are zero then the result is zero. Therefore 3 | 5 = 7 (111 in binary).
^	Computes bitwise-exclusive union. Turn the numbers into binary like & and | except when comparing the bits the result is 1 if only one of the bits is one, otherwise it is zero. Therefore 3 ^ 5 = 6.
<<	Shift bits of first variable left by the number of bits in the second variable. This concept is a little complicated and a full discussion is beyond the scope of this book, but basically it means take the first value, turn it into bits, then append zeros to the end based on the number of bits in the second operand.
>>	Shift bits of first variable right by the number of bits in the second variable.
==, !=	Test for equality or inequality. If you override the == operator, you must override the != operator as well.
>, <, >=, <=	Test for greater than, less than, greater than or equal to, or less than or equal to.

REDEFINING THE MEANING OF OPERATORS

To overload a unary operator:

1. In a new line type `public` followed by a space. (Operator overloading functions must be public.)

2. Type `static` followed by a space. (Operator overloading functions must be static.)

3. Type the name of the data type you want to return according to **Table 6.3**, followed by a space.

4. Type the word `operator` followed by the symbol for the operator you want to overload.

5. Add parentheses for parameters. Inside the parentheses add a single parameter of the same type as the class you are adding this function to (**Figure 6.18**).

Table 6.3

Return Types for Unary Operators
(What to Return when Overloading Operators)

OPERATORS	RETURN TYPE
+, -, !, ~	Can return any type.
++, --	Must return its own type. That is, if the operator overload is for a class called Checking, it must return an object of type Checking.
true, false	Must return a bool with the value of true or false.

Figure 6.18 When a developer uses the ++ operator on a variable of type rectangle, the result is a new rectangle where the width and height are increased by one.

```
class Rectangle
{
    int x,y,width,height;
    public Rectangle(int x2,
                    int y2,
                    int width2,
                    int height2)
    {
      x=x2;y=y2;
      width=width2;height=height2;
    }

    public static Rectangle operator ++(
    Rectangle orig)
    {
      Rectangle newrect = new Rectangle(
                    orig.x,orig.y,
                    orig.width+1,
                    orig.height+1);
      return newrect;
    }
}
```

Figure 6.19 For the rectangle example we are using the starting location of the first rectangle and the width and height of the second rectangle. This makes absolutely no sense, but it illustrates how to override the + operator for a class.

```
Code

class Rectangle
{
    int x,y,width,height;

    public Rectangle(int x2,
                     int y2,
                     int width2,
                     int height2)
    {
        x=x2;y=y2;
        width=width2;height=height2;
    }

    public static Rectangle operator +
    (Rectangle one, Rectangle two)
    {
        //not the most efficient way of
        //adding two rectangles
        //but you get the idea...
        Rectangle newrect = new Rectangle(
                one.x, one.y,
                two.width, two.height);
        return newrect;
    }
}
```

To overload a binary operator:

1. In a new line, type `public` followed by a space.

2. Type `static` followed by a space.

3. Type the name of the data type you want to return (it can be any type).

4. Type the word `operator` followed by the symbol for the operator you want to overload.

5. Add parentheses for parameters. Inside the parentheses add two parameters. One of the parameters must be of the same type as the class you are adding this function to; the other parameter can be of any type (**Figure 6.19**).

✔ Tips

- If you override the meaning of true or false you must override the other. It is an error to override true without overriding false.

- If you override a binary operator, it is legal to have two different definitions for the same data type—one that lists the class that the operator is in first, followed by another data type, and one that lists the other data type first then the class the operator is in. For example, it is legal to define an operator for Class1 + int and one for int + Class1.

- If you override the == operator, you must override the != operator as well, and vice versa. If you override < then you must override > as well and vice versa. If you override >= then you must override <= as well and vice versa.

REDEFINING THE MEANING OF OPERATORS

Redefining Equality by Overriding ==

You can also redefine equality in your class by overriding the == operator and the != operator. If you override the == operator the compiler warns you that you should also override the Equals function from System.Object. Also, whenever you override the == operator, the compiler forces you to override !=.

To override the == operator:

1. Type public static bool operator == (.

2. Type ClassName one where ClassName is the name of the class where you are adding this function and one is a variable to hold the first object in the comparison.

3. Type a comma , .

4. Type ClassName two where ClassName is the name of the class where you are adding this function and two is a variable to hold the second object in the comparison. For example: Checking one, Checking two.

5. Type a close parenthesis).

6. Type an open curly bracket {.

7. Type return one.Equals(two); .

8. Type a close curly bracket } (**Figure 6.20**).

Figure 6.20 The == operator usually reports whether two objects are actually identical in memory. We're overriding == to report equality. Two objects are equivalent if they are of the same type and their fields have the same values.

```
class Rectangle
{
    int x,y,width,height;

    public Rectangle(int x2,
                     int y2,
                     int width2,
                     int height2)
    {
        x=x2;y=y2;
        width=width2;height=height2;
    }

    public static bool operator ==
    (Rectangle one, Rectangle two)
    {
        if (one.x == two.x &&
            one.y == two.y &&
            one.width == two.width &&
            one.height == two.height)
            return true;
        else
            return false;
    }
}
```

Figure 6.21 If you override the == operator, the C# compiler forces you to override the != operator as well. Most developers just return the opposite of the == operator as illustrated above.

```
class Rectangle
{
    int x,y,width,height;

    public Rectangle(int x2,
                     int y2,
                     int width2,
                     int height2)
    {
        x=x2;y=y2;
        width=width2;height=height2;
    }

    public static bool operator ==
    (Rectangle one, Rectangle two)
    {
        if (one.x == two.x &&
            one.y == two.y &&
            one.width == two.width &&
            one.height == two.height)
            return true;
        else
            return false;
    }

    public static bool operator !=
    (Rectangle one, Rectangle two)
    {
        return !(one == two);
    }
}
```

- The override of the == operator is only beneficial when your class is to be used strictly inside C#. If you were to use the class from another language like Visual Basic.NET for example, the VB program wouldn't be able to use the == operator and would just have to rely on the implementation of Equals. For this reason, and because == sometimes means identity (if it isn't overridden) and sometimes means equivalence, programmers prefer to not override == and instead override only the Equals() function.

To override the != operator:

1. Type `public static bool operator != (`.

2. Type `ClassName one` where `ClassName` is the name of the class where you are adding this function and `one` is a variable to hold the first object in the comparison.

3. Type a comma `,`.

4. Type `ClassName two` where `ClassName` is the name of the class where you are adding this function and `two` is a variable to hold the first object in the comparison. For example: `Checking one, Checking two`.

5. Type a close parenthesis `)`.

6. Type an open curly bracket `{`.

7. Type `return !(one == two);`.

8. Type a close curly bracket `}` (**Figure 6.21**).

✔ Tips

- Your implementation of these functions may vary but if you override the == operator, you should really override the Equals() function. Because the Equals() function and the == operator should base their decisions on the same criteria, I have chosen to just return the result of Equals as the result of ==. Also I have chosen to return the opposite of == in !=. Other classes in the framework may choose to duplicate the code for each function in order to gain in performance. It is sometimes faster to duplicate a little bit of code than to have one function that calls another, which calls a third. Calling functions also has a little overhead.

REDEFINING EQUALITY BY OVERRIDING ==

199

Redefining Equality by Overriding Equals

Equality relates to the values of the fields: Are two variables pointing to objects that have the same values in their fields? For example, two account objects might be equivalent if the objects have the same account number and the same balance. Why is this necessary? Suppose you have an array of Person objects. Each Person has a name and an age. If you want to search the array for a particular person, the system has to know what values to use for the comparison. There is no way the system can test arbitrary fields for comparison. Instead, the .NET framework lets you define what equality means yourself. This is done by overriding two methods from the class System.Object: Equals() and GetHashCode().

To override the Equals and GetHashCode functions:

1. Type `public override bool Equals(object obj)`.

2. Type an open curly bracket {.

3. If `obj` is pointing to the same object as `this` object then return true. For example: `if (System.Object.ReferenceEquals(obj,this)) return true;`.

4. If the variable `obj` and the reference to this are not identical, then cast `obj` to the class where you are adding the Equals function. For example: `Person temp = (Person) obj;`.

5. Test the fields in `obj` to the fields in this instance of the class. For example:
   `if (temp.name == this.name && temp.age == temp.age)`

6. Return true if the fields are equal, otherwise return false.

Figure 6.22 The == operator can only be overridden in C#, not in VB.NET, so Equals is a standard way for all languages to define equivalence. When you override Equals you have to override GetHashCode as well.

```
class Person
{
    string name;
    string age;

    public Person(string Name, string Age)
    {
        name = Name;
        age = Age;
    }

    public override bool Equals(
    object obj)
    {
        if (System.Object.ReferenceEquals(
        obj,this)) return true;
        Person temp = (Person) obj;
        if (temp.name == this.name &&
            temp.age == this.age)
            return true;
        else
            return false;
    }

    public override int GetHashCode()
    {
        return this.name.GetHashCode() +
        this.age.GetHashCode();
    }
}
```

7. Type a close curly bracket }.

8. Type `public override int GetHashCode()`.

9. Type an open curly bracket {.

10. Type return fld1.GetHashCode( ) + fld2.GetHashCode( ) + ... where fld1 and fld2 are the fields that you used for determining equivalence in step 5. For example: return this.name.GetHashCode( ) + this.age.GetHashCode( );.

11. Type a close curly bracket } (**Figure 6.22**).

✔ Tip

- Whenever you override the `Equals()` function, you have to override the `GetHashCode()` function. A hash code is a numeric representation of the data in the class. Hash codes are used by the .NET Framework to group objects in tables like HashTables and dictionaries. You can return any integer number as the result of `GetHashCode()`. However, the only criteria is that if two objects return true for `Equals` they should return the same hash code. So it's a good idea to base the hash code on the fields that were used to test for equivalence.

REDEFINING EQUALITY BY OVERRIDING EQUALS

Working with Special Members

In this section you are going to create a single class that illustrates the principles of this chapter.

You may have noticed from previous Web projects a file called web.config. The wizard adds this file to all Web projects. This file is in XML format and it contains settings that let you control how your application behaves or how the Web server behaves. For example, this file has a section called compilation that tells ASP.NET what language (VB or C#) to use by default if the individual Web pages don't specify a language. In addition, ASP.NET lets you add your own configuration information to this file. One good use for this file then is to store information to open a database.

You may recall from previous chapters that to open a database you need to build a connection string. The connection string looks like this: "server=home;database=food;uid=sa;pwd=;".

Suppose then that we would like our configuration file to look like the one in **Figure 6.23**. To read the configuration information we may want to create a class as follows.

Figure 6.23 ASP.NET enables you to insert your own sections to the web.config file. The new section here is <dbConfig>; inside the section you add keys and values using the syntax <add key="whatever" value="whatever" />; the idea is you read from a section a key to obtain a value.

```
Code                                          _ □ ×
<?xml version="1.0" encoding="utf-8" ?>
<configuration>

  <dbConfig>
    <add key="server" value="Home" />
    <add key="database" value="Food" />
  </dbConfig>
```

Figure 6.24 The sCS will store the configuration string. The variable is static because the configuration string is the same no matter who reads it. So it doesn't make sense for the string to be dependent on a particular instance of the class.

```
Code                               _ □ ×

public class ConfigInfo : System.Configuration.
NameValueFileSectionHandler
{
    static string sCS;
}
```

Figure 6.25 Having a class that lets you obtain configuration information by calling a property is easier than repeating the code required to read from the configuration file.

```
Code                               _ □ ×

public static string ConnectionString
{
    get
    {
        if (sCS == "")
        {
            System.Collections.
            Specialized.NameValueCollection
            nvh;

            nvh = (System.Collections.
            Specialized.NameValueCollection)
            System.Web.HttpContext.
            GetAppConfig("DBConfig");

            sCS = "server=" + nvh["server"]
                + ";database=" +
                nvh["database"] +
                ";uid=sa;pwd=;";
        }
        return sCS;
    }
}
```

To write a class that reads configuration information:

1. Declare a public class called ConfigInfo.

2. Inherit the class from System.Configuration.NameValueFileSectionHandler. The reason it needs to be inherited from NameValueFileSectionHandler is that whenever you add a new section to the configuration file you need a class to be able to interpret the section. Later, we are going to tell the web.config file that this class is the handler for the new section.

3. Add a private static variable called sCS to hold the connection string. Your class should look like the code in **Figure 6.24**.

4. Add a public static property called ConnectionString with a get handler and no set. The get handler will first check if the configuration information has been read once. If it hasn't, then it will read it from the web.config file and set the value of the sCS variable. From then on any time ConnectionString is requested the class will just return the value stored in sCS (**Figure 6.25** shows the code to accomplish this).

continues on next page

5. Add the code in **Figure 6.26** to the configuration file. This code tells ASP.NET that your new class will serve as a handler for the dbConfig section. Notice that the type="" portion of the code is supposed to contain the name of the class you created, comma, and the name of the project (or assembly) the class is in.

That's all there is to it. All you need to do now is call ConfigInfo.ConnectionString to retrieve the connection string. As an added step you may want to enhance the ConfigInfo class to read information from any custom section you define and from any key within the section. For that you'll need to add just a little more code.

To enhance the class to read from any custom configuration section:

1. Declare a private string variable called iCS (**Figure 6.27**). Notice that this is an instance variable and not a static variable.

2. Add a constructor that takes two parameters, one string parameter for the config section you would like to read, and one string parameter for the element within the section you would like to read. Inside the constructor add the code in **Figure 6.28**.

WORKING WITH SPECIAL MEMBERS

Figure 6.26 Just adding a custom configuration section isn't enough. ASP.NET requires you to declare a section and provide a class that can read the section. That is why our class derives from NameValueFileSectionHandler.

```
<?xml version="1.0" encoding="utf-8" ?>
<configuration>

    <configSections>
        <section name="dbConfig"
        type="ConfigDB, advancedmembers" />
    </configSections>

    <dbConfig>
        <add key="server" value="Home" />
        <add key="database" value="Food" />
    </dbConfig>
</configuration>
```

Figure 6.27 iCS is an instance variable. It is instance instead of static because each instance of the class will be able to store a different element for a particular section.

```
public class ConfigInfo : System.Configuration.
NameValueFileSectionHandler
{
    static string sCS;
    string iCS;
```

Figure 6.28 The constructor code is similar to the code in the ConnectionString section except that is more generalized. The ConnectionString property always reads from dbConfig, and the constructor lets you read from any section.

```
public class ConfigInfo : System.Configuration.
NameValueFileSectionHandler
{
    static string sCS;
    string iCS;

    public ConfigInfo(string config,
                      string element)
    {
        System.Collections.
        Specialized.NameValueCollection
        nvh;

        nvh = (System.Collections.
        Specialized.NameValueCollection)
        System.Web.HttpContext.
        GetAppConfig(config);

        iCS = nvh[element];
    }
}
```

Figure 6.29 There are two versions of the + operator. One version is the binary form, requiring two parameters, for example z= x + y. The other version is the unary form, illustrated here, for example: z = +x.

```
public class ConfigInfo : System.Configuration.
NameValueFileSectionHandler
{
    static string sCS;
    string iCS;

    public ConfigInfo(string config,
                      string element)
    {
        System.Collections.
        Specialized.NameValueCollection
        nvh;

        nvh = (System.Collections.
        Specialized.NameValueCollection)
        System.Web.HttpContext.
        GetAppConfig(config);

        iCS = nvh[element];
    }

    public static string operator + (ConfigInfo
cdb)
    {
        return cdb.iCS;
    }
}
```

Figure 6.30 A default constructor is required because ASP.NET needs to create an instance of our class when it sees the custom configuration section.

```
public class ConfigInfo : System.Configuration.
NameValueFileSectionHandler
{
    static string sCS;
    string iCS;

    public ConfigInfo()
    {
    }

    public ConfigInfo(string config,
                      string element)
    {
```

3. To retrieve the string it might be interesting to use operator overloading. Unfortunately there is no way to override the = operator, which would be the best to override in this case. Instead let's say that if someone uses the + operator in front of a ConfigDB variable, we will return the configuration information stored in iCS. Then a developer would write string name=+info; where info is a variable of type ConfigDB. The code to do this is in **Figure 6.29**.

4. Now we have a little problem. We've added a parameterized constructor, which means that the default constructor is gone. The problem with that is that for our class to be a handler ASP.NET requires a default constructor. Therefore, we need to add one to our class (**Figure 6.30**).

continues on next page

WORKING WITH SPECIAL MEMBERS

✔ Tip

■ **Figure 6.31** contains all the code for the class put together.

Figure 6.31 You should now have a generic class that you can use to either read a connection string or to store different elements from a particular section in the config file.

```
public class ConfigInfo : System.Configuration.
NameValueFileSectionHandler
{
    static string sCS;
    string iCS;

    public ConfigInfo()
    {
    }

    public ConfigInfo(string config,
                      string element)
    {
        System.Collections.
        Specialized.NameValueCollection
        nvh;

        nvh = (System.Collections.
        Specialized.NameValueCollection)
        System.Web.HttpContext.
        GetAppConfig(config);

        iCS = nvh[element];
    }

    public static string ConnectionString
    {
        get
        {
            if (sCS == "")
            {
                System.Collections.
                Specialized.
                NameValueCollection
                nvh;

                nvh = (System.Collections.
                Specialized.
                NameValueCollection)
                System.Web.HttpContext.
                GetAppConfig("DBConfig");

                sCS = "server=" +
                nvh["server"] + ";database=" +
                nvh["database"] +
                ";uid=sa;pwd=;";
            }
            return sCS;
        }
    }

    public static string operator +
    (ConfigInfo cdb)
    {
        return cdb.iCS;
    }
}
```

7

TYPES

In C# all code belongs to a type. Normally we represent types as classes, but types can also be structures, enumerations, interfaces, etc. Because every code belongs in a type, a number of tasks relating to types are important to understand when writing applications. These tasks include being able to compare variables, being able to determine if an object is compatible with a certain type, and being able to convert from one type to another.

Beyond basic comparisons of variables to types and learning mechanisms for casting from one type to another, this chapter will also give you information for redefining cast operators. Cast operators let you define conversion rules for your classes.

Working with Types

As with every chapter, we start with setting up the sample application that will let you put the concepts in this chapter into practice. Of course, it's always our desire in this book to have you try out things that are practical and give you a feel for the real world, but that gets old fast. For this chapter you're going to do something different. You'll see that throughout this chapter there is a superhero theme, so it seems fitting to create a Web site that lets you offer feedback to your favorite superheroes. In this Web site superheroes will be able to register themselves as servants of humanity and describe their super powers. People will then come to the site when they are in need of superhero action, and can request a superhero to do a particular job. Then, people can rank the superhero in a scale of 1 to 5 as to how well he or she performed the task. What does this have to do with learning about types, you may ask? Well, there's a lot of database work in this Web site, and a number of database operations require you to do type comparisons and conversions. Other than that, it's just a lot of fun.

There's one more thing to discuss regarding the sample application for this chapter. To make the application fully functional, you have to add various pieces of code to four different forms—that's a little too much for this chapter. Rather, we're going to focus on making one of the forms functional. You can download the rest of the code from Peachpit's Web site. You'll find the download link in the Tips later in this section.

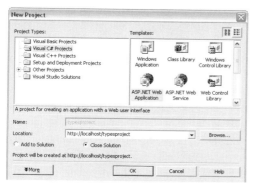

Figure 7.1 Here's the New Project dialog that you've grown to love.

Figure 7.2 The Properties window enables you to set the page's filename if you click on the page first in the Solution Explorer.

To create a test project for this chapter:

1. Launch Visual Studio .NET. (Start > All Programs > Microsoft Visual Studio .NET > Microsoft Visual Studio .NET).

2. Select File > New > Project to bring up the New Project dialog.

3. Under project types on the left side of the New Project window click the Visual C# projects folder.

4. Select the ASP.NET Web Application icon and change the name of the application to typesproject (**Figure 7.1**).

5. Visual Studio will create a new project and open WebForm1.aspx.

6. Change the form's name to mainmenu .aspx. Do so by choosing View > Solution Explorer from the top menu bar.

7. Right-click on WebForm1.aspx and choose properties. In the property grid below, change the FileName property from WebForm1.aspx to mainmenu.aspx (**Figure 7.2**).

continues on next page

8. Add four other forms to your project. Do so by selecting Project > Add Web Form. You'll see the dialog in **Figure 7.3**. Name the first register.aspx, the second helprequest.aspx, the third schedule.aspx and the fourth feedback.aspx.

9. Change the main menu form so that it looks like the form in **Figure 7.4**. Obviously this is a lot of work to do by hand. Instead you can enter the HTML directly into the editor. **Figure 7.5** on the next page shows the HTML necessary to create the form. To enter the HTML directly, click the HTML button under the editor's window. As an alternative you could download the skeleton file for this project (see Tips on the next page).

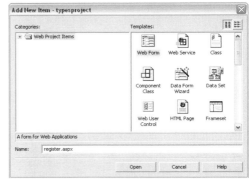

Figure 7.3 This project has five Web forms total. In the chapter you'll focus on getting the feedback.aspx form working.

Figure 7.4 The main form serves as the main menu for the application. It consists of a label and three links. The links are instances of the Hyperlink control.

Figure 7.5 Use the HTML in this figure as a reference in case you're trying to write the form from scratch.

```
[Code]                                    _ □ ×
<%@ Page language="c#"
Codebehind="mainmenu.aspx.cs"
        AutoEventWireup="false"
        Inherits="typesproject.WebForm1"
        enableViewState="False"
        enableViewStateMac="False"%>
<HTML>
   <HEAD>
      <title>WebForm1</title>
   </HEAD>
   <body MS_POSITIONING="GridLayout">
      <form id="Form1" method="post"
      runat="server">
         <asp:Label
            id="lblTitle"
            style="Z-INDEX: 101;
            LEFT: 20px;
            POSITION: absolute;
            TOP: 20px"
            runat="server"
            Font-Size="X-Large">
         Welcome to Superheroes for Hire!
         </asp:Label>
         <asp:HyperLink
            id="lnkRegister"
            style="Z-INDEX: 102;
            LEFT: 20px;
            POSITION: absolute;
            TOP: 76px"
            runat="server"
            NavigateUrl="register.aspx">
            Register
         </asp:HyperLink>
         <asp:HyperLink
            id="lnkFeedback"
            style="Z-INDEX: 103;
            LEFT: 20px;
            POSITION: absolute;
            TOP: 133px"
            runat="server"
            NavigateUrl="feedback.aspx">
            Feedback
         </asp:HyperLink>
         <asp:HyperLink
            id="HyperLink1"
            style="Z-INDEX: 104;
            LEFT: 20px;
            POSITION: absolute;
            TOP: 103px"
            runat="server"
         NavigateUrl="helprequest.aspx">
         I need help!!!
         </asp:HyperLink>
      </form>
   </body>
</HTML>
```

✔ Tips

■ In this chapter we'll focus on making the feedback form, feedback.aspx, fully functional.

■ Remember that like any other project in this book, building the project isn't necessary for learning the concepts in this chapter.

■ Skeletons for each project can be downloaded from Peachpit's Web site, http://www.peachpit.com/vqs/csharp.

Obtaining a Class's Type

You can obtain a class's type object in several ways. In this section you will learn the two most common ways. Once you have a class's type object you can use a feature called reflection to find out the type's methods, fields, constructors, etc. In Chapter 12, "Attributes," you'll learn how to use the Type object to retrieve information about the attributes in a class.

To obtain a Type object from an object:

If you already have an instance of the class in a variable then you can do the following:

◆ Type Type t1 = var.GetType(); where t1 is any variable to hold the reference to the Type object and var is the variable that holds a reference to the object from which you wish to obtain type information (**Figure 7.6**).

To obtain a Type object from a class (without creating an object):

◆ Type Type t1 = typeof(classname); where t1 is any variable to hold the reference to the Type object and classname is the name of the class (without quotation marks) from which you wish to obtain type information (**Figure 7.7**).

Figure 7.6 It's easy to get a Type object from an instance of a class. All you have to do is call the GetType method. All classes get this method from System.Object.

```
Code                                    _ □ ×
//given the following definition
class SuperheroMouse
{
    public void SaveSomeone
    {
    }
}

//use this code to get a type object
SuperheroMouse mightyMouse = new
SuperheroMouse();
Type t1 = mightyMouse.GetType();
```

Figure 7.7 Believe it or not, doing this is the same as executing the code in Figure 7.6. Whether you use an instance of the class or the typeof function with the class name, the result is the same Type object. The Type object simply describes the type itself.

```
Code                                    _ □ ×
//given the following definition
class SuperheroMouse
{
    public void SaveSomeone
    {
    }
}

//use this code to get a type object
Type t1 = typeof(SuperheroMouse);
```

Figure 7.8 I know there can only be one Mighty Mouse, but the above code creates an array of five SuperheroMouse elements. It illustrates a generic way of creating arrays: you feed the CreateInstance function the type of each element, and the number of elements, and it creates an array for you at runtime.

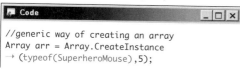

```
//generic way of creating an array
Array arr = Array.CreateInstance
↱ (typeof(SuperheroMouse),5);
```

Figure 7.9 At first glance you would think that calling obj.GetType() would return a Type object that describes the object data type. Actually, GetType always reports the type that was instantiated, not the type of the variable.

```
class Checking
{
}

object obj = new Checking();
Response.Write(obj.GetType().Name);

//outputs:
//Checking
```

✔ **Tips**

■ The first way to retrieve an object's Type object is by using a function in System.Object called GetType(). Every object derives from System.Object, so all objects have a GetType() function.

■ Why would you want to get an object's Type object? **Figure 7.8** shows you an example of using the Type object to create an array. A number of functions that can create objects dynamically at run-time require you to provide the type of object you wish to create using an instance of the Type class.

■ When you use the GetType() function, the function reports the type of the object the variable points to, not the type of the variable. For example, your code may read object obj = new Checking();. This code is legitimate because you can always assign a variable of the parent type to an instance of a derived type. If you were to call obj.GetType() and ask for the Name property you would notice that the type name reported is Checking and not object (**Figure 7.9**).

OBTAINING A CLASS'S TYPE

Testing for Type Compatibility

In the last section you learned how to retrieve an object's Type using either the GetType() function or the typeof construct. If you have two variables and you want to know if they point to the same type you could always get their Type objects and check their Name property. However, GetType() only reports the type of the object and not whether the object is compatible with another type. For example if a class called MotherInLaw is derived from ExtendedFamily, which is derived from Person, which is derived from System.Object then an object of MotherInLaw is compatible with variables of type MotherInLaw, ExtendedFamily, Person (yes, mothers-in-law are persons) and object. What's more, if a variable of type object points to an instance of MotherInLaw, just from looking at the variable it's impossible to tell whether a variable of type Person could point to the same object or not.

To test if an object is compatible with a type:

◆ Type if (var is classname) {} where var is the variable that points to the object you wish to test and classname is the name of the class you wish to compare the variable to (**Figure 7.10**).

✔ Tips

■ You don't have to have the test comparison in the context of an if statement (**Figure 7.11**).

■ Testing for compatibility is normally done before performing a conversion (also called a cast). Check out the section "Converting from One Type to Another (Casting)" for details.

Figure 7.10 The function AdviceFrequency takes any object of type Person as input. That means that you can pass to the function instances of Person, ExtendedFamily or MotherInLaw (since these classes derive from Person). The function then reports the AdviceFrequency based on the type of object that was passed in.

```
class Person
{
}

class ExtendedFamily : Person
{
}

class MotherInLaw : ExtendedFamily
{
}

class DecisionMaker
{
    static public int AdviceFrequency( Person p1)
    {
        if ( p1 is MotherInLaw)
            return 10;
        else if ( p1 is ExtendedFamily)
            return 5;
        else
            return 1;
    }
}
```

Figure 7.11 The is operator isn't limited to if statements. It simply returns true if the object the variable points to is compatible to a certain class, otherwise it returns false.

```
Person p1 = new MotherInLaw();
bool returnCall = p1 is MotherInLaw;
```

Figure 7.12 Even though mickey is of type EntrepreneurMouse, because the variable is of type Mouse, the only method the compiler lets you invoke is EatCheese.

```
Code                                      _ □ ×

class Mouse
{
    public void EatCheese()
    {
    }
}

class SuperheroMouse : Mouse
{
    public void DefeatEvildoers()
    {
    }
}

class EntrepreneurMouse : Mouse
{
    public void ChargeOutrageousPrices()
    {
    }
}

Mouse mickey = new EntrepreneurMouse();
//mickey.ChargeOutrageousPrices(); //***illegal
mickey.EatCheese();
```

Figure 7.13 When you cast (by putting a type name in parentheses in front of the variable) you're telling the compiler to treat the variable as the type in parenthesis. This makes it possible to call methods that are part of the class to which you are casting.

```
Code                                      _ □ ×

//see Figure 7.7 for details on the classes
Mouse mickey = new EntrepreneurMouse();
((EntrepeneurMouse)mickey).ChargeOutrageous
→ Prices();
mickey.EatCheese();
```

Converting From One Type to Another (Casting)

See, it's just a compiler thing . . . The C# compiler is *type safe*. You may have heard that phrase before when referring to other compilers, like the C++ or the Java compiler. To be type safe means that when you make a method call through a variable, the compiler only allows you to call methods that belong to the class of the type of the variable. If the variable is of type Mouse, then you can only call Mouse methods even if the object the variable points to is of type SuperheroMouse or EntrepreneurMouse. In **Figure 7.12** you see that even though the variable mickey points to an object of type EntrepreneurMouse, and EntrepreneurMouse has a method called ChargeOutrageousPrices, because the variable mickey is of type Mouse you can't call the method ChargeOutrageousPrices, you can only call methods that are part of the class Mouse. That's because, like I said at the beginning, it's a compiler thing. The compiler looks at the type of the variable and ensures that you only call methods that are part of the class of the type of the variable. If you wanted to call ChargeOutrageousPrices through mickey, you would have to cast mickey into EntrepreneurMouse first (**Figure 7.13**). Casting means you can turn one object into a different type as long as the object is compatible with that type. You learned how to test if an object is compatible with another in the previous section, "Testing for Type Compatibility." There are two ways to cast one type into another: one is using the explicit cast operator and one is using the as operator in C#.

To cast one type into another using explicit casts:

1. Declare a variable of the type you wish to convert to. For example: SuperheroMouse mightyMouse.

2. Type an equal sign =.

3. Type the name of the type you wish to convert to in parentheses. For example: (SuperheroMouse).

4. Type the name of the variable that contains the object you wish to convert (**Figure 7.14**).

To cast using the as operator:

1. Declare a variable of the type you wish to convert to. For example: Superhero mightyMouse.

2. Type an equal sign =.

3. Type var as Superhero, where var is the name of the variable that contains the object you wish to convert and Superhero is the type you are converting to (**Figure 7.15**).

✔ Tips

■ If the object you are converting isn't compatible with the type you are converting to—for example you are casting an object of type TwoYearOld into a QuietPerson type—and you use an explicit cast, the system will generate an exception (an error) at runtime. **Figure 7.16** shows you how to capture the error and **Figure 7.17** shows the exception you would get if you didn't capture the error.

Figure 7.14 You may be familiar with this type of cast if you have done some C++ programming.

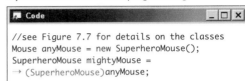

```
//see Figure 7.7 for details on the classes
Mouse anyMouse = new SuperheroMouse();
SuperheroMouse mightyMouse =
→ (SuperheroMouse)anyMouse;
```

Figure 7.15 This type of cast is new to C#. It's safer than doing the explicit cast in Figure 7.14 because if the cast fails you don't get an exception, rather the result of the cast would be null.

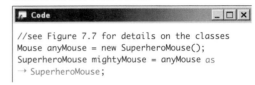

```
//see Figure 7.7 for details on the classes
Mouse anyMouse = new SuperheroMouse();
SuperheroMouse mightyMouse = anyMouse as
→ SuperheroMouse;
```

Figure 7.16 If you pay close attention to the sample code, you may notice that in the second line I use an object variable and then try to cast the object variable to QuietPerson. The reason I do that is because if I tried to cast from TwoYearOld directly to QuietPerson the compiler would stop me telling me that the conversion would fail.

```
TwoYearOld Tommy = new TwoYearOld();
object obj = Tommy;
try
{
    QuietPerson quiet = (QuietPerson)obj;
}
catch(InvalidCastException)
{
    Resonse.Write("Object is not a Quiet
Person");
}
```

Server Error in '/casterrorprep' Application.

Specified cast is not valid.

Description: An unhandled exception occurred during the execution of the current web request. Please review the stack trace for more information about the error and where it originated in the code.

Exception Details: System.InvalidCastException: Specified cast is not valid.

Figure 7.17 This is the error you would see if you fail to capture the error. The exception type is InvalidCastException. Figure 7.16 shows you how to capture the error with a try/catch block. You'll learn about try/catch blocks in Chapter 11.

Figure 7.18 The good thing about this technique is that the conversion only happens if the types are compatible; if they aren't compatible, the .NET Framework just returns a null.

```
TwoYearOld Tommy = new TwoYearOld();
object obj = Tommy;
QuietPerson quiet = obj as QuietPerson;

if (quiet == null)
{
    Response.Write(
    "Sorry, object doesn't point to a quiet
    ➞ person.");
}
```

Figure 7.19 With numeric types when there is no loss of data C# lets you do an implicit cast. However, when there is a potential loss of data, C# forces you to use an explicit cast.

```
//it's fine to go from an int to
//a float
int age = 55;
float exactAge = age;

//going back to an int from a float
//requires an explicit conversion
int normalAge = (int)exactAge;
```

Figure 7.20 The rule of thumb with classes is that you can always take a variable of a base type and assign it to an object of a derived type, but you can't go the other way without an explicit conversion.

```
class Person
{
}

class ExtendedFamily : Person
{
}

class MotherInLaw : ExtendedFamily
{
}

MotherInLaw law1 = new MotherInLaw();
ExtendedFamily ex1 = law1; //implicit conversion
//going back to a derived
//type requires an explicit conversion
MotherInLaw law2 = (MotherInLaw)ex1;
```

- It's best to first test if the type is compatible before attempting an explicit cast even if you're careful to trap the error because capturing exceptions is considered a performance costly operation (and the Microsoft police will beat you senseless).

- The advantage of using the second mechanism is that if the type isn't compatible with the type to which you are casting, the runtime returns a null. **Figure 7.18** shows you how to test for null to see if the cast succeeded.

- Some types can be converted to other types implicitly—the compiler knows how to convert between the types without you having to specify the type in parentheses. For example, a 32-bit integer (int) can be easily converted to a 64-bit integer (long) because there's no loss of information in the conversion. The rule of thumb is that you can do an implicit cast when the conversion doesn't result in loss of information. Thus, converting from a float to an integer would require an explicit cast, but converting from an integer to a float can be done implicitly (**Figure 7.19**). Along the same lines, converting from a derived object to a base type can be done implicitly, because the derived type contains all the fields and methods of the base. But converting from a base class to a derived requires an explicit conversion (**Figure 7.20**).

CONVERTING FROM ONE TYPE TO ANOTHER

Extending the Sample Application

Now that you have a taste for casting (and for working with superheroes), it's time to work on the feedback form for the sample application. Once again, you'll be working with data from a database. Therefore, before adding any code to the sample application, add a reference to the dbProvider.dll. Remember that dbProvider.dll is the DLL from eInfoDesigns that lets us talk to the MySQL database. You learned how to add a reference to this DLL in Chapter 4, "Strings."

To extend the sample application:

1. Right-click on the file feedback.aspx and select View Designer from the pop-up menu.

2. Create a form that looks like the form in **Figure 7. 21.** Optionally you could download the skeleton file for this project from Peachpit's Web site.

3. Double-click on a blank space in the form. This will cause VS.NET to open the code editor and add a Page_Load function.

4. Scroll up to the top of the file and under the last using statement add the following: using eInfoDesigns.dbProvider
   → .MySqlClient;

5. Right before the Page_Load function after all the variable declarations add the following declarations:

   protected System.Data.DataSet ds = new DataSet();
   protected const string ConnectionString = "server=localhost;
   → uid=;pwd=;database=csharpvqs;";

Figure 7.21 The job feedback form has a drop-down listbox at the top that lets you select the name of a superhero. The jobs for the superhero will be displayed in a textbox under the Select Job label, along with the ranking. A superhero may have more than one job, thus, you can scroll through the jobs for the superhero by using the < and > buttons. Once you find the job, you can change the ranking and click the Update button.

```
Code                              _ □ ×

private void Page_Load(object sender,
→ System.EventArgs e)
{
    if (IsPostBack == false)
    {
        string sql = "select * from superheroes";
        MySqlConnection conn = new
                    MySqlConnection
                        → (ConnectionString);
        conn.Open();
        MySqlCommand cmd = new MySqlCommand
        → (sql,conn);
        IDataReader reader = cmd.ExecuteReader();

        lstHeroes.DataSource = reader;
        lstHeroes.DataTextField = "Name";
        lstHeroes.DataBind();

        ViewState["index"]=0;
        SelectRecords();
    }
}
```

EXTENDING THE SAMPLE APPLICATION

Figure 7.22 One of the jobs of this code is to populate a drop-down listbox in the form that enables you to select a superhero and view all the jobs the superhero has done. Notice that the code begins with an if statement that asks if IsPostBack is false. The purpose of this statement is to execute the code only once—the very first time the form is loaded. Other events, like clicking buttons, or selecting a hero from the list will cause the Page_Load event to trigger again, but it's important we don't execute the same code again.

```
private void Page_Load(object sender,
System.EventArgs e)
{
    if (IsPostBack == false)
    {
        string sql =
        "select * from superheroes";
        MySqlConnection conn = new
        → MySqlConnection(ConnectionString);
        conn.Open();
        MySqlCommand cmd =
        new MySqlCommand(sql,conn);
        IDataReader reader =
        cmd.ExecuteReader();

        lstHeroes.DataSource = reader;
        lstHeroes.DataTextField = "Name";
        lstHeroes.DataBind();

        ViewState["index"]=0;
        SelectRecords();
    }
}
```

The first line declares a variable to store a Dataset. A Dataset is a class that stores records from a database in memory. It will help us maintain and display the information for the fields in this form. The second line declares a string variable to hold the connection string. You should already be familiar with connection strings from previous chapters.

6. Inside the Page_Load function add the code in **Figure 7.22**.

This code makes a connection to the csharpvqs database and reads the records in the superheroes table. Then it binds the heroes drop-down box to the result of the query so that the drop-down box lists the names of the heroes in the Superheroes table. The tricky part of this code is the use of ViewState. The ViewState object lets us send hidden information to the client, information that we can then retrieve each time they interact with the server. Think of ViewState as the equivalent of a cookie, if you're familiar with Web browser terminology. The difference is that ViewState doesn't require the browser to have cookie support turned on.

In this example we're using ViewState to persist an index. The reason we need that is that a superhero may have done several jobs, and each job can have its own ranking. When you select a superhero from the list, the feedback form lets you scroll through the jobs that the superhero has done and rank each one. The index number lets the application know what record is being displayed in the browser. Please note that ViewState information is only retained when we do a post back to the same page.

continues on next page

EXTENDING THE SAMPLE APPLICATION

7. After the `Page_Load` function add the `SelectRecords` function in **Figure 7.23**.

This code makes a connection to the database and runs a query that selects all the records in the herojobs table where the name of the hero is equal to the value selected in the drop-down listbox. This code also uses a class called Dataset. A full explanation of this class is way beyond the scope of this book; it's sufficient to know that the purpose of this class is to keep a copy of the records that were found in memory.

8. After the `SelectRecords` function, add the `RefreshJob` function in **Figure 7.24**.

This little function shows several situations in which casting is necessary. The purpose of this function is to display the description of the current job for the superhero and the current ranking. As I mentioned earlier, a superhero may have done a number of jobs. We keep track of the current job with the index variable that we store in ViewState. We retrieve the index from ViewState and it tells us what row in the Dataset the client is currently looking at.

Figure 7.23 The job of this function is to collect all records for jobs for the superhero selected. To fetch the records we use two classes: Dataset and DataAdapter. The DataAdapter reads the records from the database that match the criteria and saves the records it found in memory for our use in the Dataset. To find out more information about Datasets and DataAdapters consult the ADO.NET documentation in MSDN.

```
void SelectRecords()
{
    string name =
    lstHeroes.SelectedItem.Text;
    string sql = string.Format(
    "select * from herojobs where
name='{0}'",name);

    MySqlConnection conn = new
    MySqlConnection(ConnectionString);
    conn.Open();
    MySqlCommand cmd = new
    MySqlCommand(sql,conn);

    MySqlDataAdapter da = new
    MySqlDataAdapter();
    da.SelectCommand = cmd;
    da.Fill(ds);

    conn.Close();
    RefreshJob();
}
```

Figure 7.24 RefreshJob is a little function that refreshes the Job description textbox and the ranking textbox to display the currently selected record for a particular superhero.

```
void RefreshJob()
{
    int index = (int)ViewState["index"];
    System.Data.DataRow row =
    ds.Tables[0].Rows[index];
    txtJob.Text = (string)row["Job"];
    txtRanking.Text =
    (row["Ranking"] is DBNull) ? "0"
    : row["Ranking"].ToString() ;
}
```

Figure 7.25 This code triggers whenever the user selects a different superhero from the list of superheroes. The job of the code is to call `SelectRecords` again, which fetches records from the herojobs table for the selected hero.

```
private void
lstHeroes_SelectedIndexChanged(object sender,
                    System.EventArgs e)
{
   ViewState["index"]=0;
   SelectRecords();
}
```

Figure 7.26 The purpose of this code is to let the user navigate through the jobs that a superhero has done and view the description and the ranking. This code implements the next and previous button. The basic operation is to add one to the index or subtract one from the index and refresh the description and ranking textboxes.

```
private void btnNext_Click(object sender,
                    System.EventArgs e)
{
   SelectRecords();
   int index = (int)ViewState["index"];
   if (index == ds.Tables[0].Rows.Count-1)
      index = 0;
   else
      index ++;
   ViewState["index"] = index;
   RefreshJob();
}

private void btnPrevious_Click(object sender,
                    System.EventArgs e)
{
   SelectRecords();
   int index = (int)ViewState["index"];
   if (index == 0)
      index = ds.Tables[0].Rows.Count-1;
   else
      index --;
   ViewState["index"] = index;
   RefreshJob();
}
```

9. Return to the visual representation of the feedback form (right click on the file and choose View Designer from the pop-up menu). Then double-click on the hero selection drop-down listbox. This will cause the wizard to add a `SelectedIndexChanged` function to your code. Add the code in **Figure 7.25** inside this function.

This function is triggered whenever the user selects a different name from the hero listbox. The listbox control has its `AutoPostback` property set to true. This means that each time the user selects a name from the listbox, the client requests a new view of the page from the server. The server code runs the `SelectRecords` function, which reads the jobs that the selected superhero has done and resets the index value back to the first record.

10. Return to the visual designer and double-click on the < button. Repeat the process for the > button. This will cause the designer to add the skeleton for the `btnNext_Click` function and for the `btnPrevious_Click` function. Add the code in **Figure 7.26**.

The purpose of this code is to add one to the index when the > button is clicked, and to subtract one from the index when the < is clicked. Then the code calls `RefreshJob`, which refreshes the job textbox and the ranking textbox with the information for the current record.

continues on next page

11. Return to the visual designer and double-click the Update button. The wizard will add a skeleton for the `btnUpdate_Click` function. Add the code in **Figure 7.27** to this function.

The purpose of this code is to update the ranking for the particular job. All the code does is run an update query on the database that changes the ranking to whatever is in the ranking textbox.

✔ Tips

■ **Figure 7.24** has several type conversions of interest. The first one is casting the value stored in ViewState to an `int`. This is because everything in ViewState is returned as the generic data type `object`. Your job is to then cast to the appropriate type. The same thing happens when reading data from a row in the Dataset. Reading the job field in the line that reads `(string)row["Job"]` returns a generic object that you need to cast to a string in order to set the text for the job textbox.

■ **Figure 7.24** also shows an example of using the `is` operator for a type comparison. The last line uses it when comparing to the type `DBNull`. The reason we do this comparison is that sometimes a field in the database may not have a value. It's not zero, or an empty string, it's simply `null`; a value has not been saved yet. In these cases when you read the data, the .NET database layer actually creates an instance of the class `DBNull` and returns this object to you. You then have to see if the object returned from the database is of type `DBNull` before you attempt to use it.

Figure 7.27 This code updates the ranking in the database for a particular job. It runs what is called an update query. The update query takes as input the value the user entered in the ranking textbox, then uses the name of the superhero and the job the client is viewing to select the appropriate record and update it.

```
private void btnUpdate_Click(object sender,
                        System.EventArgs e)
{
    string name = lstHeroes.SelectedItem.Text;
    string job = txtJob.Text;
    string ranking = txtRanking.Text;
    string sql = string.Format(@"update herojobs
    → set ranking = {0} where name='{1}' and
    → job = '{2}'",
                        ranking,
                        name,
                        job);

    MySqlConnection conn = new
MySqlConnection(ConnectionString);
    conn.Open();
    MySqlCommand cmd = new
MySqlCommand(sql,conn);
    cmd.ExecuteNonQuery();
    conn.Close();
}
```

Defining Casting Rules (Cast Operator Overloading)

One of the most powerful features in C# is its ability to define *casting rules*. For example, you can define that your object is compatible with a type that isn't in the class's hierarchy. In the case of the SuperheroMouse class you could say that SuperheroMouse objects can be converted to EntrepreneurMouse types. Defining casting rules is done by adding a cast operator.

Cast operators come in two flavors: *explicit* cast operators and *implicit* cast operators. Choosing between them is just a matter of style. Remember that when an implicit cast is possible you can just make a variable of one type equal to a variable of a different type and the compiler takes care of the conversion. If you implement implicit cast operators, this means less typing for the users of the class but the potential for more confusion. With explicit casts the compiler allows the conversion only if the programmer does an explicit case; this means more typing but less confusion. This is known as the Law of Inverse Productivity: the less typing you do, the more confused your readers are. (I just made that up, in case you're wondering.)

To define an explicit cast operator:

1. Inside a class type `public static`.

2. Type `explicit operator`, or `implicit operator`.

3. Type the name of the type you wish to convert to. For example: `EntrepreneurMouse`.

4. Type an open parenthesis `(`.

5. Type the name of your class. For example: `SuperheroMouse`.

6. Type the name of a variable as input parameter. For example: `source`.

7. Type a close parenthesis `)`.

8. Type an open curly bracket `{`.

9. Type the statements that process the conversion and return the value of the output type.

10. Type a close curly bracket `}` (**Figure 7.28**).

Figure 7.28 Notice that the only thing SuperheroMouse and EntrepreneurMouse have in common is they are both derived from Mouse. Without the cast operator function that is highlighted, an explicit cast would be illegal.

```
class Mouse
{
    public string Name;

    public void EatCheese()
    {
    }
}

class EntrepreneurMouse : Mouse
{
    public void ChargeOutrageousPrices()
    {
    }
}

class SuperheroMouse : Mouse
{
    public void DefeatEvildoers()
    {
    }

    public static explicit operator
    EntrepreneurMouse(SuperheroMouse
    source)
    {
        EntrepeneurMouse dest =
        new EntrepreneurMouse();
        dest.Name = source.Name;
        return dest;
    }
}
```

Figure 7.29 The only way to use the explicit cast operator is to do an explicit cast. Incidentally, C# doesn't use the explicit cast operator you define if you try to cast using the *as* operator.

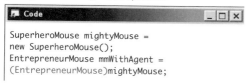

```
SuperheroMouse mightyMouse =
new SuperheroMouse();
EntrepreneurMouse mmWithAgent =
(EntrepreneurMouse)mightyMouse;
```

Figure 7.30 The difference between this code example and the previous one is that in the previous example we're defining a conversion from our type to EntrepreneurMouse. In this example we are defining a conversion from EntrepreneurMouse to SuperheroMouse. You can also choose to combine both functions.

```
class SuperheroMouse : Mouse
{

    public void DefeatEvildoers()
    {
    }

    public static explicit operator
    SuperheroMouse(EntrepreneurMouse source)
    {
        SuperheroMouse dest = new SuperheroMouse();
        dest.Name = source.Name;
        return dest;
    }
}
```

✔ Tips

■ Once you add an explicit operator to your class a developer can convert from the original type to the type specified in the operator as shown in **Figure 7.29**.

■ You can also define explicit operators that can convert from other types into the type of your class (**Figure 7.30**).

8

INTERFACES

Interfaces are types that enable you to define multiple classes that have similar functionality. Let's suppose you had a class named Escort. The Escort class has methods like Run, Stop, PlayMusic, etc. You're happy with the Escort class because it enables you to come to and from work. At some point, however, your friends begin to make fun of your Escort class, and you would like to replace the Escort class with the Ferrari class. Before you replace the Escort class with the Ferrari class, you want to make sure that the Ferrari class at least has the same functionality as the Escort class. It should Run, Stop, and PlayMusic. It may do all those things differently than the Escort class, but the point is that it at least has to have the same methods. The combination of the methods is the interface. The interface may be called ICar for example. All cars have to implement the methods of the ICar interface in order to be considered cars (in my opinion).

Our world is based on the principle of interfaces. People, for example, implement similar interfaces. A lot of us breathe and eat. (If you don't agree, please stop reading this book immediately.) Every instance of the human class may have a different way of breathing and eating, but companies like McDonald's rely on the IHuman interface having an Eat method in order to succeed.

In C# terms, interfaces are types. They're different from interface definitions in C++ for example in that they're not specialized classes; they're actually a separate type altogether. In its basic definition, an interface is a set of function definitions (just the definition without any implementation code). By themselves these functions do nothing. They're like having an IHuman interface without an instance of a human—it's just a concept and not the actual implementation. The interface must be implemented in a class to be useful. When a class implements an interface it advertises to the world that it supports all the methods defined in the interface. If a used-car salesman tells you that his cars implement the ICar interface, then he is saying that they at least Run, Stop, and PlayMusic. If they don't implement one of the methods of the interface, then the C# compiler would stop them.

With interfaces a developer can write code to use the interface rather than the implementation of the interface. This enables starting with one implementation, then substituting it at a later time without rewriting all the code. This is true for the ICar interface, for example. Drivers don't learn how to drive just one car; they learn to drive all cars because cars all follow the same basic interface.

For a real-world application, consider a technology like ADO.NET. ADO.NET enables you to connect to a database. Microsoft, believe it or not, doesn't want to force you into a single database product. Rather than making everyone use one set of classes, they define an interface of functions for connecting to the database. Database vendors then write classes that implement those interfaces. The idea is that if you code using the interfaces, then you can change what database package you use without having to rewrite your application.

Working with Interfaces

For the sample application in this chapter you're going to work on writing an ASP.NET module. It's not going to be very elaborate, but it's going to be fun, and it's going to be true to real-world applications (no super-hero applications for this chapter).

So what's an ASP.NET module? A module is a class that can intercept requests for any page in the application. Modules are used to do things like security checks. They can intercept every request and either stop the request, let the request continue, or change the request in some way. They can also optionally do something after the request page has had a chance to respond. If you've done a lot of Web programming, a module is the .NET equivalent of an IIS filter.

The ultimate goal of the module you're building is to provide each page with the dimensions of the browser's client area. The client area in the browser is the area where the Web page is displayed. (It's the inside of the browser, minus the menu bar or status bar.) It's interesting that .NET does not report these dimensions through any property. However, it's possible to obtain these measurements through client-side scripts (VBScript or JavaScript that runs on the client's machine and not on the server like ASP pages). And why do we care about these measurements, you may ask? Well, we care because sometimes it's useful to draw the page with smaller graphics if the browser window is small, and use larger graphics if the browser window is large.

To solve this problem the first time the client requests a page, the module is going to stop the request and return a page with client-side script that finds out the dimensions of the client area. The script records the dimensions in a hidden field and then immediately asks for the same page that the client first requested. The sending of the client-side script and the returning to the original page requested should happen quickly enough that it will end up being invisible. The second time the module gets a request for the same page (this time because of the client-side script requesting it), the module will detect the hidden field with the dimensions, and it will create a little object to hold the information and pass it to the page that was requested. The page can then grab the object with the information and return output to the client that takes advantage of knowing the client area's size. Our output page will just display the dimensions in text boxes.

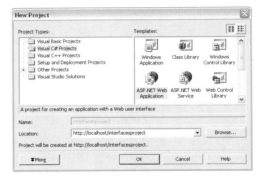

Figure 8.1 To create a custom module we only need a library project and not a full ASP.NET Web project. However, creating an ASP.NET Web project gives us the chance to write and test the module all in one project.

To write a custom module:

1. Launch Visual Studio .NET. (Start > All Programs > Microsoft Visual Studio .NET > Microsoft Visual Studio .NET).

2. Select File > New > Project to bring up the New Project dialog.

3. Under Project Types on the left side of the New Project window click the Visual C# projects folder.

4. Select the ASP.NET Web Application icon and change the name of the application to interfacesproject (**Figure 8.1**).

5. Visual Studio will create a new project and open WebForm1.aspx.

6. Change the form's name to dimensions .aspx. Do so by choosing View > Solution Explorer from the top menu bar.

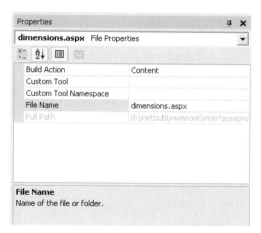

Figure 8.2 Changing the filename is probably old news by now.

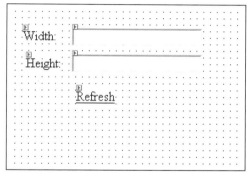

Figure 8.3 This is an easy form to recreate from scratch. It's basically two label controls, two text-boxes, and one link control.

7. Right-click on dimensions.aspx and choose Properties. In the property grid below, change the FileName property from WebForm1.aspx to dimensions.aspx (**Figure 8.2**).

8. Change the dimensions.aspx form so that it looks like the form in **Figure 8.3**. Obviously this is a lot of work to do by hand. Instead you can enter the HTML directly into the editor. **Figure 8.4** (on next page) shows the HTML necessary to create the form. To enter the HTML directly, click the HTML button under the editor's window. As an alternative you could download the skeleton file for this project (see Tips on the next page).

continues on next page

✔ Tips

- Nothing in the sample so far has to do with a custom module. The form that you are designing in this section will be used to test the module. You'll add the code for the module as soon as you learn a little about implementing interfaces.

- As with any other project in this book, building the project isn't necessary for learning the concepts in this chapter.

- Skeletons for each project can be downloaded from Peachpit's Web site, http://www.peachpit.com/vqs/csharp.

Figure 8.4 Having the HTML is good for reference purposes. With it you can see the dimension and position of each of the controls.

```
Code                                       _ □ ×

<%@ Page language="c#"
   Codebehind="dimensions.aspx.cs"
   AutoEventWireup="false"
   Inherits="interfacesproject.WebForm1" %>
<HTML>
   <HEAD>
      <title>WebForm1</title>
   </HEAD>
   <body MS_POSITIONING="GridLayout">
   <form id="Form1" method="post"
   runat="server">
   <asp:label id="lblWidth"
      style="Z-INDEX: 101; LEFT: 25px;
      POSITION: absolute; TOP: 37px"
      runat="server">
      Width:
   </asp:label>
   <asp:label id="lblHeight"
      style="Z-INDEX: 102; LEFT: 29px;
      POSITION: absolute; TOP: 70px"
      runat="server">
      Height:
   </asp:label>
   <asp:textbox id="txtWidth"
      style="Z-INDEX: 103; LEFT: 84px;
      POSITION: absolute; TOP: 36px"
      runat="server">
   </asp:textbox>
   <asp:textbox id="txtHeight"
      style="Z-INDEX: 104; LEFT: 84px;
      POSITION: absolute; TOP: 68px"
      runat="server">
   </asp:textbox>
   <asp:hyperlink id="lnkSelf"
      style="Z-INDEX: 105; LEFT: 89px;
      POSITION: absolute; TOP: 110px"
      runat="server"
      NavigateUrl="dimensions.aspx">
      Refresh
   </asp:hyperlink>
   </form>
   </body>
</HTML>
```

Table 8.1

Interface Members (Members that Can Be Added to an Interface Definition)	
NAME	EXAMPLE
Method	string Method();
Property	int Age { get; set; }
Readonly Property	int Age { get; }
Indexer	long this[int index] {get; set;}
Event	event EventHandler OnClick;

Figure 8.5 The members of an interface are only definitions, with no code inside of them. Also, they don't have an access modifier in front; all the methods in the interface are public.

```
Code                                    _ □ ×

public interface IHuman
{
    string Name { get; } //readonly property
    void Eat(int Amount); //method
    void Breathe();  //method
}
```

Defining Interfaces

Interfaces are defined with the interface keyword. Interfaces can have methods, properties, delegates, events, etc. However, each element contained in an interface must be the declaration of the element without any implementation.

To define an interface:

1. Type public or internal depending on the scope you wish to give your interface.

2. Type interface followed by a space.

3. Type any name for the interface.

4. Type {.

5. Add the definitions for valid members (**Table 8.1**).

6. Type } (**Figure 8.5**).

✔ Tips

- All interface methods are public by definition; you can't add an access modifier to the definition of the method (not even public).

- Interface types can be used in the definition of parameters or variables (**Figure 8.6**). However, interfaces are not creatable types—you can't write new IAccount, for example.

- Interfaces support method overloading (**Figure 8.7**).

- Once other developers are using the interface, it's best not to change the interface definition; otherwise you risk having their programs stop working. Instead you should add a new interface definition, as you will see later in the section "Deriving One Interface from Another."

Figure 8.6 Once you define the interface you can use it as a data type either for variable declarations or parameter declarations.

```
class DailyRoutine
{
    void Tasks()
    {
        IHuman man;
        IHuman woman;
    }

    public void GoToDinner(IHuman person)
    {
        person->Eat();
    }
}
```

Figure 8.7 Method overloading is the ability to have multiple methods with the same name. Remember that this can only be done if you change the number of parameters or change the type of one of the parameters.

```
public interface IHuman
{
    string Name { get; }
    //readonly property
    void Eat(int Amount); //method
    void Eat(string foodType, int Amount);
    //overloading
}
```

Figure 8.8 Implementing interfaces is a lot like inheriting from a class. With the implicit method all you have to do is implement the members of the interface as public methods.

```
public interface IHuman
{
    string Name { get; }
    void Sleep(short hours);
}

public class Person : IHuman
{
    public string Name
    {
        get
        {
            return "Paul";
        }
    }

    public void Sleep(short hours)
    {
        for (short counter=0;
        counter < hours; counter++)
        {
            HttpContext context =
            HttpContext.Current;
            context.Response.Write("Snore!");
        }
    }
}
```

Implementing Interface Members Implicitly

Classes implement interfaces. To implement an interface means to provide code for each one of the methods defined in the interface. The compiler forces you to add code for every single method in the interface. This is because a developer using the interface expects that the class that implements the interface will have every method in the interface defined. There are two mechanisms for implementing interfaces in a class: an implicit mechanism and an explicit mechanism. I will show you the implicit way first.

To implement an interface implicitly:

1. After the name of the class that will implement the interface type a colon followed by the name of the interface you wish to implement.

2. Add a member for each member in the interface.

3. Mark the implementation method public.

4. Provide code for the member (**Figure 8.8**).

✔ Tips

- This mechanism of implementing the interface has the side effect that every implementation function must be marked public.

- If you wish to implement more than one interface, separate each interface name with a comma (**Figure 8.9**).

Figure 8.9 The Person implements both IHuman and IManager. Implementing the interface establishes an "is a" relationship. In other words, this Person is a Human, and a Manager.

```
public interface IHuman
{
   string Name { get; }
   void Sleep(short hours);
}

public interface IManager
{
   void SpyOnEmployee(string name,
   bool IsUnaware);
}

public class Person : IHuman, IManager
{
   public string Name
   {
      get
      {
         return "Paul";
      }
   }

   public void Sleep(short hours)
   {
      for (short counter=0;
      counter < hours; counter++)
      {
        HttpContext context =
        HttpContext.Current;
       context.Response.Write("Snore!");
      }
   }

   public void SpyOnEmployee(string name,
   bool IsUnaware)
   {
      while (IsUnaware)
      {
         LookOverShoulder(name);
      }
   }
}
```

Figure 8.10 This code defines a class called Person that implements IHuman. Then, since not every person is a manager, it defines a second class just for Managers. However, since all Managers are Persons it inherits all of its functionality from Person (code inheritance) then implements the IManager interface.

```
public interface IHuman
{
   string Name { get; }
   void Sleep(short hours);
}

public interface IManager
{
   void SpyOnEmployee(string name,
   bool IsUnaware);
}

public class Person : IHuman
{
   public string Name
   {
      get
      {
         return "Paul";
      }
   }

   public void Sleep(short hours)
   {
      for (short counter=0;
      counter < hours; counter++)
      {
         HttpContext context =
         HttpContext.Current;
         context.Response.Write("Snore!");
      }
   }
}

public class Manager : Person, IManager
{
   public void SpyOnEmployee(string name,
   bool IsUnaware)
   {
      while (IsUnaware)
      {
         LookOverShoulder(name);
      }
   }
}
```

■ If your class derives from another class (not an interface) you list the non-interface class first, and then the interfaces you are implementing, all separated by commas (**Figure 8.10**).

Implementing Interface Members Explicitly

The problem with simply adding public members to implement the interface is that sometimes two interfaces have the same method name and same parameters, but the methods need to have a different implementation. If you use the implicit method, then the one public method would implement every interface method with the same name and parameters. The explicit method lets you tell the compiler which method in which interface you meant to implement.

To implement an interface explicitly:

1. After the name of the class that will implement the interface type a colon followed by the name of the interface you wish to implement.

2. Type the return type of the interface member.

3. Type `INameOfInterface.InterfaceMethod`. In other words, type the name of the interface followed by a period followed by the name of the interface method.

4. Type the parameters for the member.

5. Write the code for the member (**Figure 8.11**).

✔ Tip

■ All methods that you implement in this fashion are private. You can't add an access modifier in front of the definition.

Figure 8.11 When implementing interfaces explicitly you don't add any access modifiers, then you write the name of the interface followed by a period followed by the method name.

```
public interface IHuman
{
    string Name { get; }
    void Sleep(short hours);
}

public class Person : IHuman
{
    string IHuman.Name
    {
        get
        {
            return "Paul";
        }
    }

    void IHuman.Sleep(short hours)
    {
        for (short counter=0;
        counter < hours; counter++)
        {
            HttpContext context =
            HttpContext.Current;
            context.Response.Write("Snore!");
        }
    }
}
```

Enhancing the Sample Application

Now that you know how to define interfaces and how to implement the interfaces in a class, it's time to enhance the sample application. More specifically, you're going to add the class that serves as the custom module. To turn a class into a module the class has to implement the System.Web.IHttpModule interface. It's not very difficult to implement the interface—it only has two methods: Init and Dispose. ASP.NET calls the Init method the very first time the module gets loaded into memory. It calls Dispose when the module is unloaded. The only hard part is that you'll have to use an *event*, and events are not discussed until Chapter 10, "Delegates and Events."

We're not going to spend too much time discussing what an event is in this chapter but for now it's enough to know that an event is a method that gets triggered as a result of an action. In many ways implementing an event is like implementing an interface except that an interface can have many methods where an event has only one method. An example of an event is the `click` event of a button. Your class can request to get a click event notification from a button on a form. When the user clicks the button the server lets your class know that the event has occurred. Modules can request to listen to the `BeginRequest` event, among others. ASP.NET triggers this event in your module whenever the client's browser requests a page.

To add a custom module class:

1. Select Project > Add class from the menu bar. Type custommodule.cs for the class name and press Enter (**Figure 8.12**).

2. At the top of the code module below the line that reads using System; type using System.Web;.

3. On the line that reads public class custommodule add : IHttpModule at the end so that it reads:
   public class custommodule : IHttpModule.

4. Now it's time to cheat a little. In Visual Studio .NET there's a wizard that lets you implement an interface easily. Select View > Class View from the menu bar.

5. On the Class View window expand interfacesproject > interfacesproject > custommodule > Bases and Interfaces. Then right-click on IHttpModule and select Add > Implement Interface from the popup menu (**Figure 8.13**).

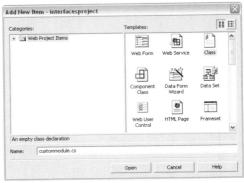

Figure 8.12 All the functionality for the custom module will go in the custommodule class. Use this dialog to have the wizard generate a skeleton for the class.

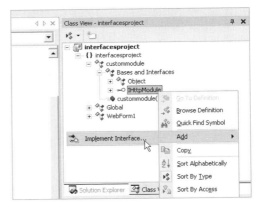

Figure 8.13 The implement interface wizard uses the implicit implementation mechanism; it adds public members for each of the members in the interface.

Figure 8.15 BeginRequest isn't part of the IHttpModule interface. It's an event in the HttpApplication class that tells you any time there's a request to any of the pages in your application.

```
Code                              _ □ ×

using System;
using System.Web;

namespace interfacesproject
{
    /// <summary>
    /// Summary description for custommodule.
    /// </summary>
    public class custommodule : IHttpModule
    {
        public custommodule()
        {
            //
            // TODO: Add constructor logic here
            //
        }

        #region Implementation of IHttpModule
        public void Init(System.Web.
        → HttpApplication context)
        {
        }

        public void Dispose()
        {
        }
        #endregion

        void BeginRequest(object sender,
        → EventArgs args)
        {
        }
    }
}
```

6. The wizard adds the method stubs for the Init and Dispose methods. Your code should look like the code in **Figure 8.14**.

7. Add a method to the class called BeginRequest (**Figure 8.15**).

continues on next page

Figure 8.14 The IHttpModule interface serves two purposes. One, it tells the ASP.NET framework that the class is in fact a custom module. Two, it gives the framework a way to tell the class when it is first loaded (Init method) and when it's no longer needed (Dispose method).

```
Code                              _ □ ×

using System;
using System.Web;

namespace interfacesproject
{
    /// <summary>
    /// Summary description for custommodule.
    /// </summary>
    public class custommodule : IHttpModule
    {
        public custommodule()
        {
            //
            // TODO: Add constructor logic here
            //
        }

        #region Implementation of IHttpModule
        public void Init(System.Web.
        → HttpApplication context)
        {
        }

        public void Dispose()
        {
        }
        #endregion
    }
}
```

ENHANCING THE SAMPLE APPLICATION

241

8. In the Init method add the code to connect the BeginRequest event to the BeginRequest method in your class (**Figure 8.16**). Don't worry about understanding this code right now; it will be explained in Chapter 10, "Delegates and Events."

Figure 8.16 Notice that to connect an event in a class to a method in your class you refer to the event as if it were a property of the object (object.eventname) then use the += operator and assign it a new object (a delegate) and pass your function as a parameter for the constructor of the object.

```
Code                                        _ □ ×

using System;
using System.Web;

namespace interfacesproject
{
  //<summary>
  //Summary description for custommodule.
  //</summary>
   public class custommodule :
   IHttpModule
   {
      public custommodule()
      {
      //
      //TODO: Add constructor logic here
      //
      }

      #region Implementation of IHttpModule
      public void
Init(System.Web.HttpApplication context)
      {
         context.BeginRequest +=
         new EventHandler(BeginRequest);
      }

      public void Dispose()
      {
      }
      #endregion

      void BeginRequest(object sender,
      EventArgs args)
      {
      }
   }
}
```

Figure 8.17 Ah, the beauty of literal strings. Notice that it's really easy to place carriage returns in a string using literal strings. You basically format the string as you want it, carriage returns and all.

```
Code                                    _ □ ×

public void Init(System.Web.HttpApplication
context)
{
    context.BeginRequest += new
EventHandler(BeginRequest);
    string html = @"
    <html>
    Loading...
    <script language=vbscript>
    Sub GetDimensions()
        Dim clientWidth
        Dim clientHeight

        clientWidth = document.body.ClientWidth
        clientHeight = document.body.ClientHeight
        document.myform.txtDimensions.Value =
        → clientWidth & "";""  & clientHeight &
        → "";""
        document.myform.submit
    End Sub
    </script>
    <body onLoad=""GetDimensions"">
    <form name=""myform"" method=""POST""
    → action=""{0}"">
    <p><input type=""hidden"" name=""txtDimensions""
    size=""20""></p>
    </form>
    </body>
    </html>";
    context.Application["__DiscoverHTML"] = html;
}
```

9. Add code to the Init method to build a string with the client-side script and save it in the Application object. Remember that the Application object is accessible to all the pages and to every client (**Figure 8.17**).

continues on next page

10. Now add the code in **Figure 8.18** to the BeginRequest method. The purpose of this code is to detect if dimension information is available. This information would be available through a hidden field. If the textbox doesn't exist, the module blocks the request to the page and sends back the client-side script. The script records the dimensions in a hidden field and immediately requests the page again. The module then sees that the textbox exists and adds the dimensions to the Item object (see sidebar on the next page for more information).

✔ Tips

■ The code in this section is all the code you need to have a custom module. However, the module does not take effect until you finish the example later in this chapter.

■ The wizard that implements interfaces adds `#region Implementation of IHttpModule` at the beginning of the implementation methods and `#endregion` at the end. These statements don't affect the compiler directly; they just provide a way for you to have a collapsible code region in the editor. If you notice in the editor you will see a minus sign to the left of the region declaration (**Figure 8.19**); if you click the minus sign then the editor will hide the code within the region, and turn the minus to a plus (**Figure 8.20**). Clicking the plus makes the code reappear.

Figure 8.18 There's a lot of code here that needs explanation. Refer to the "Walkthrough of BeginRequest Event" sidebar for details.

```
void BeginRequest(object sender,
EventArgs args)
{
    Global g = (Global)sender;
    string dimensions =
    g.Request.Form["txtDimensions"];
    if (dimensions == null ||
    dimensions == "" )
    {
        string html =
(string)g.Context.Application["__DiscoverHTML"];
        string newUrl = string.Format(html,
        g.Request.Url.AbsolutePath);
        g.Response.Write(newUrl);
        g.CompleteRequest();
    }
    else if
    (dimensions.IndexOf("ClientWidth")
    == -1)
    {
        string[] sizes =
        dimensions.Split(';');
        int clientWidth =
        System.Convert.ToInt32(sizes[0]);
        int clientHeight =
        System.Convert.ToInt32(sizes[1]);
        g.Context.Items["__ClientWidth"] =
        clientWidth;
        g.Context.Items["__ClientHeight"] =
        clientHeight;
    }
}
```

```
#region Implementation of IHttpModule
public void Init(System.Web.HttpApplication context)
{
    context.BeginRequest += new EventHandler(BeginRequest);
    string html = @"
    <html>
    Loading...
```

Figure 8.19 The #region statement adds a region of collapsible code. When the editor detects the #region directive it adds a minus sign on the left edge of the code window.

```
Implementation of IHttpModule
```

Figure 8.20 Clicking the minus collapses the code within the region and displays the description after the word #region so that you can identify the code. The #region doesn't add any functionality to the code, it's just for the editor, and you can delete it if you don't like it.

Walkthrough of BeginRequest Event

If you look at the first line in the BeginRequest function there is a cast of the sender object (the function's first parameter) into a Global object. Global is a class that the wizard generates when you create an ASP.NET project. It's derived from HttpApplication. This class gets created the first time any client accesses any page in your application. From the Global object you can access other objects like the Response and Request object.

If you look at the second line of code, you'll see that we use the Global object to get the Request object. As you may remember, Request lets you access information about the client's request. If you use the Form property, you can access the hidden field that gets created in the client-side script. The name of the hidden field is txtDimensions.

The line g.Request.Form["txtDimensions"] retrieves the text of the hidden field. If the field doesn't exist then the result will be null. If it does then the result will be the coordinates of the client area. The client-side script saves the coordinates as width;height; (800;600; for example). If the result is null then the code uses Response.Write to send the client-side script to the client. Then the code calls CompleteRequest which stops the client's request from going all the way to the page that was requested. If we didn't do this, our client-side script would be combined with the output from the page. If the dimensions are available, we split the string in the format width;height; into two values and convert to integers. Then we place the values in the Items object.

We haven't used the Items object before, but it's a lot like the Session object and the Application object. Basically it's another way to persist information; the difference is that the information is only available for the duration of one client request. With the Application object information is saved for as long as the Web server is running your application and it's accessible to any client using the application. Session information is persisted also for the duration of the program, but the information in Session is specific to each client. The Items object only lasts for one request. So if the client navigates from one page to another, the information is lost. However, within the same request, our module can put information in Items and then our page can retrieve it. You reach the Items object through g.Context.Items.

Using Objects through Interfaces

Once a developer defines an interface and implements the interface in a concrete class, a developer using the class can use the class through the interface.

To use a class through an interface:

1. Define a variable of the type of interface. Type ICar var, for example.

2. Set the interface variable equal to an instance of a class that implements the interface. Type = new Escort(); for example (**Figure 8.21**).

✔ Tip

■ You can't create instances of an interface. An interface is an abstract type, which means that it is not a creatable class. Instead you create instances of a class that implements the interface.

Figure 8:21 Although the variable's type is ICar you can't say new ICar. You have to create an instance of a class that implements the interface. Interfaces are not creatable types.

```
interface ICar
{
    string Run();
    string Stop();
    string PlayMusic();
}

class Escort : ICar
{
    public string Run()
    {
        return "I'm running as fast as I can!";
    }
    public string Stop()
    {
        return "Oh good, I finally get to stop";
    }
    public string PlayMusic()
    {
        return "We are the pirates who don't do
        → anything...";
    }
}

class Driver
{
    public string GoToWork()
    {
        ICar car = new Escort();
        string msg = "";
        msg+= car.Run();
        msg+= car.PlayMusic();
        msg+= car.Stop();
        return msg;
    }
}
```

Figure 8.22 The variable obj is of type object. That means that it can point to a Cat object or a Dog object. The code tests to see what obj contains by checking if it supports the IDog interface.

```
Code                                    _ □ ×

interface ICat
{
    string IgnoreOwner();
}

interface IDog
{
    string ListenToOwner();
}

class Poodle : IDog
{
}

class Siamese : ICat
{
}

class Owner
{
    void FeedAnimal(object obj)
    {
        if (obj is IDog)
        {
            IDog dog = (IDog)obj;
            string cmd = dog.ListenToOwner();
        }
    }
}
```

Interface Discovery

Before you attempt to use an object through an interface it's best to discover if the object in fact supports the interface. Obviously if you have the definition of the class, it's easy to look at it and see if the class implements the interface. However, sometimes you may be dealing with the `object` data type and you may want to see if the object the variable points to is compatible with the interface you want to use. There are two ways of finding out if an object supports the interface.

To discover if an object supports the interface:

1. Type `if (obj is IAnything)` where `obj` is the variable that points to the object you wish to test, and `IAnything` is the name of the interface for which you wish to test (**Figure 8.22**).

   or

   Type `IAnything var = obj as IAnything`, where `IAnything` is the interface you wish to test for, `var` is any variable to hold a reference to the object, and `obj` is the object you wish to test.

continues on next page

INTERFACE DISCOVERY

2. Type if (var != null). If after performing step one, var is equal to null then the object does not support the interface. If it returns a non null value then the object supports the interface and var now points to an interface reference (**Figure 8.23**).

✔ Tips

■ With the first mechanism, if you discover that the object in fact supports the interface, to use the object through the interface you have to declare a variable of the type of interface and cast the object to the interface.

■ With the second mechanism of discovery, both the casting of the object and the discovery are done in one step. If the object supports the interface, the var variable will point to the object, if it doesn't support the interface, the var variable will have the value of null.

■ There is a third mechanism for discovering if an object supports an interface. You could attempt to cast the object to the interface. If the object doesn't support the interface, the casting will generate an exception (an error). Exceptions will be discussed in Chapter 11, "Error Handling." Counting on an exception as a way of discovering if the object supports the interface is discouraged because exceptions have the potential of affecting program performance.

Figure 8.23 With the as command if the object does not have support for the interface the result is null.

```
interface ICat
{
    string IgnoreOwner();
}

interface IDog
{
    string ListenToOwner();
}

class Poodle : IDog
{
}

class Siamese : ICat
{
}

class Owner
{
    void FeedAnimal(object obj)
    {
        IDog dog = obj as IDog;
        if (dog != null)
            string cmd = dog.ListenToOwner();
    }
}
```

Figure 8.24 Notice that the type for the parameter in the Communicate function is type IHuman. You can pass any object to the function that implements the interface. All three classes implement the interface in different ways. The Communicate method will return a different string depending on what object you pass in.

```
interface IHuman
{
    string Speak();
}

class Baby : IHuman
{
    public string Speak()
    {
        return "Goo-goo gaa-gaa";
    }
}

class Spouse : IHuman
{
    public string Speak()
    {
        return "Can I buy a new computer?";
    }
}

class Friend : IHuman
{
    public string Speak()
    {
        return "Can I borrow some money?";
    }
}


class Person
{
    string Communicate(IHuman person)
    {
        return person.Speak();
    }

    void DailyLiving()
    {
        string answer;

        Spouse sp = new Spouse();
        answer = Communicate(sp);
        Friend fr = new Friend();
        answer = Communicate(fr);
        Baby ba = new Baby();
        answer = Communicate(ba);
    }
}
```

Using Interfaces for Polymorphism

Polymorphism is the idea that two related classes can have slightly different implementations for the same method. When using interfaces as types, a developer can define functions that accept any objects that implement the interface as parameters. Then, depending on what object you send to the function, the function will run slightly different code.

To use polymorphism:

1. In any class define a function where one of the input parameters is a type of interface.

2. Call methods of the interface.

3. Pass any object to the function that supports the interface (**Figure 8.24**).

✔ Tip

■ Before passing an object to the function, make sure that the object in fact supports the interface (see "Interface Discovery" earlier in this chapter for details).

Deriving One Interface from Another

If other developers are using your object through a particular interface, and you need to enhance the interface, it's best to leave the original interface definition intact. C# provides a mechanism by which you can extend the interface without adding methods to the original interface. The mechanism is to derive one interface from another.

To derive one interface from another:

1. Assuming you have one interface already defined, define a new interface.

2. After the name of the interface type a colon, then `NameOfFirstInterface`, where `NameOfFirstInterface` is the name of the interface you wish to extend.

3. You can implement both the original interface as well as the new interface in the same class (**Figure 8.25**).

Figure 8.25 IPresident extends IParent. That means that if you implement the IPresident, not only do you have to implement the methods in IPresident but the methods in IParent as well.

```
interface IParent
{
    void SendKidsToPlay();
}

interface IPresident : IParent
{
    void DispatchArmy();
}

class George : IPresident
{
    //implment the methods for both
    //IParent and IPresident
    public void SendKidsToPlay()
    {
    }

    public void DispatchArmy()
    {
    }
}
```

Figure 8.26 It's the same thing to implement both the parent interface and the derived interface as it is to implement just the derived (because the derived contains the parent members as well.)

```
Code                                    _ □ ×
interface IParent
{
    void SendKidsToPlay();
}

interface IPresident : IParent
{
    void DispatchArmy();
}

class George : IPresident
{
    //implment the methods for both
    //IParent and IPresident
    public void SendKidsToPlay()
    {
    }

    public void DispatchArmy()
    {
    }
}
```

Figure 8.27 Even though Telemarketer implements both IPerson and ISendsGifts, the class is not compatible with the IGivingPerson interface.

```
Code                                    _ □ ×
interface IGivingPerson : IPerson, ISendsGifts
{
}

class Grandma : IGivingPerson
{
}

class Telemarketer : IPerson, ISendsGifts
{
}
```

✔ Tips

■ The classes in **Figures 8.26** have equivalent definitions. Implementing the original and the derived interfaces is the same as implementing the derived interface only. Both result in a class that is compatible with both interfaces.

■ The classes in **Figures 8.27** are not equivalent definitions. Even though IGivingPerson is a combination of IPerson and ISendsGifts, implementing IGivingPerson is not the same as implementing IPerson and ISendsGifts separately. A good way of thinking about this is that IGivingPerson could have methods other than the combination of IPerson and ISendsGifts.

Refactoring

Refactoring is a mechanism used in object-oriented programming when working with classes and interfaces. It means that if you have two classes that have similar purposes, and these classes have code in common, it may be better to create one base class out of the common code, then write subclasses from this base class. The subclasses would only have the code that differs between the classes.

To refactor classes using interfaces:

1. If multiple classes implement the same interface in similar fashion (the implementation code is the same for all of them), create a base class.

2. Implement the interface in the base class.

3. Add implementation code for each method in the interface to the base class.

4. Derive child classes from the base class.

5. Use the derived classes through the interface (**Figure 8.28**).

✔ Tips

- If a base class implements the interface, the child classes are also compatible with the interface.

- In designing your classes, define your interfaces first, then create a base class to implement the interfaces. Then create sub-classes that inherit from the base class. Use the derived classes through the interface. This is the mechanism that experienced developers often use when writing applications.

Figure 8.28 You can use a Checking object through the IAccount interface because Checking derives from AccountImpl and AccountImpl implements the IAccount interface. In other words, if any class in the parent hierarchy implements the interface then the derived class also supports the interface.

```
interface IAccount
{
    void MakeDeposit(int Amount);
    void MakeWithdrawal(int Amount);
}

class AccountImpl : IAccount
{
    public void MakeDeposit(int Amount)
    {
    }

    public void MakeWithdrawal(int Amount)
    {
    }
}

class Checking : AccountImpl
{
}

class Savings : AccountImpl
{
}

class Bank
{
    void OpenAccount()
    {
        IAccount acct = new Checking();
        acct.MakeDeposit(100);
    }
}
```

Figure 8.29 The Dog class implements the IAnimal interface. GreatDane derives from Dog so it picks up the implementation of IAnimal. But what if GreatDane wants to implement the Speak method in IAnimal differently from Dog's implementation and keep the implementation of Eat? Then you can re-implement IAnimal in GreatDane and re-implement the methods you want to change.

```
Code                                    _ □ ×

interface IAnimal
{
    string Speak();
    string Eat();
}

class Dog : IAnimal
{
    string IAnimal.Speak()
    {
        return "woof! woof!";
    }

    string IAnimal.Eat()
    {
        return "Yum!";
    }
}

class GreatDane : Dog , IAnimal
{
    string IAnimal.Speak()
    {
        return "Big woof! Big woof!";
    }
}
```

Re-Implementing Interfaces in a Derived Class

If you read the topic of Refactoring earlier in this chapter, you know that it's possible to create a base class that supports an interface, and then write derived classes from that base class. The derived classes will also support the interface. However, sometimes it makes sense to override one or more of the implementation methods in the derived classes. For that purpose you could re-implement the interface in the derived class.

To re-implement the interface in a derived class:

1. After the name of the derived class type a colon followed by the name of the interface you wish to re-implement.

2. Add an implementation for only the methods you wish to do differently from the base class (**Figure 8.29**).

✔ Tip

- Another way of re-implementing the interface method is to mark the original implementation method as a virtual method and then override it in the sub-class (**Figure 8.30**).

Figure 8.30 This method requires the author of the base class to mark the method virtual, which isn't always possible.

```
interface IAnimal
{
    string Speak();
    string Eat();
}

class Dog : IAnimal
{
    public virtual string Speak()
    {
        return "woof! woof!";
    }

    public string Eat()
    {
        return "Yum!";
    }
}

class GreatDane : Dog
{
    public override string Speak()
    {
        return "WOOF! WOOF!";
    }
}
```

Figure 8.31 ASP.NET reads the settings of your web.config file before starting the application. The web.config file can be used to control how ASP.NET runs your application.

```
<httpModules>
    <add name="Dimensions"
    type="interfacesproject.custommodule,
    interfacesproject"/>
</httpModules>
```

Finishing the Sample Application

There are only a few steps left to make your application fully functional. In this section you will add the remaining code.

The first thing you have to do is make sure ASP.NET knows about your custom module.

To activate the custom module for your application:

1. In Solution Explorer double-click on the file web.config.

2. Scroll to the end of the file and add the code in **Figure 8.31** just before the line that reads </system.web>.

That's all it takes to activate the custom module for your application. The next step is to add code to the dimensions.aspx page to make sure that the module is working.

To finish the dimensions.aspx page:

1. Double-click on the dimensions.aspx item in the Solution Explorer.

2. Double-click on an empty space on the form to bring up the code editor. The wizard will add a Page_Load event.

3. Inside Page_Load add the code in **Figure 8.32**. This code will display the width and the height values in two textboxes (**Figure 8.33**).

✔ Tips

- To get the full effect of the module working, resize the browser, then click the Refresh button below the textboxes. The textboxes should display the new dimensions.

- Make sure you get a good night's sleep tonight.

Figure 8.32 This code looks at the Items collection and extracts the __ClientWidth and __ClientHeight values that the custom module saved.

```
private void Page_Load(object sender,
System.EventArgs e)
{
    txtWidth.Text =

((int)Context.Items["__ClientWidth"]).ToString();

    txtHeight.Text =

((int)Context.Items["__ClientHeight"]).ToString();
}
```

Figure 8.33 To test the custom module, resize the browser, and click the Refresh link. You should see the values of ClientWidth and ClientHeight change.

ARRAYS AND COLLECTIONS

Arrays are types that enable you to store a series of elements. Every array can be thought of as being two parts in one. The first part is the array object, which is an instance of the class `System.Array`. This object stores information about the array itself—things like the number of elements in the array, the number of dimensions, and whether the array has a non-zero lower bound or not. The second part is the storage for the elements in the array.

There are two main types of arrays: arrays of valuetypes and arrays of reference types. Valuetypes include the language's native data types, such as integers, longs, doubles, etc. Valuetypes also include structures. Reference types include classes that produce objects, like `System.Object`, Strings and any custom class you write.

If the array is an array of Valuetypes, the array object will also contain storage for each element in the array. For example, if an array is an array of ten integers, then creating the array object allocates enough memory to store all ten integers. As soon as the array is allocated you can start assigning values to each slot in the array.

On the other hand, if the array is an array of reference types, then creating the array object only allocates place holders for each element in it, and doesn't create each object in the array. For example, if you have an array of Checking accounts, creating the array only produces the memory required to store pointers to Checking objects. After the array is created you have to go through each entry and create Checking objects yourself before you can start manipulating each element in the array.

Whether the array is an array of reference types or of valuetypes, all arrays have a set of functions that enable you to manipulate and search through the array. In this chapter you'll learn how to create arrays and manipulate the arrays.

Aside from arrays, the .NET foundation classes offer a set of classes for storing elements that have more functionality than arrays. Those classes are normally referred to as collection classes because they are all part of a namespace called `System.Collection`. These classes include things like dynamic arrays, HashTables, queues, and others.

Working with Arrays and Collections

It this chapter we're going to do something a little different. You're going to create your own Web control—a class that can be added to a Web form. In all of the previous examples you used the Web controls that Microsoft shipped with VS.NET. They're the tools that appear in the toolbox, like the label control, the button control, the grid control, etc. Well, you're now going to write your own.

The Web control you're going to write will be a grid control. Of course, there's no way we can do a full-featured grid control in this section. However, basic grid controls are great for demonstrating how to declare arrays and other collection types.

Your grid control will have a two-dimensional array of cells. You will add a Cell class with a few properties. One of the properties will be a Text property that will store the contents of the cell. Web controls are classes that derive from `System.Web.UI.WebControls` `.WebControl`. Any public property of a standard type (int, long, string, etc.) becomes a property you can set through the VS.NET property grid. Web controls also have a Render method. Your job in the Render method is to represent your grid in an HTML form that can be displayed in a browser. You'll see that this isn't very difficult to do. One other feature you're going to add to the grid is the ability to name each cell. You'll be able to add a key to a cell, that you can use later to retrieve the contents of the cell.

To create a test project for this chapter:

1. Launch Visual Studio .NET. (Start > All Programs > Microsoft Visual Studio .NET > Microsoft Visual Studio .NET).

2. Select File > New > Project to bring up the New Project dialog.

3. Under project types on the left side of the New Project window, click the Visual C# projects folder.

4. Select the Web Control Library icon and change the name of the application to CodeControls (**Figure 9.1**).

5. Visual Studio will create a new project with a single class called WebCustomControl1. Change the name of the class to CodeGridWeb. The changes you need to make are in **Figure 9.2**. There's no way to do this through the property sheet, only through the editor.

6. Delete the code that declares a Text property. The wizard adds this property as an example of how to add properties, but we don't need it. **Figure 9.3** shows you what code to delete.

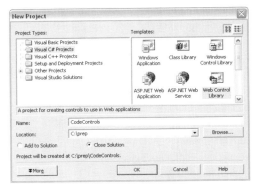

Figure 9.1 For this chapter you're creating an ASP.NET Web Control rather than an application. It doesn't create a virtual directory on your Web server, as the Web projects did.

Figure 9.2 Above the CodeGridWeb class declaration there are some attributes in square brackets. The ToolboxData attribute tells the VS.NET designer what to call instances of your control when a developer puts it on a Web page.

```
[ToolboxData(
"<{0}:CodeGridWeb runat=server>
</{0}:CodeGridWeb>")]
public class CodeGridWeb :
System.Web.UI.WebControls.WebControl
```

Figure 9.3 We don't need the text property in the control, so we can delete all the code in this figure.

```
private string text;

[Bindable(true),
Category("Appearance"),
DefaultValue("")]
public string Text
{
    get
    {
        return text;
    }
    set
    {
        text = value;
    }
}
```

Figure 9.4 The grid is basically an array of Cell objects. The Cell class has a constructor that takes in the row and column numbers for the cell as well as a pointer to the parent. The Cell will use the pointer to the parent to be able to call methods in the parent class later on.

```
public class Cell
{
   private string _text;
   CodeGridWeb _parent;
   private int _row, _col;

   public Cell(CodeGridWeb parent,
   int row, int col)
   {
      _parent = parent;
      _row = row;
      _col = col;
   }

   public string Text
   {
      get
      {
         return _text;
      }
      set
      {
         _text = value;
      }
   }

   public int Row
   {
      get
      {
         return _row;
      }
   }
   public int Column
   {
      get
      {
         return _col;
      }
   }
}
```

7. Next, add the definition for the Cell class. Remember that the grid control stores a two-dimensional array of cells. Later, you'll learn about declaring arrays. For now, let's just add the definition for the class itself. The code for the class is in **Figure 9.4.** Add the code inside the definition of the CodeGridWeb class (so that it becomes a nested class).

continues on next page

8. Declare two integers inside the CodeGridWeb to store the number of rows and the number of columns (**Figure 9.5**).

9. Add two public properties to get and set the number of rows and columns in the grid (**Figure 9.6**).

✔ Tips

- The Cell class is a nested class—a class that is a member of another class. I decided to make it a nested class because the class will need to make a call to a private function in the grid class. You'll add the private function later.

- Remember that like in any other project in this book, building the project isn't necessary for learning the concepts in this chapter.

- Skeletons for each project can be downloaded from Peachpit's Web site, http://www.peachpit.com/vqs/csharp.

Figure 9.5 _rows and _cols store the number of rows and columns in the grid. Their starting values are 10 and 5, respectively.

```
private int _rows=10;
private int _cols=5;
```

Figure 9.6 Above the property declarations for Rows and Columns there are a couple of attributes. These are read by VS.NET when the developer adds the control to a Web form. Category has to do with how the property sheet groups properties; this one will be in the appearance group. DefaultValue tells the designer that it doesn't have to write code to set this value if the value is the default.

```
[Category("Appearance"),
DefaultValue(10)]
public int Rows
{
    get
    {
        return _rows;
    }
    set
    {
        _rows = value;
    }
}

[Category("Appearance"),
DefaultValue(5)]
public int Columns
{
    get
    {
        return _cols;
    }
    set
    {
        _cols = value;
    }
}
```

Figure 9.7 Although the value in square brackets is a literal number, it could also be a variable that stores the number. This enables you to have a number of elements that are calculated at runtime.

```
Code                              _ □ ×
double[] prices = new double[20];
```

Figure 9.8 C# uses square brackets for array indexes and parenthesis for function parameters. Other languages always use parentheses, which makes things a little confusing.

```
Code                              _ □ ×
double[] prices = new double[20];
prices[0] = 5.5;
prices[1] = 2.0;
prices[19] = 3.14;
```

Figure 9.9 Structures work like classes except that they are not true objects; they behave more like integers, longs, etc. (they're valuetypes). A structure is basically a way of grouping fields that have related information. Because they're valuetypes, you can start using their fields without creating an object first.

```
Code                              _ □ ×
struct PersonalInfo
{
    public string Name;
    public string EmbarrassingMoment;
}

void Task()
{
    PersonalInfo[] diary = new PersonalInfo[365];
    diary[15].Name = "Some other Jose";
    diary[15].EmbarrassingMoment
        = "Recommending friend not to have kids";
}
```

Creating Arrays of Valuetypes

Valuetypes include all the native types as well as any structures you define. When you allocate an array of valuetypes, all the elements of the array are pre-allocated, which means that you can start using the array immediately.

To allocate and use an array of valuetypes:

1. Type the type of the array, for example: double.

2. Type an open square bracket [and a close square bracket] immediately after the type, for example: double[].

3. Type a space followed by a variable name to point to the array, for example: double[] prices.

4. Type the = sign.

5. Type new followed by the type of the array.

6. Type a set of square brackets with the size of the array inside, for example: = new double[20].

7. Type a semicolon ; (**Figure 9.7**).

✔ Tips

- Once you allocate an array of valuetypes you can begin assigning values to each element (**Figure 9.8**).

- Arrays of valuetypes include arrays of structures. **Figure 9.9** shows you how to create an array of structures and how you can address each element of the array directly without having to create individual structures manually.

continues on next page

- The array dimensions are specified inside square brackets. To address the elements of the array you refer to each element by its index number. The index can be zero through the length of the array minus one. So if the dimension is 32 the array indices are zero through 31.

- The array dimensions are immutable. That means that once you set the dimension of the array, the system creates an array of that size and the size can't be expanded or shrunk. So if you wish to change the dimensions you would need to create a brand-new array. You would also need to copy any elements you wished to preserve from the old array to the new array (**Figure 9.10**).

- Arrays in .NET are instances of the class `System.Array`. `System.Array` provides a function called `CreateInstance` that lets you create an array in a slightly different way (**Figure 9.11**).

Figure 9.10 Resizing the array can be done in two short steps. First create a second array and copy the elements from the first into it. Then point the original variable to the new array. The first array is now unreachable in memory space until the garbage collector cleans it up.

```
void Task()
{
    PersonalInfo[] diary =
    new PersonalInfo[365];
    diary[15].Name = "Some other Jose";
    diary[15].EmbarrassingMoment =
   "Recommending friend not to have kids";

    PersonalInfo[] tempdiary =
    new PersonalInfo[1000];
    System.Array.Copy(diary,0,tempdiary,0,
    365);
    diary = tempdiary;
}
```

Figure 9.11 The first parameter in the CreateInstance function is a type object—the type of the array you wish to create. The second parameter is the number of elements. The end result is an array object of the type you requested. However, the function is declared to return System.Array, so you need to cast the end result to the specific type.

```
PersonalInfo[] diary =
(PersonalInfo[]) System.Array.CreateInstance(
                typeof(PersonalInfo),365);
```

Figure 9.12 When you allocate an array of reference types, all you're doing is allocating a series of slots that will store the address to the actual objects; but you have to create the objects to go in the slots yourself.

```
Code                                _ □ ✕

class Child
{
    public string name;
    public void BegForNewVideoGame(string game)
    {
    }
}

void Task()
{
    Child[] children = new Child[5];
    children[0] = new Child();
    children[0].BegForNewVideoGame("Metroid");
}
```

Creating Arrays of Reference Types

Creating arrays of reference types requires an extra step over creating an array of value-types. Once you create an array of reference types, you have to create each individual element before you can manipulate the elements of the array.

To create an array of objects:

1. Type the type of the array, for example: `Child`.

2. Type an open square bracket and a close square bracket immediately after the type, for example: `Child[]`.

3. Type a space followed by a variable name to point to the array, for example: `Child[] children`.

4. Type the equal sign =.

5. Type new followed by the type of the array.

6. Type a set of square brackets with the size of the array inside, for example: `= new Child[5]`.

7. Type a semicolon ;.

8. For each element in the array create a new object. For example: `children[0] = new Child();` (**Figure 9.12**).

✔ Tips

■ As you can see, allocating an array of reference types is a two-step process. You first declare and create an array object like you would with valuetypes. Then you have to create a new object for each element in the array.

■ All the elements in the array are initialized to null when the array is first allocated.

continues on next page

- Arrays of reference types are compatible with arrays of parent types. In other words, if you have a class of type Child and Child is derived from a class called HeightChallengedPerson, then an array of Child is compatible with a variable of type HeightChallengedPerson [] (**Figure 9.13**). It follows that an array of the type System.Object would be compatible with any type of array (**Figure 9.14**). In fact a variable of System.Object (not an array type) could also point to an entire array (**Figure 9.15**). It's also true that if the Child class implements an interface, then the array is also compatible with an array of the interface (**Figure 9.16**).

continues on page 268

Figure 9.13 Child derives from HeightChallengedPerson, therefore, an array of Child is compatible with an array of HeightChallengedPerson.

```
class HeightChallengedPerson
{
    public string Name;
    public int Age;
}

class Child : HeightChallengedPerson
{
    public void BegForNewVideoGame(string game)
    {
    }
}

void Task2()
{
    Child[] children = new Child[5];
    children[0] = new Child();
    children[0].Name = "Ralph";
    HeightChallengedPerson[] hp = children;
    string name = hp[0].Name;
}
```

Figure 9.14 Since object is the base class to every class, an array of Child is also compatible with an array of object.

```
class Child
{
    public string name;
    public void BegForNewVideoGame(string game)
    {
    }
}

void Task()
{
    Child[] children = new Child[5];
    children[0] = new Child();
    children[0].name = "Tommy";

    object[] objChild = children;
    string name = ((Child)objChild[0]).name;
}
```

Figure 9.15 The object variable can point not only to a single object but also to any type of array.

```
Code                                          _ □ ×

class Child
{
    public string name;
    public void BegForNewVideoGame(string game)
    {
    }
}

void Task()
{
    Child[] children = new Child[5];
    children[0] = new Child();
    children[0].name = "Tommy";

    object objChild = children;
    Child[] otherchildren = (Child[])objChild;
    string name = otherchildren[0].name;
}
```

Figure 9.16 If a class implements an interface, then an array of that type is compatible with an array of the interface type.

```
Code                                          _ □ ×

interface IGoodNegotiator
{
    void BegForNewVideoGame(string game);
}

class Child : IGoodNegotiator
{
    public string name;
    public void BegForNewVideoGame(string game)
    {
    }
}

void Task()
{
    Child[] children = new Child[5];
    children[0] = new Child();
    children[0].name = "Tommy";

    IGoodNegotiator[] negs = children;
    negs[0].BegForNewVideoGame("Halo 2");
}
```

■ Because arrays are instances of the type System.Array, a variable of type System.Array can point to any array object. System.Array provides a series of functions that enable you to read and write to the array (**Figure 9.17**).

Figure 9.17 With System.Array you can create arrays and manipulate arrays without ever having to declare a variable of a specific type of array. This lets developers create arrays on the fly at runtime as needed.

```
class Child
{
   public string name;
   public void BegForNewVideoGame(string game)
   {
   }
}

void Task()
{
   Child[] children = new Child[5];

   System.Array arr = children;
   arr.SetValue(new Child(),3);
   Child tommy = (Child)arr.GetValue(3);

   double[] ages = new double[4];
   arr = ages;
   arr.SetValue(3.5,2);
   double age2 = arr.GetValue(2);
}
```

CREATING ARRAYS OF REFERENCE TYPES

Figure 9.18 Array indexes are zero based. This is a standard that .NET languages have. That means that valid indexes are zero to Length - 1.

```
Code                                    _ □ ×

class Book
{
    string _title;
    public string Read(string title)
    {
        _title = title;
        return "Once upon a time";
    }
}


void Task()
{
    Book[] library = new Book[55];
    for (int count = 0; count <
    library.Length; count++)
    {
        library[count] = new Book();
        library[count].Read("Book" +
        count);
    }
}
```

Navigating through the Array

There are two main ways of navigating through the elements of an array. Arrays let you address elements using an index number. Indices begin at zero and go up to the dimensions of the array, minus 1. The class System.Array also implements the IEnumerable interface. Any class that implements IEnumerable enables you to navigate through its members using the C# foreach command.

To navigate through the array using the index number:

1. Type for.

2. Type an open parenthesis (.

3. Type the name of the variable to serve as the index, then type an equal sign = and the number zero, followed by a semicolon ;, for example: int index = 0;.

4. Type the name of the index variable followed by a less-than sign < followed by the name of the array plus .Length, plus a semicolon ;, for example: index < accts.Length;.

5. Type the name of the index variable plus the ++ operator, for example: index++.

6. Type a close parenthesis).

7. Type an open curly bracket {.

8. Address the element of the array as follows: accts[index], where accts is the name of the array and index is the variable you used in the for declaration.

9. Type a close curly bracket (**Figure 9.18**).

To navigate through the array using the foreach command:

1. Type foreach.

2. Type an open parenthesis (.

3. Type the type of the element stored in the array, for example: Checking.

4. Type the name of a variable to hold the current item in the array, for example current.

5. Type in.

6. Type the name of the array, for example: accts.

7. Type a close parenthesis).

8. Type an open curly bracket {.

9. Use the variable current in some way, for example: current.balance += 20;.

10. Type a close curly bracket } (**Figure 9.19**).

Figure 9.19 foreach makes it easier to navigate through the array. It even works with multi-dimensional arrays.

```
Code                                    _ □ ×

class Book
{
    string _title;
    public string Read(string title)
    {
        _title = title;
        return "Once upon a time";
    }
    public void CheckOut()
    {
    }
}


void Task()
{
    Book[] library = new Book[55];
    for (int count = 0;
    count < library.Length; count++)
    {
        library[count] = new Book();
        library[count].Read("Book" +
        count);
    }

    foreach(Book singlebook in library)
    {
        singlebook.CheckOut();
    }
}
```

Figure 9.20 The variable that stores the current element in foreach is read-only. That doesn't mean you can't call a method of the object or even set a field in the object. It just means the variable itself can't be replaced with another object.

```
Code                                    _ □ ×

void Task()
{
    Book[] library = new Book[55];

    foreach(Book singlebook in library)
    {
        //*** this line results in a
        //*** compiler error
        singlebook = new Book();
        singlebook.CheckOut();
    }
}
```

Figure 9.21 As you can see, it's perfectly legal to set the fields in an object if it already has been set but we can't use foreach, for example, to initialize the array (create objects for each element).

```
Code                                    _ □ ×

class Book
{
    public string Title;
}

void Task()
{
    Book[] library = new Book[55];
    library[3] = new Book();

    int count=1;
    foreach(Book singlebook in library)
    {
        if (singlebook != null)
        {
            singlebook.Title =
    "Harry, Galactic Investigator, Part"
    + count;
            count++;
        }
    }
}
```

✔ Tips

■ In some ways it's easier to use the foreach notation (less typing). However, foreach has a limitation—the current item is read-only. This means that if the array is an array of valuetypes then you can't set the value of each element. If the array is an array of reference types, you can't set the current item equal to a new object (**Figure 9.20**). But if the element is already set to a new object, the fields in the object can be changed as you can see in **Figure 9.21**.

■ The Length property is a property available to all array types. It gives you the total number of elements in the array. When using the index, the valid index values are 0 through Length -1. The continuation test in the for loop above is written as index < Length, in other words, loop while index is less than the Length or stop when index >= Length. That means the last index value will be Length -1.

Initializing Array Elements in Place

C# offers a syntax by which you can create an array and initialize the items in place without having to navigate through all the items in the array.

To initialize an array in place:

1. Create an array of either valuetypes or reference types, for example: `int[] nums = new int[]` (without specifying a dimension).

2. Before the semicolon to end the statement, type an open curly bracket {.

3. Type the values for each element in the array separated by commas, for example: 5,4,6,3,1. The number of elements will dictate the dimension of the array.

4. Type a close curly bracket }.

5. Type a semicolon ; (**Figure 9.22**).

✔ Tips

■ You can also use this technique with reference types (**Figure 9.23**).

Figure 9.22 This notation makes it easy to create an array and initialize it in place.

```
Code                                    _ □ ×
void Task()
{
    int[] totallyRandomNums = new int[]
    → { 1,45,-35,42 };
}
```

Figure 9.23 When you initialize arrays of reference types, you can create the objects in place inside the curly brackets or create them beforehand and put the variables that store the objects in curly brackets.

```
Code                                    _ □ ×
class Fruit
{
    public string Name;
    public bool HasSeeds;

    public Fruit(string name,
    bool hasSeeds)
    {
        Name = name;
        HasSeeds = hasSeeds;
    }
}

void Task()
{
    Fruit[] salad = new Fruit[]
    {new Fruit("Banana",false),
     new Fruit("Apples",true),
     new Fruit("Watermelon",true)}
}
```

Figure 9.24 This is a common situation. You have several objects in individual variables. Then you need to make a call to a function like TransferMoney that has an array parameter. You can use the curly bracket notation to create an array for the one method call and then discard it.

```
Code                                    _ □ ✕

class Account
{
    public double Balance;
}

void TransferMoney(Account[] accts)
{
}

void Task()
{
    Account acct1 = new Account();
    acct1.Balance = 45.0;
    Account acct2 = new Account();
    acct2.Balance = -3.0;

    TransferMoney(new Account[] {acct1, acct2} );
}
```

■ This technique also is convenient for creating an array on the fly to send to a function without having to first declare the array and store it in a variable (**Figure 9.24**).

Creating Multi-Dimensional Arrays

C# also has a syntax for creating multi-dimensional arrays along with a mechanism for investigating how many dimensions an array has and the size of each dimension.

To create a two-dimensional array:

1. Type the name of the type of the array, for example: int.

2. Type an open square bracket [.

3. Type a comma ,.

4. Type a close square bracket].

5. Type the name of the variable for the array, for example: nums.

6. Type an equal sign =.

7. Type new followed by the type of the array, for example: new int.

8. Type an open square bracket [.

9. Type the size of each dimension separated by commas, for example: [4,5] .

10. Type a close square bracket].

11. Type a semicolon ; (**Figure 9.25**).

✔ Tips

- If you want to have more than two dimensions in the array, simply add more commas in the declaration of the array, for example: int[,,] nums = new int[2,1,4]; (**Figure 9.26**). A company I visited once had a need for a 20-dimensional array (yikes!).

- You can also use the curly notation for initializing the array in place with multi-dimensional arrays (**Figure 9.27**).

Figure 9.25 The number of commas in the declaration determines the number of dimensions for the array. So integer[,,,] would be a four-dimensional array of integers.

```
Code                                    _ □ ×

class Cell
{
    public string Text;
}

Cell[,] grid = new Cell[10,10];

void Task()
{
    grid[0,1] = new Cell();
    grid[0,1].Text = "Address";
}
```

Figure 9.26 And the dimensions keep growing. For homework tonight, see how many commas you can enter for dimensions before the compiler complains.

```
Code                                    _ □ ×

double[,,] spaceCoords = new double[3,4,5];
```

Figure 9.27 It starts getting difficult to see what is happening in the initialization when you have multiple dimensions. In this case we're creating a two-dimensional array of two rows by three columns.

```
Code                                    _ □ ×

double[,] angles = new double[,]
                { {-45.3,12.5,5}, {33,22,11} };
```

Figure 9.28 For some reason, it isn't possible to create arrays with a single dimension that have negative lower bounds; they have to be multi-dimensional arrays. Also, arrays that have non-zero lower bounds may not be compatible with other languages.

```
class Point
{
    public int x;
    public int y;
}

void Task()
{
    Point[,] Graph = (Point[,])
    Array.CreateInstance(
        typeof(Point), //type of array
        new int[] {10,10}, //sizes
        new int[] { -5, -5}); //lower
                               //bounds
    for (int x = -5; x < 5; x++)
    {
        for (int y = -5; y < 5; y++)
        {
            Graph[x,y] = new Point();
        }
    }
}
```

- The Length property returns the total number of elements in the array. Thus, the Length is equal to the product of all dimensions. System.Array provides a function called GetLength that returns the size of each dimension in the array. The property Rank in System.Array provides the number of dimensions for the array.

- System.Array provides a version of the CreateInstance function that enables you to create multi-dimensional arrays in which the lower bounds are not zero (**Figure 9.28**).

- C# also uses the concept of jagged arrays. That's an array in which each element is also an array, and each sub-array can be of a different size. Instead of using a comma to specify dimensions, a jagged array is declared with two sets of square brackets (**Figure 9.29**).

Figure 9.29 Jagged arrays are arrays of arrays, got that? Basically every element in the array is a sub-array ... Oh, never mind!

```
string[][] families = new string[2][];
families[0] = new string[5];
families[1] = new string[4];

families[0][0] = "Bill";
families[0][1] = "Carole";
families[0][2] = "Bradley";
families[0][3] = "Madalyn";
families[0][4] = "Duncan";

families[1][0] = "Jose";
families[1][1] = "Laurel";
families[1][2] = "Alex";
families[1][3] = "Andy";
```

CREATING MULTI-DIMENSIONAL ARRAYS

Enhancing the Sample Application

It's time to add some code to the sample application, specifically the ability to store a two-dimensional array of cells. Once we've added support for the cell array, we can also draw the grid control.

To add support for the cell array:

1. Add the definition of the two-dimensional cell array from **Figure 9.30** inside the CodeGridWeb class.

2. Next add a function to create the grid cells (**Figure 9.31**). The CreateGrid function allocates the two-dimensional array based on the number of rows and number of columns.

Figure 9.30 _cells is a two-dimensional array of the Cell class. We're going to create the array in a later function.

```
Cell[,] _cells
```

Figure 9.31 CreateGrid actually allocates the array based on the number of rows and columns. The Cell class's constructor has three parameters, the first is a pointer to the creator of the object, the second is the row number, and the third is the column number.

```
public void CreateGrid()
{
    //allocate cells
    _cells = new Cell[_rows,_cols];

    for (int r = 0; r < _rows; r++)
        for(int c = 0; c < _cols; c++)
            _cells[r,c] = new Cell(this,r,c);
}
```

Figure 9.32 Whenever the Row or the Column changes, we need to recreate the cell array. Right now, recreating the array doesn't preserve the old data. It would be great if it did, but it would also be difficult to implement.

```
Code                                        _ □ ×

[Category("Appearance"),
DefaultValue(10)]
public int Rows
{
   get
   {
      return _rows;
   }
   set
   {
      _rows = value;
      CreateGrid();
   }
}

[Category("Appearance"),
DefaultValue(5)]
public int Columns
{
   get
   {
      return _cols;
   }
   set
   {
      _cols = value;
      CreateGrid();
   }
}
```

Figure 9.33 The base class WebControl takes care of some of the rendering of our control in HTML, specifically the part of maintaining the position and size of instances of our control. However, for the base class to do its job, it needs to know what type of object we are. We pass that information through the constructor.

```
Code                                        _ □ ×

public CodeGridWeb() :
base(HtmlTextWriterTag.Table)
{
   CreateGrid();
}
```

3. With this function in place we can modify the Rows and Columns properties so that every time the dimensions change, we recreate the grid (**Figure 9.32**).

4. We also have to add a constructor, for two reasons. First, because some information, such as the dimensions and the size of our grid, can be drawn by the base class. So we need to call the base constructor and tell it what kind of control we are. Second, because we need to call CreateGrid with the default dimensions as soon as the CodeGridWeb is created (**Figure 9.33**).

continues on next page

5. The next step is to draw the grid, which we do in two stages. First of all, grid controls are tables in HTML. As you saw in the Introduction, tables in HTML are represented as <table> <tr><td></td></tr> <tr><td></td></tr> </table> Where <tr> represents a row and <td> represents a column. The outer part of the grid, the tags that have <table> and </table>, is going to be drawn by our base class (Microsoft takes care of that). The inner part is up to us. So first you add the code in **Figure 9.34** to draw the inner part of the grid.

6. Then modify the Render function so that it draws the outer part of the grid (**Figure 9.35**).

✔ Tip

■ Except for a few extra features we're going to add to the grid, the grid is now fully functional. In the later sections we'll enhance it, and then at the end of the chapter we'll create a test project to view the end result.

Figure 9.34 DrawGrid optimizes the string concatenations by using a StringBuilder object instead of plain strings. The function builds the HTML for the table using <tr> for row indicators and <td> for column indicators. It also uses the Text that's stored in each Cell object.

```
public string DrawGrid()
{
    System.Text.StringBuilder sb = new
    System.Text.StringBuilder(1024);

    for (int r = 0; r < _rows; r++)
    {
        sb.Append("<tr>");
        for(int c = 0; c < _cols; c++)
        {
            sb.Append(@"<td STYLE=""border: 'thin
black solid'"" WIDTH=50 HEIGHT=50>");
            sb.Append(_cells[r,c].Text);
            sb.Append("</td>");
        }
        sb.Append("</tr>");
    }

    return sb.ToString();
}
```

Figure 9.35 The Render function gets triggered whenever ASP.NET needs to redraw your control. The base takes care of drawing the <table></table> portion of our grid, and we then provide the HTML for the inner portion.

```
protected override void Render
(HtmlTextWriter output)
{
    output.AddStyleAttribute(
        HtmlTextWriterStyle.BorderCollapse,
        "collapse");
    base.RenderBeginTag(output);
    output.Write(DrawGrid());
    base.RenderEndTag(output);
}
```

Figure 9.36 The IndexOf function gives the zero-based index of the element. It goes through each item comparing it to the sought value until it finds a match.

```
Code                                    _ □ ×

void Task()
{
    string[] names = new string[]
    {"Fred","Martha","James","Sally"};

    int index = Array.IndexOf(names,"James");
    if (index != -1)
    {
        //we've found the name in the list
        //the index is 2
    }
}
```

Finding Array Elements Using Linear Searches

The System.Array class enables you to obtain the index number of an item. You can perform a search through the arrays using two mechanisms: linear searching or binary searching. Binary searching is faster than linear searching, but binary searching requires that the items are sorted first. If you want to sort classes you designed yourself, you'll need to implement an interface called ICompareable (for details see the "Sorting" section). Linear searches are slower than binary searches but items in the array don't need to be in any particular order.

To search through an array linearly:

1. Type int index =, where index is any variable name to store the result of the search.

2. Type System.Array.IndexOf to search for the first instance of the item in the array. Type System.Array.LastIndexOf to find the last instance of the item in the array.

3. Type an open parenthesis (.

4. Type the name of the array that you wish to search, for example: names.

5. Type a comma ,.

6. Type the value you wish to search for, for example: "Jose". Alternatively if you are searching for an instance of an object, type the name of the variable that stores the instance of the object for which you wish to search.

7. Type a close parenthesis).

8. Type a semicolon ; (**Figure 9.36**).

✔ Tips

■ Both search functions let you specify an index from which to start the search, and also limit the search to a certain range within the array (**Figure 9.37**).

■ If the item can't be located, the `IndexOf` and the `LastIndexOf` functions returns the array's lower bound -1. Since the lower-bound is 99 percent of the time zero, the function normally returns -1 if it fails to find the item.

Figure 9.37 If we were to use the first version of IndexOf to look for Martha we would always get the first instance of Martha in the list (index 1). But if we use the overloaded version that lets us specify the starting index we can tell it to skip the first one and start at index 2. The function then returns 4.

```
Code                              _ □ ✕

void Task()
{
    string[] names = new string[]
    {"Fred","Martha","James","Sally", "Martha"};

    int index = Array.IndexOf(names,"Martha",2);
    if (index != -1)
    {
        //we've found the name in the list
        //the index is 4
    }
}
```

Figure 9.38 For IndexOf to work with custom objects, your class needs to override Equals from System.Object. The rules also say that if you override Equals you have to override GetHashCode as well. A hash code is a number that represents the data. If two objects are equal they should return the same hash code.

```
class Person
{
    public string Name;
    public int Age;

    public Person(string name, int age)
    {
        Name = name;
        Age = age;
    }

    public override bool Equals(
    object obj)
    {
        if (obj is Person)
        {
            Person temp = (Person)obj;
            if (temp.Age == this.Age &&
            temp.Name == this.Name)
            {
                return true;
            }
        }
        return false;
    }

    public override int GetHashCode()
    {
        return Age.GetHashCode() +
        Name.GetHashCode();
    }
}

void Task()
{
    Person[] friends = new Person[]
        { new Person("Bill",28),
          new Person("Jim",31),
          new Person("Jason",29) };

    Person seeker = new Person("Jim",31);
    int index = Array.IndexOf(friends,
    seeker);
}
```

■ Suppose you have an array of Checking accounts, and each Checking account has an AccountNumber field that identifies the account. How would you search the array for a particular AccountNumber? The IndexOf and LastIndexOf work with any type of object, but those functions merely navigate through each item in the array and call a function in System.Object called Equals on each element passing the object you specified in your search. To make the search meaningful for custom classes, you need to override the Equals function in your class. The search functions work fine with the primitive types because Microsoft has already implemented this function. Without overriding Equals the search functions only find a match if you look for the exact same object. They wouldn't work if you create a new object and set the fields to a value you're trying to match and then search. **Figure 9.38** gives you an example of how to override Equals in a class.

FINDING ARRAY ELEMENTS

Sorting Arrays

If you have a list of names, you would most likely want to present it sorted alphabetically to the client. Or you may want to use a faster mechanism for searching through the items of the array, called a binary search. For the binary search to work properly, the items in the array need to be sorted.

To sort the elements of an array:

1. Type System.Array.Sort.

2. Type an open parenthesis (.

3. Type the name of the variable that points to the array you wish to sort: names, for example.

4. Type a close parenthesis).

5. Type a semicolon ; (**Figure 9.39**).

✔ Tips

■ Sorting only works with one-dimensional arrays.

■ String sorting is case sensitive by default. However, you can ask it to make case-insensitive comparisons using one of the versions of the Sort function that accepts the IComparer interface and passing the CaseInsensitiveComparer to it (**Figure 9.40**).

Figure 9.39 It's really easy to sort an array with the Array.Sort function. All you do is pass in a single dimensional array and the elements will be sorted.

```
void Task()
{
    string[] names = new string[]
    {"James","Bill","Angel","Sally"};
    Array.Sort(names);
    foreach(string name in names)
    {
        Response.Write(name + ",");
        //prints Angel, Bill, James, Sally,
    }
}
```

Figure 9.40 By default, string comparisons are case sensitive, but the .NET framework includes a comparer object that can perform case-insensitive comparisons.

```
void Task()
{
    string[] names = new string[]
    {"A","a","A","A","a","a"};
    Array.Sort(names);

    foreach(string name in names)
    {
        Response.Write(name + ",");
        //prints a,a,a,A,A,A
    }

    Response.Write("<br>");

    Array.Sort(names,
    System.Collections.
    CaseInsensitiveComparer.Default);

    foreach(string name in names)
    {
        Response.Write(name + ",");
        //prints A,A,A,a,a,a
    }
}
```

Figure 9.41 A comparer is a class that performs comparisons. It needs to implement the IComparer interface which has a single method called Compare. In this case we return the opposite of the default comparer so that our items end up in reverse order.

```
Code                                    _ □ X

class Reverse :
System.Collections.IComparer
{
    public int Compare(object x, object y)
    {
        int result = System.Collections.
        Comparer.Default.Compare(x,y);
        return -1 * result; //return the
                                  opposite
    }
}

void Task()
{
    string[] names = new string[]
    {"Anna","Bill","Charles"};
    Array.Sort(names,new Reverse());
    foreach(string name in names)
    {
        Response.Write(name + ",");
        //prints Charles,Bill,Anna,
    }
}
```

■ There is no version of **Sort** that enables you to sort the array in descending order, but that's not hard to do if you write your own comparer object. The **Sort** function basically tells whatever comparer object you give it to compare two items. The comparer object then returns -1 if the first item is less than the second, 1 if it is greater, and 0 if they are equal. The .NET Framework already has a class called Comparer that does this for strings, but in ascending order. All we have to do is create a class that in its compare method returns the opposite of the Comparer class. See **Figure 9.41** for details.

continues on next page

In the last section we talked about searching for items in an array of custom classes and I pointed out that searching for a custom class involved overriding the `Equals` method of your class. Sorting an array of a custom class also requires extra work. This is because it is impossible for the framework to know how to sort two instances of a custom class without your help. For that reason the .NET framework has an interface called `IComparable` that you can implement in your class to help the sort function. The `IComparable` interface has a single method: `Compare`. In this method you are given an instance of another object and asked to compare yourself to it. If you are less than the item, you return -1. If you are greater, you return 1. If you are equal, you return 0. It's up to you to determine if you are less than, greater than, or equal, based on the information in the fields of the class. For example, a class called `Person` may have a field called `Age` and you may want to sort based on the Age field. In that case you would compare the Age field of both elements and return either -1, 0, or 1 (**Figure 9.42**).

Figure 9.42 Implementing IComparable is necessary if you want to sort an array of custom objects. It has a single method called CompareTo.

```
class Person : IComparable
{
    public string Name;
    public int Age;

    public Person(string name, int age)
    {
        Name = name;
        Age = age;
    }

    public int CompareTo(object obj)
    {
        if (obj is Person)
        {
            Person temp = (Person)obj;
            return Age.CompareTo(temp.Age);
        }
        throw new ArgumentException
        ("Not a person","obj");
    }
}

void Task()
{
    Person[] friends = new Person[]
    { new Person("Bill",28),
      new Person("Jim",31),
      new Person("Jason",29) };
    Array.Sort(friends);
    //returns Bill,Jason,Jim
}
```

Figure 9.43 When BinarySearch is successful it returns a value similar to IndexOf (linear search), except that binary searches are faster than linear searches.

```
void Task()
{
    string[] names = new string[]
    {"Buffy","Kirk","Data","Wakka"};

    Array.Sort(names);
    int index = Array.BinarySearch(names,"Data");

    if (index >= 0)
    {
        //found item, index = 2
    }
}
```

Finding Array Elements Using Binary Searches

If the items in the array are sorted, you can search the array using a binary search. A binary search is optimized to eliminate parts of the array where the item can't possibly be. It does this roughly by looking at the middle of the array, seeing if the item is greater than or less than the search value, and discarding the half that does not contain the value. It then searches the middle of the portion that may contain the item and repeats the procedure until it finds the item. For binary searches to work you must sort the array but also, the class in the array must implement the IComparable interface illustrated in the section titled "Sorting." Most of the native classes already implement this interface.

To perform a binary search:

1. Type System.Array.BinarySearch.

2. Type an open parenthesis (.

3. Type the name of the array you wish to search, for example: names.

4. Type a comma ,.

5. Type the value you wish to search for, or a variable that points to the object for which you wish to search, for example: "Jose".

6. Type a close parenthesis).

7. Type a semicolon ; (**Figure 9.43**).

✔ Tip

■ If the binary search fails to find the item, the function returns a negative value equivalent to the index that comes after the place where the item would have been, minus one. (You may be thinking, "Huh? Can you say that again?" I will.) Suppose that you have an array of letters A, B, D, E and you're searching for C. C isn't in the array, so BinarySearch would return -3. That's the index of the letter *after* the item we were searching for, which is D. D's index is 2 (because the array is zero based). Because it is a failure we turn that into a negative number, which is -2. We then use what is called the *twos complement* of the number, which in lay terms means we subtract 1 from the value, which gives us -3. Why do we subtract 1? Because zero is a valid index, so if the array contained B, C, D, E and we were looking for A, the next item after A is B. B has an index of zero, but we wouldn't return zero as the result because then we would think the index of A was zero, so the function always subtracts 1. There is an easy way to find the index from a failure return code using the ~ operator (**Figure 9.44**).

Figure 9.44 Papa Smurf isn't part of the array of names, so the function returns a negative number. In this case the number would be -4. Using the ~ operator we can convert that number to the actual index the where the item would have been if it had been part of the list.

```
void Task()
{
    string[] names = new string[]
    {"Buffy","Kirk","Data","Wakka"};

    Array.Sort(names);
    int index = Array.BinarySearch(names,"Papa
    → Smurf");
    if (index >= 0)
    {
        //item not found
    }
    else
    {
        System.Console.WriteLine(
        "item should've been at " + ~index);
        → //returns 3
    }
}
```

Making Classes Behave Like Arrays (Adding Indexers)

Imagine that you're writing your own grid WebControl (it's the kind of thing I like to do for fun on the weekends). A grid control is a visual element that displays data in tabular form on a WebForm or on a WinForm. Let's say that your class name is CodeGrid. CodeGrid has a field that stores a two-dimensional array: It stores information in terms of rows and columns. A client may use your class as follows: `CodeGrid cg = new CodeGrid(5,4);` specifying that they want to create a grid of five rows by four columns. Then the client would want to set the elements of a cell, say R2,C1. How would they do that? One way is to just provide a function like `SetItem(int Row, int Column, int Value)` in which they can specify the Row, the Column, and then the Value for the cell. But a more elegant way is to provide an indexer. This is a property that makes the class look as if it were an array. The indexer would enable the programmer to set a cell in this fashion: `cg[2,1] = 45;`.

To add an indexer to your class:

1. An indexer is similar to a property declaration. Begin by typing an access modifier, for example: `public`.

2. Type a return value for the indexer, for example: `string`.

3. Type `this`.

4. Type an open square bracket [.

5. Type the parameters for the indexer. In the case of my grid control example the parameters would be: `int Row, int Column`.

6. Type a close square bracket].

7. Type an open curly bracket {.

8. Type `get`.

9. Type an open curly bracket {.

10. Return a value of the type you specified in step 2. In the case of the grid example in which items are stored in a two-dimensional array, you would write: `return m_storage[Row,Column];`.

11. Type a close curly bracket }.

12. Type `set`.

13. Type an open curly bracket {.

14. Type code that stores the value received from the programmer using the indexer. You can reference the value using the value keyword. In the case of the grid example, you would write: `m_storage[Row,Column] = value;`.

15. Type a close curly bracket }.

16. Type another close curly bracket } (**Figure 9.45**).

Figure 9.45 An indexer gives users the illusion that your tic-tac-toe board is an array of spaces.

```
class TicTacToeBoard
{
    string[,] spaces = new string[3,3];

    public string this[int x, int y]
    {
        get
        {
            return spaces[x,y];
        }
        set
        {
            spaces[x,y] = value;
        }
    }
}

void Task()
{
    TicTacToeBoard board = new TicTacToeBoard();
    board[1,1] = "O";
    board[1,2] = "X";
}
```

Figure 9.46 By default, the name of the Indexer is Item, although in C# you can't reach the indexer by using Item as a property. This code changes the name to Squares. In Languages like Visual Basic .NET you would then be able to write board.Squares(2,2) = "X" which is more intuitive than board.Items(2,2).

```
class TicTacToeBoard
{
    string[,] spaces = new string[3,3];

    [System.Runtime.CompilerServices.
    IndexerName("Square")]
    public string this[int x, int y]
    {
        get
        {
            return spaces[x,y];
        }
        set
        {
            spaces[x,y] = value;
        }
    }
}

void Task()
{
    TicTacToeBoard board =
    new TicTacToeBoard();
    board[1,1] = "O";
    board[1,2] = "X";
}
```

✔ Tips

■ Indexers can also be read-only or write-only if you omit either the set or the get portion.

■ In essence, an indexer is a property. When you look at the class with an indexer from another language like VB.NET, the Indexer appears as a property called Item. In fact, you can change the name of the resulting property from Item to something else by applying the System.Runtime.CompilerServices.IndexerName attribute to your class (**Figure 9.46**).

MAKING CLASSES BEHAVE LIKE ARRAYS

Adding Indexers to the Sample Application

It would be very handy to add to a couple of indexers to the CodeGridWeb class. With an indexer a programmer would be able to write code like grid1[3,4].Text = "Something"; Without an indexer we would have to write a function to access the cells and the programmer would have to write something like grid1.SetCellText(3,4,Text) which isn't as pretty. So, let's add an indexer to the CodeGridWeb class.

To add an indexer to the sample code:

◆ Add the code in **Figure 9.47** to the CodeGridWeb class.

✔ Tip

■ The indexer in the sample code is read-only, but that doesn't prevent someone from setting the contents of the cell, only from replacing the cell object with their own object.

Figure 9.47 The first indexer in the code lets you specify a row and a column and returns a cell from the _cells array. It's read-only, which means that a user can't create her own Cell objects and put them into the array; she can only modify existing cells.

```
Code                        _□×
public Cell this[int row, int col]
{
    get
    {
        return _cells[row,col];
    }
}
```

Figure 9.48 This code creates a new array and copies the elements from the old array into the new array. The last parameter in the Copy function is the number of elements to copy. It's not very forgiving concerning this parameter. If there's not enough room, it will give you an exception.

```
void Task()
{
  string[] moviesILike = new string[]
  {"Joe vs. the Volcano", "Pink Panther", "LOTR"};

  string[] newMovies = new string[4];
  Array.Copy(moviesILike,0,newMovies,0,moviesI
Like.Length);
  newMovies[3] = "The Princess Bride";
  moviesILike = newMovies;
}
```

Figure 9.49 This code inserts Princess Bride as the second element in the array. To do that it needs to create a new array, then copy the first half of the old array, set the new element, then copy the remainder of the array.

```
void Task()
{
  string[] moviesILike = new string[] {
  "Joe vs. the Volcano", "Pink Panther", "LOTR"};
  string[] newMovies = new string[4];

  Array.Copy(moviesILike,0,newMovies,0,1);
  newMovies[1] = "The Princess Bride";
  Array.Copy(moviesILike,1,
            newMovies,2,
            moviesILike.Length-1);

  moviesILike = newMovies;
}
```

Copying an Array

A typical thing to do while working with arrays is to expand the array. You learned earlier that array sizes are immutable. So to expand (or shrink) the array you need to create a brand-new array with the new dimensions, then copy the items from the previous array onto the new one.

To copy the elements from one array into another:

1. Type System.Array.Copy.

2. Type an open parenthesis (.

3. If the first array is called src and the second array is called dest, type src,srcstartindex,dest,deststartindex, src.Length.

4. Type a close parenthesis).

5. Type a semicolon ; (**Figure 9.48**).

✔ Tips

■ Array.Copy lets you specify the starting index in the source array from where you wish to begin copying, and the starting index in the destination to where you wish to copy, as well as the number of items that you wish to copy.

■ To insert an item within the array, create a new array. Then copy the first half of the source onto the first half of the destination array. Finally, copy the rest of the source array onto the last portion of the array, leaving a place empty for the new item (**Figure 9.49**).

Creating Dynamic Lists

As you saw in the "Copying an Array" section, it isn't easy to maintain a dynamic list in which the array can potentially grow or shrink. It involves creating new arrays and then copying the elements from the old array into the new array. However, there are a set of classes in .NET that make managing dynamic lists easier. One of these classes is System.Collections.ArrayList.

To create an ArrayList:

1. Type System.Collections.ArrayList.

2. Type the name of the variable to hold the arraylist, for example: names.

3. Type =.

4. Type new
   System.Collections.ArrayList().

5. Type a semicolon ;.

6. Type names.Add

7. Type an open parenthesis (.

8. Type the value to add to the list, for example: "William".

9. Type a close parenthesis).

10. Type a semicolon ; (**Figure 9.50**).

Figure 9.50 ArrayLists are dynamic arrays. You can keep adding items with Add and the ArrayList will grow as needed. Internally ArrayList stores information in an array. When there is no room in the array, it creates a new array and copies the elements from the old array into the new array, thus giving you the illusion that it's a dynamic array. (Knowing that sort of takes the fun out of it, doesn't it?)

```
void Task()
{
    System.Collections.ArrayList systemUsers =
    new System.Collections.ArrayList();

    systemUsers.Add("Batman");
    systemUsers.Add("Robin");
    systemUsers.Add("Cat Woman");
}
```

Figure 9.51 The capacity doesn't limit how many items you can have. It just pre-allocates space for that many items. If you go over the capacity, then ArrayList will double its capacity, but that could hurt performance.

```
🖳 Code                                    _ □ ✕
//using System.Collections;
ArrayList systemUsers = new ArrayList(500);
```

Figure 9.52 The ArrayList class lets you navigate through the items of the array using an index, just like an array. One difference, however, is that ArrayLists have a Count property instead of the Length property that arrays use to report the number of elements.

```
🖳 Code                                    _ □ ✕
void Task2()
{
    System.Collections.ArrayList
    systemUsers =
    new System.Collections.ArrayList(500);

    systemUsers.Add("Batman");
    systemUsers.Add("Robin");
    systemUsers.Add("Cat Woman");

    for(int count = 0; count <
    systemUsers.Count; count++)
    {
        string name =
        (string)systemUsers[count];
    }
}
```

Figure 9.53 You can remove based on a value, or based on an index. After the two remove functions, the only element left in the list is Cat Woman.

```
🖳 Code                                    _ □ ✕
void Task2()
{
    System.Collections.ArrayList systemUsers =
    new System.Collections.ArrayList(500);

    systemUsers.Add("Batman");
    systemUsers.Add("Robin");
    systemUsers.Add("Cat Woman");

    systemUsers.Remove("Robin");
    systemUsers.RemoveAt(0);
}
```

✔ Tips

- The array list is essentially a dynamic array. Internally it builds an array of 16 elements. If you add more than 16 elements, it doubles the size of the array and copies the elements from the old array into the new array. Every time you pass the limit, it needs to create a new array. It makes more sense to start with a large capacity if you know approximately how many items you wish to add (**Figure 9.51**).

- You enumerate through the items of the array list using an indexer (**Figure 9.52**).

- You can also remove items from the array list either specifying the object with the Remove function or specifying the index number with the RemoveAt function (**Figure 9.53**).

CREATING DYNAMIC LISTS

Creating Queues

Queues are dynamic lists in which the first item put into the collection is the first object extracted from it. Items from the queue can only be extracted in the order in which they were added.

To create a queue, add items to it, and remove items from it:

1. Type System.Collections.Queue.

2. Type the name of the queue variable that is to store the queue object, for example: msgs.

3. Type =.

4. Type new System.Collections.Queue().

5. Type a semicolon ;.

6. Type msgs.Enqueue("Task1"); where "Task1" is the item to add to the queue.

7. Type msgs.Dequeue(); to extract the first item in from the queue (**Figure 9.54**).

✔ Tip

■ You can also examine all of the items in the queue one by one, without removing them using the foreach notation (**Figure 9.55**).

Figure 9.54 With queues you Enqueue and Dequeue. Enqueue puts elements at the bottom of the list, Dequeue removes the first element in the queue (first in—first out).

```
void Task()
{
    System.Collections.Queue q1 = new
    System.Collections.Queue();

    q1.Enqueue("Task1");
    q1.Enqueue("Task2");
    q1.Enqueue("Task3");

    string s1 = (string)q1.Dequeue(); //Task1
    string s2 = (string)q1.Dequeue(); //Task2
    string s3 = (string)q1.Dequeue(); //Task3
}
```

Figure 9.55 foreach lets you navigate through the elements without removing them from the queue.

```
void Task()
{
    System.Collections.Queue q1 = new
    System.Collections.Queue();

    q1.Enqueue("Task1");
    q1.Enqueue("Task2");
    q1.Enqueue("Task3");

    foreach (string task in q1)
    {
        Response.Write(task + ",");
        //Prints: Task1, Task2, Task3,
    }
}
```

Figure 9.56 With a stack you Push and Pop. Push puts the element on top of the stack, Pop removes the top element (first in—last out).

```
void Task()
{
    System.Collections.Stack q1 = new
    System.Collections.Stack();

    q1.Push("Task1");
    q1.Push("Task2");
    q1.Push("Task3");

    string s1 = (string)q1.Pop(); //Task3
    string s2 = (string)q1.Pop(); //Task2
    string s3 = (string)q1.Pop(); //Task1
}
```

Figure 9.57 Using foreach you can peek through the elements of the stack without removing them.

```
void Task()
{
    System.Collections.Stack q1 = new
    System.Collections.Stack();

    q1.Push("Task1");
    q1.Push("Task2");
    q1.Push("Task3");

    foreach (string task in q1)
    {
        Response.Write(task + ",");
        //Prints: Task3, Task2, Task1,
    }
}
```

Creating Stacks

Stacks are the opposite of queues. A stack is a list in which the first item in is the last item to be read.

To create a stack, add items to it, and remove items from it:

1. Type System.Collections.Stack.

2. Type the name of the stack variable that is to store the stack object, for example: msgs.

3. Type =.

4. Type new System.Collections.Stack().

5. Type a semicolon ; .

6. Type msgs.Push("Task1"); where "Task1" is the item to add to the stack.

7. Type msgs.Pop(); to extract the most recent addition from the stack (**Figure 9.56**).

✔ Tip

■ As with queues, you can enumerate through the items in the stack without removing them using the foreach function (**Figure 9.57**).

Creating HashTables

A HashTable is an enhanced dynamic list in which you can assign to each item in the list a unique key. The key lets you retrieve or remove the items from the list. In other lists, such as ArrayLists, items can only be located using a numeric index. The problem with an index is that it represents a position within the list, and the position in the list can change at any given time as a result of adding or removing items from the list. With a HashTable, the keys remain fixed even when items are added or removed.

To create a HashTable:

1. Type `System.Collections.Hashtable`.

2. Type the name of the HashTable variable, for example: `list`.

3. Type `=`.

4. Type `new System.Collections.Hashtable();`.

5. Type `list.Add`.

6. Type an open parenthesis `(`.

7. Type the key for the item, for example: `"Jose Mojica"`.

8. Type the data for the item, for example: `"1111 Wellknown St."`

9. Type a close parenthesis `)`.

10. Type a semicolon `;` (**Figure 9.58**).

Figure 9.58 The first parameter in the Add function is the key that you wish to assign to each element; the second parameter is the value. You can use any type of object for the key or for the value. For the key, however, if you use a custom class you need to make sure the class overrides the Equals function so that the HashTable can find it when requested.

```
Code                                          _ □ ×

void Task()
{
    System.Collections.Hashtable ht = new
    System.Collections.Hashtable();

    ht.Add("111-11-1111","Bill Cosby");
    ht.Add("222-22-2222","Robin Williams");
    ht.Add("333-33-3333","Chevy Chase");
}
```

Figure 9.59 Notice that even though we haven't added an item with a key of "444-44-4444" when we set the element through the indexer, if the HashTable doesn't find a matching key, it will simply add the value as a new element. Thus, setting a key, either overwrites the old value or adds the value if not there.

```
void Task()
{
    System.Collections.Hashtable ht = new
    System.Collections.Hashtable();

    ht.Add("111-11-1111","Bill Cosby");
    ht.Add("222-22-2222","Robin Williams");
    ht.Add("333-33-3333","Chevy Chase");

    string nameBC = (string)ht["111-11-1111"];
    ht["444-44-4444"] = "Eddie Murphy";
}
```

Figure 9.60 HashTables are like ArrayLists in the sense that it they can grow and shrink as needed. However, HashTables have the advantage that you can remove an item based on a key. With ArrayLists you have to specify either an index (a position that may change) or the actual value, which means that the ArrayList class has to seek through all of its elements looking for a match.

```
void Task()
{
    System.Collections.Hashtable ht = new
    System.Collections.Hashtable();

    ht.Add("111-11-1111","Bill Cosby");
    ht.Add("222-22-2222","Robin Williams");
    ht.Add("333-33-3333","Chevy Chase");

    ht.Remove("111-11-1111");
}
```

✔ Tips

■ You can address each item in the HashTable using the key as a parameter to the class's indexer (**Figure 9.59**).

■ Remove items from the HashTable using the Remove function passing the key as an item (**Figure 9.60**).

CREATING HASHTABLES

Navigating through HashTables

Hashtables support an enhanced version of foreach that reports not only the value of each item but also the key for each item.

To navigate through all the items in a HashTable:

1. Type foreach (.

2. Type System.Collections.DictionaryEntry.

3. Type the name of the variable to hold the current item, for example: current.

4. Type in table, where table is the variable that points to the HashTable.

5. Type a close parenthesis).

6. Type an open curly bracket {.

7. Type current.key to extract the key.

8. Type current.value to extract the item's value.

9. Type a close curly bracket } (**Figure 9.61**).

✔ Tip

■ You can also navigate through just the keys or just the values separately (**Figure 9.62**).

Figure 9.61 The foreach support in HashTables returns a DictionaryEntry—a structure that reports both the Key and the Value. These two variables are object types, so they need to be casted to a more specific type before using them.

```
Code                                    _ □ ×

void Task()
{
    System.Collections.Hashtable ht = new
    System.Collections.Hashtable();

    ht.Add("111-11-1111","Bill Cosby");
    ht.Add("222-22-2222",
    "Robin Williams");
    ht.Add("333-33-3333","Chevy Chase");

    foreach(System.Collections.
    DictionaryEntry en in ht)
    {
        string key = (string) en.Key;
        string name = (string) en.Value;
    }
}
```

Figure 9.62 Keys and Values in a HashTable are not limited to strings. You can use any type of object for the Key and for the Value. What's nice is that the foreach statement automatically casts to whatever type you specify for the current item variable. The bad part is that if all the items are not of the same or compatible types, foreach will fail.

```
Code                                    _ □ ×

void Task()
{
    System.Collections.Hashtable ht = new
    System.Collections.Hashtable();

    ht.Add("111-11-1111","Bill Cosby");
    ht.Add("222-22-2222","Robin Williams");
    ht.Add("333-33-3333","Chevy Chase");

    foreach(string key in ht.Keys)
    {
    }

    foreach(string val in ht.Values)
    {
    }
}
```

Figure 9.63 The Hashtable field in our grid control will store the keys the developer assigns to each cell.

```
Hashtable hsCells = new Hashtable();
```

Figure 9.64 SetCellKey store Keys for each cell in a HashTable. The HashTable stores keys and values. The Key is provided by the developer. The value is a string we build that records the row and the column of the cell formatted as "row;column;" ("5;10;" for example).

```
private void SetCellKey(string key,
int row, int col)
{
    hsCells[key] = row.ToString() + ";" +
                   col.ToString() + ";";
}
```

Figure 9.65 Now you see why the Cell class needs a pointer back to the CodeGridWeb object. It needs it so that it can call the SetCellKey private function. It can call a private function on the parent because it's a nested class. It's defined inside of the CodeGridWeb class, which means that it has access to all private fields and members of the outer class.

```
public string Key
{
    get
    {
        return _key;
    }
    set
    {
        _key = value;
        _parent.SetCellKey(_key,_row,_col);
    }
}
```

Finishing the Sample Application

To illustrate how HashTables can be used in a real-world application, let's add one to the sample application. The CodeGridWeb control will let developers assign a unique name to each cell. We will implement this feature by adding the unique name to a HashTable as the key, then record the row and column for the cell as the item in the HashTable.

To finish the sample application:

1. First add the declaration for the HashTable in **Figure 9.63**.

2. The Key is a property of the Cell class. However, all the keys need to be stored in the CodeGridWeb control. So we're going to add a function to the CodeGridWeb class so that the Cell class can set the contents of the HashTable. Add the code in **Figure 9.64** to the CodeGridWeb control.

3. With that function in place, we can add a property to the Cell class to set the Key. Add the code in **Figure 9.65** to the Cell class.

continues on next page

FINISHING THE SAMPLE APPLICATION

4. Now, in order for the developer to locate a Cell based on the key, we need to add another indexer to the CodeGridWeb class. This indexer will take as a parameter a string rather than a row and a column. The code for the new indexer is in **Figure 9.66**.

✔ Tip

■ The CodeGridWeb control is now fully functional. To test the control, read the next section.

Figure 9.66 This indexer lets you specify the key for a cell. The function then looks up the key in the HashTable. The item for the key is a string in the form "row;column;". We then split the string into the row and column portions and use those values to locate the cell in the array.

```
public Cell this[string key]
{
    get
    {
        Cell retVal = null;
        string cellIndex =
        (string)hsCells[key];
        if (cellIndex != null &&
        cellIndex != "")
        {
            string[] coords =
            cellIndex.Split(';');
            int r = System.Convert.
            ToInt32(coords[0]);
            int c = System.Convert.
            ToInt32(coords[1]);
            retVal = _cells[r,c];
        }
        return retVal;
    }
}
```

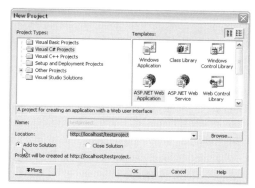

Figure 9.67 Before clicking that OK button, make sure you select the Add to Solution option. This will make it easier to debug the control at the same time as you test it.

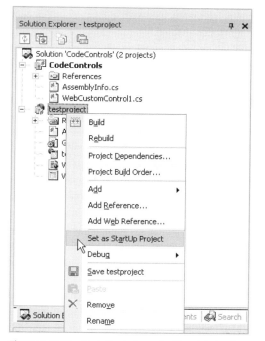

Figure 9.68 The CodeControls project is set to be the startup project by default, but we need the Test project to be the startup project. Web control projects are not executable programs—they're DLLs.

Testing the CodeGridWebControl

Visual Studio .NET offers some nice features for testing and debugging Web controls. All we have to do is add a Web Application project to the same solution and then reference the CodeControls project.

To test the sample application:

1. Before creating the test application, make sure that you build the CodeControl project first.

2. While keeping the grid control project open, choose File > New Project from the menu bar. Select ASP.NET Web application from the New Project dialog.

3. Enter testproject for the name of the application, but before you click the OK button, click on the Add to Solution option. This will make the new project and the old be in the same solution (same session of VS.NET) (**Figure 9.67**).

4. In the solution explorer, you'll see both projects. Right-click on the testproject and choose Set as Startup Project from the popup menu (**Figure 9.68**).

continues on next page

5. Right-click on the testproject again, and this time select Add Reference from the pop-up menu. Then, in the Add Reference dialog, click on the Projects tab. You'll see the CodeControls project. Double-click on the CodeControls entry to add it as a reference (**Figure 9.69**).

6. Click OK to close the dialog. If you look at the Toolbox you should now see the CodeGridWeb control there (**Figure 9.70**).

7. Add the control to the form as you would any other control; it should look like the one in **Figure 9.71**.

✔ Tips

■ Whenever you build the test project VS.NET will build both projects at once.

■ Try changing some of the properties of the grid, like Rows and Columns. You'll see that the grid repaints itself as you change the settings. You can also try writing some code to set the contents of a cell in Page_Load, for example.

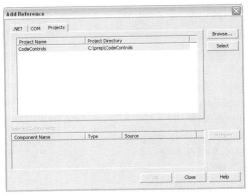

Figure 9.69 When you add a reference to the project, you also add a build dependency on that project. That means that VS.NET builds the referenced project first before building the test project.

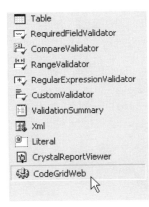

Figure 9.70 As soon as you reference the CodeControl project, the control appears in the toolbox.

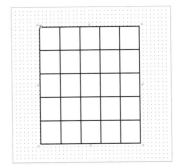

Figure 9.71 The CodeGridWeb control in all its glory. It's not as beautiful as the grid control that comes with Visual Studio .NET, but nothing beats making your own.

TESTING THE CODEGRIDWEBCONTROL

DELEGATES AND EVENTS

Delegates are the foundation of events. If you have used scripting languages before, you should be familiar with the concept of events. A user may interact with a Web page and click a button. The action of clicking generates an OnClick event. The JavaScript in the page may then do something as a result of the click action.

Delegates are classes that store functions. A developer first defines a delegate class. The definition of the delegate—as you will see in the sections in this chapter—contains a prototype for the type of functions that the delegate can store. A developer then declares a variable of the delegate type and assigns a function to it. The function could be an instance function in an object, or a static function. The only requirement is that the delegate can only store functions that match the prototype of functions used in declaring the delegate. A developer can then use the delegate variable to invoke the function that the delegate stores.

You may be tempted to think that that sounds too complicated, and that you will probably never use delegates. So how are delegates used practically? Delegates are normally used for the purpose of making callback calls. To understand callbacks consider a Modem class that has a method called Connect. Connect may do a few steps: open COM port, wait for ring tone, dial number, establish connection, etc. As a developer invoking the Connect method in the Modem class, you may want to get status information to display to the user. The question is, once you call the Connect method, how do you get notifications of the progress?

Delegates solve this problem. The Connect method could accept as a parameter a delegate to a function in the developer's caller class that offers information to the user. The Connect method then would periodically invoke the function in the developer's class as it is executing to provide progress information. This is called a *callback mechanism*. The callback function is the function in the originator code that the Modem class can call as it is executing.

Working with Delegates and Events

In this section we're going to start a project that will help you better understand the concept of using *asynchronous delegates*. Just what is an asynchronous delegate? We're going to answer that throughout the chapter, but for now let's just say that asynchronous delegates let your Web page do more than one thing at the same time.

For example, suppose you need to read a list of names and a list of states from two different database tables. The two pieces of data may be totally independent, so rather than reading from one table, waiting until we're done reading, and then reading from a different table, it may be beneficial to read from both tables at the same time. This can easily be done with asynchronous delegates.

One way in which a program can do multiple things at the same time is to use *threading*. A thread is a list of operations that must be done in order. Every application begins with one thread, and all operations occur sequentially. If an application wants to do multiple things, it needs to create another thread. The operating system then switches between the threads allowing one thread to do some work while pausing the other threads, then pausing the first thread and allow others to do work. If the machine has more than one processor, the OS can assign each thread to a different processor so that operations can happen at the same time.

One of the simplest ways of using multithreading in C# is to use asynchronous delegates.

continues on next page

For our sample application, I'm going to explain the mechanism for running multiple tasks by having your page perform three tasks concurrently. The tasks aren't anything special; they will just pause execution for a few seconds. Then we're going to first execute the tasks in order, one after the other, and then concurrently, and compare the execution times.

To create a test project for this chapter:

1. Launch Visual Studio .NET. (Start > All Programs > Microsoft Visual Studio .NET > Microsoft Visual Studio .NET).

2. Select File > New > Project to bring up the New Project dialog.

3. Under Project Types on the left side of the New Project window, click the Visual C# projects folder.

4. Select the ASP.NET Web Application icon and change the name of the application to delegatesproject (**Figure 10.1**).

5. Visual Studio will create a new project and open WebForm1.aspx.

6. Change the form's name to dispatcher.aspx by choosing View > Solution Explorer from the top menu bar.

7. Right-click on WebForm1.aspx and choose Properties. In the property grid below change the FileName property from WebForm1.aspx to dispatcher.aspx (**Figure 10.2**).

8. Create a form that looks like the form in **Figure 10.3**. This is a lot of work to do by hand, so you may want to enter the HTML directly into the editor. **Figure 10.4** shows the HTML necessary to create the form. To enter it directly, click the HTML button under the editor's window. As an alternative you could download the skeleton file for this project (see Tips on next page).

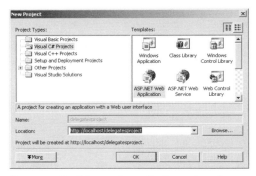

Figure 10.1 For this sample application we're going to create an ASP.NET Web Application. Name your application delegatesproject.

Figure 10.2 This application will only have a single form called dispatcher.aspx.

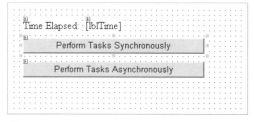

Figure 10.3 The dispatcher.aspx form is a simple form with two labels and two buttons. The first button will execute two tasks synchronously—that is, it will execute Task1, wait for it to be done, then execute Task2. The second button will execute the same tasks asynchronously (both at the same time).

WORKING WITH DELEGATES AND EVENTS

Figure 10.4 If you are trying to recreate the form by hand you may want to use this HTML for reference.

```
Code                          _ □ ×
<%@ Page language="c#"
  Codebehind="dispatcher.aspx.cs"
  AutoEventWireup="false"
  Inherits="delegatesproject.WebForm1" %>
<HTML>
   <HEAD>
     <title>WebForm1</title>
   </HEAD>
   <body MS_POSITIONING="GridLayout">
   <form id="Form1" method="post"
         runat="server">
   <asp:Button id="btnSync" style="Z-
         INDEX: 100; LEFT: 30px;
         POSITION: absolute; TOP: 52px"
         runat="server"
         Text="Perform Tasks
         Synchronously"
         Width="275px">
         </asp:Button>
   <asp:Button id="btnAsync" style="Z-
         INDEX: 104; LEFT: 30px;
         POSITION: absolute; TOP: 89px"
         runat="server"
         Text="Perform Tasks
         Asynchronously"
         Width="275px">
         </asp:Button>
   <asp:Label id="lblTimeElapsed"
         style="Z-INDEX: 102; LEFT:
         30px; POSITION: absolute; TOP:
         23px" runat="server">
         Time Elapsed:
         </asp:Label>
   <asp:Label id="lblTime" style="Z-
         INDEX: 103; LEFT: 125px;
         POSITION: absolute; TOP: 23px"
         runat="server">
         </asp:Label>
   </form>
   </body>
</HTML>
```

✔ **Tips**

■ As with the other projects in this book, building the project isn't necessary for learning the concepts in this chapter.

■ Skeletons for each project can be downloaded from Peachpit's Web site, http://www.peachpit.com/vqs/csharp.

Declaring a Delegate

A delegate is a special type that can store a function. When you declare a delegate you tell the compiler what types of functions your delegate is meant to store. The delegate declaration itself looks just like a function declaration but with the delegate keyword in front.

To declare a delegate:

1. Either outside of a class or inside of a class type delegate.

2. Write a function prototype; that is, type a return type, followed by a function name, followed by input parameters.

3. Type a semicolon ; (**Figure 10.5**).

✔ Tips

■ Just like other function declarations, delegates can either return void, or any other type.

■ At first glance it may look strange to throw a declaration of a delegate outside of a class, but the compiler takes that one line and creates a whole class out of it, so in essence what you are doing is declaring a new class. The class that it creates is derived from System.MulticastDelegate.

Figure 10.5 A delegate looks like a function declaration, except that the compiler turns the declaration into an entire class. The class name will be TaskDel, therefore TaskDel becomes a new data type.

```
delegate bool TaskDel(string desc);
```

Figure 10.6 Once you declare a delegate, you can create instances of it passing a function as the parameter of the constructor. The function can be an instance function, like Task1, or a static function like Task2.

```
Code                              _ □ ×

class Tasks
{
   public bool Task1(string desc)
   {
      return true;
   }

   public static bool Task2(string desc)
   {
      return true;
   }
}

delegate bool TaskDel(string desc);

public class WebForm1 :
System.Web.UI.Page
{
   private void Page_Load(object sender,
            System.EventArgs e)
   {
      Tasks tsks = new Tasks();
      TaskDel t1 = new TaskDel(
                  tsks.Task1);
      TaskDel t2 = new TaskDel(
                  Tasks.Task2);
   }
}
```

Creating and Invoking Delegates

Once you declare a delegate, you will want to allocate an instance of the delegate class and assign a function to it. Then you can invoke the particular function using the delegate variable.

To create a delegate:

1. Declare a variable using the delegate name as its type.

2. Type an equal sign =.

3. Type new followed by the name of the delegate type.

4. Type an open parenthesis (.

5. Type the name of the function that the delegate will store. If the function is an instance function type var.functioname, where var is a variable storing an instance of the class and functionname is the name of the function that you want to invoke through the delegate. If the function is a static function, type classname.functionname where classname is the name of the class and functionname is the name of the static function you want to invoke.

6. Type a close parenthesis).

7. Type a semicolon ; (**Figure 10.6**).

To invoke a delegate:

1. Type the name of the variable that points to a delegate object.

2. Type an open parenthesis (.

3. Enter the parameters to pass to the function assigned to the delegate object.

4. Type a close parenthesis) (**Figure 10.7**).

✔ Tip

■ You may recall that a delegate declaration is really a class declaration. The Invoke method is a method that is part of the class. It has the same parameters and output parameters as the delegate declaration. When you use the variable that stores the delegate followed by parenthesis, the compiler turns that code into a call to the Invoke method, passing the parameters after the parenthesis.

Figure 10.7 Once you assign a function to the delegate variable, you can call it by using the variable followed by parenthesis and the parameters of the function that the delegate is storing.

```
class Tasks
{
    public bool Task1(string desc)
    {
        return true;
    }

    public static bool Task2(string desc)
    {
        return true;
    }
}

delegate bool TaskDel(string desc);

public class WebForm1 :
System.Web.UI.Page
{
    private void Page_Load(object sender,
             System.EventArgs e)
    {
        Tasks tsks = new Tasks();
        TaskDel t1 = new TaskDel(
                     tsks.Task1);
        TaskDel t2 = new TaskDel(
                     Tasks.Task2);

        bool result;
        result = t1("Calling Task 1...");
        result = t2("Calling Task 2...");
    }
}
```

Figure 10.8 You can also create a delegate from the combination of two or more delegates. This enables you to call both functions with a single method call. In this example, the call to t3 actually invokes both Task1 and Task2.

```
class Tasks
{
   public bool Task1(string desc)
   {
      return true;
   }

   public static bool Task2(string desc)
   {
      return true;
   }
}

delegate bool TaskDel(string desc);

public class WebForm1 :
System.Web.UI.Page
{
   private void Page_Load(object sender,
            System.EventArgs e)
   {
      Tasks tsks = new Tasks();
      TaskDel t1 = new TaskDel(
                  tsks.Task1);
      TaskDel t2 = new TaskDel(
                  Tasks.Task2);

      bool result;
      result = t1("Calling Task 1...");
      result = t2("Calling Task 2...");

      TaskDel t3 = t1 + t2;
      t3("Call both delegates...");
   }
}
```

- The combined delegate stores a linked list of delegate objects. When you invoke a combined delegate, the framework goes through each node in the linked list and invokes the function for the particular delegate synchronously. The fact that each member in the list is invoked synchronously means that control to the program doesn't return until all the delegates have been invoked. Later in this chapter you will learn how to invoke delegates aynchronously.

Combining Delegates

Being able to combine delegates is one of their most powerful features. Combining delegates means that a single delegate object can store a chain of functions, so you can invoke multiple functions from different classes with a single method call.

To combine two delegates:

1. To combine two delegates, it's best if you have already created two other delegate objects of the same type. (For details, see the first half of "Creating and Invoking Delegates," on page 309.)

2. Declare a variable of the same type of delegate as the delegates you are combining.

3. Type an equal sign =.

4. Type the name of the first delegate variable.

5. Type a plus sign +.

6. Type the name of the second delegate variable.

7. Type a semicolon ; (**Figure 10.8**).

✔ Tips

- When you use the + sign, C# converts it to a call to the static function System.MulticastDelegate.Combine, which does the job of producing a delegate from the combination of two or more delegates.

- There are really two types of delegates in the .NET framework: delegates derived from the class System.Delegate and delegates derived from the class System.MulticastDelegate. Only classes derived from System.MulticastDelegate can be combined. (C# always uses System.MulticastDelegate.)

Removing Delegates

Removing delegates is the opposite of combining them.

To remove a delegate from a combined delegate:

1. To remove a delegate, you must have two variables: one that stores a combination of delegates and one that points to the delegate object you want to remove from the list.

2. Type the name of the variable that has the combined delegate.

3. Type -= (minus equal operator).

4. Type the name of the variable you want to remove from the list of delegates.

5. Type a semicolon ; (**Figure 10.9**).

Figure 10.9 With the -= operator we can remove one of the delegates from the combined delegate. Therefore, calling t3 now only invokes Task2.

```
class Tasks
{
    public bool Task1(string desc)
    {
        return true;
    }

    public static bool Task2(string desc)
    {
        return true;
    }
}

delegate bool TaskDel(string desc);

public class WebForm1 :
System.Web.UI.Page
{
    private void Page_Load(object sender,
                System.EventArgs e)
    {
        Tasks tsks = new Tasks();
        TaskDel t1 = new TaskDel(
                    tsks.Task1);
        TaskDel t2 = new TaskDel(
                    Tasks.Task2);

        bool result;
        result = t1("Calling Task 1...");
        result = t2("Calling Task 2...");

        TaskDel t3 = t1 + t2;
        t3("Call both delegates...");

        t3 -= t1;
        t3("Call only Task2...");
    }
}
```

Figure 10.10 The Modem class enables a user to request modem status as the modem is connecting. The Modem class has a Subscribe method that enables a user to pass a delegate variable. The Connect method then uses this variable to call a function on the subscriber's class.

```
Code                          _ □ ×

delegate void ReportStatusDel(
            string status);

class Modem
{
   static ReportStatusDel report;

   public static void Subscribe(
              ReportStatusDel del)
   {
      report += del;
   }

   public static void Unsubscribe(
              ReportStatusDel del)
   {
      report -= del;
   }

   public static void Connect()
   {
      if (report != null)
      {
         report("Initializing...");
         report("Dialing...");
         report("Authenticating...");
         report("Connected...");
      }
   }
}

public class WebForm1 :
System.Web.UI.Page
{
   private void ReportModemStatus(
             string msg)
   {
      Response.Write(msg + "<br>");
   }

   private void Page_Load(object sender,
             System.EventArgs e)
   {
      Modem.Subscribe(
          new ReportStatusDel(
          ReportModemStatus));
      Modem.Connect();
      Modem.Unsubscribe(
          new ReportStatusDel(
          ReportModemStatus));
   }
}
```

✔ Tips

■ When you use the -= operator, the C# compiler turns that code into a call to the delegate's Remove function, which lets you remove a delegate from a linked list of delegates.

■ The ability of delegates to be combined and removed makes it easy to build a subscriber class such as the Modem class (**Figure 10.10**). This class reports information for the status of the modem, and multiple classes can subscribe to receive notifications. The Modem class has a method called Subscribe and a method called Unsubscribe to enable other classes to request and cancel notifications.

REMOVING DELEGATES

Declaring and Firing Events

Events are essential entities for Web programming. They are functions that are used to report user interaction with Web forms and Web controls, among other objects. Events are built on top of delegates, so to declare an event in C# you first declare a delegate. The event declaration then tells the compiler to add a field of the delegate type and two functions: add and remove. The delegate field maintains a list of delegates by combining and removing delegates from the field. The add and remove functions enable classes to subscribe and unsubscribe from the list of delegates. By firing the event, the class invokes a method on all of the subscribers in the list.

To declare an event:

1. Declare a delegate using the instructions in the section "Declaring a Delegate," above.

2. Inside the class that is to issue event notifications, type an access modifier such as public, protected, private, etc.

3. Type event.

4. Type the name of the delegate type.

5. Type a name for the event. Event names are usually constructed by adding the prefix On to the name of the delegate type. For example, if the delegate type is ReportStatus, the event name would be OnReportStatus.

6. Type a semicolon ;.

Figure 10.11 Notice the transformation between the last figure and this one. What we have done is to turn the delegate into an event. This makes the compiler give us the added ability to subscribe and unsubscribe from status notifications.

```
Code                                    _ □ ×

delegate void ReportStatusDel(
            string status);

class Modem
{
    public static event
        ReportStatusDel OnReportStatus;

    public static void Connect()
    {
        if (OnReportStatus != null)
        {
            OnReportStatus(
                    "Initializing...");
            OnReportStatus(
                    "Dialing...");
            OnReportStatus(
                    "Authenticating...");
            OnReportStatus("Connected...");
        }
    }
}
```

To fire the event:

1. Type the name of the event. For example: OnReportStatus.

2. Type an open parenthesis (.

3. Type the parameters for the delegate type.

4. Type a close parenthesis).

5. Type a semicolon ; (**Figure 10.11** shows the Modem class from the previous section modified to use events instead of the delegate variable directly).

✔ Tips

■ Before firing an event you have to check if the event variable is not equal to null.

■ Events are used to report user interactions with various objects. For example, the Page class has a number of events. Events in Web applications execute on the server. When a client accesses a page through the browser and interacts with a control, the client HTML issues a post command. The post command is an HTTP command that executes on the server. The server then creates various objects, and those objects generate events. For example, a button control may generate a click event; you then write code to handle the event.

■ Firing the event is simply invoking a delegate. Remember, a delegate is a type that stores a reference to a function in another class. Therefore the subscriber of the event has to have a function that the delegate will invoke. For instructions on how to subscribe and unsubscribe to events, see "Subscribing to Events," later in this chapter.

DECLARING AND FIRING EVENTS

315

Adding Events that are Web Friendly

A lot of Web-related classes fire events, and some fire many events. It would be really hard to keep track of the parameters of each event if the events didn't follow certain guidelines for their parameters. To ensure that most events follow the same parameter guidelines, Microsoft defined a delegate that developers should use when declaring their events. This delegate is called EventHandler. So when you declare an event, you should use EventHandler as the type.

To declare an event that has a standard format:

1. Inside the class that will fire the event, type an access modifier, such as public.

2. Type event.

3. Type EventHandler.

4. Type the name of the event. For example: OnReportStatus.

5. Type a semicolon ; (**Figure 10.12** shows the Modem class from the previous section modified to use the standard event type, EventHandler, rather than its custom type, ReportStatusDel).

Figure 10.12 Most events in C# follow the same format because they are all based on the EventHandler delegate. This delegate has two parameters, sender and arguments. However, right now we have no way of passing arguments, so all we can do is pass Empty as our argument. To pass arguments we need to create a special class, as in Figure 10.13.

```
class Modem
{
    public event EventHandler
    OnReportStatus;

    public void Connect()
    {
        if (OnReportStatus != null)
        {
            // "Initializing..."
            OnReportStatus(this,
            EventArgs.Empty);

            // "Dialing..."
            OnReportStatus(this,
            EventArgs.Empty);

            // "Authenticating..."
            OnReportStatus(this,
            EventArgs.Empty);

            //"Connected..."
            OnReportStatus(this,
            EventArgs.Empty);
        }
    }
}
```

Figure 10.13 The ReportStatusArgs function enables us to report extra information as part of our event. All we have to do to make our event behave like other events is derive our ReportStatusArgs class from EventArgs. We then store the extra information in an instance of this class and send it as the second parameter of our event call.

```
Code

class Modem
{
    public event EventHandler
    OnReportStatus;

    public class ReportStatusArgs :
                EventArgs
    {
        public string Message;
    }

    public void Connect()
    {
        if (OnReportStatus != null)
        {
            ReportStatusArgs msg =
            new ReportStatusArgs();
            msg.Message = "Initializing...";
            OnReportStatus(this,msg);
            msg.Message = "Dialing...";
            OnReportStatus(this,msg);
            msg.Message="Authenticating...";
            OnReportStatus(this,msg);
            msg.Message = "Connected...";
            OnReportStatus(this,msg);
        }
    }
}
```

✔ Tips

- EventHandler is a delegate derived from MulticastDelegate. The delegate has two parameters. The first parameter is sender of type object. The second parameter is args of type EventArgs.

- When you fire an event of type EventHandler, the first parameter, sender, should be the class that is generating the event. Most likely this parameter would be set to this. The second parameter, args, is for sending information related to the event. If your event has related information, you would create a class derived from System.EventArgs and add a field to the class that represents the extra information. Then you would create an instance of the class and pass the instance of the class in the second parameter. In the example code in **Figure 10.12**, the event is useless for our purpose because we need to also pass in the message for the Modem status. **Figure 10.13** shows the code modified to pass the message information as well.

ADDING EVENTS THAT ARE WEB FRIENDLY

Subscribing to Events

Instead of declaring your own events, you will usually want to subscribe to events that another class has. In Web programming you will want to subscribe to events from the Page object, for example, events such as Load. Web controls also have events. For example, whenever you add a button, you will most likely want to subscribe to its click event. VS.NET has a wizard that automatically generates code to subscribe to an event, but it's good to know how to do it by hand in order to understand the subscription mechanism.

To subscribe to an event:

1. To subscribe to an event, you must have a function in your class that has the same parameters as the delegate the event is based on. Add the function to receive the event notification. If the event is based on EventHandler—as most events are—simply add a function like this:

```
private void ReportModemStatus
(object sender, EventArgs args)
{
}.
```

2. Events are instance fields of a class, so you need to have a variable pointing to an instance of the class with the event. Type var.eventname, where var is the variable pointing to the object that has the event and eventname is the name of the event. If the event is static, you can just type the name of the class followed by the name of the event.

Figure 10.14 Capturing an event is a matter of adding a function to our class that has the same format as the event's delegate (in this case EventHandler). We then type the name of the event followed by +=, followed by a new instance of the delegate with our function as the parameter for the delegate's constructor.

```
public class WebForm1 : System.Web.UI.Page
{
    private void ReportModemStatus(
    object sender, EventArgs args)
    {
        if (args is Modem.ReportStatusArgs)
        {
            Modem.ReportStatusArgs msg =
            (Modem.ReportStatusArgs) args;
            Response.Write(msg.Message
                            + "<br>");
        }
    }

    private void Page_Load(object sender,
            System.EventArgs e)
    {
        Modem m1 = new Modem();
        m1.OnReportStatus += new
        EventHandler(ReportModemStatus);
        m1.Connect();
    }
}
```

Figure 10.15 The Modem class keeps a list of listeners. If at some point we want to remove ourselves from the list, all we need to do is type the name of the event again, followed by −=, followed by a new instance of the event's delegate with our function as the parameter for the delegate's constructor.

```
█ Code                              _ □ ×
public class WebForm1 : System.Web.UI.Page
{
    private void ReportModemStatus(
    object sender, EventArgs args)
    {
        if (args is Modem.ReportStatusArgs)
        {
            Modem.ReportStatusArgs msg =
            (Modem.ReportStatusArgs) args;
            Response.Write(msg.Message
                            + "<br>");
        }
    }

    private void Page_Load(object sender,
            System.EventArgs e)
    {
        Modem m1 = new Modem();
        m1.OnReportStatus += new
        EventHandler(ReportModemStatus);
        m1.Connect();
        m1.OnReportStatus -= new
        EventHandler(ReportModemStatus);
    }
}
```

3. Type the plus equal operator +=.

4. Type new.

5. Type the name of the delegate the event is based on.

6. Type an open parenthesis (.

7. Type the name of the function in your class that you entered in step 1.

8. Type a close parenthesis).

9. Type a semicolon ; (**Figure 10.14**).

✔ Tips

■ When you use the += operator to subscribe to an event, the compiler adds code to invoke the add method of the class. Remember that when you add an event, the compiler turns the event declaration into a field and two functions, one to subscribe and one to unsubscribe.

■ To disconnect, or unsubscribe from an event, use the −= operator (**Figure 10.15**).

Firing Delegates Asynchronously

One of the most powerful features of delegates is the ability to invoke the function the delegate stores asynchronously. Executing the function asynchronously means that the system invokes the method in another thread and execution returns to the main thread immediately, before the method is done executing.

A thread is an operating system object that determines the sequence of functions that the processor will execute. What happens is that the operating system gives each thread a certain amount of time to execute some code. Even before the code is done executing, the OS may decide to halt a thread to give another thread a chance to execute.

When you execute a function asynchronously, the .NET framework allocates a pool of threads. It then takes one of the threads from the pool and uses it to execute the function. This leaves the main thread free to continue executing its code. There are two ways to execute a delegate asynchronously. One is to execute the delegate asynchronously, and then write code that waits until the delegate is done executing. The second approach is to let the system inform you when it is done by providing the system with a function in your class that it can call when it is done executing the function asynchronously.

Figure 10.16 Remember that delegate classes have an Invoke method. This method is what gets called if you use the delegate variable directly followed by parenthesis and the parameters. BeginInvoke executes the same function, but asynchronously.

```
Code                              _ □ ✕

class Tasks
{
   public bool Task1(string desc)
   {
      return true;
   }

   public static bool Task2(string desc)
   {
      return true;
   }
}

delegate bool TaskDel(string desc);

public class WebForm1 :
System.Web.UI.Page
{
   private void Page_Load(object sender,
             System.EventArgs e)
   {
      TaskDel del1 =
      new TaskDel(Tasks.Task2);

      IAsyncResult rs =
      del1.BeginInvoke(
      "Calling Task1...",null,null);
   }
}
```

To execute a delegate function asynchronously and wait:

1. Type IAsyncResult rs1, where rs1 is any variable name.

2. Type an equal sign =.

3. Type del.BeginInvoke where del is the name of a variable that stores a delegate function.

4. Type an open parenthesis (.

5. Type the parameters for the delegate function.

6. Type ,null, null after the last parameter of the delegate function.

7. Type a close parenthesis).

8. Type a semicolon ;.

9. For instructions on how to wait for the delegate to complete, read the section "Waiting for Asynchronous Delegates to Complete," later in this chapter (**Figure 10.16**).

FIRING DELEGATES ASYNCHRONOUSLY

To execute a delegate function asynchronously and let the system tell you when it is done:

1. Declare a function in your class that will be used for the system to notify you when the delegate is done executing. The function should have the following prototype:

   ```
   public void FunctionDone (
   IAsyncResult ar)
   {
   }
   ```

   You can use any function name you like as long as you match the parameters.

2. Type `AsyncCallback cb = new AsyncCallback(this.FunctionDone);` where `cb` is any variable name to store a delegate to the function that the system will use to notify you when it is done, and `FunctionDone` is the name of the function you declared in step 1.

3. Type `del1.BeginInvoke`, where `del1` is the variable that points to the delegate that you want to execute asynchronously.

4. Type the parameters for the delegate function.

5. Type `,cb, state` after the last parameter of the delegate function. `cb` is the name of the variable you created in step 2. `state` is any variable or literal value. (The system will store the value and you can retrieve it later.)

6. For information on what to do when the notification function executes in your class, read "Retrieving Results from Asynchronous Delegates," later in this chapter (**Figure 10.17**).

Figure 10.17 You can have .NET notify you when the asynchronous function is done executing by declaring a function such as FunctionDone, shown here. You then declare a delegate to contain that function and pass it as a parameter to BeginInvoke. When Task2 is done executing, the runtime will call FunctionDone.

```
class Tasks
{
    public bool Task1(string desc)
    {
        return true;
    }

    public static bool Task2(string desc)
    {
        return true;
    }
}

delegate bool TaskDel(string desc);

public class WebForm1 :
System.Web.UI.Page
{
    public void FunctionDone(
            IAsyncResult ar)
    {
    }

    private void Page_Load(object sender,
            System.EventArgs e)
    {
        TaskDel del1 =
        new TaskDel(Tasks.Task2);

        AsyncCallback cb = new
        AsyncCallback(this.FunctionDone);

        IAsyncResult rs =
        del1.BeginInvoke(
        "Calling Task1...",cb,"Task2");
    }
}
```

✔ Tips

- As you type BeginInvoke you may notice that the intellisense feature doesn't list BeginInvoke as one of the methods. That's okay; keep typing. This is one instance where intellisense doesn't work correctly.

- You can't execute combined delegates asynchronously.

- Use the first approach (execute and wait) when you want to execute multiple functions asynchronously, each in different threads, and wait until all of them have completed.

- Use the second approach (system alerts you when it's done) when you have only one function to execute asynchronously and you want to continue executing code in the main thread while the delegate function is executing.

- When you use `BeginInvoke`, the first parameters are the parameters for the delegate, but only the input parameters are important. Control returns to your code after calling `BeginInvoke` before the asynchronous function is done executing, which means that any output values are meaningless. Once the function is done executing, you can read the return values. For details, see "Retrieving Results from Asynchronous Delegates," later in this chapter.

FIRING DELEGATES ASYNCHRONOUSLY

Waiting for Asynchronous Delegates to Complete

Sometimes you want to execute multiple functions asynchronously, and then wait for all the functions to complete before continuing the execution of the program. For example, suppose your Web page is going to display an employee record. Displaying the record involves fetching multiple pieces of information from different database tables. Fetching the data from the multiple tables can be done at the same time using asynchronous delegates. But before presenting the information, you want to wait until all the delegates have fetched the particular data they were after.

To wait for several delegates to complete executing:

1. Suppose you have started multiple delegate functions asynchronously and have stored the results in the variables: IAsyncResult ar1, and IAsyncResult ar2.

2. Type System.Threading.WaitHandle[] handles = new System.Threading.
   → WaitHandle[] {ar1.AsyncWaitHandle, ar2.AsyncWaitHandle}; where handles is any name you want to assign to the array of WaitHandles.

3. Type System.Threading.WaitHandle.
   → WaitAll(handles); (**Figure 10.18**).

Figure 10.18 This looks complicated because it is. It basically tells the runtime to stop the program's main thread from running until the secondary threads are done executing. If we didn't do this, the main thread would get done before the secondary thread, and our page would be displayed before Task1 and Task2 finished.

```
class Tasks
{
    public bool Task1(string desc)
    {
        return true;
    }

    public static bool Task2(string desc)
    {
        return true;
    }
}

delegate bool TaskDel(string desc);

public class WebForm1 :
System.Web.UI.Page
{
    private void Page_Load(object sender,
            System.EventArgs e)
    {
        Tasks tsks = new Tasks();
        TaskDel del1 =
        new TaskDel(tsks.Task1);
        TaskDel del2 =
        new TaskDel(Tasks.Task2);

        IAsyncResult ar1 =
        del1.BeginInvoke(
        "Calling Task1...",null,null);

        IAsyncResult ar2 =
        del2.BeginInvoke(
        "Calling Task2...",null,null);

        System.Threading.WaitHandle[]
        handles =
        new System.Threading.WaitHandle[]
        {ar1.AsyncWaitHandle ,
        ar2.AsyncWaitHandle };

        System.Threading.WaitHandle.
        WaitAll(handles);
    }
}
```

Figure 10.19 If you don't specify a timeout, the main thread will be paused indefinitely. If the functions take longer than the timeout period, the program will continue but the WaitAll function will return false. If the Tasks finish before the timeout period, then WaitAll returns true.

```
class Tasks
{
   public bool Task1(string desc)
   {
      return true;
   }

   public static bool Task2(string desc)
   {
      return true;
   }
}

delegate bool TaskDel(string desc);

public class WebForm1 :
System.Web.UI.Page
{
   private void Page_Load(object sender,
            System.EventArgs e)
   {
      Tasks tsks = new Tasks();
      TaskDel del1 =
      new TaskDel(tsks.Task1);
      TaskDel del2 =
      new TaskDel(Tasks.Task2);

      IAsyncResult ar1 =
      del1.BeginInvoke(
      "Calling Task1...",null,null);

      IAsyncResult ar2 =
      del2.BeginInvoke(
      "Calling Task2...",null,null);

      System.Threading.WaitHandle[]
      handles =
      new System.Threading.WaitHandle[]
      {ar1.AsyncWaitHandle ,
      ar2.AsyncWaitHandle };

      bool result =
      System.Threading.WaitHandle.
      WaitAll(handles,2000,false);
   }
}
```

✔ Tip

- The WaitAll function also has over-loaded methods that enable you to wait for a certain amount of time. This is useful if you want to prevent the program from freezing if, for example, one of the delegates fails to complete within a timely manner (**Figure 10.19**).

WAITING FOR ASYNCHRONOUS DELEGATES

Retrieving Results from Asynchronous Delegates

When you execute a delegate asynchronously, control returns to the application immediately, before the delegate is done executing the function. Because the delegate hasn't completed, output parameters aren't yet known. Therefore you have to wait until the delegate is done executing to retrieve the output values. The delegate class provides a function called `EndInvoke` to retrieve output values. There are two ways of using `EndInvoke` depending on how you called `BeginInvoke`: writing code that waits, or providing a callback function.

To retrieve output parameters if you have code that waits for the delegates to finish:

1. If you invoked the delegates asynchronously and waited for the delegates to complete, you most likely have delegate variables such as del1 and del2, and `IAsyncResult` variables such as ar1 and ar2.

2. Type `object result = del1.EndInvoke(ar1, outparam1, outparam2);` where `result` is any variable to accept the result value. The type of result is shown as object, but it can be the specific type that the delegate function returns; `ar1` is the name of the variable holding the `IAsyncResult` value returned from the call to `BeginInvoke`; `outparam1` and `outparam2` are variables for each ref or out parameter specified in the delegate function (**Figure 10.20**).

Figure 10.20 Because the functions begin execution and return immediately, there's no way of knowing the return parameters on the BeginInvoke. You need to wait until they're done and then call EndInvoke to get the return values.

```
class Tasks
{
    public bool Task1(string desc)
    {
        return true;
    }

    public static bool Task2(string desc)
    {
        return true;
    }
}

delegate bool TaskDel(string desc);

public class WebForm1 :
System.Web.UI.Page
{
    private void Page_Load(object sender,
            System.EventArgs e)
    {
        Tasks tsks = new Tasks();
        TaskDel del1 =
        new TaskDel(tsks.Task1);
        TaskDel del2 =
        new TaskDel(Tasks.Task2);

        IAsyncResult ar1 =
        del1.BeginInvoke(
        "Calling Task1...",null,null);

        IAsyncResult ar2 =
        del2.BeginInvoke(
        "Calling Task2...",null,null);

        System.Threading.WaitHandle[]
        handles =
        new System.Threading.WaitHandle[]
        {ar1.AsyncWaitHandle ,
        ar2.AsyncWaitHandle };

        System.Threading.WaitHandle.
        WaitAll(handles,2000,false);

        bool retval1 = del1.EndInvoke(ar1);
        bool retval2 = del2.EndInvoke(ar2);
    }
}
```

Figure 10.21 In the case of the system telling us when it's done executing the functions, we may not have the original delegate variables and we need them to call EndInvoke and retrieve the output parameters. Luckily, the system gives us the original delegate variable through the AsyncResult parameter.

```
class Tasks
{
   public bool Task1(string desc)
   {
      return true;
   }

   public static bool Task2(string desc)
   {
      return true;
   }
}

delegate bool TaskDel(string desc);

public class WebForm1 :
System.Web.UI.Page
{
   public void FunctionDone (
            IAsyncResult ar)
   {
      TaskDel del1 = (TaskDel)
      ((System.Runtime.Remoting.
      Messaging.AsyncResult)ar).
      AsyncDelegate;
      bool result = del1.EndInvoke(ar);
   }

   private void Page_Load(object sender,
            System.EventArgs e)
   {
      Tasks tsks = new Tasks();
      TaskDel del1 =
      new TaskDel(tsks.Task1);
      TaskDel del2 =
      new TaskDel(Tasks.Task2);

      AsyncCallback cb = new
      AsyncCallback(this.FunctionDone);

      IAsyncResult ar1 =
      del1.BeginInvoke(
      "Calling Task1...",cb,null);

      IAsyncResult ar2 =
      del2.BeginInvoke(
      "Calling Task2...",cb,null);
   }
}
```

To retrieve output parameters if you have a callback function:

The trick to remember when using a callback function is that you don't have the original delegate variable when the callback function executes. But you can retrieve it from the parameter of the callback function.

1. Type DelegateTypeName del1 = (DelegateTypeName) ((System.Runtime. → Remoting.Messaging.AsyncResult)ar). AsyncDelegate; where del is any variable to hold the delegate object, and ar is the name of the input parameter.

2. Follow step 2 from the previous section to retrieve the output parameters with EndInvoke (**Figure 10.21**).

✔ Tips

■ EndInvoke can be used to retrieve the output parameter of the function, plus any ref or out parameters of the delegate function.

■ Every delegate object has a BeginInvoke function and an EndInvoke function as well as the Invoke function, which is used for synchronous operation. Other classes mimic this behavior: They provide a BeginInvoke/EndInvoke for asynchronous operations and an Invoke function for synchronous operations. For example, the class WebClient also uses the same pattern for asynchronous vs. synchronous operation.

ASYNCHRONOUS DELEGATES RESULTS

327

Finishing the Sample Application

At this point, you know enough to finish the sample application, which will show you the difference timewise between executing two functions synchronously and executing them asynchronously.

To measure the time difference, we're going to make use of the classes System.DateTime and System.TimeSpan. System.DateTime.Now reports the current date and time. We can record the date and time before and after the functions complete and print out the difference in seconds between the synchronous method and the asynchronous one.

The only other thing we need is a way to execute tasks that actually take a noticeable amount of time to execute. To do so we'll make use of a function called System.Threading.Thread.Sleep. This function enables us to stop execution for a specified amount of time, expressed in milliseconds.

To complete the sample application:

1. From the Solution Explorer window, right-click on dispatcher.aspx and choose View Code from the pop-up menu. You should see the code for the WebForm1 class inside the delegateproject namespace.

2. Add a class called Tasks. The Tasks class should have two functions, Task1 and Task2. These two functions should do nothing but pause for 5 seconds (5000 milliseconds) (**Figure 10.22**).

3. Add a definition for a delegate that can invoke either Task1 or Task2 (**Figure 10.23**).

Figure 10.22 The Tasks class has two functions, Task1 and Task2. One of them is an instance function, the other is a static function. This was done to illustrate that the same delegate type can invoke either an instance method or a static method. Both Task1 and Task2 pause execution for five seconds.

```
namespace delegatesproject
{
class Tasks
{
    public bool Task1(string desc)
    {
        System.Threading.Thread.
        Sleep(5000);
        return true;
    }

    public static bool Task2(string desc)
    {
        System.Threading.Thread.
        Sleep(5000);
        return true;
    }
}

class WebForm1 : System.Web.UI.Page
//more code here
```

Figure 10.23 The TaskDel delegate can store functions that have one string input parameter and one Boolean output parameter. So Task1 and Task2 are both valid functions to store in the delegate.

```
namespace delegatesproject
{
class Tasks
{
    public bool Task1(string desc)
    {
        System.Threading.Thread.
        Sleep(5000);
        return true;
    }

    public static bool Task2(string desc)
    {
        System.Threading.Thread.
        Sleep(5000);
        return true;
    }
}

delegate bool TaskDel(string desc);

class WebForm1 : System.Web.UI.Page
//more code here
```

Figure 10.24 The synchronous version of the function calls both Task1 and Task2 in the traditional fashion, without using delegates.

```
Code                                    _ □ ×

class WebForm1 : System.Web.UI.Page
{
    //more code here

    private void btnSync_Click(
    object sender, System.EventArgs e)
    {
        Tasks tsks = new Tasks();
        System.DateTime dt1 =
        System.DateTime.Now;

        tsks.Task1("Calling Task1...");
        Tasks.Task2("Calling Task2...");

        System.DateTime dt2 =
        System.DateTime.Now;

        System.TimeSpan tm = dt2 - dt1;
        lblTime.Text =
        tm.TotalSeconds.ToString();
    }

}
```

4. From the Solution Explorer window, right-click on dispatcher.aspx and choose View Designer from the popup menu.

5. Double-click on the Perform Tasks Synchronously button to have the wizard add the stub for the Click event of the button to the code.

6. Repeat steps 4 and 5, but this time double-click on the Perform Tasks Asynchronously button.

7. Add the code in **Figure 10.24** to the btnSync_Click function. This code first records the current time, then calls the functions Task1 and Task2 in order, and records the ending time. Finally, it displays in seconds the time it took to execute both tasks.

continues on next page

8. Add the code in **Figure 10.25** to the btnAsync_Click function. This code creates delegates for each Task function and then invokes the function asynchronously. Both functions will execute in different threads. The function then displays the time it took to execute both functions in seconds.

✔ Tips

■ The DateTime function overloads the − operator to return a TimeSpan object. When you subtract one date from another, the time difference is reported in the TimeSpan object. You can then use the TimeSpan's TotalSeconds function to report the time difference in seconds.

■ Execute the program and click on each button. You should see that in the synchronous case, the tasks complete in about ten seconds. In the asynchronous case you should see both tasks completing in about five seconds. If you have a computer with multiple processors (lucky you) then the tasks can really happen at the same time. With a single processor, the OS gives each thread some time to execute and continues to switch between each thread.

Figure 10.25 The asynchronous version of the function uses delegates to invoke both functions asynchronously. Both functions record the time before and after execution, then print out the difference in seconds.

```
class WebForm1 : System.Web.UI.Page
{
    //more code here

    private void btnSync_Click(
    object sender, System.EventArgs e)
    {
        //code entered previously
    }

    private void btnAsync_Click(
    object sender, System.EventArgs e)
    {
        Tasks tsks = new Tasks();

        TaskDel del1 = new
        TaskDel(tsks.Task1);

        TaskDel del2 = new
        TaskDel(Tasks.Task2);

        System.DateTime dt1 =
        System.DateTime.Now;

        IAsyncResult ar1 =
        del1.BeginInvoke(
        "Calling Task1...",null,null);

        IAsyncResult ar2 =
        del2.BeginInvoke(
        "Calling Task2...",null,null);

        System.Threading.WaitHandle[]
        handles = new
        System.Threading.WaitHandle[]
        {ar1.AsyncWaitHandle ,
         ar2.AsyncWaitHandle };

        System.Threading.WaitHandle.
        WaitAll(handles);

        System.DateTime dt2 =
        System.DateTime.Now;

        System.TimeSpan tm = dt2 - dt1;
        lblTime.Text =
        tm.TotalSeconds.ToString();
    }
}
```

ERROR HANDLING

It seems that every language has its own way of reporting error conditions. Take for example VBScript, which uses the error object (Err). To trap errors in VBScript, you use the On Error Resume Next function. Contrast that to the way that Windows, the operating system, reports error conditions. When you call one of the API functions, normally the function returns an error code as its output parameter. Depending on what function you call, the code may return 0 if the function was successful or a negative number if it was unsuccessful. However, other functions return 0 if the function was unsuccessful and a positive number if the function was successful. What Microsoft tried to do was unify the way that every language reports errors. They did this by adding exception handling to the .NET Framework (the underlying platform that every language uses). Exceptions are objects that report error conditions. Because C# is built on top of the .NET Framework, it has instructions for catching and throwing exceptions, as well as for allowing you to define your own exceptions. (Developers often refer to generating an exception as *throwing* the exception.)

Working with Exceptions

For this chapter we're going to work with Web security. There's a lot to security, way more than we can cover in this book, but the sample application should give you a taste for some of the security features in ASP.NET.

ASP.NET has three types of security: Windows security, Forms security, and Passport security. Windows security has to do with domain-based security. For Windows security to work, you have to add user accounts to the server, then configure the server to ask users for their user ID and password. Passport security has to do with Microsoft's Passport authentication. If you use instant messaging or have a Hotmail account you should be familiar with this type of authentication. To do Passport security you need to have the Passport SDK, and do more intense programming than what we can do in this chapter. Forms security is what you commonly see in Web applications. It involves a login screen in which a user can enter a name and a password. This is the type of security that we'll be working with.

In the sample application we're going to use the ASP.NET forms authentication module. This module intercepts all requests to your application and ensures that the user has been authenticated (user ID and password are correct). If the user hasn't been authenticated, the module routes the request to a login page.

In the past, developers would create their own security code. First, they would present the user with a login screen. Then, once they verified the name and password, they would write something to the session object—a key of some sort that told the application that the user had logged in. Finally, developers would then test in each page to see if the key was there in the session object. If it wasn't, they would route the request to the login screen. With ASP.NET you don't have to check in each page; the module takes care of intercepting requests and making sure the user has logged in.

You're going to create two pages. The first will be the login page, and the second a page in which you can perform two tasks: require Administration rights and require only User rights. When a user logs in we're going to verify the password and check what groups the user belongs to. Then we're going to create a `GenericPrincipal` object. `GenericPrincipal` is a class in the `System.Security.Principal` namespace. It can store the name of the user as well as the groups that the user belongs to (Admin, User, Guest, for example). There's a property called `HttpContext.User` that all pages have access to. This property can store our `GenericPrincipal` object. When a user clicks on one of the buttons in the secured page, we'll do a security check to see if the user is part of the group. If the user is not part of the group, then we'll generate exceptions.

It sounds like a lot of work, but it's really not that bad, since the framework does a lot of the dirty work. Also, to simplify things, we won't look up names in a database. We'll just write some code that checks a few name/password combinations in place.

To start the sample application:

1. Launch Visual Studio .NET. (Start > All Programs > Microsoft Visual Studio .NET > Microsoft Visual Studio .NET).

2. Select File > New > Project to bring up the New Project dialog.

3. Under project types on the left side of the New Project window click the Visual C# projects folder.

4. Select the ASP.NET Web Application icon and change the name of the application to exceptionsproject (**Figure 11.1**).

5. Visual Studio will create a new project and open WebForm1.aspx.

6. Change the form's name to secured.aspx. To do this, choose View > Solution Explorer from the top menu bar.

7. Right-click on WebForm1.aspx and choose properties. In the property grid below, change the FileName property from WebForm1.aspx to secured.aspx (**Figure 11.2**).

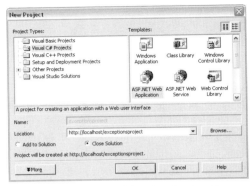

Figure 11.1 As with many of the other chapters, the sample application will be an ASP.NET Web application.

Figure 11.2 This is one way to change the name of the file. You could also click once on the filename, wait a few seconds and click again. This will let you change the name of the file in place.

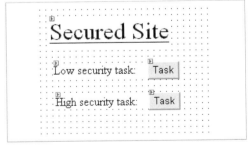

Figure 11.3 The Secured Site page has two buttons. We're going to implement a security system based on roles. The first button will require someone who is part of the Users role and the second one will require someone who is part of the Admin role.

Figure 11.4 The form is basically three labels and two buttons. The code is where the real work takes place.

```
Code                                    _ □ ×

<%@ Page language="c#"
Codebehind="secured.aspx.cs"
AutoEventWireup="false"
Inherits="exceptionsproject.WebForm1" %>
<HTML>
    <HEAD>
        <title>WebForm1</title>
    </HEAD>
    <body MS_POSITIONING="GridLayout">
    <form id="Form1" method="post"
runat="server">
        <asp:Label id="lblTitle"
        style="Z-INDEX: 100; LEFT: 37px;
        POSITION: absolute; TOP: 29px"
        runat="server" Font-Size="X-Large"
        Font-Underline="True">
        Secured Site
        </asp:Label>
        <asp:Button id="btnHighTask"
        style="Z-INDEX: 106; LEFT: 169px;
        POSITION: absolute; TOP: 130px"
        runat="server" Text="Task">
        </asp:Button>
        <asp:Label id="Label2"
        style="Z-INDEX: 105; LEFT: 44px;
        POSITION: absolute; TOP: 132px"
        runat="server" Width="124px"
        Height="20px">
        High security task:
        </asp:Label>
        <asp:Button id="btnLowTask"
        style="Z-INDEX: 102; LEFT: 168px;
        POSITION: absolute; TOP: 88px"
        runat="server" Text="Task">
        </asp:Button>
        <asp:Label id="Label1" style="Z-
        INDEX: 101; LEFT: 42px; POSITION:
        absolute; TOP: 89px" runat="server"
        Width="124px" Height="20px">
        Low security task:
        </asp:Label>
    </form>
    </body>
</HTML>
```

8. Change the secured.aspx page so that it looks like the form in **Figure 11.3**. Obviously this is a lot of work to do by hand. Instead you can enter the HTML directly into the editor. **Figure 11.4** shows the HTML necessary to create the form. To enter the HTML directly, click the HTML button under the editor's window. As an alternative you could download the skeleton file for this project (see Tips later in this section).

continues on next page

9. Select Project > Add Web Form from the menu bar. Enter login.aspx for the new filename (**Figure 11.5**).

10. Change the login.aspx page so that it looks like **Figure 11.6**. You could also input the HTML in **Figure 11.7** directly into the editor.

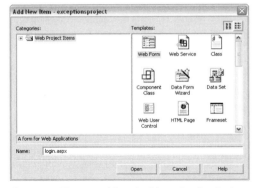

Figure 11.5 The second form in this project is a login form. If the user hasn't logged in, any attempts to reach any other page will make the authentication module present the login page instead.

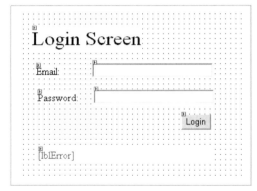

Figure 11.6 The login page asks for a user's email and a password. The user then clicks the login button.

Figure 11.7 Notice that in addition to the labels with text, there's a label below the login button that will be used to report login failures.

```
Code                                    _ □ ×

<%@ Page language="c#"
Codebehind="login.aspx.cs"
AutoEventWireup="false"
Inherits="exceptionsproject.login" %>
<HTML>
    <HEAD>
        <title>login</title>
    </HEAD>
    <body MS_POSITIONING="GridLayout">
    <form id="login" method="post"
    runat="server">
        <asp:Label id="lblEmail"
            style="Z-INDEX: 101;
            LEFT: 44px; POSITION: absolute;
            TOP: 99px" runat="server">
            Email:
            </asp:Label>
        <asp:Label id="lblPassword"
            style="Z-INDEX: 105;
            LEFT: 46px; POSITION: absolute;
            TOP: 141px" runat="server">
            Password:
            </asp:Label>
        <asp:TextBox id="txtPassword"
            style="Z-INDEX: 103;
            LEFT: 133px; POSITION:absolute;
            TOP: 137px" runat="server"
            Width="186px">
            </asp:TextBox>
        <asp:Label id="lblTitle"
            style="Z-INDEX: 102;
            LEFT: 38px; POSITION: absolute;
            TOP: 39px" runat="server"
            Font-Size="X-Large">
            Login Screen</asp:Label>
        <asp:TextBox id="txtEmail"
            style="Z-INDEX: 104;
            LEFT: 131px; POSITION:absolute;
            TOP: 95px" runat="server"
            Width="186px">
            </asp:TextBox>
        <asp:Button id="btnLogin"
            style="Z-INDEX: 106;
            LEFT: 268px; POSITION:absolute;
            TOP: 177px"
            runat="server"
            Text="Login"></asp:Button>
        <asp:Label id="lblError"
            style="Z-INDEX: 107;
            LEFT: 47px; POSITION:absolute;
            TOP: 232px" runat="server"
            Width="265px"
            ForeColor="Red"></asp:Label>
    </form>
    </body>
</HTML>
```

✔ Tips

- So far, all we have is the skeleton of the application—no security code yet. We're going to add security code throughout the chapter.

- Remember that like in any other project in this book, building the project isn't necessary for learning the concepts in this chapter.

- Skeletons for each project can be downloaded from Peachpit's Web site, http://www.peachpit.com/vqs/csharp.

Catching Exceptions

Later in this chapter you'll learn how programs generate exceptions. For now it's sufficient to know that exceptions are objects that report error conditions. More specifically, exceptions are classes derived from System.Exception. Whenever you call a function, that function may generate an exception informing you that something has gone wrong. A function may generate several types of exceptions. For example, a function called MakeDeposit may generate an AmountMustNotBeZero exception and an InvalidAccountNumber exception. There is no way to know if a function is going to generate an exception, or what kind of exceptions it will generate, except by reading the documentation. You can decide to catch only certain kinds of exceptions and let some other piece of code catch the rest, or you can decide to catch all possible exceptions.

To catch all possible exceptions:

1. Functions don't say if they're going to generate exceptions or not, so read the documentation to see if the class throws exceptions and to learn what kind of exceptions you might get.

2. Before the line that might throw an exception, type try followed by an open curly bracket {.

3. After the code you suspect may trigger an error, add a close curly bracket }.

4. In the next line type catch followed a space and an open curly bracket {.

5. Type code to handle the exception (see Tips on next page).

6. Type a close curly bracket } (**Figure 11.8**).

Figure 11.8 As this code shows, you could decide to just have one general error handler for your code.

```
Code
void OpenDatabase()
{
    string cstr =
    "Provider=Microsoft.Jet.OLEDB.4.0;"
    + @"Data Source=c:\csvqs.mdb;";

    try
    {
        IDbConnection conn = new
        OleDbConnection(cstr);
        conn.Open();
    }
    catch
    {
        Response.Write("Error!<br>");
    }
}
```

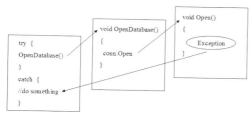

Figure 11.9 Notice that the code in the middle box doesn't have a try/catch block, so the exception flows to the first box. This would be the case also if the middle box had a try/catch block for specific exceptions only, and the exceptions being caught were different from the one being thrown.

Figure 11.10 Error pages in ASP.NET are a vast improvement over the ones in old ASP.

✔ Tips

■ Programmers normally refer to exception-handling code as *try/catch blocks*.

■ If function A calls function B and function B calls function C, and C generates an exception, function B can catch the exception first with a try/catch block. If function B doesn't have a try/catch block around the call to function C, then the exception gets propagated to function A (**Figure 11.9**). If Function A doesn't catch the exception, it's considered an *unhandled* exception. When an unhandled exception occurs in a Web application, by default you will see a message similar to the one in **Figure 11.10**.

continues on next page

CATCHING EXCEPTIONS

- Client machines by default will see the message in **Figure 11.11**. If you execute a standalone .NET application (an EXE that you double-click on, for example), an unhandled exception causes the runtime to display the message in **Figure 11.12** and then halts the program.

- You can add a function to your program to serve as a last-resort exception handler. If no code catches the exception, the runtime will invoke this function (see the topic "Catching Unhandled Exceptions" later in this chapter.)

- In your catch block you can find out information about the exception; you can write some clean-up code, like closing a file or disconnecting from a database, and then re-trigger the exception for the next level; or you can do nothing.

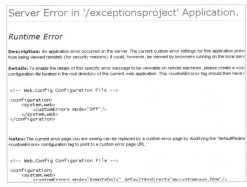

Figure 11.11 This error page doesn't reveal as much information as the one you get from a local machine. That's because we don't want potential hackers to see lines of code in our program. However, this page still isn't what you want to show your clients when something goes wrong. Later you'll learn how to customize the page.

Figure 11.12 This dialog is equivalent to the old message box with the stop icon that usually says, "An exception has occurred in your application, press ok to stop the program and cancel to debug," for non-.NET applications.

Catching Specific Exceptions

Exceptions are objects. They come from classes that derive from a runtime class called System.Exception. To catch a specific exception in your code you must know the class name of the exception or know the name of one of its parents (`System.Exception` is a parent class to all exceptions). For example, a developer may define a general exception like `AccountExceptions`. Then the developer may define more specific exceptions like `InsufficientFundsException` and `WrongAccountTypeException` that derive from `AccountExceptions`. As someone writing exception-handling code, you can decide to catch a specific exception like `InsufficientFundsException`, or you can choose to catch all exceptions of the parent type: `AccountExceptions`. Since all exceptions derive from System.Exception, you can also decide to catch all exceptions, even ones that have nothing to do with Accounts, by writing a catch block that catches System.Exception.

To catch a specific exception:

1. Surround the code that may generate an exception with a try block (see "Catching Exceptions" steps 1-3 earlier in this chapter).

2. After the closing curly bracket of the try block add a new line and type the word catch followed by an open parenthesis (.

3. Type the name of the exception class you wish to capture followed by a space.

4. Type a variable name. The variable will hold the exception object when the exception occurs. (Normally people use the variable name e or ex.)

5. Add a close parenthesis).

6. Add an open curly bracket {.

7. Type the code to handle the exception.

8. Add a close curly bracket } (**Figure 11.13**).

Figure 11.13 Exception handling is preferred over VBScript's On Error Resume Next. Rather than catching every exception (as you had to do with On Error Resume Next) you can decide which exceptions to catch, and let the others flow to the caller.

```
//using System.Data.OleDb;
void OpenDatabase()
{
    string cstr =
    "Provider=Microsoft.Jet.OLEDB.4.0;"
    + @"Data Source=c:\csvqs.mdb;";

    try
    {
        IDbConnection conn = new
        OleDbConnection(cstr);
        conn.Open();
    }
    catch(OleDbException e)
    {
        string Msg = "Database Error:<br>";
        Msg += e.Message;
        Response.Write(Msg);
    }
}
```

Figure 11.14 The C# compiler makes sure that you order the block from more specific exceptions to more general exceptions. That's because as soon as the runtime finds a matching exception block it will use that one and not consider the rest.

```
Code                                    _ □ ×

//using System.Data.OleDb;
void OpenDatabase()
{
   string cstr =
   "Provider=Microsoft.Jet.OLEDB.4.0;"
   + @"Data Source=c:\csvqs.mdb;";

   try
   {
      IDbConnection conn = new
      OleDbConnection(cstr);
      conn.Open();
   }
   catch(OleDbException e)
   {
      string Msg = "Database Error:<br>";
      Msg += e.Message;
      Response.Write(Msg);
   }
   catch(System.Exception e)
   {
      string Msg = "General error:<br>";
      Msg += e.Message;
      Response.Write(Msg);
   }
}
```

✔ Tips

- In its documentation, Microsoft is very careful to point out what exceptions a certain piece of code may generate for their system classes.

- Exception classes normally have the word Exception as the last part of their name.

- Instead of catching only one kind of exception, you can catch a number of exceptions. That's easily done by adding multiple catch blocks (**Figure 11.14**).

- When you add multiple catch blocks, make sure to order them from more specific to more general. The compiler will issue an error if you don't. This must be done because the runtime simply chooses the first handler that applies to the exception. Thus if you were to write two handlers, one for a specific exception like InsufficientFundsException, and one for a more general exception like AccountException, and you put the general handler first, the runtime would always choose that handler and not the more specific handler.

Obtaining Exception Information

Once you catch an exception, you may want more information about the error. Exception classes may contain proprietary information (as you will see in the section "Declaring Your Own Exception" later in this chapter), but since all exceptions derive from `System.Exception` there are a few pieces of information that all exception objects must have.

To extract exception information:

1. First trap the exception with a try/catch block (see "Catching Exceptions" above).

2. The catch block must catch a particular type of exception and use a variable to hold the exception object (see "Catching Specific Exceptions" earlier in this chapter).

3. Inside the catch block type the name of the variable that holds a reference to the exception object and use one of the properties in **Table 11.1**.

✔ Tips

■ If you look at **Table 11.1** you will find a property called `TargetSite`. This property provides information about the method that generated the error. You can use a functionality known as *reflection* to extract information from this object such as the class name that contains the method, the method name, and even the method parameters. You'll learn about reflection in Chapter 12, "Reflection and Attributes." You can use `e.TargetSite.Name` to obtain the name of the method that produced the error, `e.TargetSite.DeclaringType.FullName` to obtain the name of the class that contains the method, and `e.Targetsite.DeclaringType.Assembly.Location` to get the path and name of the DLL that generated the error.

■ It's usually not a good idea to pass the exception information directly to the client. In other words, don't simply write `Response.Write(ex.Message)`. Error information is often meaningless to the client, and error information can provide hackers with information on how to exploit your system.

Table 11.1

System.Exception Properties and Methods (Properties and Methods that Enable You to Get More Information About the Exception)		
PROPERTY	EXPLANATION	TYPE
HelpLink	A URL to a page or file that provides more information about the error.	Property string read/write
InnerException	Sometimes a function needs to report more than one exception, and may choose to create an exception chain. This property returns the next exception object in the chain.	Property System.Exception readonly
Message	A brief description of the error.	Property string readonly
Source	Describes the origin of the error. It could be the application name plus the class name plus the method that triggered the error, for example, Banking- Checking- MakeDeposit.	Property string read/write
StackTrace	A list of all the functions that were executing when the error occurred. The StackTrace reports something along the lines of "function a called function b which called function c and then an error occurred in line 5."	Property string readonly
TargetSite	An object that represents the method that triggered the error. You can use this object to retrieve information about the method, such as the method name, and parameter types.	Property System.Reflection.MethodBase readonly
GetBaseException	If there is a chain of exceptions, this method returns the root exception in the chain.	Method System.Exception
ToString	Returns information about the exception. Usually this information includes the name of the exception class, the exception Message, plus the StackTrace information.	Method string

OBTAINING EXCEPTION INFORMATION

Working with Exception Chains

Suppose you write a class called Checking, and Checking inherits from a class called Account. Then suppose that the Checking class has a method called `OrderChecks`. Some code in your program creates an instance of the Checking class and calls the `OrderChecks` method, and gets an exception. Let's say the exception object is of type `OrderChecksException`.

But perhaps the exception originated as the result of another exception in the Account class. Let's say that there is a $5 fee for ordering checks, and the particular account involved in the request has a balance of zero dollars (the story of my life). So the exception might have originated in Account as `AccountOverdrawnException`, but the `OrderChecks` method catches the exception and decides to throw a different exception that is specific to ordering checks (`OrderChecksException`). Instead of discarding the `AccountOverdrawnException` object, a developer may choose to chain the exceptions. The developer calling the `OrderChecks` method would then be able to catch the `OrderChecksException` but would also be able to obtain information about the `AccountOverdrawnException` and any other exceptions involved in the process of ordering checks.

Figure 11.15 This loop ensures that you record the message for every inner exception.

```
//using System.Data.OleDb;
void OpenDatabase()
{
    string cstr =
    "Provider=Microsoft.Jet.OLEDB.4.0;"
    + @"Data Source=c:\csvqs.mdb;";

    try
    {
        IDbConnection conn = new
        OleDbConnection(cstr);
        conn.Open();
    }
    catch(OleDbException e)
    {
        string Msg = "Database Error:<br>";
        Msg += e.Message;
        Response.Write(Msg);
    }
    catch(System.Exception e)
    {
        string Msg = "General error:<br>";
        Msg += e.Message;

        while (e.InnerException != null)
        {
            e = e.InnerException;
            Msg += e.Message + "<br>";
        }

        Response.Write(Msg);
    }
}
```

To navigate through an exception chain:

1. In a catch block for a specific exception, test if the InnerException property is not equal to null.

2. If the InnerException property is not null, save the value of InnerException in a variable.

3. The new variable now contains another exception object that also has an InnerException property.

4. Repeat steps 1 through 3 until InnerException is null.

✔ Tips

■ Steps 1-4 can easily be combined into a simple while loop (**Figure 11.15**).

■ Whenever you catch an exception, it's a good idea to check if the InnerException property is not null to ensure that you aren't neglecting other information about the exception.

continues on next page

WORKING WITH EXCEPTION CHAINS

■ Every exception object has an
InnerException property, but some
classes may choose to report chains of
errors with a custom property. For example, ADO .NET classes often use an
Errors property. The Errors property is an
array of errors rather than a chain. (In a
chain one node points to another node,
which points to another, and so on.) In
an array, you can jump to any one error
at a given time. **Figure 11.16** shows how
to handle ADO.NET exceptions.

Figure 11.16 Even though .NET has a mechanism for
reporting nested exceptions with the InnerException
property, ADO.NET reports related errors through the
Errors collection. This lets you jump directly to a
particular error rather than navigate through a chain
to find it.

```
//using System.Data.OleDb;
void OpenDatabase()
{
    string cstr =
    "Provider=Microsoft.Jet.OLEDB.4.0;"
    + @"Data Source=c:\csvqs.mdb;";

    try
    {
        IDbConnection conn = new
        OleDbConnection(cstr);
        conn.Open();
    }
    catch(OleDbException e)
    {
        string Msg = "Database Error:<br>";
        foreach (OleDbError err in
                e.Errors)
        {
            Msg += e.Message + "<br>";
        }
        Response.Write(Msg);
    }
    catch(System.Exception e)
    {
        string Msg = "General error:<br>";
        Msg += e.Message;
        Response.Write(Msg);
    }
}
```

Figure 11.17 You'll need to use this technique later when we talk about unhandled exceptions. What happens with ASP.NET unhandled exceptions is that the error reported is just a general "there was an error" object. To get the specific exception that caused the program to halt you need to use the GetBaseException method.

```
//using System.Data.OleDb;
void OpenDatabase()
{
    string cstr =
    "Provider=Microsoft.Jet.OLEDB.4.0;"
    + @"Data Source=c:\csvqs.mdb;";

    try
    {
        IDbConnection conn = new
        OleDbConnection(cstr);
        conn.Open();
    }
    catch(OleDbException e)
    {
        string Msg = "Database Error:<br>";
        Msg += e.GetBaseException()
            .Message;
        Response.Write(Msg);
    }
    catch(System.Exception e)
    {
        string Msg = "General error:<br>";
        Msg += e.Message;
        Response.Write(Msg);
    }
}
```

■ You can use the function GetBaseException to navigate directly to the root exception: the first exception that was generated (**Figure 11.17**).

Declaring Your Own Exceptions

Exceptions are classes that derive from System.Exception. However, the .NET framework distinguishes between two types of exceptions: system exceptions, exceptions Microsoft defined that have to do with the .NET Framework; and application exceptions, custom exceptions for a particular application. System exceptions derive from System.SystemException. Application exceptions derive from the class System.ApplicationException. Both System.SystemException and System.ApplicationException derive from System.Exception.

To declare an exception class:

1. Add a new class definition. You can name the class anything you wish, but as a standard convention developers add the word Exception as the last part of the name.

2. Inherit the class from System.ApplicationException.

3. Add properties and methods to your class that may help the developer obtain more information about the error (**Figure 11.18**).

Figure 11.18 In addition to having fields that report extra error information, you could add methods that try to fix the problem, for example. Exception classes are full classes and as such you can add to them any type of member that other classes could have.

```
class AccountOverdrawnException :
    ApplicationException
{
    public int AccountNumber;
    public string LastCheckNumber;
}
```

Figure 11.19 Because we're looking for a specific exception, our exception variable is already of the same type as the exception we're catching, and so we can ask for members that are specific to our exceptions class. If we were catching general exceptions, we would have to cast to our exception type first before trying to get the account number.

```
try
{
    MakeWithdrawal(5000);
}
catch(AccountOverdrawnException ex)
{
    string acctInfo = FetchAccountInfo(
                      ex.AccountNumber);
    Response.Write(acctInfo);
}
```

Figure 11.20 This is the same approach that Microsoft takes—a hierarchy of exceptions. With this structure you can decide to catch all banking exceptions, or more specific kinds of banking exceptions.

```
class AccountException : ApplicationException
{
    public int AccountNumber;
}

class CheckingException: AccountException
{
    public string LastCheckNumber;
}

class SavingsException : AccountException
{
    public bool IsPreferredCustomer;
}
```

✔ Tips

■ In the section titled "Obtaining Exception Information" you learned about properties like Message, Source, TargetSite, etc. You don't have to add these properties to your class by hand; they come from the base class System.Exception. However, you may want to add custom properties to provide extra information about your class. For example, if the class is AccountException, you may want to add a property like AccountNumber that tells the developer receiving the exception the account number of the account responsible for the error (**Figure 11.19**).

■ If you're creating a number of exception classes, it's good to divide the exceptions into categories and declare base classes for each category. For example, if you have a number of exceptions that relate to Checking accounts and other exceptions that relate to Savings accounts, it's a good idea to create a base class called AccountExceptions and perhaps create separate CheckingExceptions and SavingsExceptions classes (**Figure 11.20**).

DECLARING YOUR OWN EXCEPTIONS

Setting the Error Message

The base class to all exceptions, System.Exception, has a property called Message that gives a brief description of the error. However, the Message property is read-only. So how do you set the error message of your custom exception objects?

To set the error message for custom error classes:

1. Add a constructor to your custom exception class.

2. In the body of the constructor call the base constructor passing the error message as a parameter (**Figure 11.21**).

✔ Tip

■ A developer using your class may want to set the error message of your class instead of using the default error message you provide. To enable a developer to set a custom error message in your class add a constructor that accepts a string parameter, then pass the string in the constructor to the base constructor (**Figure 11.22**).

Figure 11.21 Remember that the only time you can set a read-only property is in the constructor of the class. The Message property happens to be a read-only property.

```
class AccountException :
ApplicationException
{
    public int AccountNumber;
    public AccountException() : base(
    "There was an error while accessing "
    + "a  bank account")
    {
    }
}
```

Figure 11.22 It's convenient to add several constructors to your exception class. Normally there should be a default constructor so that it's easy to create and throw the exception. But it's also good to add a constructor that lets the user modify the message, as the one in the figure.

```
class AccountException :
ApplicationException
{
    public int AccountNumber;
    public AccountException(string msg) :
        base(msg)
    {
    }
}
```

Figure 11.23 The only types of objects that can be thrown are objects that derive from System.Exception.

```
class AccountOverdrawnException :
ApplicationException
{
    public int AccountNumber;
    public int Amount;
    public AccountOverdrawnException()
    {
    }
    public AccountOverdrawnException(
    string msg) : base(msg)
    {
    }
}

class Checking
{
    public int AccountNumber;
    private double Balance;

    public void MakeWithdrawal(
    double Amount)
    {
        if (Amount > Balance)
        {
            AccountOverdrawnException ex =
            new AccountOverdrawnException();
            throw ex;
        }
    }
}
```

Figure 11.24 If you don't need to set any of the properties of the exception, it's easier to combine the throw with the new command.

```
class Checking
{
    public int AccountNumber;
    private double Balance;

    public void MakeWithdrawal(
    double Amount)
    {
        if (Amount > Balance)
        {
            throw new
            AccountOverdrawnException();
        }
    }
}
```

Generating an Exception

As the author of a class, you may want to generate your own exceptions to notify other developers of various error conditions. You can choose to write your own exception classes (as in the section "Declaring Your Own Exceptions"), or you can choose to generate a predefined Microsoft error like DivideByZeroException or ArgumentNullException.

To throw an exception:

1. Create a new instance of the exception class you want to generate and store it in a variable.

2. In the next line type throw followed by the name of the variable that holds the instance of the exception class followed by a semicolon ; (**Figure 11.23**).

✔ Tips

■ You can also combine the creation of the new exception and the throw statement into one statement (**Figure 11.24**).

■ If you use the throw statement within the try portion of a try/catch block the catch portion of the block will catch the exception. In other words you will catch your own exception.

■ If you throw an exception within the catch portion of a try/catch block, the function will exit and the exception will be passed on to the caller of the function.

■ Don't use an exception in the try section of your code as a means to execute code in the catch section. Some developers have used this technique in the past—they write code as part of a catch block, then in certain instances they generate a "phony" error to trigger that code. Shame on them! This is a poor practice because exceptions are only intended to report error conditions.

Catching and Re-throwing Exceptions

When catching exceptions, you may want to log some exception information but afterwards pass on the same exception to the caller. Logging information about the exception requires a catch block. Catching the exception nullifies the effect of the exception and lets the program continue executing normally after the catch block executes.

To reactivate the exception for the caller:

◆ Inside the catch block (either for a general exception or for a specific exception) type throw followed by a semicolon (**Figure 11.25**).

✔ Tip

■ Alternatively you can allow the original exception to dissipate and generate a new exception. If you still want to provide information about the original exception you could chain the exceptions as illustrated in "Building an Exception Chain."

Figure 11.25 While throw; by itself looks awkward, it's a quick way of re-throwing the same exception. Alternatively, you could just write throw ex; in the code here.

```
public void OrderChecks(int Amount)
{
  try
  {
    MakeWithdrawal(5.00);
  }
  catch (AccountOverdrawnException ex)
  {
    LogProblemAccount(ex.AccountNumber);
    throw;
  }
}
```

Figure 11.26 The only way to nest the exceptions is to pass the previous exception up to the base in the constructor.

```
class AccountOverdrawnException :
ApplicationException
{
    public AccountOverdrawnException() {}
}

class OrderChecksException :
ApplicationException
{
    public OrderChecksException(
        string msg,
        Exception inner) :
        base(msg,inner)
    {
    }
}

class Checking
{
    public void OrderChecks(int Amount)
    {
        try
        {
            MakeWithdrawal(5.00);
        }
        catch (
        AccountOverdrawnException ex)
        {
            throw new OrderChecksException(
            "Unable to order checks",ex);
        }
    }
}
```

Building an Exception Chain

In certain instances, a single method call may cause multiple related errors to occur. A developer may choose to provide the caller with a chain of errors that report all the exceptions that were triggered. It's called an *error chain* because the developer catching the exception only sees one of the exceptions in the chain, then the developer uses the InnerException property to get the next exception in the chain. Using the InnerException object, the developer can ask that object for its InnerException and so on, until InnerException returns null. The difficult part of chaining exceptions is that the InnerException property is read-only. This means that chaining exceptions is not just a matter of setting an exception object's InnerException property.

To build an exception chain:

1. Inside a catch block that captures a specific exception, create a new exception object to throw as the new exception.

2. In the parameters for the constructor of the new exception object, pass the exception's error message followed by the variable storing the original exception (**Figure 11.26**).

✔ Tip

■ As you can see from the example, it's a good idea to add a constructor that enables the caller to set the inner exception property. In the constructor for your class, simply pass the inner exception object to your base constructor.

Adding Code that Executes Before Exiting the Function

Part of the difficulty of handling exceptions is doing clean-up. Suppose you open a database and move a record from one table to another, but you receive an exception before you have a chance to close the database. If you leave the function without closing the database, your program will consume more memory and limit the number of connections from other users to the same database. C# provides a language construct that works in conjunction with the try/catch block that enables you to specify code that should run before you exit a function (whether you exit because of an exception or simply exit because the function is done executing). To add code that triggers automatically before a function exits, you must add a *finally block*.

To add a finally block:

1. Put the code for the function inside a try block. Adding a catch section is optional.

2. After the closing curly bracket for the try section, on the next line, type `finally` followed by a space and an open curly bracket {.

3. Add clean-up code—code that you wish to execute before exiting the function.

4. Add a close curly bracket } (**Figure 11.27**).

Figure 11.27 The finally block doesn't require you to have a catch block, only a try. It will always execute even if an exception doesn't occur.

```
void OpenDatabase()
{
    string cstr =
    "Provider=Microsoft.Jet.OLEDB.4.0;"
    + @"Data Source=c:\csvqs.mdb;";

    IDbConnection conn = new
    OleDbConnection(cstr);

    try
    {
        conn.Open();
        OleDbCommand cmd = new
        OleDbCommand(
        "select * from authors",conn);
        IOleDbReader reader =
        cmd.ExecuteReader();
    }
    catch(OleDbException e)
    {
        string Msg = "Database Error:<br>";
        Msg += e. Message;
        Response.Write(Msg);
    }
    finally
    {
        conn.Close();
    }
}
```

Figure 11.28 In each iteration of the loop, whether there was an exception or not, the program will execute the code in the finally. Notice that if the code gets an exception that isn't being caught, the program will not only exit the loop, but the entire function as well, yet the finally will still execute.

```
Code                            _ □ ×

void FetchAuthors()
{
    string cstr =
    "Provider=Microsoft.Jet.OLEDB.4.0;"
    + @"Data Source=c:\csvqs.mdb;";

    OleDbConnection conn = new
    OleDbConnection(cstr);

    using(conn)
    {
        conn.Open();
        OleDbCommand cmd = new
        OleDbCommand(
        "select * from authors",conn);
        IDataReader reader =
        cmd.ExecuteReader();
    }
}
```

✔ Tips

- After try, you can add many catch handlers and one finally block. You have to put all catch blocks before the finally block.

- Whether you catch an exception or not before leaving the function the .NET runtime will execute the code in the finally block.

- It's not necessary to have a catch block to use finally.

- You can use try/finally anywhere in your code—the try section doesn't need to contain all the code of the function (**Figure 11.28**). The code in the finally block executes whenever you exit the try section of the try/finally block.

Using *using*

In Chapter 3, "Conditionals and Loops," you learned how to use the *using* statement for namespace declarations. However, there's another command with the same name, using, that has a different purpose.

Throughout the book you've learned that the way the .NET runtime reclaims memory from objects is with a mechanism called garbage collection. But garbage collection doesn't happen immediately, only when the runtime feels it needs to reclaim memory. The problem is that certain resources must be reclaimed immediately. A good example is a database connection. A database engine only allows a certain number of simultaneous connections. Therefore, classes that have expensive resources often have a method called Dispose that the developer using the object can invoke to release those resources. If you're using such an object, you may want to put the code that calls the Dispose method inside a finally block so that the method executes before exiting the function. The C# using method puts your code automatically within a try/finally block and adds code to call the Dispose method of the object for you.

Figure 11.29 The using command is unique to C#. In VB.NET, you have to write a try/finally block yourself. With using, the compiler is the one that writes the try/finally for you.

```
Code                                    _ □ ×

void FetchAuthors()
{
    string cstr =
    "Provider=Microsoft.Jet.OLEDB.4.0;"
    + @"Data Source=c:\csvqs.mdb;";

    OleDbConnection conn = new
    OleDbConnection(cstr);

    using(conn)
    {
        conn.Open();
        OleDbCommand cmd = new
        OleDbCommand(
        "select * from authors",conn);
        IDataReader reader =
        cmd.ExecuteReader();
    }
}
```

To use an object with the using statement:

1. Look in the documentation for the class you want to enclose in the using statement and make sure the class implements the IDisposable interface.

2. In a new line, type using followed by an open parenthesis (.

3. Type the name of the variable that holds a reference to an object.

   or

   Declare a new variable by typing the class name, followed by a space, followed by the variable name. Set the variable equal to a new instance of the class.

4. Type a close parenthesis).

5. Type an open curly bracket {.

6. Enter code that is related to the class type inside the using.

7. Type a close curly bracket } (**Figure 11.29**).

✔ Tips

■ When you use the using method the compiler turns using into a try/finally block. It moves the code from inside the using block into the try section, then adds the following code to the finally section:

   ```
   IDisposable disp = (IDisposable) var;
   If (disp != null) disp.Dispose();
   ```

■ The limitation of the using statement is that it can only be used with a single object. If you need to ensure that your code calls the Dispose method in multiple objects it's best to add a try/finally block manually and put the code that calls the Dispose method inside the finally block.

USING using

Adding Form Security to the Sample Application

At this point your sample application has two pages: One is a login form and the other is basically a form with two buttons (one that says High security task and one that says Low security task). Let's make the login form fully functional.

To add form security to the sample application:

1. Open the file Web.config.

2. If you look through the file you'll find a section called authentication. It currently says <authentication mode="Windows" />. Replace the entry with the code in **Figure 11.30**.

3. Open the login.aspx page and double-click on the login button so that the wizard adds a skeleton for the Click event.

4. Inside the Click event, add the code in **Figure 11.31**. As you can see the code doesn't really look up names in a database (although it wouldn't be very difficult to do this). It just recognizes three emails: robertjordan@fantasy.com, douglasadams@funny.com, and josemojica@tech.com. (In case you're wondering who this Jose Mojica guy is, he's just the guy who wrote the book you're reading. Thank you for buying it, by the way).

Figure 11.30 The trick to having the program always transfer control to the login page first is the line that's highlighted. The question mark stands for unauthenticated users. In other words, deny access to all pages for unauthenticated users.

```
<authentication mode="Forms" >
    <forms loginUrl="login.aspx"
    protection="All" />
</authentication>

<authorization>
    <deny users="?" />
</authorization>
```

Figure 11.31 I don't recommend storing all the names of your users and their passwords in plain text in your code, but it makes it easier to write the sample code.

```
private void btnLogin_Click(
object sender, System.EventArgs e)
{
    string username = "";
    switch (txtEmail.Text)
    {
        case "robertjordan@fantasy.com":
        if (txtPassword.Text == "password")
        {
            username="Robert Jordan";
        }
        break;
        case "douglasadams@funny.com":
        if (txtPassword.Text == "password")
        {
            username="Douglas Adams";
        }
        break;
        case "josemojica@tech.com":
        if (txtPassword.Text == "password")
        {
            username="Jose Mojica";
        }
        break;
    }
    if (username != "")
    {
        FormsAuthentication.
        RedirectFromLoginPage(
        username,false);
    }
    else
    {
        lblError.Text =
        "Incorrect userid or password";
    }
}
```

Figure 11.32 When the user attempts to reach another page without being authenticated, the authentication module routes the call to the login page but records in the query string the name of the page that the user had requested. This method marks the user as authenticated and tells the module to forward the request to the page the user had intended to go.

```
Code                                    _ □ ×

private void btnLogin_Click(
object sender, System.EventArgs e)
{
    string username = "";
    switch (txtEmail.Text)
    {
        case "robertjordan@fantasy.com":
        if (txtPassword.Text == "password")
        {
            username="Robert Jordan";
        }
        break;
        case "douglasadams@funny.com":
        if (txtPassword.Text == "password")
        {
            username="Douglas Adams";
        }
        break;
        case "josemojica@tech.com":
        if (txtPassword.Text == "password")
        {
            username="Jose Mojica";
        }
        break;
    }
    if (username != "")
    {
        FormsAuthentication.
        RedirectFromLoginPage(
        username,false);
    }
    else
    {
        lblError.Text =
        "Incorrect userid or password";
    }
}
```

5. Right-click on the file global.aspx and select View code from the code menu.

6. Find the function called `Application_AuthenticateRequest` and replace it with the code in **Figure 11.32**. This function executes on each request after the `FormsAuthenticationModule` has had a chance to verify that the user is authenticated. If the user has been authenticated, you can get the user's name with `Context.User.Name`. The code then creates a `GenericPrincipal` object that has the user's name plus the groups that the user belongs to.

continues on next page

ADDING FORM SECURITY

7. Open the secured.aspx form and double-click on the first task button. The wizard will add code to handle the Click event. Enter the code in **Figure 11.33** inside the Click event. This code is actually quite amazing, because it shows how little code we have to write to implement group-based (or role-based) security in our code. This code creates a PrincipalPermission object. The first parameter in the constructor is the user name (null means any user). The second parameter is the role we require. Then, when we call the Demand method in the object, the code will trigger an error if the current user is not part of the role.

8. Go back to the secured.aspx form view and double-click on the second button. The wizard will add code to handle the Click event. Add the code in **Figure 11.34**. This code is similar to the code in **Figure 11.33** except that it demands that the user be part of the Admin group.

9. Execute the program by pressing F5. Try entering different names in the login screen and clicking the login button. Once the program transfers control to the secured form, try clicking each of the buttons.

✔ Tips

- If you attempt to go to any page without logging in, ASP.NET will transfer control to the login window. Then after you've logged in, it will transfer control to the page you request.

- Right now, if you enter a user that doesn't have Admin rights and click the High security task button, you'll get an unhandled exception. In the next section we'll take care of displaying something nice when there's an error.

Figure 11.33 Checking if the user has rights to access the code is a matter of creating a PrincipalPermission object and calling Demand on it. After those two lines of code you can write all the rest of the code for the function. If the user doesn't have permission, the function will exit with an exception; otherwise it will continue normally.

```
private void btnLowTask_Click(object
sender, System.EventArgs e)
{
    PrincipalPermission perm = new
    PrincipalPermission(null,"User");
    perm.Demand();
}
```

Figure 11.34 The High task button click function ensures that the user is a member of the Admin group. In the code, Jose Mojica is the only user to have Admin rights.

```
private void btnHighTask_Click(
object sender, System.EventArgs e)
{
    PrincipalPermission perm = new
    PrincipalPermission(null,"Admin");
    perm.Demand();
}
```

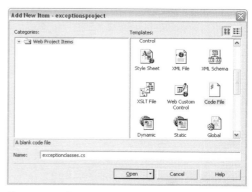

Figure 11.35 This time, instead of creating a class, we're just adding an empty file. This is because when you tell the wizard to add a class file, the wizard adds a class definition as well. We don't want a single class definition. We want this module to be a repository for any exception class we define in the future.

Handling Unhandled Errors in Web Applications

If you handle unhandled errors, doesn't that make them handled, by definition? The answer is "not quite," as you'll see shortly.

When the ASP.NET framework detects an unhandled exception, it cancels the response for the page that triggered the exception. Then it fires the application's error event in the Global.asax file. From here you can find out what exceptions you have and even clear the exceptions, if you like. Nothing can resurrect the page where you had the exception, but by clearing the exceptions you can prevent the application from sending an error page back to the user. So one way to handle unhandled exceptions is to clear them from the errors collection.

The other way to handle unhandled exception is to print a nice error message. Sometimes no matter how hard you try to debug your program, something always ends up breaking. In that case you can tell ASP.NET to display a custom error page when an unhandled exception occurs.

In summary, there are three things you can do with exceptions. You can handle them with try/catch blocks; you can handle them in the application's error event; or you can design a nice page for your user in case something gets missed. Let's add all three mechanisms to the sample application.

To add error catching in the sample application:

1. Choose Project > Add New Item from the menu bar. Enter exceptionclasses.cs for the file name (**Figure 11.35**).

2. Add the code in **Figure 11.36**. This code defines the NotAMemberOfRoleException custom exception. The class has a single member with the name of the role that was requested.

3. In the High security task button, let's modify the code so that when a security error occurs we throw the NotAMemberOfRoleException exception instead, with information about the role that was needed to execute the function. Right-click on the secured.aspx file and choose View Code from the pop-up menu. Find the btnHighTask_Click function and add the highlighted code from **Figure 11.37**.

4. Right-click on the file Global.asax and choose View Code from the pop-up menu.

Figure 11.36 NotAMemberOfRoleException is a simple exception object with a field called RoleRequested that tells the error handling code what role was needed for the function to execute.

```
using System;

namespace exceptionsproject
{
    public class NotAMemberOfRoleException
    : ApplicationException
    {
        public string RoleRequested;
    }
}
```

Figure 11.37 The High task button catches the general security exception and then throws the more specific NotAMemberOfRoleException to the caller so that they know what role the function was expecting.

```
private void btnHighTask_Click(
object sender, System.EventArgs e)
{
    try
    {
        PrincipalPermission perm = new
        PrincipalPermission(null,"Admin");
        perm.Demand();
    }
    catch(
    System.Security.SecurityException ex)
    {
        NotAMemberOfRoleException newex =
        new NotAMemberOfRoleException();

        newex.RoleRequested = "Admin";
        throw newex;
    }
}
```

(sidebar) HANDLING UNHANDLED ERRORS

Figure 11.38 If you were to examine Contex.Error you would just see a generic System.Web.HttpUnhandledException exception. To get at the NotAMemberOfRoleException you need to call the GetBaseException function.

```
Code                                    _ □ ×

protected void Application_Error(
Object sender, EventArgs e)
{
    if (Context.Error.GetBaseException()
        is NotAMemberOfRoleException)
    {
        string role =
        ((NotAMemberOfRoleException)
        Context.
        Error.
        GetBaseException()).RoleRequested;

        Response.Write(
        "You can upgrade now to " + role +
        " for only 9.95 a month!");

        Context.ClearError();
    }
}
```

5. Locate the function `Application_Error` and add the highlighted code from **Figure 11.38** to it. This code checks to see if the error generated was a `NotAMemberOfRoleException`. If so, it clears the errors and sends a friendly message to the client.

6. The only thing missing is a custom error page for when there are unhandled exceptions, and in fact there's at least one unhandled exception. Select Project > Add Web Form from the menu bar.

7. In the dialog in **Figure 11.39** enter niceerror.aspx for the file name.

continues on next page

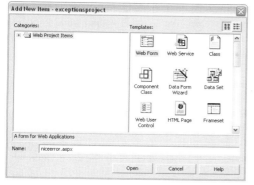

Figure 11.39 niceerror.aspx will be our custom error page. If there's an unhandled exception that we didn't account for, they'll see this nice error page.

8. Add a label control to the niceerror.aspx page that gives a friendly error message. I chose "Oops!" for mine (**Figure 11.40**).

9. Open the Web.config file and locate the section that reads customErrors. Replace the section with the code in **Figure 11.41**.

✔ Tips

- The customErrors section in Web.config has three settings: RemoteOnly, On, or Off. The default is RemoteOnly, which means: Display a custom error page only when a machine outside your server gets the error. If you're testing the pages in your own server then you'll get a detailed error. Off means that ASP.NET will always display a detailed error and never a custom error. On is the opposite, and means: Always display a custom error. In the sample code we're changing the setting to On so that you can see the custom error while debugging, but normally RemoteOnly is what you want.

- To test the application, log in as Douglas Adams and try both buttons. The Low security task button should display the custom error page. The High security task should display a nice message asking the you to subscribe to Admin rights—for only $9.95 a month.

Figure 11.40 You'll probably want to have more than Oops! for your custom error page, but you get the idea.

Figure 11.41 It's very simple to tell ASP.NET what our custom error page is and when to display it, it's just a matter of adjusting some settings in Web.config.

```
<customErrors defaultRedirect=
"niceerror.aspx" mode="On" />
```

REFLECTION AND ATTRIBUTES

C# programs are self-describing. When you compile a C# program, part of the EXE or DLL you generate contains metadata (extra information) that tells you the classes that your EXE or DLL contains. It also tells you about the members of each class: the fields, properties, methods, delegates, events, etc. This information is always available to your program and other programs, and can be reached through a mechanism known as *reflection*. In addition to being able to read information about a particular class and its members, it's also possible to extend this metadata with *attributes*. Attributes are classes that extend the metadata about a certain class or member in the class. You can create your own attributes easily, as you will see shortly.

Attributes are inert classes, in the sense that they don't consume memory unless a program looks for them. If a program specifically looks for a certain attribute, the runtime will then activate the attribute. It does this by creating an instance of the attribute class and calling one of its constructors.

Working with Reflection and Attributes

In this chapter, you're going to work on two separate tasks. The first will teach you how to load a DLL dynamically based on a setting in your configuration file. The second will teach you how to use attributes in an application. Both tasks use the same sample application.

The sample application features an order-tracking system. In this system you'll be able to manage a list of customers, view a list of items, and enter an order for a particular customer. There's too much code in the sample application to write it all from scratch. Therefore, you'll need to download the sample code from Peachpit's Web site (see Tips later in this section) if you haven't already done so.

Let's focus on task one first. The order-tracking system gives you two options for saving records. You can save records to memory or to XML files. To accomplish this, the application has two separate DLLs for storing records: one that uses Hashtables in memory and one that uses MySQL. You can guess that the memory one isn't going to be as popular as the XML one: Any orders you save to memory will be lost five minutes after you shut the application down. Nevertheless, using memory does make it easy to work with data and to learn the concepts.

Through a configuration setting, you'll be able to tell the application which mechanism you wish to use, and the application will load the appropriate DLL. For the application's code to work with either DLL you will use a concept you learned in Chapter 8, "Interfaces," known as *polymorphism*.

Polymorphism occurs when two classes implement the same interface but have slightly different implementations. You can write generic functions that use classes through the interfaces; the results of the functions will be different depending on what object you pass to them. The application has already been written to use interfaces. However, you may recall that interfaces are not creatable types; you have to create an object that implements the interface. Right now the application creates the objects in the ordersMemory.DLL. So if we want to make it work with the objects in ordersXML.DLL, we have to rewrite some of the code. Ideally, we want to change it only once and make it flexible enough to account for all the future DLLs we may write—and that's what the first task is about.

The first step in doing task one is to get familiar with the sample application. After you've learned a few tricks about loading DLLs dynamically, we'll work on changing the code.

To start working on the sample application:

1. Download the sample code from Peachpit's Web site (see Tips on next page) if you haven't already done so. You'll notice that for Chapter 12 there are four projects. OrdersSystem is the Web application that enables you to enter customers and orders. The ordersInterfaces project has the definitions for the interfaces that all the other projects use ordersMemory and ordersXML take care of managing the data for the project.

2. In the OrdersSystem directory, double-click on the file OrderSystem.sln to open the project in Visual Studio.

3. Press F5 to run the application.

4. You'll see the dialog in **Figure 12.1**. Enter a customer's name in the Name field and click the Add button. This will add a customer to the list of customers.

5. After you add a few names, your screen will look like **Figure 12.2**. You can delete names with the Delete link, or you can click View Orders to view all the orders for the selected customer and to add new orders. Click on View Orders for one of the customers in the list.

Figure 12.1 Probably Order Systems need to have more information than the person's name, but I'll leave adding that functionality "as an exercise for the reader."

Customer Manager Main Menu

Name: _____ [Add]

William Gates IV	View Orders	Delete
Steve Apple Jobs II	View Orders	Delete
Jose Mojica	View Orders	Delete
Steve Dell Dude	View Orders	Delete

Figure 12.2 The grid has a hidden column that stores an ID number for each customer. The View Orders link column has a property called DataNavigateUrlFormatString which is set to "orders.aspx?ID={0}"; when you click on it, it calls orders.aspx passing the ID number from column one (hidden) to the orders page.

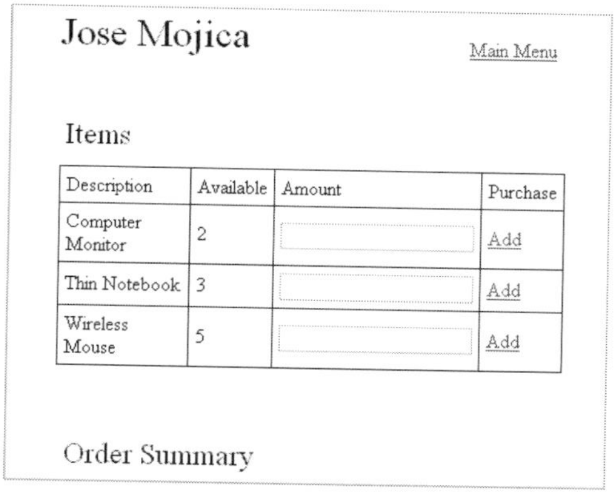

Figure 12.3 The first time you use this screen you'll only see the top grid with the products that are available. Enter an amount next to the item you wish to purchase and press Add.

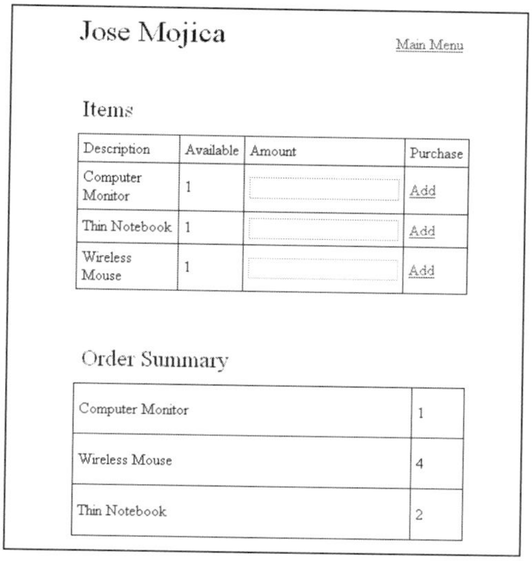

Figure 12.4 After you've added a few items, your orders grid should resemble the grid in the figure. You can also put negative numbers in the purchase amount and click add, to subtract the quantity from the amount purchased.

6. You should see the dialog in **Figure 12.3**. The top grid on this page lists all the items in inventory and their available quantities. To purchase an item, enter the amount next to the item you want and click the Add button.

7. After adding a few items to the list your page should resemble **Figure 12.4**.

8. Play around with the program until you feel you're familiar with it. Be gentle with the data—I didn't put in a lot of safeguards. For example, right now the program will let you purchase more items than there are in inventory.

✔ Tips

■ As with the other projects in this book, building the project isn't necessary to learn the concepts in this chapter.

■ Skeletons for each project can be downloaded from Peachpit's Web site, http://www.peachpit.com/vqs/csharp.

Identifying an Assembly

The term assembly refers to DLLs and EXEs built with one of the .NET compilers (csc.exe, the C# compiler, is of course included in that category). You already know a little about how the runtime uses the assembly concept. In Chapter 5, "Class Inheritance," you learned that types have a *scope*—they're either internal or public. The meaning of the scope modifiers is defined in terms of the assembly concept. If two source files are part of the same assembly, the two files can share internal types; if they're part of separate assemblies, they can't share internal types, only public types.

Certain functions (some of which you'll learn about in this chapter) will ask you to specify the assembly that you want to work with. There are two ways to identify an assembly. Assemblies can be identified with a display name or with a path string. You're going to learn about display names and path strings in the next two sections.

Figure 12.5 This is also known as a fully qualified display name as you will learn later in the chapter. Notice that it has four parts, separated by commas.

```
SoapSudsCode,
Version=1.0.3300.0,
Culture=neutral,
PublicKeyToken=b03f5f7f11d50a3a
```

Working with Display Names

Figure 12.5 shows an example of a display name. Display names are strings that can be used to identify assemblies. They have four parts.

The first part is the name of the DLL or EXE minus the extension. So if the DLL is named ChildCare.DLL, the first part of the display name is ChildCare.

The second part is the version number. The version number is a string in the form "version=1.2.3.4." Version numbers in .NET have four elements: major, minor, build, and revision. *Major* and *minor* numbers are the ones that people normally use to refer to a software version, "Tools version 1.5," for example. *Build* numbers and *revision* numbers are normally used for internal purposes.

When a company is working on the next version of their software, they might refer to the version as 1.5, but every time someone fixes a major bug, they rebuild the code and assign a different build number to the latest code. In this way when the boss comes around and says, "I thought you were going to fix that major bug we had," you can say, "Oh, it should be there in the latest build. Do you have build number 245?" The last number is for when you have to build multiple times on the same day, or when something minor is changed and you don't really want to do a full build of all the source code. The rule of thumb is that if you change major functionality in the software you should change at least the major or the minor numbers. The other two numbers can be used at your discretion.

The third part of the display name is the *culture*. The culture is written in the form "Culture=en_us" or "Culture=neutral". Cultures have two parts, the language, and the region in which the language is spoken. They're used in situations in which programs need to be translated into different languages. Any assembly that contains executable code has a Culture=neutral, which means it can be used from anywhere. You can also put resources into an assembly without code, like a list of strings, and then assign it a culture. Writing assemblies for resources is beyond the scope of this book; for the most part you will leave the culture as neutral.

The third part of the display name is the PublicKeyToken, which is written in the form "PublicKeyToken= a5d015c7d5a0b012." The last number is a part of the public key in a public/private encryption key. With public/private key encryption, a private key is used to encrypt information, while the public key is used to decrypt it. Only information encrypted with the private key can be decrypted with the public key.

In Chapter 13, "C# Web projects," you'll learn how to add public key tokens to an assembly. You add a public key token for two purposes: one is to prevent "bad guys" (or bad people, rather) from tampering with the assembly. The second reason is that you need to add a public key if you want to share your assembly with multiple Web applications.

Many times display names are used to refer to assemblies that are in the Global Assembly Cache (GAC). The GAC has assemblies that are shared by multiple applications. In Chapter 13 you'll learn how to add an assembly to the GAC. For now, let's see how to obtain the display name of an assembly that is in the GAC.

Figure 12.6 This is assembly heaven! The GAC is really a bunch of directories under Windows\Assembly, but Microsoft installs a viewer that lets you see a nice list of assemblies if you navigate there with Windows Explorer. If you navigate there through a command prompt, you'll uncover the true nature of the GAC.

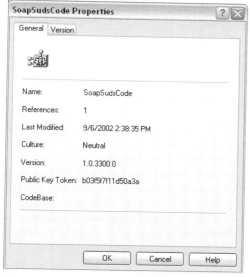

Figure 12.7 Even though you can see most of this information without getting the Properties dialog, this dialog makes it easier to select the information and copy it into your code.

To build the display name for an assembly in the GAC:

1. Using Windows Explorer, navigate to the Windows\Assembly directory (**Figure 12.6**).

2. Write the assembly name from the first column followed by a comma.

3. Write `Version=` followed by the value in the version column, followed by a comma.

4. Write `Culture=neutral` followed by a comma.

5. Write `PublicKeyToken=` followed by the value in public key token.

✔ Tips

■ If you right-click on an assembly in the GAC and choose properties, you'll see a dialog like the one in **Figure 12.7**. From there you can copy the version number or the PublicKeyToken and paste it into your code.

■ The order in which you write the different parts of the display string isn't important. The only part that needs to go first is the assembly name.

WORKING WITH DISPLAY NAMES

Working with Path Strings

Another way to refer to an assembly is to specify its location. Paths are normally relative to the location of the application. There's no big mystery to identifying an assembly by its path name, but there are a few tips to keep in mind.

To identify assemblies using path strings:

◆ Use URLs in the form file:// or http://. For example:
file://c:/chapter12/ordersXML.DLL or
http://www.josemojica.com/games.DLL

◆ Include the name of the DLL plus the extension.

✔ Tips

■ Sometimes Web applications have problems locating files (DLLs and others) using relative paths. For example, the sample application creates a few XML files. Ideally we would like to save these files to the same directory where the application resides. The problem is that if you try to open a file using a relative path, your Web application is hosted by ASPNET_WP.EXE, and this EXE lives in the Windows/System32 directory. You can obtain the path to your application directory by using the code in **Figure 12.8**.

■ A tip for the tip above: MapPath only works if you ask it to map a file in the current directory or in a subdirectory below your application directory. It doesn't work if you request a path above the directory where your application is. For example requesting "..\..\something.txt" won't work properly. It'll return something in relation to where your Web server is installed rather than your Web application.

Figure 12.8 You use MapPath by requesting it to give you the full path of a file or of a directory. The file or directory doesn't need to exist. It's a way of asking, "if I had a file shared/myfile.txt, what would be its full path?"

```
string filePath =
System.Web.HttpContext.Current.
Server.MapPath("filename.txt");
```

Figure 12.9 The Load statement uses a display string to locate the assembly. It will look for the assembly in the GAC first. (A number of the examples assume that you have a using System.Reflection; at the top of the code.)

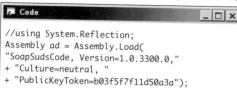

```
//using System.Reflection;
Assembly ad = Assembly.Load(
"SoapSudsCode, Version=1.0.3300.0,"
+ "Culture=neutral, "
+ "PublicKeyToken=b03f5f7f11d50a3a");
```

Figure 12.10 The GAC can actually store multiple versions of the same assembly. They can do this because the GAC is really a series of subdirectories, and they create a different subdirectory for each version. With Load you have to specify a version number or .NET won't even search the GAC. With LoadWithPartialName you can omit version and have .NET just get the latest version.

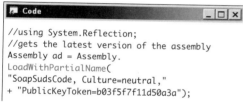

```
//using System.Reflection;
//gets the latest version of the assembly
Assembly ad = Assembly.
LoadWithPartialName(
"SoapSudsCode, Culture=neutral,"
+ "PublicKeyToken=b03f5f7f11d50a3a");
```

■ When you use the Load mechanism or LoadWithPartialName .NET looks for the DLL in the GAC first. If it doesn't find it there, it searches in the bin subdirectory of your application directory. It doesn't use the traditional PATH environment variable that DOS and some Windows programs rely on. It won't search the application directory either (just the bin subdirectory).

Loading a Program Dynamically with a Display String

Now that you know how to identify an assembly, let's talk about some of the functions that use that information. The .NET framework includes a class called System.Reflection.Assembly. This class does two things: It lets you hold a reference to a loaded assembly, and it provides methods for loading assemblies dynamically. You can load an assembly dynamically using the assembly's display name or using its string path.

To load a program using its display name:

1. Type `System.Reflection.Assembly ad`, where *ad* is the name of the variable to hold a reference to the assembly you're going to load.

2. Type an equal sign =.

3. Type `System.Reflection.Assembly.Load (`.

4. Type a display string for the assembly.

5. Type a close parenthesis, followed by a semicolon (**Figure 12.9**).

✔ Tips

■ The example in **Figure 12.9** shows what is called a fully qualified display name—it has all four parts (Assembly name, Version, Culture, and PublicKeyToken). The function works differently if you omit any of the parts, and it will fail if you're trying to locate a DLL in the GAC. However, it's possible to have multiple versions of the same DLL in the GAC, or even multiple cultures. There's another function you can use if you don't know all the parts of the display string. It's called LoadWithPartialName (**Figure 12.10**).

Loading a Program Dynamically with a Path String

To load a program using its path:

1. Type System.Reflection.Assembly ad, where ad is the name of the variable to hold a reference to the assembly you're going to load.

2. Type an equal sign =.

3. Type System.Reflection.Assembly.LoadFrom (.

4. Type the path to the DLL either in the traditional fashion ("c:\path\file.dll") or in URL form (with file:// or http://).

5. Type a close parenthesis, followed by a semicolon (**Figure 12.11**).

✔ Tips

■ The LoadFrom mechanism isn't recommended for loading DLLs that are in the GAC. Instead, for DLLs in the GAC use the Load mechanism. However, if you need to download a DLL from a server in your network or from a Web site, LoadFrom is the preferred method.

■ You can specify a relative path with LoadFrom, but Web applications have problems with this approach, as I mentioned in an earlier tip. The problem is that they run from inside ASPNET_WP.EXE, which lives in the Windows\System32 directory. To find a file using a relative path, you first have to get the path to your application directory using the Server.MapPath function (**Figure 12.12**).

Figure 12.11 LoadFrom uses the path to the assembly rather than the display string. You can use a URL to a local resource, to a network resource, or even to a Web site.

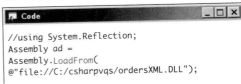

```
//using System.Reflection;
Assembly ad =
Assembly.LoadFrom(
@"file://C:/csharpvqs/ordersXML.DLL");
```

Figure 12.12 You can't really use relative paths with LoadFrom because they end up being mapped to Windows\System32 rather than your application directory. MapPath lets you get full paths based on your application directory.

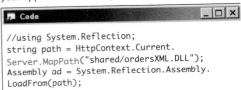

```
//using System.Reflection;
string path = HttpContext.Current.
Server.MapPath("shared/ordersXML.DLL");
Assembly ad = System.Reflection.Assembly.
LoadFrom(path);
```

LOADING WITH A DISPLAY STRING

Instantiating a Class in the Assembly

Once you have a reference to a loaded assembly, you can create an instance of a class in the assembly. The only problem is that the function that lets you do this has a return type of object. Of course it needs to use object as its return type since you can use the function to create any class. However, this doesn't help us much, since we can only make calls for methods in the object class. We could cast the variable to a more concrete type, but in order to do a cast we need to have the type defined ahead of time, and that means we need to have a reference to the assembly containing the type. Having a reference to the assembly sort of defeats the whole purpose of loading an assembly dynamically. The answer to this is to use interfaces. The sample application uses this approach. It puts the definitions for the interfaces in a separate DLL. Then the Web application has a reference to the interface DLL. When we load an assembly dynamically and create an object, we can cast the object to the interface type. This makes it possible for us to use the object through the interface methods.

To create an instance of a class in an assembly:

1. First make sure that the class implements an interface you define. Put the interface definition in a separate DLL, and reference this DLL from both the class project and the client project.

2. Type `ISomeInterface var = (ISomeInterface)ad.CreateInstance` → `("classname");` where `ISomeInterface` is an interface that the class implements, `var` is the name of the variable that will hold the reference to the object, `ad` is the variable that points to the assembly you loaded dynamically, and `"classname"` is the name of the class plus the namespace (**Figure 12.13**).

✔ Tip

■ The tricky part with `CreateInstance` is that people (me included) often forget that the class name isn't just the short name you give to the class but also the namespace name. And as you may know already, the C# wizards by default put your classes inside of a name space with the name of your project.

Figure 12.13 CreateInstance takes in a class name and creates an instance of the class. Remember that the full name of the class includes the namespace name.

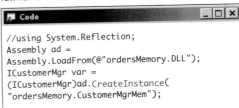

```
//using System.Reflection;
Assembly ad =
Assembly.LoadFrom(@"ordersMemory.DLL");
ICustomerMgr var =
(ICustomerMgr)ad.CreateInstance(
"ordersMemory.CustomerMgrMem");
```

Figure 12.14 GetTypes returns an array of System.Type objects. From there you can navigate through all the items in the array and find information about each type, like its names, its base class's name, etc.

```
Code                                    _ □ ✕

//using System.Reflection;
Assembly ad =
Assembly.LoadFrom(@"ordersMemory.DLL");
foreach (System.Type currtype in
        ad.GetTypes() )
{
   HttpContext.Current.Response.Write(
   currtype.Name + "<br>");
}
```

Enumerating Through the Classes in an Assembly

There are a few other tricks you can do once you have a reference to an assembly. Some aren't very practical but they're good to know nonetheless—the one in this section falls under that second category.

It's possible to list all the classes in an assembly. Class information is obtained through a reference to a System.Type object. You learned about System.Type in Chapter 7, "Types." In the following example we obtain an array of System.Type objects for all the classes in the assembly.

To enumerate through all classes in an assembly:

1. Obtain a reference to an assembly using any of the mechanisms described in "Loading a Program Dynamically," earlier, and store it in a variable, ad for example.

2. Type
   ```
   foreach (System.Type currtype in
   ad.GetTypes() )
   ```
   where currtype is any variable name to store the current System.Type object.

3. Type an open curly bracket {.

4. Type Response.Write(currtype.Name + "<br>");

5. Type a close curly bracket } (**Figure 12.14**).

✔ Tip

■ You can use this technique if you want to generate documentation about an assembly. For example, suppose your boss wants you to write a report of all the classes you have in your DLL. You can write a function where you pass in the name of the assembly, and the function outputs HTML with a list of all the classes in the assembly.

Listing the Members of a Class

Reflection is all about obtaining information about classes. With the reflection classes you can find out information about all the fields, properties, constructors, methods, delegates, events and even nested types of a class. If your program has enough security, you can even list all the private members of a class. (Security is beyond the scope of this book. For more information, consult MSDN for the subject of Code Access Security.)

To obtain the members of a class:

1. Obtain a reference to a class's System.Type object. You can do that by listing all the classes in an assembly, like you saw in the section "Enumerating Through the Classes in an Assembly." Alternatively, Chapter 7, "Types," shows several mechanisms for obtaining System.Type objects.

2. Type
   foreach(System.Reflection.MemberInfo
   mi in currtype.GetMembers()).

3. Type an open curly bracket {.

4. Type Response.Write(mi.Name + "...");

5. Type Response.Write(mi.MemberType + "<br>");

6. Type a close curly bracket } (**Figure 12.15**).

Figure 12.15 Once you have a Type object, you can ask it to give you a list of all of the type's members. You could also ask it for more specific things like, "list all the properties." This is done with GetProperties instead of GetMembers. If you want all of the type's fields, there's a GetFields function, and so on.

```
//using System.Reflection;
Assembly ad =
Assembly.LoadFrom(@"ordersMemory.DLL");
foreach (System.Type currtype in
        ad.GetTypes() )
{
    HttpContext.Current.Response.Write(
    "<b>" + currtype.Name + "</b><br>");

    foreach(MemberInfo mi in
          currtype.GetMembers())
    {
        HttpContext.Current.
        Response.Write(mi.Name + "...");
        HttpContext.Current.Response.Write(
        mi.MemberType + "<br>");
    }
}
```

Figure 12.16 The code here asks for all the members that were declared in the type itself (none of the members from the base) that are private. You can only do this if you have enough security, and by default you do.

```
//using System.Reflection;
Assembly ad =
Assembly.LoadFrom(@"ordersMemory.DLL");
foreach (System.Type currtype in
        ad.GetTypes() )
{
    HttpContext.Current.Response.Write(
    "<b>" + currtype.Name + "</b><br>");

    foreach(MemberInfo mi in
            currtype.GetMembers(
            BindingFlags.DeclaredOnly |
            BindingFlags.NonPublic |
            BindingFlags.Static |
            BindingFlags.Instance))
    {
        HttpContext.Current.
        Response.Write(mi.Name + "...");
        HttpContext.Current.Response.Write(
        mi.MemberType + "<br>");
    }
}
```

✔ Tips

- The previous steps output to a Web client the names and types of each member in each class in the ordersMemory assembly. These members include by default all public members inherited from base classes and all public members declared in the class itself. The list includes both instance and static members. It does not include non-public members, or interfaces.

- There is an overloaded version of the `GetMembers()` function that enables you to specify `BindingFlags`. `BindingFlags` enable you to filter the member types you want to obtain from the `GetMembers()` function. To list all the members of a class including non-public members, and to limit the members to those declared in the type itself (not inherited members), type the following:

  `currtype.GetMembers(BindingFlags.DeclaredOnly | BindingFlags.NonPublic | BindingFlags.Static | BindingFlags.Instance )`

  (**Figure 12.16**).

Setting or Getting a Field Dynamically

Reflection gives you the ability to do late binding. Late binding lets you set or get the value of a field dynamically at runtime based on the field's name, or to invoke a method based on the method's name and its parameters. You can always code to an interface, which is easier than using late binding, but if you don't have an interface and you really need to set or get the contents of a field this would be the way to do it.

The terms *late binding* and *early binding* have to do with the information that the compiler has at compile time. Early binding, the opposite of late binding, means invoking a method by writing C# code that the compiler can turn into a method invocation. Late binding is really about turning a method name in string form into a method invocation.

To set or get the value of the field through late binding, you have to have two things: an instance of the class for which you wish to set or get the field (unless the field is static in which case you don't need an instance of the class to set it or get it), and an instance of the class System.Reflection.FieldInfo.

Figure 12.17 It isn't very difficult to set or get the value of a field using reflection. Notice that reflection is just a more generic way of making a method invocation. You get a pointer to a field from its string name, then you call the SetValue or GetValue functions.

```
📩 Code                          _□✕

//get a reference to our assembly
//that's where we have the definition for
//the Address class
Assembly ad =
Assembly.GetExecutingAssembly();
object objAddress = ad.CreateInstance(
            "ordersystem.Address");

Type typeAddress = typeof(Address);
FieldInfo fldStreet =
typeAddress.GetField("Street");
FieldInfo fldLastModified =
typeAddress.GetField("LastModified");

//set the Street field (instance field)
fldStreet.SetValue(objAddress,
            "123 Elm St.");
//set the LastModified field
//(static field)
fldLastModified.SetValue(null,
            System.DateTime.Now);

//get the Street field
string Street =
(string)fldStreet.GetValue(objAddress);
//get the LastModified field
DateTime LastModified =
        (DateTime)fldLastModified.
        GetValue(null);
```

To set or get the value of a field at runtime:

1. Assuming that you have an object of type System.Type in a variable called currtype, type: System.Reflection.FieldInfo fi = currtype.GetField("fieldname"); where fieldname is the name of the field in the class you wish to set or get.

2. to get the value of a static field, type fieldtype result = (fieldtype) fi.GetValue(null); where fieldtype is the type of the field, for example, int so that the line reads: int result = (int)fi.GetValue(null);

   or

   If the field isn't static, then type fieldtype result = (fieldtype) fi.GetValue(obj); where fieldtype is the type of the field and obj is the variable that holds an instance of the object containing the field.

3. To set the value of a static field type fi.SetValue(null,val); where val is a variable or a literal dictating the value, for example: fi.SetValue(null, 50);

   or

   If the field is an instance field type fi.SetValue(obj, val); where obj is a variable containing an instance of the class with the field you wish to set and val is a variable or a literal dictating the value to which you wish to set the field, for example: fi.SetValue(obj,100); (**Figure 12.17**).

SETTING OR GETTING A FIELD DYNAMICALLY

✔ Tips

■ Unless an administrator uses code access security to block reflection permissions, you can set and read the value of private fields as well as non-private fields for any class. Without reflection permission you can only set and get the value of public fields.

■ Setting and getting properties is done in the same fashion as setting and getting fields. Information about the property is stored in an object of type System.Reflection.PropertyInfo instead of a FieldInfo object, and you use GetProperty() instead of GetField() to get information about the property. Other than that, you use GetValue() and SetValue() just like in fields (**Figure 12.18**).

■ If your class has an indexer, you can reach that indexer using GetProperty() and asking for the Item property (**Figure 12.19**).

Figure 12.18 For properties, you follow the same procedure as for fields except you call GetProperty and use a PropertyInfo object rather than FieldInfo. The SetValue and GetValue functions have an extra parameter for properties, because a property can be an indexer, and indexers can have arguments, whereas fields never have arguments.

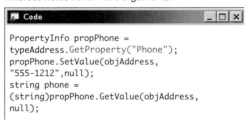

```
PropertyInfo propPhone =
typeAddress.GetProperty("Phone");
propPhone.SetValue(objAddress,
"555-1212",null);
string phone =
(string)propPhone.GetValue(objAddress,
null);
```

Figure 12.19 An indexer is basically a property called Item that has arguments. In other languages, like VB.NET, you can create properties with any name that have arguments.

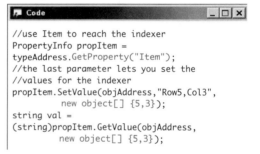

```
//use Item to reach the indexer
PropertyInfo propItem =
typeAddress.GetProperty("Item");
//the last parameter lets you set the
//values for the indexer
propItem.SetValue(objAddress,"Row5,Col3",
          new object[] {5,3});
string val =
(string)propItem.GetValue(objAddress,
          new object[] {5,3});
```

Figure 12.20 Invoke returns an object with the return value of the function. You can then cast the object to the type the function returns.

```
// Code                              _ □ ×

//this is the definition for the method
//we want to invoke
//public bool SendLetter(string letter)

MethodInfo mi =
typeAddress.GetMethod("SendLetter");
//the second parameter is an array of
//parameters
bool result = (bool)mi.Invoke(
        objAddress,
        new object[] {"Dear Mr. Rogers"});
```

Invoking a Method Dynamically

In the same way that you can set or get the value of a field, you can also invoke a method dynamically. Invoking a method dynamically is done with a MethodInfo object.

To invoke a method dynamically at runtime:

1. Assuming that you have an object of type System.Type in a variable called currtype, type: System.Reflection.MethodInfo mi = currtype.GetMethod("methodname"); where fieldname is the name of the field in the class you wish to set or get.

2. Type object[] params = new object[] {"val1",val2, val3} where val1, val2, and val3 are the variables or literals representing the parameters for the method.

3. If the method is static, type object result = mi.Invoke(null,params); If you know the return type, use the specific type when declaring the result variable. For example, instead of object result, type int result = (int) mi.Invoke(null,params).

   or

   If the method is an instance method, type mi.Invoke(obj, params), where obj is an instance of a class containing the method (**Figure 12.20**).

✔ Tips

■ The preceding steps enable you to locate a method within the class using the method name. It is possible that the class has overloaded methods, and therefore has more than one method with the same name. However, overloading is legal only if you change the casing of the method, add or remove parameters from the parameter list, or change the type of some of the parameters. You can call a version of GetMethod() that lets you specify the parameters types for the method to use in cases where overloading is a possibility (**Figure 12.21**).

■ With enough security you can invoke a private method in a class (see Code Access Security in the MSDN documentation for details).

Figure 12.21 For you to have overloaded functions, something needs to be different in each function's parameter list. GetMethod lets you pass in an array of types. The function will then match the types and the number of elements to the types and number of arguments in one of the overloaded functions.

```
//there are two definitions of the
//Demolish method
//public void Demolish()
//public void Demolish(string reason)

//the second parameter is an array of
//types that the function uses to find
//which version of Demolish to use
MethodInfo methodDem =
typeAddress.GetMethod(
        "Demolish",
        new Type[] {typeof(string)});
methodDem.Invoke(objAddress,
        new object[] {"Highway"});
```

Figure 12.22 Web.Config can be used to store settings for your application and it's now the preferred method for storing application settings rather than the registry. In this case we're storing the path to the DLL and the name of the class we want to create.

```
string ordersDLL = System.Configuration.
                ConfigurationSettings.
                AppSettings["OrdersDLL"];

string className = System.Configuration.
                ConfigurationSettings.
                AppSettings["CustomerMgrClass"];
```

Figure 12.23 Once we know the full path to the DLL, we can load it and create an instance of a CustomerMgr class. Then we cast the object returned to the interface that all versions of the class implement.

```
public class VisibleColumnAttribute :
System.Attribute
{
    private bool _visible;
    public bool IsReadOnly;

    public VisibleColumnAttribute(
    bool value)
    {
        _visible=value;
    }
}
```

Completing Task One in the Sample Application

You now know enough to complete task one in the sample application. You may recall from earlier sections that what you're going to be working on is the ability to have your Web application choose between two DLLs at runtime: one that saves information to memory, and one that uses XML files. The names of the DLLs that you're going to load are: ordersMemory.DLL and ordersXML.DLL. Both DLLs are in a subdirectory called shared under the application's directory.

To complete task one in the sample application:

1. In the OrdersSystem project select View Solution Explorer from the menu bar.

2. Double-click on the file utilities.cs to open it in the editor.

3. Locate the functions CreateCustomerMgr, CreateInventoryMgr, and CreateOrderMgr. This is where you will add your work. You'll notice that all of these three functions create objects by calling new on one of the classes in ordersMemory. Let's focus on the CreateCustomerMgr function.

4. Above the line that reads `retVal = new ordersMemory.CustomerMgrMem();` add the code in **Figure 12.22**. This code reads the path to the DLL we want from the Web.config file. You'll add the configuration setting to the file shortly.

5. Replace the line that reads `retVal = new ordersMemory.CustomerMgrMem();` with the code in **Figure 12.23**.

continues on next page

6. Now that the code loads the ordersMemory.DLL dynamically, we can take off the reference to the ordersMemory.DLL file in the project references. Expand the references for the project (**Figure 12.24**).

7. Highlight ordersMemory from the list and press the Delete key.

8. Open the file Web.config from the Solution Explorer window. Just after the line that reads `<configuration>` copy the code in **Figure 12.25**.

9. Repeat steps 4 and 5 for the other two functions: CreateInventoryMgr, and CreateOrderMgr.

✔ Tips

- To test the application, go to the web.config file and change the path to the DLL to point to the ordersXML.DLL.

- Notice from step 8 that you can add custom configuration to web.config and read it with the code in **Figure 12.23**.

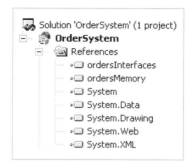

Figure 12.24 We no longer need the reference to the ordersMemory DLL. You can highlight it and delete it.

Figure 12.25 You can add an appSettings section to Web.config and in there add your application's custom configuration information. This is a lot easier than creating registry keys.

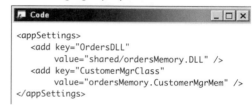

```
<appSettings>
    <add key="OrdersDLL"
        value="shared/ordersMemory.DLL" />
    <add key="CustomerMgrClass"
        value="ordersMemory.CustomerMgrMem" />
</appSettings>
```

Figure 12.26 Serializable and NonSerialized are attributes provided by Microsoft. They tell certain classes in the framework (conveniently known as serializers) that the contents of your class can be persisted either to memory, or to the drive. NonSerialized tells the class not to persist the contents of a field.

```
Code                                    _ □ ✕

[Serializable()]
class Address
{
    public string Street;
    public string City;
    public string ZipCode;
    [NonSerialized]
    public string SecurityCode;
}
```

Figure 12.27 You can combine multiple attributes by separating them with commas.

```
Code                                    _ □ ✕

[VisibleColumn(false),ColumnWidth(200)]
public string ID
{
    get
    {
        return _id;
    }
    set
    {
        _id = value;
    }
}
```

✔ Tip

■ You can combine more than one attribute per element by separating the attributes with commas (**Figure 12.27**).

Applying Attributes to Code

Attributes are classes that expand the information about other programming elements. You can apply attributes to various elements including: the assembly, classes, members, parameters, etc. Microsoft has defined a number of attributes that control how the compiler works and how the runtime works. You can also define your own attributes, as you will see later.

To apply attributes to code elements.

1. In front of the element, type an open square bracket [.

2. If the attribute is for the assembly (project level) type `assembly:` otherwise continue to step 3.

3. Type the name of the attribute without the attribute suffix. Attribute classes are named "SomethingAttribute" but when applying the attribute you can omit the Attribute suffix and just use the word "Something." For example, `ColorAttribute` would be applied as: [Color....

4. Type an open parenthesis (.

5. Type any parameters for the constructor of the attribute class separated by commas. Parameters vary depending on the attribute. To know what parameters to set you have to look it up in the documentation.

6. You can also set the attributes of any public field in the class, type `fieldname = value`, where fieldname is the name of a public field in the class. Check documentation for the names of public fields.

7. Type a close parenthesis).

8. Type a close square bracket] (**Figure 12.26**).

Defining Attributes

Microsoft has created a number of attributes to apply to various programming elements. You can also define your own attributes. Of course yours won't have any effect unless you write code that specifically looks for the attributes and does something with the information. Remember that attributes are there to extend the information about an element.

To define a custom attribute:

1. Write a class where the class name has the suffix attribute, for example: `public class VisibleColumnAttribute`.

2. Derive the class from `System.Attribute`.

3. Add one or more constructors to the class. If you add only parameterized constructors then the parameters of the constructor will become required arguments for the attribute. For example: `VisibleWidthAttribute(bool value) { }`

4. Add public fields or properties to the attribute. Public fields or properties define optional arguments for the attribute. For example: `public bool ReadOnly;`

5. Apply the attribute to any programming element using square brackets. For example: `[VisibleColumn(true,ReadOnly=true)]` (**Figure 12.28**).

Figure 12.28 A custom attribute is just a class that's derived from System.Attribute. The parameters of the constructor will be the parameters of the attribute.

```
public class VisibleColumnAttribute :
System.Attribute
{
    private bool _visible;
    public bool IsReadOnly;

    public VisibleColumnAttribute(
    bool value)
    {
        _visible=value;
    }
}
```

<image type="sidebar_label">**DEFINING ATTRIBUTES**</image>

Figure 12.29 AttributeUsage is an attribute for your attribute class. It controls how the attribute can be applied.

```
[AttributeUsage(AttributeTargets.
Property)]
public class VisibleColumnAttribute :
System.Attribute
{
    private bool _visible;
    public bool IsReadOnly;

    public VisibleColumnAttribute(
    bool value)
    {
        _visible=value;
    }
}
```

Figure 12.30 There are two types of parameters for attributes: named and unnamed. Named parameters correspond to a parameter in the attribute's constructor. Unnamed parameters correspond to public fields or properties in the class.

```
[VisibleColumn(true,IsReadOnly=true)]
public string Name
{
    get
    {
        return _name;
    }
    set
    {
        _name = value;
    }
}
```

✔ Tips

- An attribute is a class that derives from System.Attribute.

- By default the attribute can be applied to any programming element: assembly, class, members, delegates, events, parameters, etc. You can control the usage for the attribute by applying an attribute to the attribute. Let me explain. The attribute you apply to the attribute is called System.AttributeUsage. This attribute has one parameter, a constant from the enum System.AttributeTargets. The constants in this enum include: All, Assembly, Class, Constructor, Delegate, Enum, Event, Field, Interface, Method, Module, Parameter, Property, ReturnValue, and Struct. You can combine the constants in this enum using the | operator. For example:
  [AttributeUsage(AttributeTargets
  .Class | AttributeTargets.Delegate)]
  tells the compiler that the attribute can only be applied to classes and delegates (**Figure 12.29**).

- If you add a default constructor, then the attribute can be applied without arguments. If you add only parameterized constructors, then the compiler requires that you add arguments when applying the attribute. After specifying the arguments for a constructor you can set any public fields or properties for the attribute by typing the name of the field followed by the equal sign and the value of the field (**Figure 12.30**).

continues on next page

DEFINING ATTRIBUTES

393

- By default, an attribute can be applied only once to a programming element. For example if the attribute is ColumnWidth, you can't say [ColumnWidth(500),ColumnWidth(300)], because that's illegal. However, at times it may make sense to apply the same attribute twice. Imagine an attribute named Author that lets you specify the developers that worked on a class. In that case you may enter [Author("Jose"), Author("Bill")]. To allow an attribute to be applied twice, you can set the public field AllowMultiple in AttributeUsage to true (**Figure 12.31**).

- By default, attributes are inheritable. That means that if you apply an attribute to a base class and then write a derived class, the derived class gets all the attributes from the base class. In the same fashion if the attribute is applied to a virtual method and you override the method in the derived class the attribute is available in the derived class. You can prevent this behavior by setting the Inherited field of the AttributeUsage class (**Figure 12.32**).

Figure 12.31 By default, the same attribute can't be applied more than once to the same element. With the AllowMultiple setting in AttributeUsage you can change that behavior.

```
[AttributeUsage(AttributeTargets.All,
AllowMultiple=true)]
class Author : System.Attribute
{
    public string Name;

    public Author(string val)
    {
        Name = val;
    }
}
```

Figure 12.32 By default, attributes are inherited. That means that derived classes get the attributes of the base class. For the Author attribute that may not make sense since the author of the base class isn't necessarily the author of the derived class.

```
[AttributeUsage(AttributeTargets.All,
Inherited=false)]
class Author : System.Attribute
{
    public string name;
}
```

Searching Code for Attributes

Attributes in themselves don't do anything unless a program or the runtime looks for them. When you ask a certain type for its custom attributes, the runtime creates an instance of the attribute class and invokes one of the class's constructors. The runtime looks at the arguments of the attribute to determine which constructor to invoke. The runtime then sets the value of any of the named fields.

For the following example, assume that we're looking for custom attributes of type VisibleColumn and that these attributes can only be applied to a class's fields.

To search for custom attributes:

1. Get a Type object for the class you wish to search. For example: `System.Type typeClass = typeof(Person);` where Person is the class we are inspecting.

2. Enumerate through all the fields in the class. For example: `foreach(System.Reflection.FieldInfo fi in typeClass.GetFields() ) {.`

3. Get all the custom attributes of a specific type using the `GetCustomAttributes()` function and passing a type object for the attribute class. The function returns an array of attributes that have been applied to the element. Normally this array will contain either zero elements or one element (since attribute by default can only be applied once to an element). You can use `foreach` to enumerate through the array returned by `GetCustomAttributes()`. For example: `foreach( object attrobj in fi.GetCustomAttributes` → `(typeof(VisibleColumnAttribute)){}.`

4. Cast the object element to the particular attribute class type so that you can examine the properties of the attribute. For example: `VisibleColumnAttribute attr = (VisibleColumnAttribute) attrobj;` (**Figure 12.33**).

Figure 12.33 GetCustomAttributes can give an array of every type of attribute that has been applied to an element, or you can get all the attributes of a certain type as you see from the example here.

```
//get a reference to our assembly
//that's where we have the definition for
//the Address class
Assembly ad =
Assembly.GetExecutingAssembly();
object objAddress = ad.CreateInstance(
                    ordersystem.Address");
Type typeAddress = typeof(Address);
FieldInfo fldStreet =
typeAddress.GetField("SecurityCode");

//get the custom attributes for the field
object[] attrs =
fldStreet.GetCustomAttributes(
        typeof(Author),false);

//we only apply the attribute once, so it
should be the first one of its type
Author author1 = (Author)attrs[0];
Response.Write(author1.Name);


//below are the class definitions we're
//working with
/*
[AttributeUsage(AttributeTargets.All,AllowMul
tiple=false)]
class Author : System.Attribute
{
    public string Name;
    public Author(string name)
    {
        Name = name;
    }
}

class Address
{
    public string Street;
    public string City;
    public string ZipCode;
    [NonSerialized,Author("Jose")]
    public string SecurityCode;
}
*/
```

Figure 12.34 When you call GetCustomAttributes the framework creates an instance of all the attributes that have been applied to the element. Sometimes all you want to know is if it's been applied to an element. In that case you can use the IsDefined function, which doesn't cause the framework to instantiate the attributes.

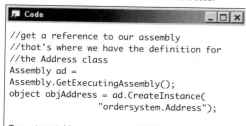

```
//get a reference to our assembly
//that's where we have the definition for
//the Address class
Assembly ad =
Assembly.GetExecutingAssembly();
object objAddress = ad.CreateInstance(
                "ordersystem.Address");

Type typeAddress = typeof(Address);
Bool Defined= typeAddress.
IsDefined(typeof(Serializable),false);
```

✔ Tips

■ When you call GetCustomAttributes() the runtime creates an instance of all the attribute classes that are applied to the particular element if any. Each of the element types MethodInfo, PropertyInfo, ConstructorInfo, etc. has a GetCustomAttributes() function and invoking it only creates instances of the attributes applied to that particular element.

■ If you want to find out if an element has an attribute without having the runtime create instances of the element, you can use the IsDefined() method. This lets you input the type object for the attribute for which you are searching. It also lets you specify if inheritance should be taken into account. In other words, does the base class have this attribute? (**Figure 12.34**)

Completing Task Two in the Sample Application

We've hardly talked about task two. Task two in the sample application involves attributes, and your goal is to create a custom attribute. As you might have guessed from the previous sections, you're going to define an attribute called VisibleColumnAttribute. The idea is to create a function that automatically configures a grid control according to the attributes that have been added to a class. So if the grid is going to have inventory items, we can pass the grid and the InventoryItem class to a function and the function will look at the attributes and format the grid according to the attributes.

To finish task two in the sample application:

1. In the sample code directory for Chapter 12, find the subdirectory called ordersInterfaces. In there you'll find a file called ordersInterfaces.sln. Double-click on this file to open it with VS.NET.

2. If you look at the Solution Explorer you'll see that the solution has three projects in it. We're going to be working with the files in the ordersInterfaces project highlighted in bold (**Figure 12.35**).

3. Open the file interfacedef.cs.

4. Inside the namespace declaration before the definition of ICustomer add the code in **Figure 12.36**. This code defines the VisibleColumnAttribute class.

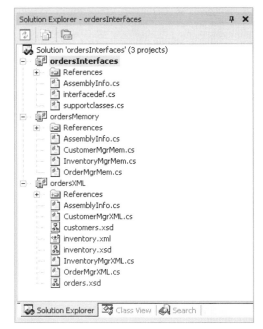

Figure 12.35 The ordersInterfaces solution file has three projects in one. They're each stored in a different subdirectory. Grouping projects into one solution makes it easier to work with multiple related projects.

Figure 12.36 The VisibleColumn attribute can be applied to properties. It tells our grid function whether we want the property information displayed or not.

```
[AttributeUsage(AttributeTargets.Property)]
public class VisibleColumnAttribute :
System.Attribute
{
    public bool Visible;

    public VisibleColumnAttribute(bool value)
    {
        Visible=value;
    }
}
```

Figure 12.37 Notice that it's very easy for a developer of a class to specify whether a column should be displayed or not.

```
Code                              _ □ ✕

public class Customer : ICustomer
{
   string _id;
   string _name;

   [VisibleColumn(false)]
   public string ID
   {
      get
      {
         return _id;
      }
      set
      {
         _id = value;
      }
   }

   [VisibleColumn(true)]
   public string Name
   {
      get
      {
         return _name;
      }
      set
      {
         _name = value;
      }
   }
}
```

5. Now that you've defined the attribute, we can apply it to some of the properties in a class. Open the file supportclasses.cs.

6. In the definition of Customer locate the properties ID and Name. Above ID apply the VisibleColumn attribute with a value of false, and above Name apply it again with a value of true (**Figure 12.37**).

7. Build the application to make sure everything is in order.

8. Open the OrdersSystem solution file (OrdersSystem/OrderSystem.sln).

9. Open the file customers.aspx.

continues on next page

COMPLETING TASK TWO

399

10. Before the Page_Load function, add the code in **Figure 12.38**. It defines the PrepareCustomerGrid that searches for the attribute and configures the grid control to display columns or hide columns depending on the attribute settings.

11. Inside the function Page_Load before the line that reads RefreshGrid add a call to the PrepareCustomerGrid function.

✔ Tip

- It seems to me that with more work it would be possible to create a nice function that could format any grid based on attributes you set in the class. You could for example define attributes to control colors, type of cell, width of column, whether the column is editable or not, and drive a lot of the functionality with attributes.

Figure 12.38 PrepareCustomerGrid uses reflection to find all the properties in the customer class and adds a column to the grid for each one. It then looks for a VisibleColumn attribute to see if it should make the column visible or not.

```
void PrepareCustomerGrid()
{
    Type typeCustomer =
    typeof(ordersInterfaces.Customer);
    grdCustomers.Columns.Clear();
    foreach(PropertyInfo prop in
            typeCustomer.GetProperties())
    {
        BoundColumn grdcol =
        new BoundColumn();
        bool visible = false;

        if (prop.IsDefined(
        typeof(VisibleColumnAttribute),
        false))
        {
            object[] attrs =
            prop.GetCustomAttributes(
            typeof(ordersInterfaces.
            VisibleColumnAttribute),
            false);

            VisibleColumnAttribute viscol =
            (VisibleColumnAttribute)
            attrs[0];
            visible = viscol.Visible;
        }

        grdcol.HeaderText = prop.Name;
        grdcol.DataField = prop.Name;
        grdcol.Visible = visible;
        grdCustomers.Columns.Add(grdcol);
    }

    HyperLinkColumn linkcol =
    new HyperLinkColumn();
    linkcol.Text = "View Orders";
    linkcol.DataNavigateUrlField = "ID";
    linkcol.DataNavigateUrlFormatString=
                "orders.aspx?ID={0}";
    grdCustomers.Columns.Add(linkcol);

    ButtonColumn buttoncol =
    new ButtonColumn();
    buttoncol.Text = "Delete";
    buttoncol.CommandName = "Delete";
    buttoncol.HeaderText = "Delete";
    grdCustomers.Columns.Add(buttoncol);
}
```

C# WEB
PROJECTS

This chapter gives you a preview of various Web projects. Throughout the book you have gotten a taste of various Web technologies such as Web controls, Web forms, Data Binding, String parsing, etc. In this chapter you will learn some techniques that you might have missed that have to do with Web development. In particular we will look at how to enhance Web projects with DLLs and how to add these DLLs to the global assembly cache for the purpose of sharing them among various applications.

Because this chapter is project oriented, there's no need to build one application that encompasses all the tasks. However you will find that the sample code for this book contains small projects with the code presented in this chapter.

Creating a DLL Project with Visual Studio .NET

Part of Web development involves properly partitioning your code. As a general rule, developers put business logic (code that has to do with business rules) in a separate DLL and put code that has to do with the visual elements of the program in another DLL. This enables one set of developers to write the business logic while another set works on the front end. DLLs also enable you to share the same code with multiple applications. So it's important to learn how to move code to other DLLs and call them from your Web application.

To create a DLL in VS.NET:

1. Start VS.NET.

2. Select File > New Project.

3. In the New Project Dialog select Class Library from the list of Visual C# projects.

4. Type the name you want to assign to the project in the Name field of the New Project Dialog. For example: BankLib (**Figure 13.1**).

5. Click OK.

6. The wizard will generate a project with two source files: AssemblyInfo.cs and Class1.cs. The wizard will also open the file Class1.cs. AssemblyInfo.cs contains attributes for the DLL (or more specifically, the assembly). Class1.cs contains code for a simple class.

7. Rename the file for the first class to Account.cs. Do this by right-clicking on the file Class1.cs from the Solution Explorer window and selecting Properties. In the Properties window type a new name in the File Name field (**Figure 13.2**).

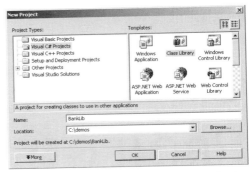

Figure 13.1 The Class Library project creates a stand-alone DLL that can be used with Web applications as well as Windows Form applications.

Figure 13.2 The default name for the main file is Class1.cs. For this example, change the filename to Account.cs.

Figure 13.3 Renaming the file doesn't change the class's name, unfortunately. The default class name is Class1. Change it to something more meaningful, like Account, and remember to change the constructor name as well.

```
Code                                    _ □ ×

using System;

namespace BankLib
{
    /// <summary>
    /// Summary description for Class1.
    /// </summary>
    public class Account
    {
        public Account()
        {
            //
            // TODO: Add constructor logic here
            //
        }
    }
}
```

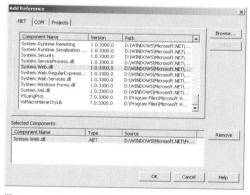

Figure 13.4 Because DLLs aren't just for Web applications, the wizard doesn't automatically add a reference to System.Web.Dll. If we want to have our DLL interact with the Web objects, we need to add this reference.

8. Change the class name for the wizard-generated class to **Account**. Remember also to rename the constructor function (constructors have the same name as the class name) (**Figure 13.3**).

To have your DLL code interact with the Web objects (like Response, Request, etc.) continue on to step 9. Otherwise, you're done.

9. Right-click on the References branch in the Solution Explorer window and choose Add Reference. You will see the Add Reference dialog (**Figure 13.4**).

10. Find System.Web.Dll in the list of assemblies and double-click on the entry. This will add System.Web.Dll to the Selected Components list. Then click OK.

11. Type using System.Web; at the top of the code file.

continues on next page

12. Inside of a function for your class, type:

```
HttpContext ctx=HttpContext.Current;
if (ctx != null)
ctx.Response.Write(msg);
```

(**Figure 13.5**).

Figure 13.5 HttpContext.Current is a static property. If the DLL code is being executed by a Web application, the property will be a non-null value. If the property is null, the application is not being run by a Web application.

```
Code                                    _ □ ×

using System;
using System.Web;

namespace BankLib
{
    /// <summary>
    /// Summary description for Class1.
    /// </summary>
    public class Account
    {
        decimal _amount;

        public Account()
        {
            //
            // TODO: Add constructor logic here
            //
        }

        void MakeDeposit(decimal amount)
        {
            _amount=amount;
        }

        void PrintBalance()
        {
            HttpContext ctx = HttpContext.Current;
            if (ctx != null)
                ctx.Response.Write(msg);
        }
    }
}
```

✔ Tips

- Steps 9-12 explain how to interact with the Web objects. To do so you first add a reference to System.Web.dll to your project. From that assembly you will use the HttpContext class. This class has a static property called Current (see step 12). If your function is being invoked in the context of a Web application, the Current property will point to an object of type HttpContext that will enable you to interact with the Web server. Otherwise Current will return null.

- **Table 13.1** shows a list of the most common properties in the HttpContext object. With this object you can find out about the client's request and participate in the response.

Table 13.1

Properties of HttpContext Object (Most Common Properties in HttpContext Object)	
PROPERTY	PURPOSE
Request	The request object is of type HttpRequest and it encapsulates the user's request. The HttpContext.Request.QueryString returns the information the user entered in the browser's address box after the URL. HttpContext.Request. Forms can be used to examine the contents of fields on a form, and HttpContext.Request. Cookies can be used to get cookie information sent from the client.
Response	The response object is of type HttpResponse and it is used to build the client's output. HttpContext.Response. Write is a common method for sending output to the client. HttpContext.Response. StatusCode can be used to read or set the server status code; for example 200 means ok, 400 means bad request, 301 means page moved. For more information on status codes look for "HttpStatusCode Enumeration" in the documentation. HttpContext.Response.Redirect tells the client's browser to go to a different page.
Server	Returns an HttpServerUtility object. HttpContext.Server.MapPath is a favorite of many, it gives the physical path of a file in your machine when given a virtual path. Remember that IIS (the Web Server) works with virtual directories. HttpContext.Server.Transfer switches to a different page without notifying the client's browser. HttpContext.Server.Execute lets you collect the output for another web page.
Session	Returns an HttpSessionState object. We have been using the Session object throughout the book to store information that gets sent back and forth between the client and the server. A session is the term used for communication with a single client.
Application	Returns an HttpApplicationState object. We have been using the Application object to store information pertaining to all users of the application.

Referencing and Executing DLL Code

Once you partition your code so that some of the code runs from a separate DLL, you will want to create instances of the classes in that DLL from your Web application. There are two ways to reference that DLL from a Web application. **To reference a DLL from a Web application:**

1. In a Web application project, right-click on the References item in the Solution Explorer window and select Add Reference.

2. In the References dialog, click the Browse button. You will see the Select Component dialog. Find your DLL file (**Figure 13.6**).

3. Click OK to close the References dialog.

4. When you run the application in a production environment (outside of VS.NET) copy the DLL to the bin sub-directory under your Web application's virtual directory. Chapter 2, "C# Building Blocks," explains how to set up a virtual directory for your Web application.

5. Add the DLL to the Global Assembly Cache (GAC). The GAC (**Figure 13.7**) is a special directory for DLLs that are to be shared among various applications. To add a DLL to the GAC you need to first digitally sign the DLL. For details, read the section "Making DLLs Globally Available" on the next page.

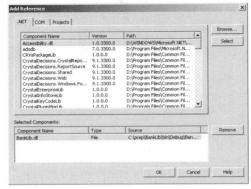

Figure 13.6 Once you compile the DLL project from the previous section you can add a reference to it in your Web application. This makes the wizard copy the DLL to the application's bin directory. Whenever you build the Web project, the copy of the DLL is refreshed.

Figure 13.7 Assembly heaven! This is where assemblies that have been protected against tampering reside. Every Web and Windows Forms application can share the same copy of the DLL if it is in the Assembly cache.

✔ Tip

■ VS.NET takes all the code for your Web Form pages and turns it into a single DLL file. Your Web Form forms in .aspx files reference this DLL. VS.NET automatically creates a bin subdirectory under your Web application's directory and copies the main DLL there. You can also copy to the bin directory any other DLLs your application needs.

Figure 13.8 The resulting .snk file contains a private and public key pair. This is the file that you want to keep in a safe place. If the bad guys get hold of this file, they can tamper with the code in the DLL.

Making DLLs Globally Available

For a DLL to be available to more than one Web application, the DLL needs to be installed in the Global Assembly Cache (GAC). Before a DLL can be installed in the GAC it must be digitally signed. A digital signature is created by running the compiler with certain attributes set. The compiler gathers information about the DLL (this is called creating a hash of the DLL) and uses a private/public key file to encrypt it. This information becomes a digital signature and gets embedded into the resulting DLL. The public key is published as part of the metadata for the DLL. The runtime uses the public key to decrypt the information in the signature, and then compares the file hash to the current DLL file to see if any tampering occurred.

To digitally sign a DLL and add it to the GAC:

1. Create a Class Library Project.

2. From the Start menu select All Programs > Microsoft Visual Studio .NET > Visual Studio Tools > Visual Studio .NET Command Prompt.

3. In the command prompt window, change the current directory to the directory of the class library project (use the cd command to do so).

4. Type sn –k mykey.snk, where mykey.snk is any name to give to your private/public key file (**Figure 13.8**).

5. Back in the class library project, double-click on the AssemblyInfo.cs file in the Solution Explorer.

continues on next page

6. In the `AssemblyKeyFile` attribute, type the complete path to the digital signature file, for example: `[assembly: AssemblyKeyFile(@"c:\prep\BankLib → \mykey.snk")]` (**Figure 13.9**).

7. Select Build > Build Solution from the menu bar.

8. Back in the command prompt window, switch directories to the directory where the DLL was generated; usually this is done as follows: `cd bin\debug`.

9. Type `gacutil -i nameofdll.dll` where `nameofdll.dll` is the name of the DLL (**Figure 13.10**).

✔ Tips

■ You can view all of the DLLs in the GAC by opening Windows Explorer and switching to the Windows\Assembly directory. You should see something like what you saw in **Figure 13.7**.

■ When you digitally sign an assembly, the assembly gets a public key token, also known as the originator or the strong name for the assembly. **Figure 13.11** highlights the public key token column.

■ You can also add a DLL to the GAC (once you digitally sign it) by dragging and dropping the file into the Windows\Assembly directory.

Figure 13.9 The Assembly.cs file contains attributes that apply to the entire project. In this case we're setting the path of the public/private key, the compiler will use the private portion to create a digital signature to protect the file.

```
[assembly: AssemblyDelaySign(false)]
[assembly:
AssemblyKeyFile(@"c:\prep\BankLib\mykey.snk")]
[assembly: AssemblyKeyName("")]
```

Figure 13.10 Once a DLL has been digitally signed, you can move it to the GAC. This means that every Web application can then share the same copy of the DLL. You can either transfer the file visually by dragging it to the Windows\Assembly directory, or you can do it manually with the gacutil tool that ships with the .NET Framework.

Global Assembly Name	Type	Version	Culture	Public Key Token
Accessibility		1.0.3300.0		b03f5f7f11d50a3a
ADODB		7.0.3300.0		b03f5f7f11d50a3a
BankLib		1.0.1097.40377		d0de54ffaf11ff41
CRVsPackageLib		1.0.0.0		692fbea5521e1304
CrystalDecisions.CrystalReports.Engine		9.1.3300.0		692fbea5521e1304
CrystalDecisions.ReportSource		9.1.3300.0		692fbea5521e1304

Figure 13.11 The Public Key Token is useful in identifying the DLL (or assembly). Remember that the assembly's full name is the name of the file minus the extension, the version number, the culture, and the number highlighted in the picture, the Public Key Token.

Figure 13.12 The version number becomes very important when you digitally sign the DLL. By default, the application that is compiled using a certain version of the DLL will always want to use the same version. The GAC can store many versions of the same DLL.

```
// 
// Version information for an assembly consists
of the
// following four values:
// 
//      Major Version
//      Minor Version
//      Build Number
//      Revision
// 

[assembly: AssemblyVersion("2.0.0.0")]
```

- Once you digitally sign the DLL, the version number becomes very important. Version numbers have four parts: major.minor.buildnumber.revision. Your Web application can only use the DLL with the version you referenced. Version numbers can be set by changing the AssemblyVersion attribute (**Figure 13.12**). By default this version number is set to 1.0.*. The asterisk tells the compiler to auto-generate the build and revision numbers based on the calendar date and system clock. However, you should change the version number to a more specific number (containing all four parts) and leave it like that until you make a significant change.

- You can remove a DLL from the GAC by pressing the Delete key after highlighting the DLL in the Windows\Assembly directory. You can also use gacutil -u dllname, where dllname is the display name of the DLL. This means: nameminusextension, Version=1.2.3.4, Culture=neutral, PublicKeyToken= 874e23ab874e23ab.

MAKING DLLS GLOBALLY AVAILABLE

Creating Web Services

Web Services are programs that enable a client program to run a task on the server without needing a visual front end. For example, suppose you created a function for converting currency from one country to another. Users may reach these functions in one of two ways. You could add a Web Form to your application that lets users visually enter an amount, the origin and destination countries, and then press a button named Convert that displays the conversion results.

Another possibility is to offer a Web Service. A Web Service doesn't have a visual front end. It is a program that listens for requests to a function, such as the Convert function. Companies then write programs with their own visual front end that interact with your Web Service. These programs communicate through the Internet with your Web Service and invoke your conversion function, passing you all the parameters you need; your Web Service then transmits the answer through the Internet. A Web Service gives the illusion that the client is simply making a method call; it's just that the method call happens through the Internet.

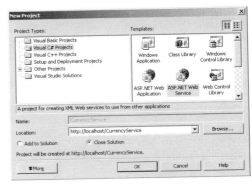

Figure 13.13 A Web Service is conceptually equivalent to having a DLL running remotely on a Web server. It doesn't provide visual elements, only functions.

To create a Web Service:

1. Run VS.NET.

2. Select File > New Project from the menu bar.

3. Click the ASP.NET Web Service icon from the New Project dialog (**Figure 13.13**).

4. Enter a name for the Web Service in the Location field and press OK. For example: CurrencyService.

5. Right-click on the Service1.asmx file (the wizard generated this file) in the Solution Explorer window, and select Properties.

Figure 13.14 The extension .asmx is very important because that is the way ASP.NET knows to treat the file as a Web Service.

6. Change the File Name in the Properties. For example: CurrencyConverter.asmx (**Figure 13.14**).

7. Right-click on the newly named file on the Solution Explorer window and select View Code.

8. Change the class name from Service1 to something more meaningful like CurrencyConverter. Don't forget to rename the constructor to match the class name (**Figure 13.15**).

continues on next page

Figure 13.15 The easiest way to write a Web Service is to write a public class that is derived from System.Web.Services.WebService. Deriving from WebService gives the class access to the ASP.NET intrinsic objects, like Session and Application.

```
using System;
using System.Collections;
using System.ComponentModel;
using System.Data;
using System.Diagnostics;
using System.Web;
using System.Web.Services;

namespace CurrencyService
{
    public class CurrencyConverter :
    System.Web.Services.WebService
    {
        public CurrencyConverter()
        {
            //CODEGEN: This call is required
            //by the ASP.NET
            //Web Services Designer
            InitializeComponent();
        }
    }
}
```

9. Add a public function to the class that you want other programs to invoke through the Web. In front of the method declaration add the [WebMethod] attribute (**Figure 13.16**). For example: [WebMethod] public decimal Convert(decimal original, string srcCountry, string dstCountry).

10. On top of the class declaration, type: [WebService(Namespace="http://www .josemojica.com/CurrencyServices/")], where www.josemojica.com is any URL that you want to associate with your service. This attribute gives your classes a unique name to distinguish it from other companies' classes (**Figure 13.17**).

11. Select Build > Build Solution from the menu bar to create the service.

Figure 13.16 The WebMethod attribute tells ASP.NET that the method should get exposed through the Internet. This attribute also has other properties that are useful, for example: Description, EnableSession, etc.

```
using System;
using System.Collections;
using System.ComponentModel;
using System.Data;
using System.Diagnostics;
using System.Web;
using System.Web.Services;

namespace CurrencyService
{
    public class CurrencyConverter :
    System.Web.Services.WebService
    {
        public CurrencyConverter()
        {
            //CODEGEN: This call is required
            //by the ASP.NET
            //Web Services Designer
            InitializeComponent();
        }

        [WebMethod] public decimal Convert(
                decimal original,
                string srcCountry,
                string dstCountry)
        {
            //of course, a full currency
            //conversion function
            //is beyond the scope of this
            //book
            return original - 1;
        }
    }
}
```

Figure 13.17 The WebService attribute lets you assign a unique namespace to the service. This is necessary to distinguish your service from other companies' services. The WebService attribute has other useful properties, like Description and Name for example.

```
namespace CurrencyService
{
    [WebService(Namespace=
    "http://www.josemojica.com/CurrencyServices/")]
    public class CurrencyConverter :
    System.Web.Services.WebService
    {
        public CurrencyConverter()
```

Figure 13.18 SOAP is a text-based protocol on top of XML for making method calls through the Internet. If you notice, the parameters are being sent in literal form; the tags, original, srcCountry, dstCountry dictate the parameters the values are for, and the first element in the soap:Body is the name of the function we want to invoke: Convert.

```
<?xml version="1.0" encoding="utf-8"?>
<soap:Envelope ...>
   <soap:Body>
        <Convert ...>
            <original>5.25</original>
            <srcCountry>USA</srcCountry>
            <dstCountry>CAN</dstCountry>
        </Convert>
   </soap:Body>
</soap:Envelope>
```

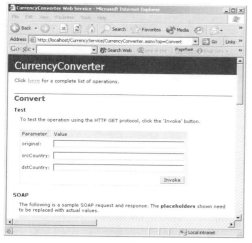

Figure 13.19 The method Convert is meant to be invoked via SOAP (other mechanisms are possible, but normally SOAP is used). If you enter the name of the file directly, the Web Service generates a help page that lets you test the Web Service.

✔ Tips

- Web Service consumers communicate with the Web Service through XML, a text-based markup protocol. On top of XML we use a protocol called SOAP (Simple Object Access Protocol). SOAP is a specification that describes how to format XML to make a method call and receive a result (**Figure 13.18**).

- A client can get information about a Web Service by entering `http://www.josemojica.com/CurrencyService/CurrencyConverter.asmx`, where `www.josemojica.com` is the URL to the server hosting the service, `CurrencyService` is the name of the project (or, more exactly, the name of the virtual directory that VS.NET creates for you) and `CurrencyConverter.asmx` is the name you assigned to the file with the Web Service class. When a client accesses the Web Service directly through the browser they will see a help page telling them how a program can talk to the Web Service (**Figure 13.19**). You can change the look of this page by modifying the configuration file and adding the code in **Figure 13.20**. `Myhelp.aspx` is a file you create. When a client tries to access the Web Service the runtime will call this page for you.

Figure 13.20 If you don't want to display the usual help page you can create your own, and change it in the Web Service's configuration file `web.config`.

```
<?xml version="1.0" encoding="utf-8" ?>
<configuration>
   <system.web>
      <webServices>
         <wsdlHelpGenerator href="myhelp.aspx" />
      </webServices>
```

Consuming Web Services

If you read the last section, then you know the basics of creating a Web Service with the wizard. Of course, there is a lot more to creating robust Web Services. For example, there are issues with how to transfer various data types through the Web using the SOAP protocol. One important issue is the issue of using a Web Service. VS.NET offers a wizard that lets you connect easily to a Web Service.

To use a Web Service:

For this example let's assume you want to create a desktop application that connects to the Web Service without the use of a browser.

1. Run VS.NET.

2. Select File > New Project from the menu bar.

3. Click the Windows Application icon from the New Project dialog.

4. Enter a name for the Windows Application, `CurrencyClient` for example, in the Name field and press OK (**Figure 13.21**).

5. Right-click on the References item in the Solution Explorer and choose Add Web Reference (**Figure 13.22**).

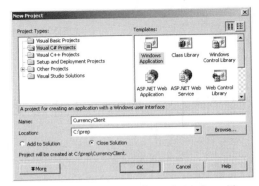

Figure 13.21 This is a change for us, but we're writing a Windows Form application to illustrate that you can still have a traditional Windows application (non-Web front end) communicate through the Internet with a service.

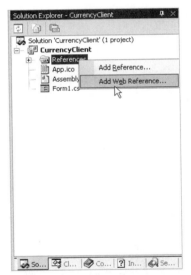

Figure 13.22 We normally use the Add Reference option when the DLL is present in the same machine. Web References are used when we want to talk to a Web Service. The process creates what is called a proxy. It is a class that looks just like the class in the Web Service but when you call one of its methods it forwards the call to the Web Service.

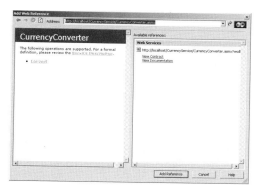

Figure 13.23 The Web Service provides a mechanism that reports to the wizard what methods it contains so that the wizard can create a client-side proxy that looks like the service.

Figure 13.24 CurrencyConverter is the client-side proxy class that the wizard created. Its full name is CurrencyClient.localhost.CurrencyConverter. CurrencyClient is the name of our client application. Localhost is the name of the Web server. If the server had been www.ibm.com, then the name of the class would have been CurrencyClient.ibm.com.www. CurrencyConverter.

```
Code                                    _ □ ✕
//using CurrencyClient.localhost;
private void cmdConvert_Click(
             object sender,
             System.EventArgs e)
{
   CurrencyConverter conv =
   new CurrencyConverter();
}
```

6. You will see the Add Web Reference dialog (**Figure 13.23**). In the address field enter the path to the Web Service. For example: `http://www.josemojica.com/CurrencyService/CurrencyConverter.asmx`

7. Click the Add Reference button. VS.NET will add several files to your application. One of the files is hidden, but contains source for a class with the same name as the class you authored for the service in the previous section.

8. Write code that creates an instance of the Web Service class and uses it. For example: `CurrencyConverter conv = new CurrencyConverter();` (**Figure 13.24**).

✔ Tips

■ When you add a Web Reference with the wizard, the wizard creates a file called `Reference.cs`. It creates a subdirectory under your application directory called Web References, and a subdirectory under that called the same thing as the server name; that's where it puts the `References.cs` file. You can take a look at it from the Solution Explorer if you click the Show All Files icon (**Figure 13.25**).

■ The Web Service client class contains a property called `Url`. This property points to the address of the Web Service at the time you added the Web Reference. It could be that this property will change over time. **Figures 13.26** and **13.27** show you how to read this property from the `app.config` file and set the `Url` property at runtime. With this code you can modify the Web Service's address at any time by editing the `web.config` file.

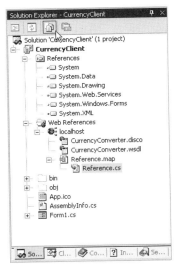

Figure 13.25
After you add a Web Reference, a few files are created but to view them you have to click on the View All icon at the top of the Solution Explorer window.

Figure 13.26 You may recall from other chapters that the web.config file lets you add custom configuration information. You can either define your own section or use the appSettings section to add your own information. In this case we're saving the Url to the Web Service in appSettings.

```
<configuration>
    <appSettings>
        <add key="Url"
        value="http://localhost/CurrencyService/
        CurrencyConverter.asmx;"/>
    </appSettings>
</configuration>
```

Figure 13.27 Once we add the information for the Url to the config file reading it is a simple matter of using the ConfigurationSettings.AppSettings property passing the name of the key.

```
private void cmdConvert_Click(
object sender, System.EventArgs e)
{
    CurrencyConverter conv = new
    CurrencyConverter();
    conv.Url = System.Configuration.
            ConfigurationSettings.
            AppSettings["Url"];
}
```

INDEX

Symbols

(? :) (conditional operators), 92
[ ] (square brackets), array indexes, 263
&& (and) clause, 87, 100
% binary operator, 195
& binary operator, 195
* binary operator, 195
/ binary operator, 195
<< binary operator, 195
<= binary operator, 195
>> binary operator, 195
>= binary operator, 195
^ binary operator, 195
| binary operator, 195
, (comma), multi-dimensional arrays, 274–275
{} (curly brackets), 26
   arrays, 272–273
   multi-dimensional arrays, 274–275
== (equals to) operator, 82, 85–86
   binary operator, 195
   overriding, 198–199
   strings, 120
\ (escape) character, strings, 132–133
> (greater than) operator, 82, 122
   binary operator, 195
>= (greater than or equal to) operator, 82
< (less than) operator, 82, 122
   binary operator, 195
<= (less than or equal to) operator, 82
-= (minus equal) operator
   removing delegates, 312–313
   subscribing to events, 319
!= (not equal to) operator, 82
   binary operator, 195
   overriding, 198–199
+ operator
   binary, 195
   unary, 123, 194
+= operator, 123
   subscribing to events, 319
- operator
   binary, 195
   unary, 194
| | (or) expression, 87, 100
() (parenthesis), function parameters, 263
; (semicolons), 26
\\ sequence, 132
* sequence, 132
! unary operator, 194
++ unary operator, 194
– unary operator, 194
~ unary operator, 194

A

Abstract classes, 179
Active Server Pages (ASP), xiv
Add Class command (Project menu), 173
Add function, arrays, 296
Add New Item dialog box, 70
Add Reference dialog box, 49
Add Web Form command (Project menu), 107
Add Web Reference dialog box, 415

INDEX

INDEX

T